How to Do
Everything

iPod®, iPhone™
& iTunes®

Fifth Edition

About the Author

Guy Hart-Davis is the author of more than 50 computer books, including *PC QuickSteps, Second Edition*; *Mac OS X Leopard QuickSteps*; *How to Do Everything with Microsoft Office Word 2007*; and *How to Do Everything with Microsoft Office Excel 2007*.

About the Technical Editor

Marc Campbell is a technology author, graphic designer, and instructor, whose popular guides to computer topics have appeared around the world in eight languages. To date, he has written or co-written 12 books, including *iPod Repair QuickSteps*. In his spare time, he plays rock keyboards and records in his home studio.

How to Do
Everything

iPod®, iPhone™
& iTunes®

Fifth Edition

Guy Hart-Davis

New York Chicago San Francisco Lisbon
London Madrid Mexico City Milan New Delhi
San Juan Seoul Singapore Sydney Toronto

The McGraw·Hill Companies

Cataloging-in-Publication Data is on file with the Library of Congress

McGraw-Hill books are available at special quantity discounts to use as premiums and sales promotions, or for use in corporate training programs. To contact a special sales representative, please visit the Contact Us page at www.mhprofessional.com.

How to Do Everything: iPod®, iPhone™ & iTunes®, Fifth Edition

234567890   DOC DOC   0

ISBN   978-0-07-163024-5
MHID   0-07-163024-4

Sponsoring Editor	**Technical Editor**	**Composition**
Megg Morin	Marc Campbell	International Typesetting and Composition
Editorial Supervisor	**Copy Editor**	**Illustration**
Janet Walden	Bill McManus	International Typesetting and Composition
Project Manager	**Proofreader**	
Vasundhara Sawhney, International Typesetting and Composition	Claire Splan	**Art Director, Cover**
	Indexer	Jeff Weeks
	Claire Splan	**Cover Designer**
Acquisitions Coordinator	**Production Supervisor**	Jeff Weeks
Meghan Riley	Jean Bodeaux	

Cover image used by permission from Apple Inc.
Jack Johnson and Matt Costa images used by permission from Brushfire Records.
Cro-Mag Rally image used by permission from Reverb Inc.

Product images are used by permission from:

RadTech LLC	DecalGirl	Edifier International Ltd.
Speck Products	Griffin Technology Inc.	Sonnet Technologies, Inc.

This book is dedicated to the people who gave us MP3, AAC, Apple Lossless Encoding, the various iPods, and the iPhone.

Contents at a Glance

Contents

PART III   Learn Advanced Techniques and Tricks

CHAPTER 11   Use Multiple iPods or iPhones, Multiple Computers, or Both 263

Acknowledgments

I'd like to thank the following people for their help with this book:

- Megg Morin for developing the book—for the fifth time
- Meghan Riley for handling the acquisitions end of the book
- Marc Campbell for reviewing the manuscript anew for technical accuracy and contributing many helpful suggestions
- Bill McManus for editing the manuscript once more
- Vasundhara Sawhney for coordinating the production of the book again
- Janet Walden for returning for an encore assisting with the production of the book
- International Typesetting and Composition for laying out the pages

Introduction

iPods are the best portable music players available. Small enough to fit easily into a hand or a pocket, an iPod classic can hold the contents of your entire CD collection in compressed audio files, your entire photo collection, and enough hours of video to keep you entertained for a week or more. An iPod nano holds much less but is correspondingly smaller and cuter. And an iPod shuffle, the tiniest of the lot, not only holds enough music to keep you listening all day but also has enough battery life to play it all.

The iPhone is the best mobile phone for anyone who enjoys music and video on the move. And the iPod touch—like an iPhone without the phone bits—is a terrific mobile entertainment device, Internet tablet, notepad, and even game platform.

Whichever model of iPod or iPhone you have, you can download a dozen CDs' worth of music from your computer to it in less than a minute, and you can recharge the iPod or iPhone quickly either from your computer or from any handy power outlet. And whether you use Windows or Mac OS X, you can enjoy music on your computer with iTunes, the best all-round jukebox and music-management application available.

But you can also do more—much more.

This book shows you how to get the most out of your iPod or iPhone.

What Does This Book Cover?

Chapter 1, "Choose an iPod or iPhone and Get Your Computer Ready to Work with It," explains what the iPods and iPhone are and what they do; how to distinguish the current models from each other; and how their capabilities differ. The chapter then suggests how to choose the model that's best for you and shows you how to get your PC or Mac ready to work with it.

Chapter 2, "Configure iTunes and Load the iPod or iPhone with Music, Video, and Data," runs you through the steps of installing iTunes on your PC or Mac and connecting the iPod or iPhone for the first time. The chapter then shows you how to start creating your library and how to load the iPod or iPhone with songs, videos, and data—and then disconnect it safely.

Chapter 3, "Enjoy Music and Video on the iPod or iPhone," shows you how to connect your speakers or headphones to the iPod or iPhone, how to use its controls, and how to use its main features.

Chapter 4, "Get More Out of the iPod or iPhone with Hardware Accessories," discusses the various types of accessories available for the iPod and iPhone, from mainstream accessories (such as cases and stands) to more esoteric accessories (wait and see).

Chapter 5, "Use an iPod or iPhone as Your Home Stereo or Car Stereo," discusses how to connect the iPod or iPhone to your home stereo or car stereo. You'll also learn how to control iTunes on your computer from an iPod touch or iPhone.

Chapter 6, "Create Audio Files, Edit Them, and Tag Them," shows you how to use iTunes and other tools to build a library stuffed with high-quality, accurately tagged song files. You'll learn how to choose the best location to store your library, how to configure iTunes to get exactly the audio quality you need, and how to work with compressed audio in ways that iTunes itself can't manage. You'll also learn how to convert other audio file types to MP3, AAC, Apple Lossless Encoding, WAV, or AIFF so you can play them on your iPod or iPhone, how to create audio files from cassettes or vinyl records, and how to save audio streams to disk so you can listen to them later.

Chapter 7, "Buy and Download Songs, Videos, and More Online," explains your options for buying song and video files online. The chapter starts by covering what digital rights management (DRM) is, what it means for computer users, and how Apple is now getting rid of most of it. It then discusses what the iTunes Store is, how to set up an account, how to find music and videos by browsing and searching, and how to buy and download music, videos, and other items. The chapter also discusses other online music stores that you may want to examine (although the song files many of the stores sell aren't directly compatible with the iPod or the iPhone) and points you to sites where you can find free (and legal) songs online.

Chapter 8, "Create Video Files That Work with the iPod or iPhone," shows you how to create video files for the iPod and iPhone. You can buy video files from the iTunes Store or from other online stores, but unless you're as rich as Croesus, you'll also want to make suitable files from your own video content. You can, easily enough—but it helps to understand the legalities involved, particularly before you rip your DVDs.

Chapter 9, "Make Your Music Sound Great and Customize the iTunes Window," shows you how to make the most of iTunes for playing back music—with or without the monstrous graphical visual effects the application can give. You'll learn how to use audio features such as the graphical equalizer, crossfading, and Sound Enhancer; and you'll find out how to control iTunes both via keyboard shortcuts and via the iTunes widget on Mac OS X.

Chapter 10, "Manage Your Music and Video Library with iTunes," explains how to browse, mix, and import and export music and videos; how to share items with others and access the items that others are sharing; and how to tune into podcasts. You'll also learn how to move your library from one folder to another, remove duplicate items from your library, and even use multiple libraries on the same computer.

Chapter 11, "Use Multiple iPods or iPhones, Multiple Computers, or Both," explains how to synchronize several iPods or iPhones with the same computer and shows you how to load an iPod or iPhone from multiple computers. The chapter walks you through the processes of moving an iPod or iPhone from Mac OS X to Windows or the other direction and shows you how to change the computer to which your iPod is linked.

Chapter 12, "Use an iPod as an External Drive or Backup Device," shows you how to use an iPod as an external drive for backup and portable storage. You'll learn how to enable disk mode on an iPod and transfer files to or from an iPod.

Chapter 13, "Recover Your Songs and Videos from an iPod or iPhone," shows you how to transfer files from the iPod's or iPhone's library to your computer—for example, to recover songs and other items from the iPod or iPhone after the hard disk on your computer fails.

Chapter 14, "Use the iPod or iPhone with Software Other Than iTunes," explains why you might want to use software other than iTunes to control the iPod or iPhone, and gives examples of several Windows applications that are viable alternatives to iTunes. On the Mac, iTunes rules almost unchallenged, but Clutter provides a wonderful super-graphical interface that makes iTunes even easier to use.

Chapter 15, "Troubleshoot the iPod, iPhone, and iTunes," discusses how to troubleshoot the iPod, the iPhone, and iTunes when things go wrong. You'll learn how to avoid making the iPod or iPhone unhappy, how to approach the troubleshooting process in the right way, and how to perform essential troubleshooting maneuvers. Plus, you'll find solutions for problems that occur frequently on the iPod, on the iPhone, and in iTunes.

Chapter 16, "Make Phone Calls with the iPhone," shows you how to make calls with the iPhone, including conference calls. You'll also learn how to receive calls, how to get your messages with Visual Voicemail, how to choose phone settings that suit you, and how to work with contacts on both the iPhone and the iPod touch.

Chapter 17, "Connect the iPhone or iPod touch to Wireless Networks and VPNs," covers connecting the iPhone and iPod touch to wireless networks so that you can connect to the Internet at full speed rather than relying on the cell-phone network. In corporate settings, you may also need to connect to a company network via a virtual private network (VPN); this chapter tells you what you need to know and do.

Chapter 18, "Send E-mail and Surf the Web," shows you how to set up an e-mail account, send and receive e-mail and attachments, and surf the Web with the Safari browser on the iPhone or iPod touch. You'll also learn how to connect to Exchange Server mail servers on corporate networks if you need to.

Chapter 19, "Install Applications and Play Games," tells you how to make the most of the third-party software that's available through Apple's App Store. You'll learn how to find, download, and install applications; synchronize, configure, and update them; rearrange them so they're at your fingertips—and delete applications you no longer want. You'll also find pointers for playing games on the iPhone or iPod touch and information about "jailbreaking" the devices so that you can install non-approved software on them.

Conventions Used in This Book

To make its meaning clear without using far more words than necessary, this book uses a number of conventions, four of which are worth mentioning here:

- Note, Tip, and Caution paragraphs highlight information to draw it to your notice.
- The pipe character or vertical bar denotes choosing an item from a menu. For example, "choose File | Open" means that you should click the File menu and select the Open item on it. Use the keyboard, mouse, or a combination of the two as you wish.
- The ⌘ symbol represents the COMMAND key on the Mac—the key that bears the Apple symbol and the quad-infinity mark on most Mac keyboards.
- Most check boxes have two states: *selected* (with a check mark in them) and *cleared* (without a check mark in them). This book tells you to *select* a check box or *clear* a check box rather than "click to place a check mark in the box" or "click to remove the check mark from the box." (Often, you'll be verifying the state of the check box, so it may already have the required setting—in which case, you don't need to click at all.) Some check boxes have a third state as well, in which they're selected but dimmed and unavailable. This state is usually used for options that apply to only part of the current situation.

PART I

Enjoy Audio with an iPod or iPhone and iTunes

1

Choose an iPod or iPhone and Get Your Computer Ready to Work with It

HOW TO...

- Understand what iPods are and what they do
- Understand what the iPhone is
- Distinguish the different types of current iPods
- Choose the right iPod or iPhone for your needs
- Get your PC or Mac ready to work with an iPod or iPhone

If you don't already have an iPod or iPhone, you'll need to beg, borrow, or buy one before you can make the most of this book. This chapter tells you about the iPhone and the iPods available at this writing, and suggests how to choose the one that will best suit your needs. After that, it shows you how to get your PC or Mac ready to work with an iPod or iPhone.

If you're already the proud owner of an iPod or iPhone, you may prefer to skip directly to Chapter 2, which shows you how to get up and running with it.

What Are iPods and iPhones?

iPod is the umbrella term for the wildly popular portable music and video players built by Apple Inc. *iPhone* is Apple's cell phone that has an iPod built right into it.

At this writing, there are four main families of iPod, shown left to right on the front cover of the book:

- **iPod touch**   This is the iPod that looks like the iPhone, with a large, touch-sensitive screen.
- **iPod classic**   This is the full-sized iPod, with a control wheel on the front.
- **iPod nano**   This is the smallest iPod with a screen.
- **iPod shuffle**   This is the tiny iPod that doesn't have a screen and just clips onto your clothing.

Apart from these current models, Apple has also produced—and discontinued—five earlier generations of regular iPod, three earlier generations of the iPod nano, one earlier generation of the iPod shuffle, and one generation of the iPod mini, a medium-sized iPod built around a miniature hard disk called a Microdrive. The second-generation iPod shuffle has been supplanted by the third, but Apple has not discontinued it yet.

All current iPods and the iPhone connect to your PC or Mac via USB, enabling you to transfer files quickly to the player using a regular USB port on your computer. (Older models connected via FireWire, an alternative connection technology that Apple has now phased out of iPods and the iPhone.) At the iPod or iPhone's end, the connector cable plugs into a narrow, wide port called the Dock Connector port. The exception is the iPod shuffle, which recharges through an extra connector buried deep inside its headphone socket.

What the iPods and the iPhone Do

Before we dive into what the iPhone and each of the different models of iPod do, let's look at the features they have in common: playing back audio and video, storing photos, synchronizing your contacts and calendars, and more.

 In capabilities, the iPod shuffle is the odd one out for reasons you'll grasp immediately. Without a screen, it can't display video, photos, or textual information, so it concentrates on playing back audio. However, you can store files on the iPod shuffle just as you can on its larger siblings.

The Main Event: Audio and Video Playback

The main feature of the iPods (and one of the main features of the iPhone) is high-quality audio and video playback. Let's look at this briefly here so that we don't need to cover it for each individual player.

The iPods and iPhone can play audio files in these formats:

- **Advanced Audio Coding (AAC)**   This is Apple's preferred format for getting high audio quality on small devices.
- **MP3**   This is the rest of the world's preferred format for getting high audio quality on small devices.

- **Audible**   This is the MP3-derived format used by Audible.com for its audiobook files.
- **Apple Lossless Encoding**   This is Apple's format for full-quality audio. The second-generation iPod shuffle doesn't play these files, but the third-generation iPod shuffle does.
- **WAV**   This is an industry-standard format for full-quality, uncompressed audio.
- **AIFF**   This is an industry-standard but Mac-based format for full-quality, uncompressed audio.

The iPod and iPhone don't support other formats—such as Microsoft's Windows Media Audio (WMA), RealNetworks' RealAudio, and the open-source audio formats Ogg Vorbis and FLAC—but you can convert audio files in those formats to AAC, MP3, or another supported format easily enough (see Chapter 6 for details).

The iPod (apart from the iPod shuffle) and the iPhone can play several types of video files, including H.264 files and MPEG-4 files. If you have video files in other formats, you can convert them to one of these formats (see Chapter 8 for details).

Carrying Contacts, Calendars, and Photos

The iPods and iPhone also act as a contact database, calendar, and notebook, enabling you to carry around not only all your music but your vital information as well. You can also put other textual information on an iPod or iPhone so you can carry that information with you and view it on the screen. On the iPod touch and the iPhone, you can edit your contacts, calendars, and notes and create new ones as needed.

The iPhone and the iPods (except the iPod shuffle) can also carry your photos and display them, which is great for taking them with you and sharing them with others.

Carrying Your Vital Files

You can also use an iPod or iPhone as an external disk for your PC or Mac. This provides an easy and convenient means of backing up your data, storing files, and transporting files from one computer to another. And because the iPod and iPhone are ultra-portable, you can take those files with you wherever you go, which can be great for school, work, and even play.

Synchronizing with Your Computer and Buying Songs and Videos Online

The iPods and iPhone are designed to communicate seamlessly with iTunes, which runs on both Windows and the Mac. If you prefer, you can use the devices with other software as well on either operating system (Chapter 14 discusses some of the applications you can use).

If you use an iPod or iPhone with iTunes, you can buy songs or videos from the iTunes Store, download them to your computer, and play them on either your computer or the device.

The iPhone and What It Does

The iPhone (see Figure 1-1) is a cell phone that includes all the features of an iPod. Apart from playing music and video, the iPhone's capabilities include:

- Making phone calls, including conference calls
- Checking your voicemail messages either in the order received or out of order
- Connecting to the Internet either via the cell network or via a wireless network connection
- Browsing the Web with the Safari browser
- Sending and receiving e-mail messages via your existing e-mail account
- Taking pictures with the built-in camera—and sending them immediately via e-mail if you so wish
- Watching videos from YouTube
- Getting maps, weather reports, stock quotes, and other handy information
- Running applications you download from Apple's App Store—everything from productivity-enhancing business tools to brain-bending study tools and entertaining games

FIGURE 1-1   The iPhone includes full iPod functionality—along with normal cell-phone capabilities, mail, and web browsing. (Image used courtesy of Apple Inc.)

Did You Know?

The Advantages and Disadvantages of Flash Memory

Except for the iPod classic, which uses a hard drive, all iPods and the iPhone use flash memory chips for storage.

Flash memory has two main advantages:

- Flash memory is shockproof, so the iPod won't skip unless you damage it badly enough to prevent it from playing.
- Flash memory uses far less power than a hard disk—around 1/30 of the amount a hard drive takes—so the iPod or iPhone can run for a good time on a smaller battery than it would otherwise need.

The disadvantage of flash memory is that it is still much more expensive per gigabyte than hard disks. This is why there is such a vast difference in capacity between the iPod classic (120GB) and the next-most capacious iPod, the iPod touch (32GB).

The iPod touch and What It Does

The iPod touch (see Figure 1-2) resembles an iPhone without the phone, the camera, and the waistline. Like the iPhone, the iPod touch has a large, touch-sensitive screen that you use to control most of its functions, from playing back songs and videos to surfing the Web via a wireless network and sending mail.

The iPod touch has an on/off button on the top, a volume rocker button on the side, and the Home button below the screen. It has a minimalist built-in speaker that's just about adequate for games, but you'll want to use headphones or external speakers for listening to any audio you want to hear well.

FIGURE 1-2   The iPod touch resembles the iPhone but is marginally smaller and substantially slimmer. (Image used courtesy of Apple Inc.)

The iPod classic and What It Does

The iPod classic is the sixth generation of regular iPod. The iPod classic is a portable music and video player with a huge capacity, a rechargeable battery good for 8 to 15 hours of music playback (less if you watch a lot of video), and easy-to-use controls.

The iPod classic is built around the type of hard drive used in small laptop computers and comes at this writing only in a 120GB capacity. (The capacity is engraved on the back of the iPod.) Larger hard disks are available, but not yet in the slimline format that the iPod classic needs. So far, as hard-disk manufacturers have released higher-capacity hard disks, Apple has continued to release higher-capacity iPods, so the maximum capacity seems certain to rise. The more space on the iPod's hard disk, the more songs, video, or other data you can carry on it.

The iPod classic (see Figure 1-3) has a 2.5-inch color screen with a resolution of 320 × 240 pixels, which is called Quarter VGA resolution, or QVGA for short. (VGA resolution is 640 × 480 pixels—twice as much in each direction, so four times as much overall.) The screen can display videos, photos, and album covers as well as the iPod's menus, information about the song that's currently playing, and text-based items, such as your contacts, calendars, and notes.

FIGURE 1-3 The iPod classic is the latest of the full-size iPods. (Image used courtesy of Apple Inc.)

Below the screen is a control device called the Click wheel. The Click wheel has four buttons built into it, which you click by pressing the wheel so that it tilts slightly in the required direction. You drag your finger around the surface of the Click wheel to scroll through items such as menus. You press the Select button or Center button, in the middle of the Click wheel, to access the item you've selected by scrolling.

At the top is a headphone socket and a Hold switch that you slide to put the iPod on hold (which locks all its controls) or to take it off hold again.

Note With extra hardware, you can extend an iPod's capabilities even further. For example, with a custom microphone, you can record audio directly onto it. With a custom media reader, you can transfer digital photos to the iPod's hard disk directly from a digital camera without using a computer. This capability can make an iPod a great travel companion for a digital camera—especially a camera that takes high-resolution photos.

Why the iPod's or iPhone's Capacity Appears to Be Less Than Advertised

One hundred twenty gigabytes is a huge amount of music—around 30,000 four-minute songs at the iPod classic's default audio quality, or enough for about 80 days' solid listening. It's also a decent amount of video: about 700 hours at the compression rate the iTunes Store uses. But unfortunately, you don't actually get the amount of hard disk space that's written on the iPod or iPhone.

There are two reasons for this. First, you lose some hard-disk space to the device's operating system (OS—the software that enables it to function) and the file allocation table that records which file is stored where on the disk. This happens on all hard disks and solid-state devices that contain operating systems, and costs you anywhere from a few megabytes on the iPod shuffle to a few hundred megabytes on the iPhone.

Second, the capacities of the iPods and the iPhone are measured in "marketing gigabytes" rather than in real gigabytes. A real gigabyte is 1,024 megabytes, a megabyte is 1,024 kilobytes, and a kilobyte is 1,024 bytes. That makes 1,073,741,824 bytes (1,024 × 1,024 × 1,024 bytes) in a real gigabyte. By contrast, a marketing gigabyte has a flat billion bytes (1,000 × 1,000 × 1,000 bytes)—a difference of 7.4 percent.

So an iPod or iPhone will actually hold 7.4 percent less data than its listed size suggests (and minus more for the OS and file allocation table). You can see why marketing folks choose to use marketing megabytes and gigabytes rather than real megabytes and gigabytes—the numbers are more impressive. But customers tend to be disappointed when they discover that the real capacity of a device is substantially less than the device's packaging and literature promised.

FIGURE 1-4 The iPod nano is very small and contains flash memory rather than a hard disk. Its controls and ports are similar to those on an iPod classic, but its headphone socket is on the bottom rather than the top. (Image used courtesy of Apple Inc.)

The iPod nano and What It Does

The iPod nano (see Figure 1-4, above) is the smallest iPod that has a screen. At this writing, the iPod nano comes in 8GB and 16GB models and in various colors.

The iPod nano has a similar layout to the iPod classic, with a screen at the top of the front, the main control buttons built into the Click wheel, and a Dock Connector port on the bottom. The only major difference in layout is that the headphone socket is on the bottom of the iPod nano rather than on the top.

Despite its diminutive size, the iPod nano can play back video as well as songs, and can even output that video to a TV. The iPod nano can also display photos and album art on its screen or on a TV. The iPod nano's capacity is engraved on the back.

 You can turn the iPod nano sideways and use the screen in landscape (wider) orientation, which is great for pictures and videos.

The iPod shuffle and What It Does

The iPod shuffle is the smallest and least expensive iPod. At this writing, two generations of iPod shuffle are available:

- **Third-generation iPod shuffle** This iPod is a sleek metal slab with a clip on the back, a single switch on the top, and its remaining controls integrated into the headset cord.

FIGURE 1-5   The iPod shuffle clips onto your clothing. (Image used courtesy of Apple Inc.)

- **Second-generation iPod shuffle**   This iPod (shown in Figure 1-5) has a rectangular metal case with controls on the front and a clip on the back for attaching the player to your clothing.

The iPod shuffle has no screen and two play modes, either playing back an existing playlist in order or "shuffling" the songs into a random order—hence its name. To change from playlist mode to shuffle mode, you move the switch at the top of the third-generation iPod shuffle or one of the two switches on the bottom of the second-generation iPod shuffle.

You control the third-generation iPod shuffle via the three buttons on its headset cord (see Chapter 3 for details). You control the second-generation iPod shuffle via the five buttons (Play/Pause, Previous Track and Next Track, and Volume Up and Volume Down) laid out in a circular arrangement on its face.

Because the iPod shuffle has no screen, the only way you can navigate through your playlist is by using the Previous button and Next button and listening to the song that plays. The shuffle mode makes a virtue out of this limitation by offering to mix up the songs for you.

The iPod shuffle is great for exercise or extreme activities that would threaten a larger iPod, especially as the controls are easy to use without looking. But it's also great if you often get new music and want to focus your listening on it without being distracted by your existing collection, or if you want to force yourself to listen to artists or albums that you normally neglect.

Because of the iPod shuffle's limitations, much of what you'll read in the rest of this book doesn't apply to it. For example, you can't put your contacts, your calendar, or notes on the iPod shuffle, because it has no way to display them to you; likewise, you can't watch video on it. The iPod shuffle doesn't use equalizations, but it does support the Start Time and End Time options in iTunes, which allow you to skip part of the beginning or end of a track.

But the iPod shuffle isn't only for playing music. You can also use the iPod shuffle as a portable disk, and because of its diminutive size, the iPod shuffle is a great way to take your key documents with you.

The second-generation iPod shuffle plays AAC, MP3, WAV, AIFF, and Audible.com files, but it can't play Apple Lossless Encoder files. The third-generation iPod shuffle does play Apple Lossless Encoding files as well as all the other types.

Choose the iPod or iPhone That's Best for You

By ruthlessly discontinuing earlier iPod models even when they were selling strongly, Apple has made the process of choosing among the different iPods pretty straightforward:

- If you need a mobile phone that includes an iPod (or vice versa), buy an iPhone.
- If you need the smallest player possible, or a player for active pursuits, get an iPod shuffle.
- If you want the cutest medium-capacity player, go for an iPod nano. The iPod nano is great for smaller libraries, or for carrying only the newest or most exciting songs and videos in your colossal library with you, but its lower capacity makes it a poor value alongside the iPod classic.
- If you want to carry as many songs and videos as possible with you, buy the iPod classic model.
- If you want to watch videos, send mail, surf the Web, and run applications on the iPod, but you don't want to pay for an iPhone contract, get an iPod touch.

Table 1-1 shows you how much music you can fit onto the current iPod models at widely used compression ratios for music. For spoken audio (such as audio books, plays, or talk radio), you can use lower compression ratios (such as 64 Kbps or even 32 Kbps) and still get acceptable sound with much smaller file sizes. The table

TABLE 1-1   iPod Capacities at Widely Used Compression Ratios

iPod or iPhone Nominal Capacity	iPod Real Capacity	128 Kbps		160 Kbps		320 Kbps		Apple Lossless Encoder[1]	
		Hours	Songs	Hours	Songs	Hours	Songs	Hours	Songs
1GB	950MB	17	240	14	200	8	100	n/a[2]	n/a
2GB	1.9GB	34	500	28	400	16	200	n/a	n/a
4GB	3.7GB	65	950	55	775	30	375	10	150
8GB	7.2GB	135	2,000	110	1,600	55	800	20	290
16GB	14.7GB	270	4,000	220	3,200	110	1600	40	580
32GB	29.6GB	550	8,000	440	6,400	220	3,200	80	1,160
120GB	111.5GB	2,000	30,000	750	24,000	820	12,000	300	4,300

[1]Apple Lossless Encoder encoding rates vary; these figures are approximations.
[2]The second-generation iPod shuffle cannot play Apple Lossless Encoder files.

How to... **Buy an iPod or iPhone for Less Than Full Price**

If you'd prefer not to pay full price for an iPod or iPhone, consider these alternatives:

- **Buy a refurbished iPod or iPhone from Apple**   Apple sells refurbished iPods and iPhones at a discount—sometimes up to a third off the normal price. To find them, search the Apple store (http://store.apple.com) for **refurbished iPod** or **refurbished iPhone**. These iPods and iPhones have a one-year limited warranty, which you should read before buying one (look for a link to the warranty on any page that offers a refurbished iPod). You can also buy AppleCare to extend the coverage, although this is typically worthwhile only for the most expensive models.
- **Buy a reconditioned iPod or iPhone from another vendor**   eBay and other sites carry reconditioned iPods and iPhones. However, you will not normally get a warranty, and it may be hard to determine the quality of the reconditioning.
- **Grab an old iPod or iPhone when a relative or sibling upgrades**   If you know someone who simply must have the latest technology, get ready to jump in line for their existing device.

assumes a "song" to be about four minutes long and rounds the figures to the nearest sensible point. The table doesn't show less widely used compression ratios such as 224 Kbps or 256 Kbps. (For 256 Kbps, halve the 128 Kbps numbers.)

The iPod, iPhone, and iTunes refer to tracks as "songs"—even if they're not music—so this book does the same. Similarly, Apple and this book refer to "artists" rather than "singers," "bands," or other terms.

Get Your PC or Mac Ready to Work with an iPod or iPhone

If your PC or Mac is a recent model, it probably is ready to work with whichever new iPod you choose. If it's older, or if it's a budget model, or if you've picked up an older iPod, you may need to add new components.

Here are the requirements for an iPod classic, an iPod touch, an iPod nano, an iPod shuffle, or an iPhone:

- A PC running Windows Vista (Home Premium, Business, Ultimate, or Enterprise Edition) or either Windows XP Home Edition or Windows XP Professional with Service Pack 3, or a Mac running Mac OS X 10.4.10 (Tiger) or Mac OS X 10.5 (Leopard).
- A USB port. It's best to have a high-power USB 2.0 port, although you can scrape by with a USB 1.x port if you're prepared to be patient. The USB port must deliver

Did You Know?

Why USB 2.0 Makes a Huge Difference to Using an iPod or iPhone

USB 2.0 is up to 40 times faster than USB 1.x, so you'll definitely want USB 2.0 if you have the choice. USB 1.x has a top speed of 12 megabits per second (Mbps), which translates to a maximum transfer of about 1.5MB of data per second; USB 2.0 has a top speed of 400 Mbps, which gives a data transfer rate of about 60MB per second.

As a result of this difference, loading an iPod via a USB 2.0 port will go far faster than via a USB 1.x port. The difference is most painful when you're loading an iPod classic, but you'll feel the pinch of USB 1.x even with the lower capacity of an iPod shuffle or an iPod nano.

Apple will no doubt release higher-capacity iPods and iPhones in the years to come, but USB will be improving its act too. USB 3.0, known as SuperSpeed USB, will provide up to 5 gigabits per second (Gbps), will be backward compatible with USB 2.0, and is expected to arrive in 2010.

enough power to recharge the iPod or iPhone. If your keyboard has a built-in USB port (as many Apple keyboards do), chances are that it doesn't deliver enough power for recharging.

- An optical drive (a CD drive or a DVD drive) if you want to be able to rip songs from CDs to put on the iPod or iPhone.
- A CD burner if you want to burn CDs from iTunes, or a DVD burner if you want to be able to burn both DVDs and CDs. (Most modern optical drives include burning capabilities.)

Get Your PC Ready to Work with an iPod

If you bought your PC in 2003 or later, it most likely has everything you need to start using an iPod or iPhone and iTunes:

- A USB 2.0 port
- Windows Vista (Home Premium, Business, Ultimate, or Enterprise Edition) or Windows XP (either Home Edition or Professional) with Service Pack 3. (If you don't yet have Service Pack 3, you can download it from the Microsoft website for free.) Windows 7 will also be fine when Microsoft releases it.
- A 500-MHz or faster processor (you can get away with a slower processor, but it won't be much fun).
- 512MB RAM (for Windows Vista) or 128MB RAM (for Windows XP). Much more RAM is much better.

- Enough hard-disk space to contain your library, on either an internal hard disk or an external hard disk.
- A CD or DVD burner.

If your PC can't meet those specifications, read the following sections to learn about possible upgrades.

Add USB 2.0 if Necessary

Most PCs manufactured in 2003 or later include one or more USB 2.0 ports—some have a half-dozen or more USB ports. If your PC has one or more, you're all set. If your computer has only USB 1.*x*, you can add USB 2.0 by installing a PCI card in a desktop PC or by inserting a PC Card in a laptop PC.

If you don't know whether your computer's USB ports are USB 1.*x* or USB 2.0, simply plug in the iPod or iPhone and set it up. Either iTunes or Windows itself will warn you if the device is using a USB 1.*x* port rather than a USB 2.0 port. The Windows warning is usually a notification-area pop-up saying "HI-SPEED USB Device Plugged into non-HI-SPEED USB Hub" or "This USB device can perform faster if you connect it to a Hi-Speed USB 2.0 port," while the iTunes warning is an easy-to-understand message box.

Check Your Operating System Version

Make sure your PC is running Windows Vista or Windows XP with Service Pack 3. If you're in doubt about which version of Windows your computer is running, press WINDOWS KEY–BREAK, and then look at the System window (on Windows Vista; see Figure 1-6) or the General tab of the System dialog box (on Windows XP; see Figure 1-7). If you don't have one of these versions of Windows, upgrade to one of them—or to Windows 7 if Microsoft has released it by the time you're reading this.

 If you want to use an iPod or iPhone with an older version of Windows—such as Windows 98 Second Edition, Windows Me, or Windows 2000 Professional—you'll need to use third-party software. See Chapter 14 for details.

Check Memory and Disk Space

If you don't know how much memory your computer has, check it. As in the previous section, press WINDOWS KEY–BREAK, and then look at the System window (on Windows Vista) or the General tab of the System dialog box (on Windows XP).

To check disk space, follow these steps:

1. Open a Windows Explorer window to display all the drives on your computer:
   - **Windows Vista**   Choose Start | Computer.
   - **Windows XP**   Choose Start | My Computer.
2. Right-click the drive you want to check, and then choose Properties from the shortcut menu to display the Properties dialog box for the drive.

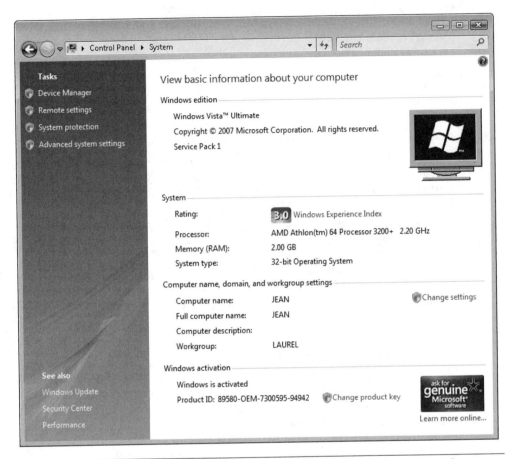

FIGURE 1-6 In Windows Vista, the System window shows which version of Windows you're using, which Service Pack is installed, and how much RAM the computer contains.

3. Look at the readout on the General tab of the Properties dialog box to see the amount of free space and used space on the drive. Figure 1-8 shows an example using Windows Vista.
4. Click the OK button to close the Properties dialog box.

Add a Burner Drive if Necessary

If you want to be able to burn CDs or DVDs from iTunes, add a burner drive to your computer. Which drive technology is most appropriate depends on your computer type and configuration:

- For a desktop PC that has an open 5.25-inch bay and a spare internal drive connector, an internal burner drive is easiest.

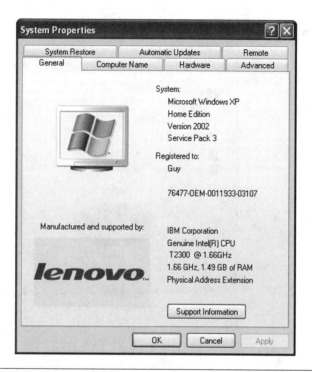

FIGURE 1-7   The readouts on the General tab of the System Properties dialog box typically include the version of Windows, the latest Service Pack, and the amount of RAM in your PC.

- For a desktop PC that has no open 5.25-inch bay or no spare internal drive connector, or for a portable PC, get a USB 2.0 burner drive.

Note   Because USB 1.*x* is relatively slow, USB 1.*x* CD recorders can manage only 4*x* burning speeds. Therefore, you'll probably want to use USB 1.*x* only when you must—for example, if you have a USB 1.*x* drive available and can't afford to upgrade.

Get Your Mac Ready to Work with an iPod or iPhone

If you bought your Mac in 2004 or later, chances are it's already all set to work with an iPod or iPhone: It has one or more USB 2.0 ports, Mac OS X (Tiger, Leopard, or Snow Leopard) with iTunes, plenty of disk space and memory, and a CD or DVD burner drive as well.

But if you have an older Mac, it may lack a USB 2.0 port; that means you'll either need to add a USB 2.0 port or suffer slow USB 1.*x* transfer speeds instead. And if your Mac doesn't have a CD or DVD burner drive, you may need to add a burner drive to get the best out of iTunes.

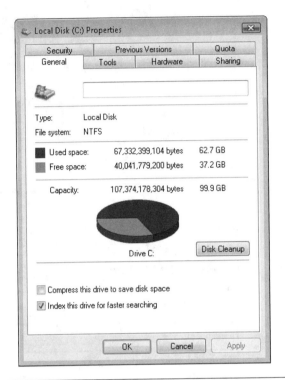

FIGURE 1-8   The General tab of the Properties dialog box for a drive shows you how much space has been used and how much remains free.

Add USB 2.0 if Necessary

If your Mac lacks a USB 2.0 port, add one or more USB 2.0 ports:

- **Desktop Mac**   Insert a PCI card in a vacant slot.
- **Laptop Mac**   Insert a PC Card.

If you have an iPod shuffle and your Mac has only a USB 1.x port, you probably don't need to upgrade, because the USB 1.x port will fill an iPod shuffle in a tolerably short time.

Check Your Operating System Version

Make sure your version of Mac OS is advanced enough to work with the iPod. You need Mac OS X 10.4.11 (Tiger with updates) or 10.5 (Leopard) or 10.6 (Snow Leopard) to use current iPods or the iPhone. Upgrade if necessary, or use Software Update (choose Apple | Software Update) to download the latest point releases.

How to...   # Check the Speed of Your Mac's USB Ports

If you're not sure of the speed of your Mac's USB ports, check them like this:

1. Choose Apple | About This Mac to display the About This Mac dialog box.
2. Click the More Info button to launch the System Profiler utility, which displays more detailed information about the Mac.
3. Expand the Hardware entry in the Contents pane if it's collapsed. Then click the USB item to display its contents.
4. Select one of the USB Bus items in the USB Device Tree pane and check the Speed readout in the lower pane, as shown here. If the readout says "Up to 12 Mb/sec," it's USB 1.*x*. If the readout says "Up to 480 Mb/sec," it's USB 2.0.

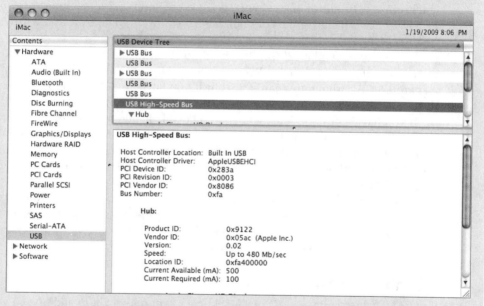

5. Press ⌘-Q or choose System Profiler | Quit System Profiler to close System Profiler.

If you're not sure which version of Mac OS X you have, choose Apple | About This Mac to display the About This Mac window. Then look at the Version readout.

   Tip   Apple frequently adds new features to iTunes, the iPods, and the iPhone. To get the latest features and to make sure that iTunes and the iPod or iPhone work as well as possible, keep Mac OS X, iTunes, and the device up to date. To check for updates, choose Apple | Software Update.

Check Disk Space and Memory

Make sure your Mac has enough disk space and memory to serve the iPod or iPhone adequately.

In most cases, memory shouldn't be an issue: If your Mac can run Mac OS X and conventional applications at a speed you can tolerate without sedation, it should be able to handle the iPod or iPhone. Technically, either Leopard or Snow Leopard requires a minimum of 512MB, but you'll get far better performance with 1GB or more—preferably much more.

Disk space is more likely to be an issue if you will want to keep many thousands of songs and videos in your library. The best situation is to have enough space on your hard drive to contain your entire library, both at its current size and at whatever size you expect it to grow to within the lifetime of your Mac. That way, you can easily synchronize your entire library with the iPod or iPhone (if your library fits on the device) or just whichever part of your library you want to take around with you for the time being.

For example, to fill a 120GB iPod with music and video, you'll need 120GB of disk space to devote to your library. Recent desktop Macs have hard disks large enough to spare 120GB without any hardship, but if you have an older desktop Mac or a MacBook, you may not be able to spare that much space.

If you have a desktop Mac, you should be able to add another hard drive without undue effort. Typically, the least expensive option will be to add another EIDE hard drive or SCSI drive (depending on the configuration of your Mac) to the inside of your Mac. Alternatively, you can go for an external FireWire, USB, or SCSI drive (if your Mac has SCSI).

If you have a MacBook, an iMac, or a Mac mini, your best bet is probably to add an external FireWire or USB hard drive. Replacing the internal hard drive on these Macs tends to be prohibitively expensive—not to mention that you must transfer or reinstall the operating system, your applications, and all your data after the upgrade.

Add a Burner Drive if Necessary

If your Mac doesn't have a CD or DVD burner, you may want to add one so you can burn CDs or DVDs from iTunes and other applications.

For a desktop Mac that has a full-sized drive bay free, an internal burner drive is the least expensive option. Or for either a desktop Mac or a MacBook, add an external FireWire or USB burner drive.

2

Configure iTunes and Load the iPod or iPhone with Music, Video, and Data

HOW TO...

- Identify the different components included with the iPod or iPhone
- Set up the iPod or iPhone and connect it to your PC or Mac
- Install iTunes
- Start creating your library from existing files and CDs
- Load music, video, and data onto the iPod or iPhone
- Connect and load the iPod shuffle
- Eject and disconnect the iPod or iPhone

In this chapter, you'll unpack the iPod or iPhone (if you haven't already done so), give it an initial full charge if it needs one, and connect it to your PC or Mac. You'll install iTunes if you don't already have it installed. Then you'll start creating your library from any existing digital audio and video files you have and from your audio CDs. Finally, you'll load the iPod or iPhone with songs, videos, contacts, calendars, and other information.

This chapter discusses how to proceed on both Windows and the Mac. Most of the way, the process is the same for both operating systems. Where they differ, the chapter presents Windows first and then the Mac, so you'll need to skip past the sections that cover the operating system that you're not using.

Unpack the iPod or iPhone

The different models of iPod and iPhone ship with different components and accessories, but most have the following basics:

- The iPod or iPhone itself.
- A pair of ear-bud headphones. The iPhone headphones include a microphone and control button, which the iPod headphones don't include. The third-generation iPod shuffle headphones include three control buttons.
- A USB cable for attaching the iPod or iPhone to your computer.
- Booklets containing basic instructions and technical information.

The iPhone also includes a power adapter. This is built to accept AC input from 100 to 240 volts, so with the right adapters, you can use it to power the iPhone most of the way around the world.

 The Apple Store (http://store.apple.com) sells a World Travel Adapter Kit for the iPod. You can also get clumsier but less expensive adapters at RadioShack or any competent electronics store.

The second-generation iPod shuffle also includes a dock on which to stand, charge, and load the device. You can buy docks for the other iPods and the iPhone from the Apple Store (http://store.apple.com) and many other sources. The iPod classic, the iPod touch, and the iPod nano include adapters for docks that meet the Apple iPod Universal Dock specification, a standard design that works with these iPods and several earlier models.

Install iTunes if It's Not Already Installed

Before you connect the iPod or iPhone, you need to install iTunes on your computer—unless you have it installed already, as is likely on a Mac. The process is a little different on Windows and on the Mac, so the next two sections discuss the operating systems separately.

Install iTunes on Your PC

To install iTunes on your PC, follow these steps:

1. Open your browser, go to the iTunes Download page on the Apple website (www.apple.com/itunes/download/), and then download the latest version of iTunes.
2. If Internet Explorer displays a File Download – Security Warning dialog box like the one shown here, verify that the name is iTunesSetup.exe. Then click the Run button.

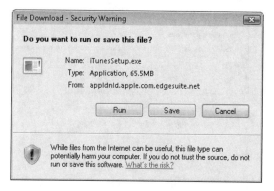

3. If Internet Explorer displays an Internet Explorer – Security Warning dialog box like the one shown here, verify that the program name is iTunes and the publisher is Apple Inc. Then click the Run button.

4. On the Welcome To The iTunes Installer screen, click the Next button.
5. On the License Agreement screen, read the license agreement, select the I Accept The Terms In The License Agreement option button if you want to proceed, and then click the Next button.
6. On the Installation Options screen (see Figure 2-1), choose installation options:
   - **Add iTunes And QuickTime Shortcuts To My Desktop** Select this check box only if you need shortcuts on your desktop. The installation routine creates shortcuts on your Start menu anyway. The Start menu is usually the easiest way to launch iTunes.
   - **Use iTunes As The Default Player For Audio Files** Select this check box if you plan to use iTunes as your main audio player. If you plan to use iTunes only for synchronizing the iPod or iPhone and use another player (for example, Windows Media Player) for music, don't make iTunes the default player. iTunes associates itself with the AAC, MP3, Apple Lossless Encoding, AIFF, and WAV file extensions.
   - **Default iTunes Language** In this drop-down list, choose the language you want to use—for example, English (United States).
   - **Destination Folder** The installer installs iTunes in an iTunes folder in your Program Files folder by default. This is fine for most computers, but if you want to use a different folder, click the Change button, choose the folder, and then click the OK button.

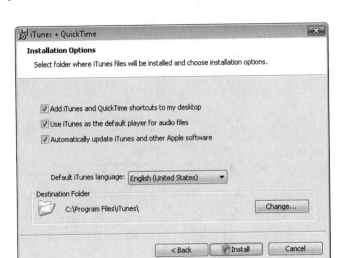

FIGURE 2-1 Choose whether to create shortcuts for iTunes and QuickTime on your Desktop, use iTunes as the default audio player, and update iTunes and QuickTime automatically.

7. Click the Install button to start the installation.
8. The installer displays the iTunes + QuickTime screen while it installs iTunes and QuickTime. On Windows XP, you need take no action until the Congratulations screen appears, telling you that iTunes and QuickTime have been successfully installed. However, on Windows Vista, you must go through several User Account Control prompts for different components of the iTunes installation (unless you've turned User Account Control off).

 On Windows Vista, the User Account Control prompts may get stuck behind the iTunes + QuickTime screen. Look at the taskbar now and then to see if there's a flashing User Account Control prompt that you need to deal with before the installation can continue. Don't leave the installation unattended, because if you don't answer the User Account Control prompt, it times out and cancels the installation of the component.

9. When the Congratulations screen appears, leave the Open iTunes After The Installer Exits check box selected if you want to run iTunes immediately; otherwise, clear it. Then click the Finish button to close the installer.

Configure iTunes the First Time You Run It

After installing iTunes, you must configure it.

If you allowed the installer to run iTunes, the program now opens. If not, choose Start | iTunes | iTunes when you're ready to start running iTunes. After you accept the iTunes Software License Agreement, the iTunes Setup Assistant starts, and walks you through the setup process.

**Decide Whether to Convert Your
WMA Files to AAC Files**

Converting your unprotected WMA files to AAC files is usually a good idea. WMA files can be protected with digital rights management (DRM) restrictions that control which computers can play the files. iTunes can't convert protected WMA files to AAC files.

Technically, the AAC files you end up with contain all the flaws of the original WMA files plus any flaws that the AAC encoding introduces. This is because all "lossy" audio formats lose audio quality, introducing flaws into the resulting audio files.

In practice, however, if the WMA files sound great to you, the AAC files will probably sound at least acceptable—and you can play them on the iPod, which you cannot do with the WMA files.

In any case, the conversion process leaves the original WMA files untouched, so if you don't like the resulting AAC files, you can simply delete them. One thing to bear in mind is that the AAC files will probably take up around the same amount of space on your computer's hard disk as the WMA files, so you should make sure you have plenty of free space before you convert the files.

During the setup process, you make the following decisions:

- **Whether to have iTunes scan your Music folder or My Music folder for any music files so that it can add them to your library**   Scanning now is usually a good idea (see Figure 2-2), but you may prefer to add files manually later (see "Add Existing Song Files to Your Library," later in this chapter). Select the Add MP3 And

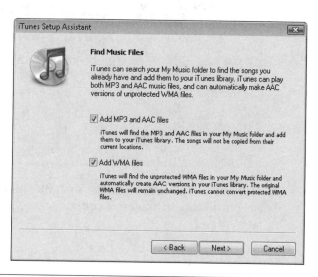

FIGURE 2-2   iTunes offers to scan your Music folder or My Music folder for AAC and MP3 files. You can also have iTunes create AAC files from any WMA files you have.

AAC Files check box if you want to find files of these types and add them to the library. Select the Add WMA Files check box if you want iTunes to find unprotected WMA files and create AAC files from them.

- **Whether to let iTunes keep your Music folder organized** On the Keep iTunes Music Folder Organized screen (see Figure 2-3), decide whether to let iTunes rename files for you. See the sidebar "Decide Whether to Let iTunes Organize Your Music Folder" for details on this decision.

Once you've finished the iTunes Setup Assistant, the iTunes window appears.

If your computer is connected to the Internet, iTunes checks to see if an updated version is available. If one is available, iTunes prompts you to download it (which may take a few minutes, depending on the speed of your Internet connection) and install it. Usually, after updating iTunes, you'll need to run through the iTunes Setup Assistant again. You may also need to restart your PC.

Connect the iPod or iPhone to Your PC

Next, connect the iPod or iPhone to your PC. Connect the USB end of the iPod's cable to your computer, and then connect the other end to the iPod or iPhone.

FIGURE 2-3   iTunes can automatically rename song files and folders for you to keep your library in apple-pie order.

How to...

Decide Whether to Let iTunes Organize Your Music Folder

Take a moment to think about the Keep iTunes Music Folder Organized setting, because it decides whether you or iTunes controls the organization of the files in your library.

If you turn this feature on, iTunes stores a song in a file named after the track number (if you choose to include it). iTunes places the song in a folder named after the album; this folder is stored within a folder named after the artist, which is placed in your iTunes Music folder.

For example, if you rip the album *How to Save a Life* by The Fray, iTunes stores the first song as \The Fray\How to Save a Life\01 She Is.aac on Windows or as /The Fray/How to Save a Life/01 She Is.aac on Mac OS X. If you then edit the artist field in the tag to "Fray" instead of "The Fray," iTunes changes the name of the artist folder to "Fray" as well.

This automatic renaming is nice and logical for iTunes, but you may dislike the way folder and file names change when you edit the tags. If so, turn off the Keep iTunes Music Folder Organized feature. You can change this setting at any time on the Advanced tab in the iTunes dialog box (in Windows) or the Preferences dialog box (on the Mac), but it's least confusing to make a choice at the beginning and then stick with it.

At this point, depending on the iPod or iPhone and the version of iTunes you have, either or both of two things may happen:

- **Restore**   iTunes may prompt you to "restore" the device to change it from Macintosh formatting to PC formatting. Click the OK button and follow through the prompts. iTunes formats the iPod's hard disk or flash memory, reinstalls its operating system, and then displays a message box telling you it has done so.
- **Update**   iTunes may tell you that the device's software isn't up to date and prompt you to update it. Doing so is almost always a good idea, but be prepared to wait for a few minutes while iTunes downloads the update.

Install or Update iTunes on the Mac

If you have a Mac running Mac OS X, you most likely have iTunes installed already, because iTunes is included in a default installation of Mac OS X.

Even if you explicitly exclude iTunes from the installation, Software Update offers you each updated version of iTunes that becomes available, so you need to refuse the updates manually or tell Software Update to ignore them. (To tell Software Update to ignore updates, select the iTunes item in the list, and then press ⌘-BACKSPACE or choose Update | Ignore Update.)

Get and Install the Latest Version of iTunes

If you've managed to refuse all these updates, the easiest way to install the latest version of iTunes is to use Software Update:

1. Choose Apple | Software Update to launch Software Update, which checks automatically for updates. (Your Mac must be connected to the Internet to use Software Update.)
2. If Software Update doesn't turn up a version of iTunes that you can install, choose Software Update | Reset Ignored Updates. Software Update then checks automatically for the latest versions of updates you've ignored and presents the list.
3. Make sure the iTunes check box is selected, and then click the Install Items button. Follow through the update process, entering your password in the Authenticate dialog box and accepting the license agreements.
4. Restart your Mac when Software Update prompts you to do so. iTunes Setup then runs automatically (see the next section).

Set Up iTunes if You Haven't Already Done So

If you haven't used iTunes before, or if you've just installed it, follow the steps in the iTunes Setup Assistant to configure iTunes.

If the iTunes Setup Assistant isn't running yet, click the iTunes icon on the Dock. If there's no iTunes icon on the Dock, click the Finder icon on the Dock (or click the desktop), choose Go | Applications or press ⌘-SHIFT-A to open your Applications folder, and then double-click the iTunes icon.

During the setup process, you make three key decisions:

- **Whether to use iTunes for Internet audio content** If you accept the default setting (leaving the Yes, Use iTunes For Internet Audio Content option button selected, as shown in Figure 2-4), iTunes becomes the helper application for audio you access through your web browser (for example, Safari). This is normally a good idea unless you prefer to use another music player.
- **Whether to have iTunes scan your Home folder for any music files so that it can add them to your library** Scanning now is usually a good idea (see Figure 2-5), but you may prefer to add files manually later (see "Add Existing Song Files to Your Library," later in this chapter).
- **Whether to let iTunes keep your Music folder organized** On the Keep iTunes Music Folder Organized screen, decide whether to let iTunes rename files for you. See the sidebar "Decide Whether to Let iTunes Organize Your Music Folder," earlier in this chapter, for details on this decision.

During setup, iTunes also displays an information screen telling you that it can download album artwork when you add songs to your library and that you need to sign into the iTunes Store to use this feature.

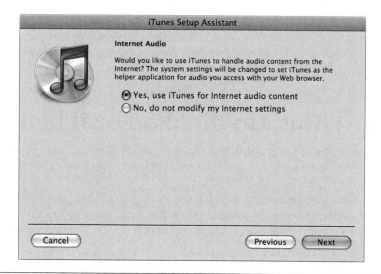

FIGURE 2-4   Choose whether to use iTunes for Internet audio content.

 iTunes requires QuickTime for some of its features to work. The iTunes Setup Assistant may prompt you to use Software Update (choose Apple | Software Update) to install the latest version of QuickTime so that all the iTunes features work.

Now connect the USB end of the cable that came with the iPod or iPhone to your computer, and then connect the other end to the Dock Connector port on the bottom

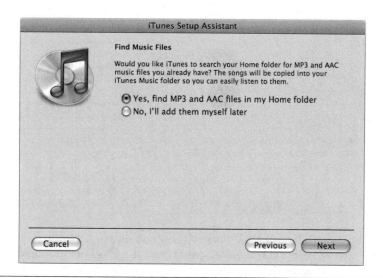

FIGURE 2-5   iTunes offers to scan your Home folder for AAC and MP3 files. If your files are in other folders, you can add them manually later.

of the device. For a third-generation iPod, slide the other end of the cable into the headphone socket. For a second-generation iPod shuffle, connect the dock's cable to a USB port on your computer, and then impale the iPod shuffle's headphone socket on the connector spike.

Finish Setting Up the iPod or iPhone

After you install iTunes and connect the iPod or iPhone, iTunes recognizes the device, adds it to the Devices list in the Source list, and displays the Set Up Your iPod screen shown in Figure 2-6 (for an iPod).

For an iPhone, iTunes displays the Set Up Your iPhone screen, which lets you make similar choices for the iPhone. Before this, though, iTunes walks you through registering your iPhone and specifying which iTunes account (if you have one) to use with the iPhone.

 Hackers have devised various ways of bypassing iPhone activation so that they can use the nonphone features of their iPhones. To learn more about this topic, search for **iPhone activation hack** on the Internet.

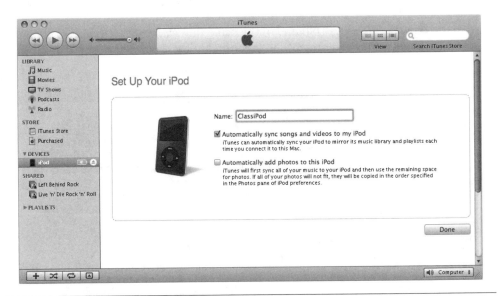

FIGURE 2-6   The Set Up Your iPod screen (shown here) or the Set Up Your iPhone screen lets you name the iPod or iPhone, choose whether to update it automatically from the start, and decide whether to synchronize pictures.

Follow these steps to finish setting up the iPod or iPhone:

1. In the Name text box, you can change the name that iTunes has suggested for the iPod or iPhone—for example, Max's iPod.
2. Choose what to synchronize for an iPod:
   - If the iPod has enough space to store your entire library, and you want to synchronize all items in your library with the iPod, select the Automatically Sync Songs And Videos To My iPod check box. If you want to update the iPod manually from the start, clear this check box.
   - If you want to synchronize photos automatically with the iPod, select the Automatically Add Photos To This iPod check box. On Windows, open the Sync Photos From drop-down list and select the source of the photos—for example, your Pictures folder on Windows Vista, or your My Pictures folder on Windows XP.
3. Choose what to synchronize for an iPhone:
   - Select the Automatically Sync Contacts, Calendars, Email Accounts, And Bookmarks check box if you want to synchronize all these items.
   - Select the Automatically Sync Applications check box if you want iTunes to automatically sync any applications you buy (or get for free) from the App Store.
4. Click the Done button to apply your choices.

Start Creating Your Library

Before you can add any songs or other items to the iPod or iPhone, you must add them to your library in iTunes. This section gets you started with the basics of adding songs to your library either from CDs or from existing digital audio files. Chapter 10 covers this topic in far greater depth, discussing how to plan, create, and manage an effective library for iTunes, an iPod or iPhone, and your household.

Add Existing Song Files to Your Library

While setting up iTunes, you probably let iTunes add song files automatically to your library from your Music folder (on Windows Vista), your My Music folder (on Windows XP), or your Home folder (on the Mac). You can quickly add further songs to your library from other folders—but before you do, check whether iTunes is set to copy the songs to your Music folder.

Decide Whether to Copy All Song Files to Your Library

The ideal setup is to store all your songs and videos within your Music folder (on Windows Vista), your My Music folder (on Windows XP), or your Home folder (on the Mac). Typically, this folder is on your computer's hard drive (or on its primary hard drive, if it has more than one hard drive).

That means your hard drive must have enough space for all your songs, videos, and other items (for example, podcasts), not to mention the operating system, your applications, and all your other files (for example, documents, pictures, and video files). For a modest-sized library, this is easy enough. But for the kind of library that most music enthusiasts accumulate over the years, it means your computer must have a huge hard drive. Most modern desktop computers do, but at this writing laptop hard drives are limited to around 300GB—and most laptops have hard drives that are far smaller than this.

Another possibility is to store your entire library on a server or on an external disk. See Chapter 10 for a discussion of this option.

If your computer does have a huge hard drive, all is well. But if it doesn't, you'll have to either make do with only some of the songs and videos you want or store some of the files on other drives or other computers. You can tell iTunes to store references to where files are located rather than store a copy of each file in the library folder on your hard drive.

Even if your computer has enough hard drive space for all your songs, you may prefer not to store them in your Music folder, My Music folder, or Home folder so that you can more easily share them through the file system with other members of your household. iTunes' Sharing features (discussed in Chapter 10) enable you to share even files stored in your private folders, but they limit other users to playing the songs (rather than adding them to their music libraries) and work only when iTunes is running. For more flexibility, you may prefer to store shared songs on a server or in a folder that all members of your household can access.

To control whether iTunes copies song files or merely stores references to where the song files are, follow these steps:

1. Display the iTunes dialog box or the Preferences dialog box:
   - In Windows, choose Edit | Preferences or press CTRL-COMMA or CTRL-Y to display the iTunes dialog box.
   - On the Mac, choose iTunes | Preferences or press ⌘-COMMA or ⌘-Y to display the Preferences dialog box.
2. Click the Advanced tab to display its contents.
3. Select the Copy Files To iTunes Music Folder When Adding To Library check box if you want to copy the files (see Figure 2-7). Otherwise, clear this check box.
4. Click the OK button to close the dialog box.

Storing references is great when you have too little space free on your hard disk to accommodate your colossal library. For example, if you have a laptop whose hard disk is bulging at the seams, you might choose to store in your library only references to songs located on an external hard disk rather than trying to import a copy of each song.

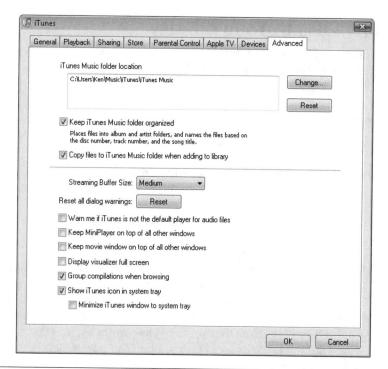

FIGURE 2-7   Clear the Copy Files To iTunes Music Folder When Adding To Library check box if you don't want to store a copy of each song file on your hard disk.

However, you won't be able to play any song stored on the external hard disk when your laptop isn't connected to it.

Add Songs to Your Library

To add songs to your library, follow these instructions:

- In Windows, to add a folder of songs, choose File | Add Folder To Library. In the Browse For Folder dialog box, navigate to and select the folder you want to add. Click the OK button, and iTunes either copies the song files to your library (if you selected the Copy Files To iTunes Music Folder When Adding To Library check box) or adds references to the song files (if you cleared this check box).
- In Windows, to add a single file, choose File | Add File To Library or press CTRL-O. In the Add To Library dialog box, navigate to and select the file you want to add. Click the OK button, and iTunes adds it.
- On the Mac, choose File | Add To Library or press ⌘-O. In the Add To Library dialog box, navigate to and select the folder or the file you want to add and then click the Choose button to add the folder or file.

Copy CDs to Your Library

The other way to add your existing digital music to your library is to copy it from CD. iTunes makes the process as straightforward as can be, but you should first verify that the iTunes settings for importing music are suitable.

Check iTunes' Settings for Importing Music

Follow these steps to check iTunes' settings for importing music:

1. Display the iTunes dialog box or the Preferences dialog box:
   - In Windows, choose Edit | Preferences or press CTRL-COMMA or CTRL-Y to display the iTunes dialog box.
   - On the Mac, choose iTunes | Preferences or press ⌘-COMMA or ⌘-Y to display the Preferences dialog box.
2. Click the General tab if it's not already displayed.
3. In the When You Insert A CD drop-down list, choose the action you want iTunes to take when you insert a CD: Show CD, Begin Playing, Ask To Import CD, Import CD, or Import CD And Eject. When you're building your library, Show CD is usually the best choice, as it gives you the chance to scan the CD information for errors that you need to correct before you import the CD.
4. Click the Import Settings button to open the Import Settings dialog box (see Figure 2-8).
5. Verify that AAC Encoder is selected in the Import Using drop-down list.
6. In the Setting drop-down list, choose High Quality if you want good audio quality with a compact file size—for example, if you have an iPod shuffle or a low-capacity iPod nano or iPhone. Choose iTunes Plus if you're prepared to use twice as much disk space to improve the audio quality.

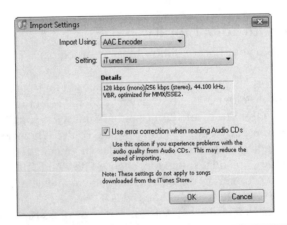

FIGURE 2-8   Before importing music, open the Import Settings dialog box and make sure that iTunes is configured with suitable settings.

7. Click the OK button to close the Import Settings dialog box.
8. Click the OK button to close the iTunes dialog box or Preferences dialog box.

iTunes can store the music extracted from CDs in several different formats, including Advanced Audio Coding (AAC, the default), MP3, and Apple Lossless Encoding. Chapter 6 discusses the pros and cons of the various formats and how to choose between them. For the moment, this book assumes that you are using AAC.

Add a CD to Your Library

To add a CD to your library, follow these steps:

1. Start iTunes if it's not already running.
2. Insert the CD in your computer's optical drive (CD drive or DVD drive). iTunes loads the CD and displays an entry for it in the Source list. If your computer is connected to the Internet, iTunes retrieves the CD's information and displays it (see Figure 2-9).
3. Look at the CD's information and make sure that it is correct. If not, click twice (with a pause between the clicks) on the piece of information you want to change, type the correction, and then press ENTER (Windows) or RETURN (Mac).

You can also change CD or song information in other ways. See Chapters 6 and 9 for the details.

4. Clear the check box for any song you don't want to import.
5. Click the Import CD button. iTunes extracts the audio from the CD, converts it to the format you chose, and saves the files to your library.

FIGURE 2-9 Load a CD, check that the data is correct, and then click the Import CD button to import its songs into your library.

How to... Associate Your Music Files with iTunes on Windows

If iTunes notices that it's not the default player for the audio file types it normally plays, it displays the dialog box shown here telling you about the problem (as iTunes sees it). On Windows Vista, iTunes prompts you to go to the Default Programs control panel to set it up, as shown on the left here. On Windows XP, iTunes simply suggests you make iTunes the default player, as shown on the right here.

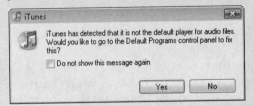 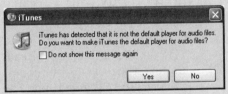

If you've set up another program to play these audio files, select the Do Not Show This Message Again check box and click the No button. Otherwise, click the Yes button. On Windows XP, iTunes simply grabs the file associations. On Windows Vista, iTunes opens the Set Program Associations window, shown here.

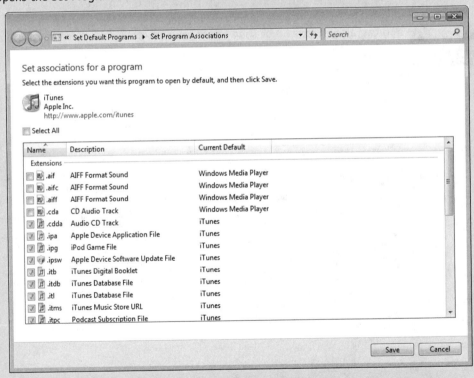

In the list box, select the check box for each of the files you want to associate with iTunes. Select the Select All check box if you're sure you want to associate all of them.

You can click the Current Default column heading to sort the list by program, which lets you quickly see which file types are assigned to other applications. Click the heading again if you need to sort in reverse order—for example, to bring the Windows Media Player–assigned file types to the top of the list.

When you've selected all the file types you want to associate, click the Save button. Windows closes the Set Program Associations window.

If you want Windows Vista to prompt you to show or import songs every time you insert an audio CD, choose Start | Control Panel, click the Classic View button link in the upper-left corner, and then double-click the AutoPlay icon. In the Audio CD drop-down list, choose Show Songs Using iTunes or Import Songs Using iTunes (as appropriate), and then click the Save button.

Check That the Songs You've Added Sound Okay

After adding the first CD, click the Music item under the Library category in the Source list, double-click the first song you imported from the CD, and listen to it to make sure there are no obvious defects (such as clicks or pauses) in the sound. If you have time, listen to several songs, or even the entire CD.

If the songs sound fine, you probably don't need to use error correction on your CD drive. But if you do hear defects, turn on error correction and copy the CD again. Here's how:

1. Display the iTunes dialog box or the Preferences dialog box:
   - In Windows, choose Edit | Preferences or press CTRL-COMMA or CTRL-Y to display the iTunes dialog box.
   - On the Mac, choose iTunes | Preferences or press ⌘-COMMA or ⌘-Y to display the Preferences dialog box.
2. Click the General tab if it's not already displayed.
3. Click the Import Settings button to open the Import Settings dialog box.
4. Select the Use Error Correction When Reading Audio CDs check box.
5. Click the OK button to close each dialog box.

In your library, click the first song that you ripped from the CD, hold down SHIFT, and click the last song from the CD to select all the songs. Press DELETE or BACKSPACE on your keyboard, click the Yes button in the confirmation dialog box, and then click the Yes button in the dialog box that asks whether you want to move the files from your Music folder to the Recycle Bin (on Windows) or the Trash (on the Mac).

Click the CD's entry in the Source list, and then click the Import CD button to import the songs again. Check the results and make sure they're satisfactory before you import any more CDs.

Load the iPod or iPhone with Music, Video, and Data

If you chose to let iTunes update the iPod or iPhone automatically, iTunes performs the first update after you connect the device. If the device is an iPod, and your library will fit on it, iTunes copies all the songs to the iPod. All you need to do is wait until the songs have been copied and then disconnect it (see "Eject and Disconnect the iPod or iPhone," later in this chapter).

Load Only Some Songs from Your Library on an iPod or iPhone

If your library is larger than the capacity of the iPod or iPhone, iTunes warns you of the problem (see Figure 2-10). Click the Yes button to let iTunes put an automatic selection of songs on the iPod or iPhone; iTunes creates a playlist named *device's name* Selection (where *device's name* is the name you've given the iPod or iPhone), assigns a selection of songs to it, and copies them to the iPod or iPhone. Click the No button if you want to make the selection yourself.

Configure How the iPod or iPhone Is Loaded

If you decide against having iTunes load the iPod or iPhone automatically, change the device's settings as follows:

1. Click the device's entry in the Source list.
2. On the Summary tab, select the Manually Manage Music And Videos check box. iTunes displays a confirmation message box, as shown here.

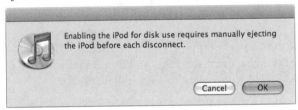

3. Click the OK button to close the message box.
4. Click each of the other tabs in turn, and choose the items you want to sync. For example, here's how to choose settings on the Music tab:
   - Select the Sync Music check box.
   - Select the All Songs And Playlists option button to synchronize your entire library. Select the Include Music Videos check box if you want to include music videos with the songs.
   - Select the Selected Playlists Only option button if you want to synchronize the iPod or iPhone with the playlists whose check boxes you select in the list box. This is a good choice when the device doesn't have enough capacity to hold your entire library.
5. Click the Apply button.

Why Your First-Ever Synchronization May Take Much Longer than Subsequent Synchronizations

USB 2.0 connections are fast, but your first-ever synchronization of an iPod or iPhone may take an hour or two if your library contains many songs or videos. This is because iTunes copies each song or video to the device.

Subsequent synchronizations will be much quicker, because iTunes will need only to transfer new songs and videos you've added to your library, remove songs you've deleted, and update the data on items whose tags (information such as the artist name and song name) you've changed.

If you're using USB 1.x rather than USB 2.0 to synchronize an iPod or iPhone, the first synchronization will take several hours if your library contains many songs and videos. You might plan to perform the first synchronization sometime when you can leave your computer and the iPod or iPhone to get on with it—for example, overnight, or when you head out to work.

Tip   iTunes 8.1 and later versions let you use AutoFill to fill the iPhone and lower-capacity iPods as well as the iPod shuffle. See the section "Load the iPod shuffle Using AutoFill," later in this chapter, for instructions on using AutoFill.

Load Music on the iPod or iPhone Manually

If you decided against automatic updating of either your entire library or iTunes' automatic selection from it, you need to load the iPod or iPhone manually. You can perform either of the following actions:

- Connect the device to your computer, wait until its entry appears in the Source list, and then drag songs, artists, albums, or playlists to its entry. When you drop the items, iTunes copies the songs to the device, which takes a few seconds.

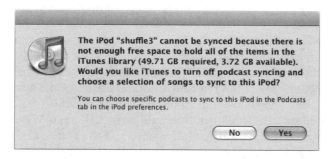

FIGURE 2-10   If your library is too large to fit on the iPod or iPhone, decide whether to let iTunes choose a selection of songs for it automatically.

- Create a playlist for the iPod or iPhone by choosing File | New Playlist, typing the name in the text box, and then pressing ENTER (Windows) or RETURN (Mac). Drag songs, albums, or artists to the playlist to add them. When you're ready to load the playlist, connect the iPod or iPhone to your computer, wait until its entry appears in the Source list, and then drag the playlist to the entry. iTunes then copies the songs to the device all at once.

To force iTunes to copy to an iPod or iPhone any song files that lack the tag information the device normally requires, add the songs to a playlist. Doing so can save you time over retagging many files manually and can be useful in a pinch. (In the long term, you'll probably want to make sure all your song files are tagged properly.)

Choose Custom Synchronization Settings

Setting up synchronization of songs, videos, and maybe photos with the iPod or iPhone is a good start, but you'll probably want to choose custom synchronization settings so that you can get exactly the files and data you want on the iPod or iPhone.

To choose custom settings, connect the iPod or iPhone, click the iPod or iPhone's entry in the Devices category in the Source list, and then set options on the device's settings tabs (discussed next). Click the Apply button in the lower-right corner of the window to apply your changes.

Choose Info or Contacts Synchronization Settings

On the Info tab (for the iPhone or iPod touch; see Figure 2-11) or the Contacts tab (for the iPod classic and iPod nano), choose which information you want to synchronize with the iPod or iPhone:

- **MobileMe (iPhone only)** Click the Learn More button to learn about how you can use Apple's MobileMe online service to push data to an iPhone.
- **Contacts** On Windows, select the Sync Contacts With check box and choose the source in the drop-down list: Yahoo! Address Book, Windows Address Book or Windows Contacts, Google Contacts, or Outlook. On Mac OS X, select the Sync Address Book Contacts check box. On either OS, either select the All Contacts option button, or select the Selected Groups option button and select the check box for each group of contacts you want. For the iPod classic and iPod nano, select the Include Contacts' Photos check box if you want to include photos. For the iPhone, select the Put New Contacts Created On This iPhone Into The Group check box and choose the group in the drop-down list.
- **Calendars** On Windows, select the Sync Calendars With check box and choose the source in the drop-down list—for example, Outlook. On the Mac, select the Sync iCal Calendars check box. On either OS, either select the All Calendars option button, or select the Selected Calendars option button and select the check box for each calendar you want.

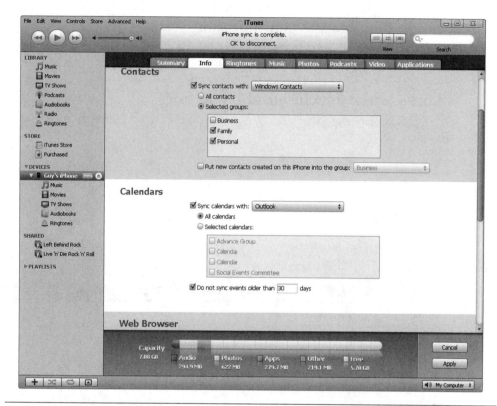

FIGURE 2-11   The Info tab lets you choose exactly which data to synchronize with the iPhone or iPod touch. For an iPod classic or iPod nano, use the Contacts tab to choose which contacts and calendars to synchronize.

- **Mail Accounts (iPhone and iPod touch only)**   On Windows, select the Sync Selected Mail Accounts From check box, and then choose the mail program in the drop-down list: Outlook, Outlook Express, or Windows Mail. On the Mac, select the Sync Selected Mail Accounts check box. On either OS, select the check box for each account you want to synchronize.
- **Web Browser (iPhone and iPod touch only)**   On Windows, select the Sync Bookmarks With check box, and then choose the browser (Internet Explorer or Safari) in the drop-down list. On the Mac, select the Sync Safari Bookmarks check box.
- **Advanced (iPhone and iPod touch only)**   If you need to overwrite the data on the iPhone or iPod touch with the data on your computer, select the Contacts check box, the Calendars check box, the Mail Accounts check box, or the Bookmarks check box, as appropriate. Normally, you won't need to do this—you'll need to synchronize the iPhone's or iPod touch's data with your computer's data instead.

Choose Ringtones Synchronization Settings

On the Ringtones tab, which appears only for the iPhone, select the Sync Ringtones check box, and then choose which ringtones to synchronize.

Choose Music Synchronization Settings

On the Music tab (see Figure 2-12), choose whether to synchronize music and, if so, which music:

1. If you want to synchronize music, select the Sync Music check box. If you prefer to load the iPod or iPhone manually, clear this check box and skip the rest of this list.

FIGURE 2-12   Use the Music tab to tell iTunes which playlists to put on the iPod or iPhone.

2. To synchronize all your songs and playlists, select the All Songs And Playlists option button. This is the best choice if the device has plenty of space. Otherwise, select the Selected Playlists option button, and then select the check box for each playlist you want to include.

3. Select the Include Music Videos check box if you want to synchronize music videos as well.

Choose Photos Synchronization Settings

To tell iTunes which photos to put on the iPod or iPhone, select the Sync Photos From check box, and then choose the source in the drop-down list.

Once you've done that, choose which photos to include:

- **Windows**   Select the All Photos option button to add all the photos. To add just some, select the Selected Folders option button, and then select the check box for each folder you want.
- **Mac OS X**   Select the All Photos And Albums option button if you want to include all the photos. To choose by Events, select the Events option button, and then choose which Events from the pop-up menu: All, 1 Most Recent, 3 Most Recent, 5 Most Recent, 10 Most Recent, or 20 Most Recent. (An *Event* is a group of photos in iPhoto that are organized by date or by topic.)

For the iPod classic and iPod nano, you can select the Include Full-Resolution Photos check box if you want to put the full-resolution versions of the pictures on the iPod as well as the smaller versions that iTunes prepares for you. Select this check box only if you want to have the original photos with you—for example, because you may need to share the photo files with people by connecting your iPod to their computer and transferring the files.

Choose Podcasts Synchronization Settings

On the Podcasts tab, select the Sync check, and then choose which episodes to synchronize:

- All the episodes (the simple choice)
- From 1 to 10 of the most recent episodes
- From 1 to 10 of the most recent unplayed episodes
- From 1 to 10 of the least recent unplayed episodes
- All the new episodes
- From 1 to 10 of the most recent new episodes
- From 1 to 10 of the least recent new episodes

Then select the All Podcasts option button if you want the setting to apply to all podcasts. Otherwise, select the Selected Podcasts option button, and then select the check box for each podcast you want to include.

Choose Video Synchronization Settings

On the Video tab (for an iPhone or iPod touch) or the Movies tab and TV Shows tab, choose which rented movies, movies, and TV shows you want to synchronize with the device. The settings vary for the different devices but are easy to use.

Choose Applications Synchronization Settings

For the iPhone and iPod touch, select Sync Applications on the Applications tab if you want to synchronize applications (as most likely you will on your primary computer). Then either select the All Applications option button—usually the best choice—or select the Selected Applications option button and then select the check box for each application you want to synchronize.

Recharge the iPod or iPhone

As with most devices, the battery icon on the iPod's or iPhone's display shows you the status of the device's battery power.

The easiest way to recharge the iPod or iPhone is to plug it into a high-power USB port on a computer. If the USB port provides enough power, you will see the battery indicator add a charging symbol. (If the port doesn't provide enough power, try another port.)

Alternatively, you can use an iPod or iPhone power adapter, an optional accessory. See Chapter 4 for details. The power adapter is useful when you need to recharge the iPod or iPhone away from any computer. You can also run the iPod or iPhone from the adapter even while the battery is charging.

 Using the power adapter to charge an iPod or iPhone is more reliable than using the USB cable, and the power adapter is useful for troubleshooting problems such as the device becoming nonresponsive. For this reason, a power adapter is a great accessory to have, even if you normally charge directly from the computer.

Most batteries take between three and five hours to recharge. After about half of the charging time, the battery should be at about 80 percent of its charge capacity—enough for you to use the iPod or iPhone for a while. (This is because the battery charges quickly at first, up to around the 80 percent level, and then charges more slowly the remainder of the way so as not to overcharge.)

Connect and Load the iPod shuffle

Because the iPod shuffle is different from the regular iPod, the iPod touch, the iPod nano, and the iPhone, connecting it and loading it are different too. This section discusses both the second-generation and third-generation iPod shuffle models, as Apple is selling both at this writing.

Connect the iPod shuffle

To connect a third-generation iPod shuffle, connect its cable to a high-power USB port on your computer, and then slide the other end of the cable into the iPod shuffle's headphone socket.

To connect a second-generation iPod shuffle, connect its dock to a high-power USB port on your computer, and then impale the iPod shuffle's headphone socket on the connector in the dock.

The iPod shuffle is formatted with the FAT32 file system for use with both PCs and Macs, so the iPod Software doesn't need to reformat it the first time you connect it to a PC.

Load the iPod shuffle

Because the iPod shuffle doesn't have enough capacity to hold any but the most modest library, iTunes includes a feature called Autofill for loading the iPod shuffle. Autofill lets you tell iTunes to fill the iPod shuffle to capacity with songs from either your library or a specified playlist. You can also load an iPod shuffle manually if you prefer.

Configure the iPod shuffle

Before you load the iPod shuffle for the first time, check that it is correctly configured:

1. Click the iPod shuffle's entry in the Source list to display its screens. Click the Settings tab if it isn't already displayed (see Figure 2-13).
2. Select the Open iTunes When This iPod Is Attached check box if you want your computer to automatically launch or activate iTunes when you connect the iPod. This is usually handy.
3. Select the Sync Only Checked Songs check box if you want to prevent iTunes from putting on the iPod any song whose check box you've cleared. This setting is usually helpful; it's not available if you select the Manually Manage Music check box.
4. Select the Enable Sound Check check box if you want to use the Sound Check feature to "normalize" the volume on the iPod. This helps prevent wide variations in the volume of songs, but it tends to make them sound less interesting because it squashes down the dynamic range—the difference in volume between the quietest bits and the loudest bits.
5. Select the Convert Higher Bit Rate Songs To 128 Kbps AAC check box if you want to get as many songs as possible on the iPod shuffle.

 Converting songs to 128 Kbps prevents higher-bitrate songs from sneaking onto the iPod shuffle and hogging its limited space. For a second-generation iPod shuffle, there's another benefit: This setting enables you to load songs in formats that the iPod shuffle doesn't support (for example, Apple Lossless Encoding). The drawbacks are that the conversion slows down the loading process a bit and reduces sound quality somewhat.

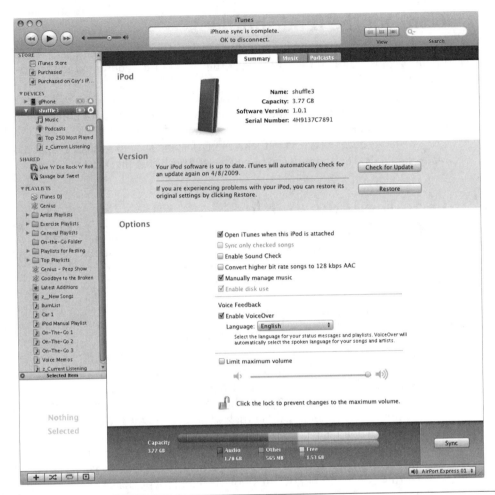

FIGURE 2-13 On the iPod shuffle, you can make iTunes convert higher-bitrate songs to 128 Kbps AAC files, and you can specify the amount of space you want to reserve for data.

6. If you want to load the iPod shuffle manually, select the Manually Manage Music check box, and then click the OK button in the confirmation message box that iTunes displays.

7. If you want to be able to store data on the iPod shuffle as well as songs, select the Enable Disk Use check box. iTunes displays a message box warning you that you will need to eject the iPod manually. Click the OK button to dismiss the message box. (The Enable Disk Use check box is automatically selected and unavailable when you've selected the Manually Manage Music check box.)

8. If you want to be able to use the third-generation iPod shuffle's VoiceOver feature for hearing song and artist names and switching playlists, select the Enable VoiceOver check box and choose your language in the Language pop-up menu.
9. If you want to prevent the iPod from playing louder than a certain volume, select the Limit Maximum Volume check box, and drag the slider to set the maximum volume.
10. Click the Apply button to apply the changes.

Load the iPod shuffle Using Autofill

The easiest way to load an iPod shuffle is to use Autofill:

1. Connect the iPod shuffle to your computer and wait for iTunes to add its entry to the Source list.

 You can use Autofill to load other low-capacity iPods and the iPhone as well.

2. Click the iPod shuffle's entry in the Source list to display the iPod shuffle's control screens.
3. Click the Music item under the iPod shuffle's entry. You may need to click the disclosure triangle to expand the items under the iPod shuffle's entry.
4. Open the Autofill From drop-down list and choose the source. Select the Music entry if you want iTunes to choose songs from your entire library. Choose a playlist if you want to confine the selection to just that playlist.
5. Click the Settings button to display the Autofill Settings dialog box (see Figure 2-14). The first time you use Autofill, configure it:

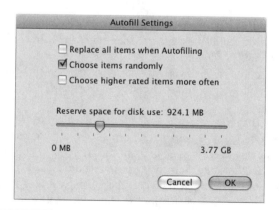

FIGURE 2-14   Autofill is the fast-and-easy way to fill an iPod or iPhone with songs chosen by iTunes either from your entire library or from a specific playlist.

6. Select the Replace All Items When Autofilling check box if you want iTunes to remove the songs that are currently on the iPod shuffle. Clear this check box if you want to keep the existing songs.

7. Select the Choose Items Randomly check box if you want a random selection on the iPod. Clear this check box if you want iTunes to choose from your chosen playlist (or your library) in order, starting from the first song and using all the available space.

8. Select the Choose Higher Rated Items More Often check box if you want iTunes to prefer the songs you've given a higher rating.

9. If you're using the iPod as a disk, drag the Reserve Space For Disk Use slider to tell iTunes how much space to reserve for files.

10. Click the OK button to close the Autofill Settings dialog box.

Once you've configured Autofill, you can load songs on the iPod by clicking the Autofill button. Wait until the display shows that the update is complete, and then check the list for songs you don't want to hear. If you find any, select them, and press the Delete button to remove them. You can then either add replacement songs manually or click the Autofill button again (with the Replace All Items When Autofilling check box cleared in the Autofill Settings dialog box) to fill up the remaining space with other songs.

How to... Keep the iPod shuffle Loaded with Your New Music

If you want to load an iPod shuffle with the latest music you've added to your library, use the Recently Added Smart Playlist that iTunes automatically creates.

Check that the iPod shuffle is set up to use the Recently Added Smart Playlist by following these steps:

1. Connect the iPod shuffle to your computer.
2. Click the iPod shuffle's entry in the Source list, and then click the Contents tab to display the iPod shuffle's contents.
3. Expand the iPod shuffle's entry if necessary, and then click the Music item.
4. Select Recently Added in the Autofill From drop-down list.

Next, check that the Recently Added Smart Playlist is set to track songs added during a suitably long period of time. The default setting is two weeks. If you add music frequently, you may need to specify a shorter interval; if you seldom add music, you may need a longer interval. You can choose among days, weeks, and months.

Right-click (or CTRL-click on the Mac) the Recently Added item in the Source list, and then choose Edit Smart Playlist from the shortcut menu to display the Smart Playlist dialog box. Check the condition, change it if necessary, and then click the OK button to close the dialog box.

With its limited capacity, the iPod shuffle is a great target for a well-thought-out Smart Playlist. See the section "Automatically Create Smart Playlists Based on Your Ratings and Preferences" in Chapter 10 for details on Smart Playlists. See the previous sidebar, "Keep the iPod shuffle Loaded with Your New Music," for a way to use Smart Playlists to put the latest songs you've acquired onto the iPod shuffle.

Load an iPod shuffle Manually

Instead of using Autofill, you can load an iPod shuffle manually. The most direct way is to connect the iPod shuffle to your computer, wait until the iPod shuffle's entry appears in the Source list, and then drag songs, artists, albums, or playlists to its entry. iTunes copies the songs to the iPod shuffle when you drop them.

Another option is to create a playlist for the iPod shuffle and then drag songs to the playlist. When you're ready to load the playlist, connect the iPod shuffle to your computer, wait until the iPod shuffle's entry appears in the Source list, and then drag the playlist to the entry. iTunes then copies the songs to the iPod shuffle all at once.

Eject and Disconnect the iPod or iPhone

When iTunes has finished loading songs onto the iPod or iPhone, you can disconnect it unless it's an iPod you're using in disk mode (or you need to continue recharging its battery). iTunes displays the message saying that the update is complete and "OK to disconnect." The iPod displays the message "OK to disconnect." When you see this message, you can unplug the iPod from the cable or from your computer.

If you're using an iPod in disk mode, however, iTunes doesn't prepare the iPod for disconnection after it finishes loading songs. Instead, it leaves the iPod mounted on your computer as a disk so that you can transfer files to and from it manually. When the iPod is in disk mode like this, it displays the message "Eject Before Disconnecting." In Mac OS X, an icon for the iPod appears on the desktop unless you have specifically chosen to exclude it (see the "Prevent the iPod from Appearing on the Desktop in Mac OS X" sidebar). See Chapter 12 for more information about disk mode.

At this writing, the iPhone and iPod touch have no disk mode, so you can safely remove either at any time that it is not showing the Sync In Progress screen. When the iPhone or iPod touch is showing this screen, you can drag your finger across the slider at the bottom of the screen to cancel the sync—for example, if you receive a phone call while the sync is running on the iPhone.

If you forget to eject the iPod or iPhone before you log out of Mac OS X, you shouldn't need to log back in to eject the device. If it's an iPod classic or an iPod nano, make sure that the screen is displaying the "OK to disconnect" message, and then disconnect the iPod. If it's an iPod shuffle, make sure that the orange or amber light isn't blinking. If it's an iPhone or iPod touch, make sure it's not displaying the Sync In Progress screen.

How to... **Prevent the iPod from Appearing on the Desktop in Mac OS X**

When the iPod is mounted in disk mode, it appears on the Mac OS X desktop by default. You can prevent it from appearing, but doing so also prevents CDs and DVDs from appearing. Here's how:

1. Click the Finder button on the toolbar, or click the desktop.
2. Choose Finder | Preferences to display the Finder Preferences window.
3. Click the General tab if it isn't already displayed.
4. Clear the CDs, DVDs, And iPods check box.
5. Click the Close button on the window, or choose File | Close Window or press ⌘-w, to close the window.

You can eject the iPod in any of the following ways:

- Click the Eject button that appears next to the device's entry in the Source list (see Figure 2-15).
- Right-click (or CTRL-click on the Mac) the device's entry in the Source list and then click the Eject item on the shortcut menu.
- Click the device's entry in the Source list and then choose Controls | Eject *device's name* or press CTRL-E (Windows) or ⌘-E (Mac).

FIGURE 2-15 The easiest way to eject the iPod or iPhone is to click its Eject button in the Source list.

3

Enjoy Music and Video
on the iPod or iPhone

HOW TO...

- Connect your headphones or speakers to an iPod or iPhone
- Play music and video on the iPhone or iPod touch
- Play music and video on an iPod classic or iPod nano
- Choose settings to make the iPod or iPhone easier to use
- Use key extra features
- Play music on the second-generation iPod shuffle
- Play music on the third-generation iPod shuffle

This chapter shows you the essentials of using an iPod or iPhone. You'll start by connecting your headphones or speakers, and then quickly get the hang of playing music and video, first on the iPhone and iPod touch and then on the iPod classic and iPod nano. After that, the chapter explains how to choose settings to make the iPhone or iPod easier and faster to use, and how to use other features such as the sleep timer, stopwatch, and passcode lock.

The second-generation iPod shuffle and third-generation iPod shuffle are substantially different from the other iPods and the iPhone, so this chapter discusses them separately in their own sections at the end of the chapter.

Connect Your Headphones or Speakers

The easiest way to get sound out of an iPod or iPhone is to connect your headphones or speakers to the headphones port. The headphones port is on the top of the iPod classic, the second-generation iPod shuffle, and the iPhone; on the iPod nano and the iPod touch, the port appears on the bottom. You can't miss it: a $\frac{1}{8}$-inch (3.5mm) round hole, into which you slide a miniplug of the corresponding size.

Connecting the miniplug and the port couldn't be easier, but a couple of things are worth mentioning:

- The headphone port delivers up to 60 milliwatts (mW) altogether—30 mW per channel. To avoid distortion or damage, turn down the volume when connecting the player to a different pair of headphones, powered speakers, or an amplifier. Make the connection, set the volume to low on the speakers or amplifier, and then start playing the audio.
- If you have a dock for the iPod or iPhone, you can play music from the device when it's docked. (The exception is the iPod shuffle, whose dock is for charging only.) Plug a cable with a stereo miniplug into the Line Out port on the Dock, and then connect the other end of the cable to your powered speakers or your stereo. Use the iPod's or iPhone's controls to navigate to the music, play it, pause it, and so on. Use the volume control on the speakers or the receiver to control the volume at which the songs play.

 The Line Out port delivers a standard volume and better audio quality than the headphone port, so it's well worth using a dock if you have one.

Use Headphones with an iPod or iPhone

Each iPod comes with a pair of ear-bud headphones—the kind that fit in your ear rather than sit on your ear or over your ear. The iPhone includes a similar pair of headphones that incorporates a pause button and a microphone in the cord. The third-generation iPod shuffle's headphones include playback and volume controls.

The headphones are designed to look good with the iPod—and in fact their distinctive white has helped muggers in many countries target victims with iPods and iPhones rather than those with less desirable audio players and phones.

Beyond that, these are good-quality headphones with a wide range of frequency response: from 20 Hz (hertz) to 20 kHz (kilohertz; 1,000 hertz), which is enough to cover most of the average human's hearing spectrum. Apple emphasizes that the headphones have drivers (technically, *transducers*) made of neodymium, a rare earth magnet that provides better frequency response and higher sound quality than alternative materials (such as cobalt, aluminum, or ceramics).

A wide range of frequency response and high sound quality are desirable, but what's more important to most people is that their headphones be comfortable and that they meet any other requirements, such as shutting out ambient sound or enhancing the wearer's charisma. See the sidebar "Choose Headphones to Suit You" for suggestions on evaluating and choosing headphones.

 If you're looking for the ultimate sound quality, look into having custom earphones molded to fit your ears. You can find these online (terms vary, but try searching for "in-ear monitors"), but you may also want to consult your local musical instruments store.

How to... # Choose Headphones to Suit You

If you don't like the sound the iPod's headphones deliver, or if you just don't find them comfortable, use another pair of headphones instead. Any headphones with a standard miniplug will work; if your headphones have a quarter-inch jack, get a good-quality miniplug converter to make the connection to the iPod. You don't need to break the bank by buying the most expensive converter, but those with gold-plated contacts tend to give noticeably better audio quality than ones with base metals, as well as costing more.

You can use another set of headphones with the iPhone, but you lose the benefit of the Pause button and microphone built into the headphone cord. For the third-generation iPod shuffle, you need either headphones with built-in playback and volume controls or an adapter from Apple that includes the controls.

Headphones largely break down into three main types, although you can find plenty of exceptions:

- **Ear-bud headphones**   The most discreet type of headphones and the easiest to fit in a pocket. Most ear buds wedge in your ears like the iPod's ear buds do, but others sit on a headband and poke in sideways.
- **Supra-aural headphones**   These headphones sit on your ears but don't fully cover them. Supra-aural headphones don't block out all ambient noise, which makes them good for situations in which you need to remain aware of the sounds happening around you. They also tend not to get as hot as circumaural headphones, because more air can get to your ears.
- **Circumaural headphones**   These headphones sit over your ears, usually enclosing them fully. *Open* circumaural headphones allow external sounds to reach your ears, whereas *sealed* circumaural headphones block as much external sound as possible. Sealed headphones are good for noisy environments, but even better are noise-canceling circumaural headphones such as Bose's QuietComfort headphones (www.bose.com), which use electronics to reduce the amount of ambient noise that you hear.

Headphones can cost anywhere from a handful of dollars to many hundred dollars. Even ear buds can be impressively expensive: Shure's top-of-the-line set, the SE530 ear buds, cost $499 (www.shure.com), and Etymotic Research, Inc.'s hf5 in-ear phones go for $149 (www.etymotic.com). When choosing headphones, always try them on for comfort and listen to them for as long as possible, using a variety of your favorite music on the iPod or iPhone, to evaluate their sound as fully as you can.

Whichever type of headphones you choose to use, don't turn the volume up high enough to cause hearing damage. Instead, if you use an iPod or iPhone often with a high-end pair of headphones, get a headphone amplifier to improve the sound. A headphone amplifier plugs in between the sound source and your headphones to boost and condition the signal. You don't necessarily have to listen to music *louder* through a headphone amplifier—the amplifier can also improve the sound at a lower volume. Many headphone amplifiers are available from various manufacturers, but HeadRoom's Total AirHead and Total BitHead seem especially well regarded (www.headphone.com). You can also find plans on the Web for building your own headphone amplifier.

Use Speakers with an iPod or iPhone

Instead of using headphones, you can also connect an iPod or iPhone to a pair of powered speakers, a receiver or amplifier, or your car stereo. Chapter 5 discusses this topic in detail, but briefly, there are two main ways of making such a connection:

- **Direct connection** Use a standard cable with a $\frac{1}{8}$-inch stereo headphone connector at the iPod end and the appropriate type of connector at the other end. For example, to connect an iPod to a conventional amplifier, you need two phono plugs on the other end of the cable.
- **Dock connection** If you have a dock for the iPod or iPhone, you can get higher-quality sound by connecting the receiver or amplifier to the dock's line-out port instead of the player's headphone port. The line-out port on the dock also gives a consistent level of signal, so you won't need to adjust the volume on the iPod or iPhone.

Powered speakers are speakers that contain an amplifier, so you don't need to use an external amplifier. Many speaker sets designed for use with portable CD players, MP3 players, and computers are powered speakers. Usually, only one of the speakers contains an amplifier, making one speaker far heavier than the other. Sometimes the amplifier is hidden in the subwoofer, which lets you put the weight on the floor rather than on the furniture.

The iPod and iPhone will work with any pair of speakers or stereo that can accept input, but you can also get various speakers designed specifically for these players. Chapter 4 discusses some of the options and suggests how to choose among them.

Play Music and Video on the iPhone or iPod touch

This section shows you how to play music and video on the iPhone or iPod touch. As usual, you use the touch screen to control everything.

Switch to iPod Mode

To play a song, first switch to iPod mode. Follow these steps:

1. Press the Home button to go to the Home screen unless you're already there (or you're already in iPod mode).
2. On the iPhone, touch the iPod button at the bottom of the Home screen. The iPhone switches to iPod mode and displays the last browse category you were using. On the iPod touch, touch the Music button if you want to play music; touch the Videos button if you want to play videos.

FIGURE 3-1   Use the browse buttons at the bottom of the screen to switch among playlists, artists, songs, videos, and other items (touch the More button).

Switch to the Browse Category You Want

In iPod mode, four browse buttons appear at the bottom of the screen: Playlists, Artists, Songs, and Videos or Albums, together with a More button. Touch the browse button by which you want to browse. For example, touch the Songs browse button to browse by song name, as shown on the left in Figure 3-1, or touch the Artists browse button to browse by artist name, as shown on the right in Figure 3-1.

The Playlists list contains the On-The-Go playlist that the iPhone or iPod touch creates for you, together with any other playlists you've created in iTunes.

The Songs list has a Shuffle item at the top that you can touch to play the songs in random order.

To browse by albums, audiobooks, compilations, composers, genres, or podcasts, touch the More button. The iPhone or iPod touch displays the More screen (shown on the left in Figure 3-2). From here, you can touch one of the browse categories to browse by that category. For example, touch the Albums category to browse by album name, as shown on the right in Figure 3-2.

How to... **Change the Browse Buttons at the Bottom of the iPod Screen**

To change the browse buttons at the bottom of the iPod screen, follow these steps:

1. Touch the More button to display the More screen.
2. Touch the Edit button to display the Configure screen, shown here with the Genres icon being moved.

3. Drag the icon from the main part of the screen to the browse button whose current icon you want to replace. (You can't replace the More button.)
4. Change other browse buttons as needed, and then touch the Done button.

The icon you removed from the browse button appears on the More screen, so you can easily restore it if you want to.

Find the Song or Other Item You Want to Play

To move down one of the lists, either drag your finger up the screen to pull the list upward, or touch one of the letters on the right to jump to that letter's section of the list. Once you find the song, playlist, album, artist, or other item you want to

FIGURE 3-2   The More screen lets you browse by any albums, audiobooks, compilations, composers, genres, or podcasts.

play, touch it. If the item is a song, video, or podcast, the iPhone or iPod touch starts playing it. If the item contains other items (such as songs), the iPhone or iPod touch displays a list of the contents. Touch the item you want to start playing.

Play a Song or Other Item

When you start a song or other item playing, the iPhone or iPod touch displays any available art for it, together with play controls. Figure 3-3 shows an example of a song playing.

Touch the Track List button to display the list of tracks from the album (touch a track to play it) and a row of five stars you can use to apply a rating to the song. The iPhone or iPod touch synchronizes this rating back to iTunes the next time you synchronize the device (see Figure 3-4). Touch the Track List button again to return to the album art.

Touch the Back button to go back to the screen from which you started the song or other item playing.

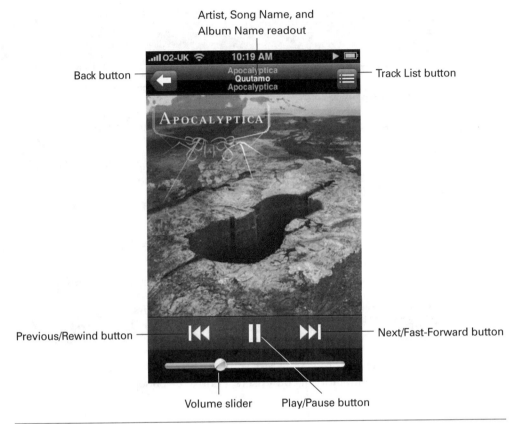

Artist, Song Name, and Album Name readout

Back button

Track List button

Previous/Rewind button

Next/Fast-Forward button

Volume slider   Play/Pause button

FIGURE 3-3 The iPhone or iPod touch displays the cover art for the item you're playing.

Touch the cover art to display the additional play controls (see Figure 3-5). You can then:

- **Play a different part of the song** Drag the Playhead (the dot that shows the current playing position in the song) back or forward.
- **Turn repeat on or off** Touch the Repeat button once to repeat the album or playlist, a second time to repeat the playing item, and a third time to turn off repeating.
- **Turn shuffle on or off** Touch the Shuffle button to toggle shuffle on or off.

Use Cover Flow View

Once you've started a song or other audio item playing, you can turn the iPhone or iPod touch to landscape orientation to switch to Cover Flow view (see Figure 3-6).

FIGURE 3-4   The Track List screen lets you rate the playing item or go to another item on the album or playlist.

You can then browse through songs by touching the cover whose songs you want to view. Drag your finger left or right to scroll through the covers more quickly.

Apply an Equalization to the Music

To apply an equalization on the iPhone or iPod touch, follow these steps:

1. Press the Home button to go to the Home screen unless you're already there.
2. Touch the Settings button to display the Settings screen.
3. On the iPhone, scroll down to the iPod button, and then touch it to display the settings screen titled iPod (shown on the left in Figure 3-7). On the iPod touch, touch the Music button to display the Music settings screen, which has the same settings as the Music section of the iPod screen.
4. Touch the EQ item to display the EQ screen (shown on the right in Figure 3-7).
5. Touch the iPod button or Music button at the top to return to the iPod screen or Music settings screen, or simply press the Home button to go to the Home screen.
6. On the iPhone, touch the iPod button to switch to iPod mode. On the iPod touch, touch the Music button.

Playhead

Elapsed Time readout

Repeat button

Remaining Time readout

Shuffle button

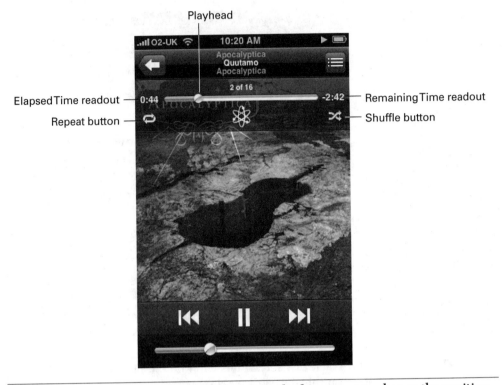

FIGURE 3-5 Display the additional play controls if you want to change the position of the Playhead or turn repeating or shuffle on or off.

FIGURE 3-6 Cover Flow view lets you browse through songs or other items by their covers.

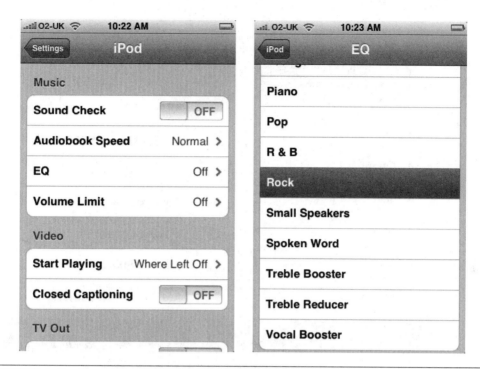

FIGURE 3-7   From the settings screen called iPod (left) or the Music settings screen, use the EQ screen (right) to apply an equalization to the iPhone or iPod touch.

  Usually, it's easier to apply the required equalization to each song, but you may need to adjust EQ directly on the iPhone or iPod touch sometimes—for example, when you've connected it to speakers or are using different headphones than usual.

Create a Genius Playlist

Like iTunes, the iPhone and iPod touch have a Genius feature that automatically creates a playlist based on a song you choose, drawing from the songs on the device at the time. See the section "Create Powerful Playlists with iTunes' Genius" in Chapter 10 for a fuller explanation of this feature.

To create a Genius playlist on an iPhone or iPod touch, follow these steps:

1. Touch the Playlists button to display the Playlists screen.
2. At the top of the list, touch Genius to display the Choose A Song To Create A Genius Playlist screen (shown on the left in Figure 3-8).

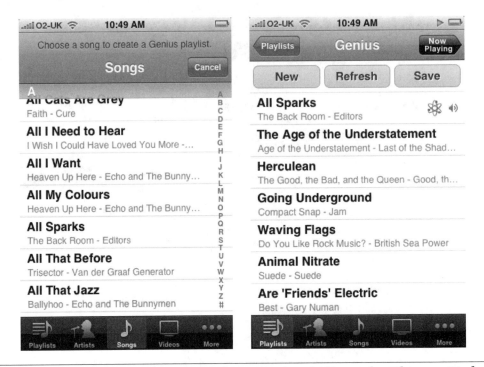

FIGURE 3-8 You can quickly put together a Genius playlist on the iPhone or iPod touch. If you don't like the result, touch the Refresh button.

3. Touch the song on which you want to base the Genius playlist. Genius puts together a playlist, displays it momentarily (see the right screen in Figure 3-8), and starts playing the first song (the song you chose).

4. To check or change the playlist, touch the Back button in the upper-left corner to go back to the Genius playlist. You can then take one of these actions:
   - **Play another song** Touch the song you want to play.
   - **Refresh the playlist** Touch the Refresh button to tell Genius to try again, still basing the list on the song you chose.
   - **Save the playlist** Touch the Save button. The iPhone or iPod touch saves the playlist under the name of the first song. (You can change this later in iTunes after you synchronize the iPhone or iPod touch.)
   - **Create a new playlist** Touch the New button to go back to the Choose A Song To Create A Genius Playlist screen.

Create an On-The-Go Playlist

If none of your playlists appeals, and you want a playlist of songs you've chosen rather than Genius' best efforts, you can create a playlist directly on the iPhone or iPod touch. This is called the On-The-Go playlist.

To create an On-The-Go playlist on an iPhone or iPod touch, follow these steps:

1. Touch the Playlists button to display the Playlists screen.
2. Near the top of the list, touch the On-The-Go item to display the Add Songs To The On-The-Go Playlist screen (shown on the left in Figure 3-9).
3. Touch the first song you want to add to the playlist. The iPhone or iPod touch turns the song's listing gray instead of black to show that you've added it to the playlist. This helps you avoid getting duplicates on the playlist.

 While adding to the On-The-Go playlist, you can switch to another browse category. For example, touch the Artists button to view songs by artist.

4. Touch additional songs in the order in which you want to add them.
5. When your playlist is complete, touch the Done button. The iPhone displays the On-The-Go playlist screen (shown on the right in Figure 3-9). From here, you can start the playlist playing (by touching a song or the Shuffle button) or touch the Edit button to edit it further:
   - **Delete a song from the playlist** Touch the red button on the left, and then touch the Delete button that appears (see the left screen in Figure 3-10).

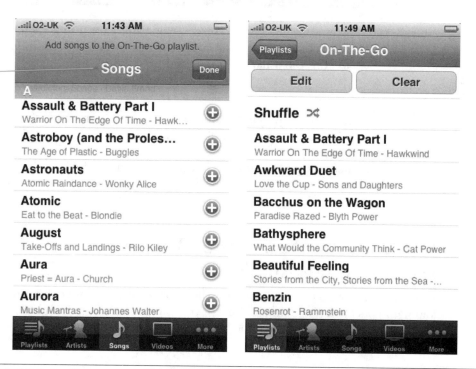

FIGURE 3-9 You can quickly pull together a playlist on the iPhone or iPod touch by using the On-The-Go feature.

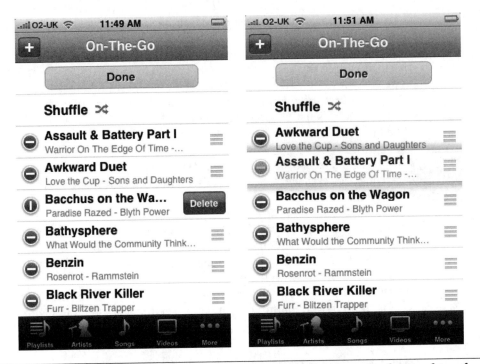

FIGURE 3-10   From this On-The-Go screen, you can delete a song by touching the red button on the left or drag a song to a different position by using the three-bar handle on the right.

- **Add songs to the playlist**   Touch the + button in the upper-left corner, and then work as described above. Touch the Done button when you've finished adding songs.
- **Move a song up or down the playlist**   Touch the three-bar handle on the right, and then drag the song to where you want it (see the right screen in Figure 3-10).

Control Your Music While You're Using Another Application

When you're listening to music on the iPhone or iPod touch but you've moved to another application (for example, Safari), you can pop up a panel of play controls (shown next) by pressing the Home button twice. These controls let you check the song information, pause and restart play, move forward and back, change the volume, or simply jump to the iPod or Music application.

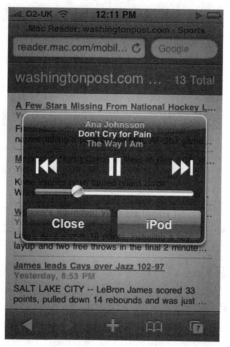

When you've finished using the play controls, touch the Close button to hide the panel again.

Play Videos

Playing videos on the iPhone or iPod touch could hardly be easier:

1. Display the list of videos:
   - **iPhone** Touch the iPod button at the bottom of the Home screen, and then touch the Videos button.
   - **iPod touch** Touch the Videos button at the bottom of the Home screen.
2. Find the video you want, and then touch it to start it playing. The iPhone or iPod touch switches automatically to landscape orientation if you're holding it in portrait orientation.
3. If you need to display the playback controls (shown in Figure 3-11), touch the screen. You can then pause, fast-forward, or rewind the video; move the Playhead manually by dragging its dot; control the volume; or zoom the video to fill as much of the screen as possible. Touch the screen again when you're ready to hide the playback controls.

FIGURE 3-11 The onscreen playback controls let you easily control video playback on the iPhone or iPod touch.

Play Music and Video on an iPod classic or iPod nano

This section shows you how to get up to speed with an iPod classic or iPod nano, play music and video, choose settings, and make the most of the iPod's extra features.

 For instructions on the iPod shuffle's controls, see the section "Play Music on the iPod shuffle," later in this chapter.

Read the iPod's Display

The iPod has an LCD display that shows a handful of lines of text (exactly how many depends on the model of iPod) and multiple icons. Figure 3-12 shows the display with labels.

FIGURE 3-12 The iPod's LCD display contains around six lines of text and key icons.

The title bar at the top of the display shows the title of the current screen—for example, "iPod" for the main menu (the top-level menu), "Now Playing" when the iPod's playing a song, "Cover Flow" when you're browsing using Cover Flow, or "Artists" when you're browsing by artist.

To turn on the display's backlight, hold down the Menu button for a moment. The backlight uses far more power than the LCD screen, so don't use the backlight unnecessarily when you're trying to extract the maximum amount of playing time from a single battery charge. You can configure how long the iPod keeps the backlight on after you press a button (see "Set the Backlight Timer or Auto-Lock," later in this chapter).

Use the iPod's Controls

Below the iPod's display are the iPod's main controls, which you use for accessing songs and playing them back. The control buttons are integrated into the Click wheel. Figure 3-13 shows an iPod classic.

Use the Buttons and the Click Wheel

Use the buttons and the Click wheel as follows:

- Press any button to switch on the iPod.
- Press the Menu button to move up to the next level of menus. Hold down the Menu button for a second to turn the backlight on or off.

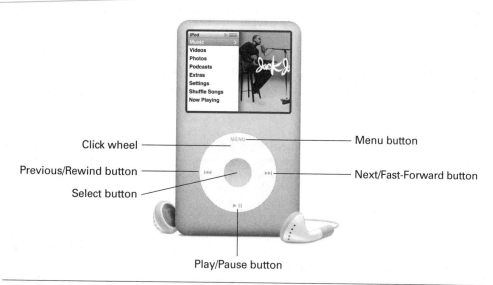

Click wheel

Previous/Rewind button

Select button

Menu button

Next/Fast-Forward button

Play/Pause button

FIGURE 3-13   The control buttons on the iPod classic (shown here) and the iPod nano are integrated into the Click wheel. (Image used courtesy of Apple Inc.)

- Press the Previous/Rewind button or the Next/Fast-Forward button to navigate from one song to another and to rewind or fast-forward the playing song. Press one of these buttons once (and release it immediately) to issue the Previous command or the Next command. Hold down the button to issue the Rewind command or the Fast-Forward command. The iPod rewinds or fast-forwards slowly at first, but then speeds up if you keep holding down the button.
- Press the Play/Pause button to start playback or to pause it. Hold down the Play/Pause button for three seconds or so to switch off the iPod.
- Press the Select button to select the current menu item.
- Scroll your finger around the Click wheel to move up and down menus, change the volume, or change the place in a song.

The Click wheel adjusts the scrolling speed in response to your finger movements on the Click wheel and the length of time you scroll for: When you're scrolling a long list, it speeds up the scrolling as you continue the scroll, and then slows down as you ease back on the scroll. This behavior makes scrolling even long lists (such as the Songs list, which lists every song on the iPod) swift and comfortable once you get used to it.

Browse and Access Your Music

The iPod's menu-driven interface makes browsing and accessing your music as easy as possible on the device's compact display.

Once you've accessed a list of songs—a playlist, an album, or a listing of all songs by an artist or composer—simply press the Play button to play the list from the start. Alternatively, scroll down to another song, and then press the Play button to start playing from that song.

 You can customize the main menu on the iPod (see the "Customize the Main Menu and Music Menu for Quick Access to Items" sidebar for details). This chapter assumes you're using the default menu layout.

Play a Playlist

To access your playlists, choose the Music item and press the Select button, then scroll to the Playlists item and press the Select button again. On the resulting screen, scroll down to the playlist you want to play, and then press the Select button.

Browse Your Music

To browse your music, select the Music item on the main menu. The iPod displays the Music menu, which contains entries for the various ways you can browse the songs and other audio items on the iPod.

Scroll to the browse category you want to use, and then press the Select button to access that category. Here's what you need to know about the browse categories:

- **Cover Flow** Displays the songs as a sequence of CD covers, as shown here. You can move from one cover to the next by pressing the Previous button or

How to...   Customize the Main Menu and Music Menu for Quick Access to Items

You can customize the iPod's main menu by controlling which items appear on it. By removing items you don't want, and adding items you do want, you can give yourself quicker access to the items you use most. For example, you might want to promote the Playlists item from the Music menu to the main menu, or you might want to put the Screen Lock item on the main menu so that you can lock the iPod's screen more easily.

To customize the main menu, follow these steps:

1. Choose Settings | Main Menu to display the Main Menu screen.
2. Scroll to the item you want to affect.
3. Press the Select button to toggle the item's setting between on (with a check mark next to it) and off (without a check mark).
4. Make further changes as necessary. Then press the Menu button twice to return to the main menu and see the effect of the changes you made.

To reset your main menu to its default settings, choose the Reset Main Menu item at the bottom of the Main Menu screen, and then choose Reset from the Menus screen.

Another way of resetting your main menu is to reset all settings on the iPod by choosing the Reset Settings item at the bottom of the Settings screen. Resetting all settings includes the main menu.

You can also customize the Music menu in a similar way by selecting the Music Menu item on the Settings screen, and then working on the Music Menu screen.

If you listen to many compilation albums—*Ultimate Aerosmith Hits*, *Lost Stoner Rock of the Desert*, and so on—you may want to add the Compilations item to the Music menu or the Main menu. This makes it much easier to browse your compilations.

the Next button. To flick through the covers faster, scroll to the left or to the right. When you've highlighted the cover you want, press the Play button to start it playing.

- **Playlists** Displays an alphabetical list of the playlist folders and playlists you have created. To access a playlist within a folder, choose the folder, and then press the Select button to display its contents. Once you've chosen the playlist you want, press either the Select button or the Play button to start it playing.
- **Artists** Displays an alphabetical list of all the songs on the iPod sorted by artist. The first entry, All Albums, displays an alphabetical list of all the albums on the iPod. Otherwise, scroll down to the artist and press the Select button to display a list of the albums by the artist. (If there's only one album, the iPod displays that album's songs immediately.) This menu also has a first entry called All Songs that displays an alphabetical list of all songs by the artist.
- **Albums** Displays an alphabetical list of all the albums on the iPod. Scroll down to the album you want, and then press the Select button to display the songs it contains.

The data for the artist, album, song title, genre, composer, and so on comes from the tag information in the song file. (See Chapter 6 for instructions on editing the tag information.) An album shows up in the Artists category, the Albums category, the Genre category, or the Composers category even if only one file on the iPod has that album entered in the Album field on its tag. So the entry for an album doesn't necessarily mean that you have that entire album on the iPod—you may have only one song from that album.

- **Songs** Displays an alphabetical list of every song on the iPod. Scroll down to the song you want to play, and then press the Select button to start playing the song.
- **Genres** Displays a list of the genres you've assigned to the music on the iPod. (The iPod builds the list of genres from the Genre field in the tags in AAC files, Apple Lossless Encoding files, and MP3 files.) Scroll to a genre, and then press the Select button to display the artists whose albums are tagged with that genre. You can then navigate to albums and songs by an artist.
- **Composers** Displays a list of the composers for the songs on the iPod. (The iPod builds the list of composers from the Composer field in the tags in the song files.) Scroll to a composer, and then press the Select button to display a list of the songs by that composer.
- **Audiobooks** Displays a list of the audiobooks on the iPod. (The iPod can play audiobooks in the Audible format, which you can buy either from the iTunes Store or from the Audible.com website.) Scroll down to the audiobook you want, and then press the Select button to start it playing.
- **Search** Displays a screen for searching by strings of text you dial in using the Click wheel—for example, the key word in a song title. Searching initially seems clumsy, but once you get the hang of it, you may find it a handy way to find songs whose full names escape you.

How to... **Use the Composers Category Effectively to Find Music**

The Composers category is primarily useful for classical music, because these songs may be tagged with the name of the recording artist rather than that of the composer. For example, an album of The Fargo Philharmonic playing Beethoven's *Ninth Symphony* might list The Fargo Philharmonic as the artist and Beethoven as the composer. By using the Composers category, you can access the works by composer: Bach, Beethoven, Brahms, and so on.

However, there's no reason why you shouldn't use the Composers category to access nonclassical songs as well. For example, you could use the Composers category to quickly access all your Nick Drake cover versions as well as Drake's own recordings of his songs. The only disadvantage to doing so is that the tag information for many CDs in the online CD Database (CDDB) that iTunes uses doesn't include an entry in the Composer field, so you'll need to add this information if you want to use it. In this case, you may be better off using iTunes to create a playlist that contains the songs you want in the order you prefer.

There's also no reason why you should confine the contents of the Composer field to information about composers. By editing the tags manually, you can add to the Composer fields any information by which you want to be able to sort songs on the iPod or iPhone.

Create a Playlist on the iPod

As well as synchronizing playlists from iTunes, you can create a playlist directly on the iPod. This is called the On-The-Go playlist, and you create it like this:

1. If you've previously created an On-The-Go playlist, decide whether to clear it or add to it. To clear it, choose Music | Playlists | On-The-Go | Clear Playlist | Clear.
2. Navigate to the song, album, artist, or playlist you want to add to the playlist.
3. Press the Select button and hold it down until the item's name starts flashing.
4. Repeat Steps 2 and 3 for each additional item that you want to add to the On-The-Go playlist.

To play your On-The-Go playlist, choose Playlists | On-The-Go. (Until you create an On-The-Go playlist, selecting this item displays an explanation of what the On-The-Go playlist does.)

To save your On-The-Go playlist under a different name, choose Playlists | On-The-Go | Save Playlist. The iPod saves the playlist under the name *New Playlist 1* (or *New Playlist 2*, or the next available number). After synchronizing the iPod with iTunes, click the playlist in the Source list, wait a moment and click it again, type the new name, and then press ENTER (Windows) or RETURN (Mac).

Play Songs

Playing songs on the iPod is largely intuitive.

Start and Pause Play

To start playing a song, take either of the following actions:

- Navigate to the song, and then press the Play/Pause button or the Select button.
- Navigate to a playlist or an album, and then press the Play/Pause button or the Select button.

To pause play, press the Play/Pause button.

Change the Volume

To change the volume, scroll counterclockwise (to reduce the volume) or clockwise (to increase it) from the Now Playing screen. The volume bar at the bottom of the screen shows the volume setting as it changes (see Figure 3-14).

Change the Place in a Song

As well as fast-forwarding through a song by using the Next/Fast-Forward button, or rewinding through a song by using the Previous/Rewind button, you can *scrub* through a song to quickly change the location.

Scrubbing can be easier than fast-forwarding or rewinding because the iPod displays a readout of how far through the song the playing location currently is. Scrubbing is also more peaceful, because whereas Next/Fast-Forward and Previous/Rewind play blips of the parts of the song you're passing through (to help you locate the passage you want), scrubbing keeps the song playing until you indicate you've reached the part you're interested in.

FIGURE 3-14 Scroll counterclockwise or clockwise to change the volume from the Now Playing screen.

FIGURE 3-15   To "scrub" forward or backward through the current song, press the Select button, and then scroll clockwise (to go forward) or counterclockwise (to go backward).

To scrub through a song, follow these steps:

1. Display the Now Playing screen.
2. Press the Select button to display the scroll bar (see Figure 3-15).
3. Scroll counterclockwise to move backward through the song or clockwise to move forward through the song.
4. Press the Select button to cancel the display of the scroll bar, or wait a few seconds for the iPod to cancel its display automatically.

 To display the lyrics for the currently playing song (if it contains lyrics), press the Select button twice from the Now Playing screen. Scroll down to see more lyrics (if there are more). Press the Select button again to access the Ratings screen, again to reach the repeat-mode screen, and press it once more to return to the Now Playing screen. Some artists include lyrics in song files distributed online, but you'll need to add them yourself to other files or to files you rip from your CDs.

Rate a Song as You Play It

To assign a rating to the song that's currently playing, follow these steps:

1. Display the Now Playing screen if it's not currently displayed. For example, from the main screen, scroll to the Now Playing item, and then press the Select button.
2. Press the Select button three times. (If the song has no CD cover art, you need only press twice.) The iPod displays five hollow dots under the song's name on the Now Playing screen.
3. Scroll to the right to display the appropriate number of stars in place of the five dots. Then press the Select button to apply the rating.

The iPod synchronizes the rating with iTunes at the next synchronization.

Use the Hold Switch

The Hold switch (also called the Lock switch), located on the top of the iPod classic and the iPod nano, locks the iPod controls in their current configuration. The Hold switch helps protect the controls against being bumped in active environments—for example, when you're exercising at the gym or barging your way onto a packed bus or subway train. When the Hold switch is pushed to the Hold side so that the orange underlay shows, the iPod is on hold.

The Hold switch is equally useful for keeping music playing without unintended interruptions and for keeping the iPod locked in the Off position, which prevents the battery from being drained by the iPod being switched on accidentally when you're carrying it.

If the iPod seems to stop responding to its other controls, check first that the Hold switch isn't on.

Navigate the Extras Menu

The Extras menu provides access to the iPod's Clocks, Calendars, Contacts, Alarms, Games, Notes, Screen Lock, and Stopwatch features:

- To use the iPod's clock features, scroll to the Clocks item on the Extras menu, and then press the Select button. On the first Clock screen, which lists the clocks already configured, select the clock you want, or press the Select button to pop up a panel that allows you to add a new clock or either edit or delete an existing clock.
- To use the calendars, scroll to the Calendars item on the Extras menu, and then press the Select button. The iPod displays the list of calendars you've synchronized with the iPod (see Chapter 2 for instructions on how to do this). Scroll to the calendar you want and press the Select button to display the calendar in month view. Scroll to access the day you're interested in, and then press the Select button to display the events listed for that day. The one-month display shows empty squares for days that have no events scheduled and dots for days that have one or more events. If the day contains more appointments than will fit on the iPod's display, scroll up and down.
- To access a contact, scroll to the Contacts item on the Extras menu, and then press the Select button. On the Contacts screen, scroll to the contact, and then press the Select button.
- To play the games included with the iPod, scroll to the Games item on the Extras menu, and then press the Select button. From the Games menu, scroll to the game you want, and then press the Select button.

 You can buy further games for the iPod from the iTunes Store. Not all games work on all iPod models, so before you buy a game, verify that it supports your iPod model.

- To access your text notes, scroll to the Notes item on the Extras menu, and then press the Select button.

Choose Settings for the iPod or iPhone

This section shows you how to choose settings on an iPod classic, iPod nano, iPod touch, or iPhone. Broadly speaking, the devices have similar settings, but because of their differences in software and hardware, you access and set the settings in different ways. To reach the settings:

- **iPhone or iPod touch** Press the Home button to reach the Home screen, and then touch the Settings icon.
- **iPod classic or iPod nano** Go to the main menu (press the Menu button however many times is needed), scroll to the Settings item, and then press the Select button.

Check the "About" Information

To see the details of the iPhone or iPod, display the About information:

- **iPhone or iPod touch** Touch Settings, touch General, and then touch About.
- **iPod classic or iPod nano** Scroll to the About item, and then press the Select button. Press the Select button to move on to the second About screen, and then press again to display the third About screen.

The About screen (or screens) includes the following information:

- The number of songs, videos, photos, podcasts, games, contacts, and other items the iPod or iPhone contains
- The device's capacity and the amount of space available
- The device's name, serial number, and model
- The version number of the device's software
- On some iPod models, whether the iPod is formatted for Windows or for the Mac (at the end of the Version readout)

Apply Shuffle Settings to Randomize Songs or Albums

Instead of playing the songs in the current list in their usual order, you can tell the iPod or iPhone to shuffle them into a random order. Here's what you can do:

- **iPhone or iPod touch** When you're playing a song, touch the screen to bring up the play controls. Touch the Shuffle button to turn shuffling on (so that the icon is blue) or off (so that the icon is white).
- **iPod classic or iPod nano** Scroll to the Shuffle item on the Settings menu and press the Select button to choose the Shuffle setting you want. The settings are Off (the default), Songs (to shuffle the songs in the album or playlist you're playing), and Albums (to shuffle the albums by a particular artist or composer into a random order).

To shuffle songs on an iPod shuffle, move the slider on the bottom to the Shuffle position.

Repeat One Song or All Songs

Instead of playing each song just once, you can either repeat a single song or repeat all the songs in the current album or playlist. Here's what to do:

- **iPhone or iPod touch**   When you're playing a song, touch the screen to bring up the play controls. Touch the Repeat button on the left once to repeat all songs (turning the curving arrows blue), again to repeat just the current song (adding a circle bearing 1 to the curving arrows), or a third time to turn off repeating (turning the curving arrows white).
- **iPod classic or iPod nano**   Scroll to the Repeat items on the Settings menu, and then press the Select button to choose One (to repeat the current song), All (to repeat all the songs in the current list), or Off (to turn repeating off).

Set the Volume Limit

To prevent the iPod or iPhone from playing back audio too loudly, connect the headphones that you (or the listener) will use, and set a song playing. Then set the volume limit like this:

- **iPhone or iPod touch**   Touch iPod (on the iPhone) or Music (on the iPod touch), and then touch Volume Limit. Drag the slider to the maximum volume you want to allow, and then touch Lock Volume Limit. On the Set Code screen, enter a four-digit locking code twice.
- **iPod classic or iPod nano**   Scroll to the Volume Limit item, and then press the Select button. On the Volume Limit screen, scroll to set the maximum audio volume, and then press the Select button to apply the change. On the Enter Combination screen, dial each of the four digits to create the combination number for locking the volume limit, and then press the Select button to apply the locking.

Set the Backlight Timer or Auto-Lock

To customize the length of time that the display backlight stays on after you press one of the iPod's controls, or until the iPod touch or iPhone locks itself:

- **iPhone or iPod touch**   Touch General, touch AutoText-Lock, and then touch the number of minutes (from 1 Minute to 5 Minutes) or Never.
- **iPod classic or iPod nano**   Scroll to the Backlight option, press the Select button, and then choose Off (to keep the backlight off until you turn it on manually by holding down the Menu button for a second), the number of seconds to keep the backlight on, or Always On.

The Never setting (on the iPhone or iPod touch) or the Always On setting (on an iPod classic or iPod nano) is useful when you're using the iPod as a sound source in a place that's too dark to see the display without the backlight and when you need to change the music frequently. Be warned that these settings get through battery power surprisingly quickly.

Set the Screen Brightness

You can choose how bright the iPhone's or iPod's screen shines like this:

- **iPhone or iPod touch**   Touch Brightness, and then drag the slider on the Brightness screen. If you want the iPhone or iPod touch to adjust the brightness automatically to suit the prevailing light conditions, move the Auto-Brightness switch to On.
- **iPod classic or iPod nano**   Scroll to the Brightness item, press the Select button, and then select the brightness you want on the Brightness screen.

Change the Speed at Which Audiobooks Play

If you listen to audiobooks on an iPod or iPhone, you may want to make them play faster or slower. Here's how to do so:

- **iPhone or iPod touch**   Touch iPod (on the iPhone) or Music (on the iPod touch), and then touch Audiobook Speed. On the Audiobook Speed screen, touch Slower, Normal, or Faster, as needed.
- **iPod classic or iPod nano**   Scroll to the Audiobooks item, press Select, and then choose Slower, Normal, or Faster, as needed.

Choose Equalizations to Make Your Music Sound Better

The iPod and iPhone contain a graphical equalizer—a device that alters the sound of music by changing the level of different frequency bands. Here are two examples of how equalizations work:

- A typical equalization for rock music boosts the lowest bass frequencies and most of the treble frequencies, while reducing some of the midrange frequencies. The normal effect of this arrangement is to punch up the drums, bass, and vocals, making the music sound more dynamic.
- A typical equalization for classical music leaves the bass frequencies and midrange frequencies at their normal levels while reducing the treble frequencies, producing a mellow effect overall and helping avoid having the brass section blast the top off of your head.

The iPod shuffle doesn't include a graphical equalizer.

The iPod and iPhone include the following equalizations, which are also built into iTunes: Acoustic, Bass Booster, Bass Reducer, Classical, Dance, Deep, Electronic, Flat, Hip Hop, Jazz, Latin, Loudness, Lounge, Piano, Pop, R & B, Rock, Small Speakers, Spoken Word, Treble Booster, Treble Reducer, and Vocal Booster. You might long for a Vocal Reducer setting for some artists or for karaoke, but the iPod doesn't provide one.

The names of most of these equalizations indicate their intended usage clearly, but Flat and Small Speakers deserve a word of explanation:

- Flat is an equalization with all the sliders at their midpoints—an equalization that applies no filtering to any of the frequency bands. If you don't usually use an equalization, there's no point in applying Flat to a song, because the effect is the same as not using an equalization. But if you *do* use an equalization for most of your songs, you can apply Flat to individual songs to turn off the equalization while they play.
- Small Speakers is for use with small loudspeakers. This equalization boosts the frequency bands that are typically lost by smaller loudspeakers. If you listen to the iPod or iPhone through portable speakers, you may want to try this equalization for general listening. Its effect is to reduce the treble and enhance the bass.

 Don't take the names of the equalizations too literally, because those you find best will depend on your ears, your earphones or speakers, and the type of music you listen to. For example, if you find crunk sounds best played with the Classical equalization, don't scorn the Classical equalization because of its name. Or you may prefer to use different equalizations even for different songs that belong to the same genre—or even to the same CD.

Here's how to apply an equalization:

- **iPhone or iPod touch** From the Settings screen, touch iPod (on the iPhone) or Music (on the iPod touch), and then touch EQ. On the EQ screen, touch the EQ you want, or touch the Off "equalization" at the top of the list if you want to turn equalization off.
- **iPod classic or iPod nano** On the Settings menu, scroll to the EQ menu, and then press the Select button. On the EQ screen, scroll to the equalization you want, and then press the Select button to apply it. Choose Off at the top of the list if you want to turn equalizations off.

Specifying an equalization like this works well enough when you need to adjust the sound balance for the music you're playing during a listening session. But if you want to use different equalizations for the different songs in a playlist, set the equalization for each song in iTunes, as described in the section "Specify an Equalization for an Individual Item" in Chapter 9. iTunes, the iPod, or the iPhone then applies this equalization each time you play back the song.

Use Sound Check to Standardize the Volume

Sound Check is a feature for normalizing the volume of different songs so you don't have to crank up the volume to hear a song encoded at a low volume and then suffer ear damage because the next song was recorded at a far higher volume.

To set Sound Check:

- **iPhone or iPod touch**   From the Settings screen, touch iPod (on the iPhone) or Music (on the iPod touch), and then move the Sound Check switch to the On position or the Off position.
- **iPod classic or iPod nano**   Scroll to the Sound Check item on the Settings menu, and then press the Select button to toggle Sound Check on or off.

 For Sound Check to work on the iPod or iPhone, you must also turn on the Sound Check feature in iTunes. Press CTRL-COMMA or choose Edit | Preferences to display the iTunes dialog box in Windows, or press ⌘-COMMA or choose iTunes | Preferences on the Mac to display the Preferences dialog box. Click the Playback tab to display its controls. Select the Sound Check check box, and then click the OK button to close the dialog box. iTunes then scans through the songs in your library and determines the loudest point of each, so that it knows how much to damp them down during playback.

Turn the Clicker Off or Redirect the Clicks

By default, the iPod classic and iPod nano play a clicking sound as you move the Click wheel, to give you feedback. You can turn off this clicking sound if you don't like it. Choose Settings | Clicker | Off.

On the iPod nano, you can also choose to direct the clicking sound to the headphones, the iPod's tiny built-in (and hidden) speaker, or both, instead of turning them off: choose Settings | Clicker | Headphones, Settings | Clicker | Speaker, or Settings | Clicker | Both.

Set the Date and Time

You can set the date and time, or switch between using the 12-hour clock and the 24-hour clock, like this:

- **iPhone or iPod touch**   Touch General, scroll down, and then touch Date & Time.
- **iPod classic or iPod nano**   Choose Extras | Date and Time.

 On the iPod classic and iPod nano, you can display the time in the title bar by setting the Time In Title item on the Date & Time screen to On.

Choose How to Sort and Display Your Contacts

The iPod and iPhone can sort and display your contacts either by first name or last name. Usually, you'll want to sort by "Last, First" so that your contacts appear in alphabetical order by last name, but display by "First, Last" so that the names appear the right way around: Tom Anderson, Jane Banks, Paul Callan, and so on.

To control how the device sorts your contacts:

- **iPhone or iPod touch** Touch the Mail, Contacts, Calendars button, scroll down to the Contacts area, touch Sort Order, and then choose First, Last or Last, First. Touch the Mail... button (it would be Mail, Contacts, Calendar, but that's too much text to fit) to go back to the previous screen, touch Display order, and then choose First, Last or Last, First again.
- **iPod classic or iPod nano** On the Settings screen, scroll to the Sort By item, and then press the Select button to toggle between First (sorting the contacts by their first names) and Last (sorting them by their last names). On these devices, you can't choose to display the contacts' last names first.

Use Key Extra Features

This section draws your attention to some of the extra features on the iPod and iPhone that are easy to miss—but that you almost certainly won't want to miss.

Lull Yourself to Sleep with a Sleep Timer

Here's how to set music to play for a length of time and then switch off—for example, when you're going to sleep:

- **iPhone or iPod touch** From the Home screen, touch Clock, and then touch the Timer button at the bottom. Use the spin wheels to choose the number of hours and minutes. Touch the When Timer Ends button, touch Sleep iPod, and then touch Set. Touch the Start button, and then go to the iPod and start your music playing.
- **iPod classic or iPod nano** Choose Extras | Alarms, and then choose Sleep Timer. Scroll to the number of minutes (15, 30, 60, 90, or 120), and then press the Select button. The Sleep Timer starts running. To turn off the Sleep Timer, access the Sleep screen again, and then select the Off setting.

Set an Alarm to Wake You Up or Remind You of an Appointment

Before you lull yourself to sleep, you may also want to set an alarm to blast yourself awake. Or you may simply want to set an alarm for a mustn't-miss appointment.

On the iPhone or iPod touch you can set a sound for the alarm, but on the iPod classic and iPod nano you can start a playlist playing.

Set an Alarm on the iPhone or iPod touch

To set an alarm on the iPhone or iPod touch, follow these steps:

1. From the Home screen, touch Clock to open the Clock application.
2. Touch the Alarm button at the bottom of the screen to display the Alarm screen (shown on the left in Figure 3-16).
3. Touch the + button in the upper-right corner of the screen to display the Add Alarm screen (shown on the right in Figure 3-16).
4. If you want to repeat the alarm, touch the Repeat button, and then choose the day or days on the Repeat screen—for example, Every Monday, Every Tuesday, Every Wednesday, Every Thursday, and Every Friday for a workweek alarm. Touch the Back button after making your choice.
5. Touch the Sound button to display the Sound screen, and then touch the sound you want. Again, touch the Back button.
6. Move the Snooze switch to the On position or the Off position to choose whether to allow snoozing.

FIGURE 3-16 You can quickly set an alarm on the iPhone or iPod touch. The clock icon to the left of the battery icon indicates that an alarm is set.

7. If you want to change the name of the alarm, touch the Label button, type the name for the alarm, and then touch the Back button.
8. Use the spin wheels to set the time for the alarm.
9. Touch the Save button. The alarm appears on the Alarm page, with a switch for turning it on or off. When the alarm is on, a clock icon appears to the left of the battery icon.

Set an Alarm on the iPod classic or iPod nano

To use the Alarm Clock on the iPod classic or iPod nano, follow these steps:

1. Create a custom playlist for waking up if you like (or create several—one for each day of the week, maybe). If you don't have your computer at hand, and the iPod or iPhone doesn't contain a suitable playlist, create an On-The-Go playlist on the iPod.
2. Choose Extras | Alarms, and then choose Create Alarm to display the Alarm Clock screen.
3. Scroll to the Alarm item, and then press the Select button to toggle the alarm on or off, as appropriate.
4. Scroll to the Date item, and then press the Select button to access a screen on which you can set the date for the alarm.
5. Scroll to the Time item, and then press the Select button to access a screen on which you can set the time for the alarm.
6. If you want the alarm to repeat, scroll to the Repeat item, and then press the Select button to access a screen on which you can set up repeating. The default is Once (in other words, without repeating), but you can also choose Every Day, Weekdays, Weekends, Every Week, Every Month, or Every Year.
7. Scroll to the Sound item, and then press the Select button to display a screen on which you can choose between Tones and Playlists. If you just want a beep, select the Tones item, and then select the Beep item on the following screen. More likely, you'll want a playlist—in which case, select the Playlists item, and then choose the playlist on the resulting screen.
8. If you want to name the alarm, scroll to the Label item, and then press the Select button to access a screen on which you can choose from various predefined labels—for example, Wake Up, Work, Class, or Prescription.
9. If you're setting an alarm to wake you, connect the iPod to your speakers or stereo (unless you sleep with headphones on), and then go to sleep. Otherwise, use the iPod as normal.

When the appointed time arrives, the iPod wakes itself (if it's sleeping) and then unleashes the alarm.

Note The iPod classic and iPod nano can remind you of appointments in your calendar when their times arrive. Choose Extras | Calendars, scroll down to the Alarms item, and then press the Select button. Choose the Beep setting for Alarms to receive a beep and a message on the screen. Choose the None setting to receive only the message. Choose the Off setting to receive neither the beep nor the message.

Use the iPod or iPhone as a Stopwatch

You can also use the iPod or iPhone as a stopwatch:

- **iPhone or iPod touch**   Touch Clock, and then touch Stopwatch.
- **iPod classic or iPod nano**   Choose Extras | Stopwatch, and then press the Select button.

Lock the iPod or iPhone with a Passcode

To protect the contents of the iPod or iPhone, you can lock it with a four-digit passcode. Set the passcode like this:

- **iPhone or iPod touch**   Touch Settings, touch General, and then touch Passcode Lock. On the Set Passcode screen (shown on the left in Figure 3-17), type the passcode you want, and then type it again to confirm. On the Passcode Lock screen (shown on the right in Figure 3-17), you can turn the passcode off, change the passcode, or set the iPhone or iPod touch to erase the data on it after ten failed attempts to guess the passcode. Now, whenever you put the iPhone or iPod touch to sleep, it locks itself, and you must enter the passcode before you can use it.

FIGURE 3-17   Set the passcode for the iPhone or iPod touch on the Set Passcode screen (left), and then choose how to apply the passcode on the Passcode Lock screen (right).

- **iPod classic or iPod nano** Choose Extras | Screen Lock, and then use the resulting screen to set the four-digit code you want. Scroll each number to the appropriate digit, and then press the Select button to move to the next digit. Reenter the passcode on the Confirm Combination screen and press the Select button. On the Screen Lock screen, select the Lock button and press the Select button to lock the iPod. Now you must enter the passcode before you can use the iPod again.

 If you forget your combination, all shouldn't be lost: Just connect the iPod or iPhone to its home computer, and it unlocks. But if this doesn't work (don't ask why not), you'll need to restore the device's software to unlock it. See Chapter 15 for instructions on restoring the software.

Play Music on the Second-Generation iPod shuffle

With no screen, the second-generation iPod shuffle needs only a limited set of controls for playing music (see Figure 3-18). These are largely intuitive but have a couple of hidden tricks:

- To start playing the songs on the iPod shuffle in the order of the playlist, move the mode switch on the bottom of the iPod shuffle to play mode, and then press the Play/Pause button.

 If the iPod shuffle blinks green and amber several times in succession when you press the Play/Pause button, it probably contains no songs. Move the switch to the Off position, wait for five seconds or more, move the switch back to the On position, and press the Play/Pause button again. If you see green and amber blinking again, connect the iPod shuffle to your computer and make sure that some songs are loaded on it.

- To start playing the songs in random order, move the mode switch to shuffle mode, and then press the Play/Pause button. When you hit a part of the playlist

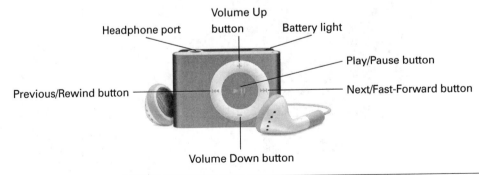

FIGURE 3-18   The iPod shuffle's limited set of controls includes a couple of hidden tricks. (Image used courtesy of Apple Inc.)

that you want to hear in sequence, move the mode switch to play mode to continue in sequence.

- Press the Play/Pause button three times in immediate succession to move to the start of the playlist. To get to the end of the playlist, press the Play/Pause button three times, and then press the Previous/Rewind button once.

 When the iPod shuffle is in shuffle mode and you move to the beginning of the playlist, it shuffles the playlist again.

- Press the Next/Fast-Forward button to skip to the next song. Hold it down to fast-forward through the song.

 When the iPod shuffle is paused, you can press the Next/Fast-Forward button to start the next song playing, or press the Previous/Rewind button to start the previous song playing. The iPod shuffle doesn't remain paused when you press the Next/Fast-Forward button or the Previous/Rewind button, unlike other iPod models.

- Press the Previous/Rewind button to return to the start of the current song; press it again to go to the start of the previous song. Hold the button down to rewind through the current song.
- Press the Volume Up button to increase the volume, or press the Volume Down button to decrease the volume.
- To put the iPod shuffle on hold, hold down the Play/Pause button for several seconds. The top light gives three orange blinks to indicate that hold is applied. To remove hold, press the Play/Pause button for several seconds again until the status light blinks green.
- To reset the iPod shuffle, turn it off, wait five seconds, and then turn it on again.

 If, when you press a button on the iPod shuffle, you see only the top light blink orange, it means that the iPod shuffle is on hold. Hold down the Play/Pause button for several seconds until the green light blinks three times to take it off hold.

The iPod shuffle's lights give you feedback on the battery's status, as explained in the following list.

Battery Light Color	Battery Status
Green (when in dock)	30 percent or more charge
Amber (bottom light, when in dock)	10 to 30 percent charge
Red (bottom light, when in dock)	Critically low (less than 10 percent)—needs more charging
No light (bottom light, when in dock)	No charge
Blinking red (top light, while playing)	Critically low—recharge at once

Play Music on the Third-Generation iPod shuffle

With its expressionless faceplate and single switch, the third-generation iPod shuffle is even more inscrutable than the second-generation iPod shuffle—but you can easily play music with it.

First, move the switch at the top of the iPod shuffle from the Off position to the loop symbol (if you want to play the songs in order) or to the shuffle position (if you want to play the songs in random order).

Then use the three buttons on the headset cord like this:

- **Play/Pause**   Click the middle button once to start play. Click again to pause.
- **Next song**   Double-click the middle button.
- **Previous song**   Triple-click the middle button.
- **Announce the current song and artist**   Hold down the middle button until the iPod shuffle turns the music down and starts speaking at you, then release the button.
- **Change playlist**   Hold down the middle button so that the iPod shuffle announces the current song and artist, but keep holding the button down until the iPod announces the current playlist. Release the button. Wait until the iPod announces the playlist you want, and then click the button again.
- **Increase the volume**   Click the upper button on the headset cord—the one nearest your ear.
- **Decrease the volume**   Click the lower button on the headset cord.

To check the battery status, turn the iPod shuffle off and then back on. You'll see a color-coded status light on top of the iPod and hear an announcement of battery status:

- **Green light**   The battery is 50 percent or more full. The announcement is more helpful: "Battery full," "Battery 75 percent," or "Battery 50 percent."
- **Orange light**   The battery is between 25 and 50 percent full. The announcement is "Battery 25 percent."
- **Red light**   The battery is less than 25 percent full. The announcement is "battery low."

4

Get More Out of the iPod or iPhone with Hardware Accessories

HOW TO...

- Approach buying accessories the right way
- Select cases for an iPod or iPhone
- Learn about power adapters and car adapters for the iPod or iPhone
- Choose iPod stands, docks, and remote controls
- Choose a radio transmitter

Like many consumer products that have been a runaway success, the iPods and iPhone have spawned a huge market for accessories—from cases to stands, from microphones for input to speakers for output, from radio transmitters to remote controls. Apple makes some of the accessories, and third-party companies make far more. Some of these accessories are widely useful (although you may not need any of them yourself). Others are niche products, some of which are for very small niches.

This chapter discusses the major categories of accessories (leaving you to choose the types you need) and highlights some of the less obvious and more innovative accessories that you might want to know about for special needs. This chapter focuses primarily on the current iPods—the iPod classic, iPod touch, iPod nano, and iPod shuffle—and the iPhone, but also mentions some accessories for earlier iPods where appropriate.

Approach Buying iPod or iPhone Accessories

Before you buy any iPod or iPhone accessory, run a quick reality check:

- *Do you really need the accessory, or is it just cool or cute?* These are your dollars, so this is your decision.
- *Is there a less expensive alternative?* For some types of accessories, such as power adapters and cassette adapters, you don't need to restrict your horizons to iPod- or iPhone-specific accessories—you can choose generic accessories as well. Often, generic accessories are substantially less expensive than custom accessories, give you much more flexibility, or both.
- *Will this accessory work only with your current iPod or iPhone, or will it work with other devices you may buy in the future?* (You can be sure that Apple will release such compelling new iPod or iPhone models that you'll want to upgrade sooner or later.) For example, if you get a radio transmitter designed for the iPod nano only, you'll need to upgrade the transmitter as well if you buy an iPod touch or an iPhone. In this case, buying a perhaps less stylish but more flexible accessory might make better financial sense.

Cases

The iPod and iPhone are built to be carried, so it's hardly surprising that a wide variety of cases has been developed for them—everything from bifold cases to armband cases to armored cases and waterproof cases. Early iPod models included sturdy cases, but Apple has dropped the cases along with the prices, so the first accessory you might need is a protective case for the iPod or iPhone.

 Many stores sell iPod cases and iPhone cases, but at this writing, the prime sources are the Apple Store (http://store.apple.com), Digital Lifestyle Outfitters (www.dlo.com), and the stores searchable through iLounge (http://ilounge .pricegrabber.com).

The Apple Store has user ratings for most cases, which can help you weed out superficially attractive losers.

Choosing a Case

Choosing a case is as fiercely personal as choosing comfortable underwear or choosing a car. Different aspects of cases are important to different people, and although one size may suit many, it doesn't fit all. As with underwear (or a car), you may prefer not to use a case at all—but the iPod's or iPhone's shiny surfaces will tend to get scratched, and you'll need to be careful not to drop the device onto any unforgiving surface.

But as with underwear (and, to a lesser extent, a car), it's vital to make sure the case you choose is the right size for the model of iPod or iPhone you have. For example, the iPhone 3G is a different size than the original iPhone, and the iPod touch is slimmer than either of them; the iPod classic 120GB model is slimmer than its 160GB predecessor; and each of the last three generations of the iPod nano has a completely different shape.

Beyond getting the size right, the remaining choices are yours. The following paragraphs summarize the key ways in which the cases differ. You get to decide which points are important for you:

- **How the case attaches to you (if at all)**   Many cases attach to your belt, whereas some hook on to a lanyard that goes around your neck or a strap that goes over your shoulder. Still others attach to an armband, which some people find better for performing vigorous activities. Some cases come with a variety of attachments—for example, a belt clip and an armband, or a mounting for sticking the iPod to a flat surface. Other cases are simply protective, designed to be carried in a pocket or a bag.
- **The amount of protection the case provides**   In general, the more protection a case provides, the larger and uglier it is, the more it weighs, and the more it costs. Balance your need for style against the iPod's or iPhone's need for protection when gravity gets the better of your grip.
- **Whether or not the case is waterproof**   If you plan to take the iPod or iPhone outdoors for exercise, you may want to get a case that's water-resistant or waterproof. Alternatively, carry a sturdy plastic bag in your pocket for weather emergencies. Either way, protect the device's Dock Connector port and headphone port.
- **Whether or not the case lets you access the iPod's or iPhone's controls**   Access to the controls is pretty vital unless you have a remote control for the device, in which case your need to access the controls once you've set the music playing will be much less. Generally speaking, the more waterproof the case, the less access it offers to the controls—although some case makers have been more successful than others at letting you reach the device's buttons and sensitive parts.
- **Whether or not the case can hold the iPod's or iPhone's headphones and remote control**   If you'll be toting the iPod or iPhone in a bag or pocket, a case that can hold the ear-bud headphones and remote control as well as the player itself may be a boon. You may even want a case that can accommodate a USB cable and power adapter for traveling. But if you're more interested in a case that straps firmly to your body and holds the iPod or iPhone securely, you probably won't want the case to devote extra space to store other objects.

If you're looking for an inexpensive case that'll take the iPod's or iPhone's complete entourage, consider the type of case designed for portable CD players and built into a padded belt.

- **Whether or not you need to take the iPod or iPhone out of the case to dock or recharge it**   Some cases are designed to give you access to the Dock Connector port, so you can leave the iPod or iPhone in the case unless you need to admire it. With more protective cases, usually you need to remove the iPod or iPhone more often.
- **What the case is made of and how much it costs**   Snug cases tend to be made of silicone or neoprene. Impressive cases tend to be made of leather or armor. Leather and armor cost more than lesser materials.
- **Whether the case is single-purpose or multipurpose**   Most cases are designed for carrying, either in your pocket or attached to your belt or clothing. Some cases convert to mount the iPod or iPhone in your car or home.

When shopping for a case, look for special-value bundles that include other accessories you need—for example, a car cassette adapter or cables for connecting the iPod or iPhone to a stereo.

Examples of Cases

Most manufacturers who make cases worth having produce a range of them for most or all current models of iPod and the iPhone. Here are examples of interesting cases you may want to look at.

Rugged-Lifestyle Cases

When delicate electronics meet a rugged lifestyle, the results are often unfortunate—but who can leave their communications and entertainment behind just because reality can be harsh?

Here are four cases for the rugged lifestyle:

- **Diving protection**   If you need to take the iPod or iPhone to the seabed, look at H2O Audio iDive 300 Deep Dive Waterproof Housing and Over Ear Speakers. These are available at the Apple Store (http://store.apple.com), cost the earth ($350), and let you take your death metal to a depth of 300 feet (where it arguably belongs).
- **Military-grade protection**   The Otterbox Defender from RadTech ($49.95; www.radtech.us) offers "waterproof impact protection" and a fully sealed audio jack interface that lets you use an iPod on the water—or even in the water. The Otterbox Defender (see Figure 4-1) works with any headphones, but RadTech's H2O Audio Waterproof iPod Headphones ($39.95) seem an obvious match.

Knights Armaments even makes a mount for attaching the iPod touch to an M110 sniper rifle—and this mount attaches to some Otterbox models. The sniper can then not only enjoy songs or videos while reducing the population but also use ballistics-calculator applications such as Bullet Flight or iSnipe to calculate where to aim given the distance, wind speed, altitude, ammo type, and so on. (You can find these applications in the App Store.)

FIGURE 4-1   The Otterbox Defender provides waterproof protection for the iPod. You can even mount some models on a sniper rifle.

- **Protection for lively activities**   The Matias Armor cases from Matias Corporation (from $9.95 but mostly more; http://matias.ca/armor/index.php) cradle the iPod or iPhone in a full metal jacket made of anodized aluminum padded with open-cell EVA foam. If you land on this case, you're more likely to damage yourself than the device, so plan your pratfalls ahead of time.
- **Everyday rough-and-tumble protection**   The ToughSkin from Speck Products ($24.95; www.speckproducts.com) is a series of ruggedized covers for various iPods, including the iPod classic. The ToughSkin (see Figure 4-2) is a polymer case with rubber bumpers, providing protection, a good grip, and easy access to the iPod's controls.

Sports Cases

If you take the iPod or iPhone out for a jog or a hike, you'll want either an iPod shuffle, which you can clip firmly to your least sweaty piece of clothing, or a case

FIGURE 4-2   The ToughSkin cases provide a stylish way to protect an iPod or iPhone from everyday threats.

that's snug on both the iPod or iPhone and you—and comfortable on you both. Normally, this means an armband. Here are three examples of cases to look at:

- **AeroSport Armband**   The Griffin AeroSport series ($29.99; www.griffintechnology .com) includes low-profile sport armbands that keep an iPod or iPhone firmly attached to your upper arm. You can also clip the case onto a belt or—for gentler activities—a strap.
- **Incase Sports Armband**   The Incase Sports Armband series (from $29.95; http://store.apple.com) includes a case for each type of iPod and for the iPhone. It's worth reading the reviews, as some cases get much better user ratings than others.
- **Sportwrap**   The Sportwrap from XtremeMac ($29.95; www.xtrememac.com) is a series of lightweight neoprene armbands that bind the iPod or iPhone firmly to your quivering muscles.

Everyday Cases

For everyday use, you probably won't want the iPod or iPhone armored to the teeth or clamped immovably to your bulging biceps. Here are examples of cases that protect the iPod or iPhone from minor dings but slip into your pocket without leaving an awkward bulge:

- **Gelz**   The Gelz series from RadTech ($8.95; www.radtech.us) offers skintight silicone cases for iPods and iPhones. The Gelz cases come in various bright colors (plus black and white) and two styles named Ultra Sheer and Ribbed Grip. If those names remind you of awkward moments in the drugstore, don't worry—you can order Gelz online without embarrassment.

- **Reflect**   The Reflect series from Griffin Technology ($9.99–$24.99; www .griffintechnology.com) includes tough polycarbonate cases for iPods and the iPhone. The front of each Reflect has a mirrored chrome finish that hides the device's screen until you turn the device on. If you wear mirror shades, you'll want one of these.
- **PixelSkin**   The PixelSkin cases from Speck Products (from $19.95; www .speckproducts.com) are lightweight, form-fitting cases with a soft-touch tiled pattern that gives you a better grip on the iPod or iPhone. The PixelSkins come in various bright colors and give you full access to the device's ports and controls.
- **DecalGirl Skins**   The DecalGirl Skins (mostly $6.99; www.decalgirl.com) come in various flashy designs and hug the iPod or iPhone like a friendly anaconda. Figure 4-3 shows an example.
- **Incase Leather Sleeve**   The Incase Leather Sleeve series (from $29.99; http:// store.apple.com) is a protective leather case that lets you easily access the iPod's or iPhone's controls and ports. The Sleeve includes a belt clip.

Quick-Draw Cases for the iPhone

The iPhone presents a challenge for cases, because even if you use the headphones for listening to music, you'll presumably need to be able to whip the iPhone out at any moment to take or make a phone call—or to surf the Web, check your e-mail, watch a YouTube video, or use many of the other features. At the same time, the iPhone is an expensive gadget and is worth protecting.

FIGURE 4-3   The DecalGirl iPod nano Skins come in a variety of striking designs.

How to... Choose a Case for the iPod shuffle

The second-generation iPod shuffle is small and tough in its aluminum shell, so you may prefer not to put it in a case. Besides, its built-in clip provides an effective means of securing the iPod shuffle to your clothing or belt.

But if you need a case, here are three to consider:

- **RhinoSkin Accents** The RhinoSkin Accents ($19.95 for a pack of four different colors; http://store.apple.com) are machined aluminum cases with a neoprene lining.
- **Wraptor** The Wraptor cases from Mophie ($19.95 for a pack of three different colors; http://store.apple.com) are see-through polycarbonate shells that fit the iPod shuffle securely. The earphone cord wraps around the case to prevent snags.
- **H2O** The H2O Audio Waterproof Case from H2O Audio ($39.95; http://store.apple.com) is a waterproof case that includes a sport armband. Designed for swimming, surfing, and monsoon conditions, this case is best used with waterproof headphones such as the H2O Audio Waterproof ones.

The disadvantage to using any of these cases is that you need to remove the case before you can recharge or load the iPod shuffle.

At this writing, the third-generation iPod shuffle is brand new, and case manufacturers seem to be puzzling over its shape and its needs.

To solve this problem, various makers have developed quick-draw holsters for the iPhone. Here are two examples:

- **SLAM** The SLAM for iPhone from RadTech ($14.95 for the iPhone 3G model; www.radtech.us) is a hard-shell clip case that secures the iPhone either face in or face out. You press the Eject button to release the iPhone from its bindings.
- **QwickDraw** The QwickDraw (see Figure 4-4) from Speck Products ($29.95; www.speckproducts.com) is a spring-loaded, quick-release holster that promises to make you the "fastest iPhone in the West." (You can use it in other geographical areas too.) Flick the quick-release switch and the iPhone's in your hand and coming up to the aim, ready to shoot snap shots...with the camera.

FIGURE 4-4 A holster such as the QwickDraw can be a great way to keep your iPhone both safe and to hand.

If you want to make the most of the iPhone's built-in camera, check out the Clarifi case from Griffin Technology ($34.99; www.griffintechnology.com/products/clarifi). The Clarifi includes a macro lens that you can slide over the iPhone's built-in lens, which lets you take close-up pictures. This is great for snapping text you want to keep from hard copy—for example, a business card (which you can associate easily with a contact), a map you want to take with you, a shopping list, or an article in a magazine or newspaper.

Stands and Docks

Cases can be great, but you won't always want to carry the iPod or iPhone. Sometimes, you'll want to park it securely so that you can use it without worrying about knocking it down, or so that you can crank up the volume on an external speaker—either one with a dock built right in or one to which you connect the iPod with a cable.

 Another option for docking the iPod or iPhone is to get a set of portable speakers designed to include a stand for the device. See "Portable Speakers for the iPod and iPhone," later in this chapter, for examples.

Early iPods and iPhones included docks, but Apple has gradually phased them out; now the second-generation iPod shuffle is the only iPod that includes a dock, and that's only because the dock houses its custom power connection. However, plenty of iPod docks are available from Apple and from third-party manufacturers.

 The advantage of playing audio from an iPod dock that includes a line-out port is that the port delivers a standard volume rather than a variable volume. The standard volume means that you're less likely to damage your receiver or speakers by putting too great a volume through them. It also means that you can't adjust the volume on the iPod, only on the receiver or speakers.

Apple Universal Dock

If you want standard dock features, start by looking at the Apple Universal Dock ($49; http://store.apple.com). This dock works with the iPhone or with any iPod that has the Dock Connector port, and includes assorted Dock Adapters to make the devices fit well. The Universal Dock includes a line-out port for producing high-quality audio (via the Dock Connector port) and an S-video out port for displaying photos, videos, or slideshows on a TV.

Apple Docks for the iPhone and Individual iPods

Apart from the one-size-fits-almost-all Universal Dock, Apple also sells docks for the iPhone and some individual iPods. For example, you can buy the Apple iPhone 3G

Dock ($29.00; http://store.apple.com) to get a dock that fits only the iPhone 3G and any smaller iPods that you can shoehorn onto the Dock Connector.

Generally speaking, the Universal Dock is a better choice, first because you can use it for any current or past iPhone or iPod, and second because you should be able to use it for future iPhone or iPod models as well.

Third-Party Stands and Docks

If you decide that an Apple Universal Dock or device-specific dock isn't what your iPod or iPhone needs, you should be able to find third-party alternatives that offer an appealing design, extra features, or both. Here are several of the possibilities:

- **Simplifi** The Simplifi from Griffin Technology ($69.99; www.griffintechnology .com) is an iPod or iPhone dock that incorporates a media-card reader and a USB hub. This means you can plug into the Simplifi not only the iPod or iPhone but also your memory cards and other USB devices—a neat idea that can reduce the clutter on your desk by several cables and devices. Simplifi includes Universal Dock adapters to fit most iPods and the iPhone.

 Griffin Technology also makes a Dock Adapter for iPod shuffle ($19.95; www .griffintechnology.com) that lets you connect an iPod shuffle to a device that uses the Dock Connector. In other words, the Dock Adapter goes from the iPod shuffle's headphone-spike connector to a standard Dock Connector port. So you can connect the iPod shuffle to powered speakers via a Dock Connector and let rip.

- **AirCurve** The AirCurve from Griffin Technology ($19.99; www.griffintechnology .com) is an acoustic amplifier for the iPhone. You plug the iPhone into the stand part on top of the AirCurve, and the sound from the iPhone's bottom speaker travels through a waveguide "horn" that amplifies the sound and launches it into the room. The AirCurve is a compact device, but it amplifies the iPhone's sound by about 10 decibels.
- **Ampli-Phone** The Ampli-Phone from Gryphon Corporation ($34.95; www.ampli-phone.com) is an acoustic amplifier for the iPhone. The Ampli-Phone is similar in concept to the AirCurve but considerably larger at 8 inches wide by 5.5 inches high and 6.5 inches deep. The Ampli-Phone amplifies the iPhone's sound by 10 decibels.

 You can also find cases that double as stands. For example, Speck Products' SeeThru case series ($29.95; www.speckproducts.com) lets you slide off the bottom section of the case and snap it on as a tilted stand for watching videos on the iPhone or iPod touch. Similarly, the Power Support Crystal Jacket for iPhone 3G ($39.95; http://store.apple.com) includes a holster clip that doubles as a stand.

Car and Bike Mounting Kits

The iPod or iPhone on your body or desk gets you only so far. To get further, you'll probably want to use the device in your car or on your bike. To prevent it from shifting around as you shift gears, you'll probably want to secure it.

Car Mounts

The ideal way of securing an iPod or iPhone in a car is one of the "iPod-integration" units that car manufacturers are increasingly building into cars. If your car came without an iPod-integration unit, you can add a third-party one easily enough—see the next chapter for details—but in many cases you will need to replace your existing stereo.

For a less invasive solution, try a holder or mount such as these:

- **TuneDok**   The TuneDok Car Holder series from Belkin (from $29.99; www.belkin.com) lets you mount various iPod models in your car's cup holder.
- **VentMount**   The VentMount series from DLO ($24.99; www.dlo.com) lets you mount an iPod or iPhone on—yes, you've guessed it—the AC vent, where it stays cool and within reach.
- **WindowSeat**   The WindowSeat from Griffin Technology ($29.99; www.griffintechnology.com) lets you mount an iPhone or iPod touch on your car's windshield, putting your maps and music at eye level. The WindowSeat attaches using a suction cup, and the angled bracket lets you turn and tilt the screen to the right position for viewing. The WindowSeat includes an audio cable for connecting the iPhone or iPod to your car stereo. If you need to power the iPhone or iPod, you can add an in-car charger such as the PowerJolt (discussed later in this chapter). Resist the temptation to play the Cro-Mag Rally driving game on the desert stretches of I-80.

All-in-One Adapters for the Car

If your car doesn't have an iPod-integration unit, securing the iPod or iPhone tends to be only half the problem. The other half is playing the sound from the iPod or iPhone through the car's stereo system. Chapter 5 discusses this problem in more detail, but one solution is to use an all-in-one gadget. Most of these combine three main components:

- A power adapter that connects to your car's 12-volt accessory outlet or cigarette-lighter socket.
- A means of piping the iPod's or iPhone's output to your stereo. This can use a direct cable connection, a cassette adapter, or a radio transmitter.
- A cradle or other device for holding the iPod or iPhone, either built onto the power adapter (using the power adapter as its support) or fitting into a cup holder or onto the dash.

Many different all-in-one gadgets are available, including the following:

- **TransDock** TransDock from Digital Lifestyle Outfitters (www.dlo.com) is a series of car gadgets for iPods. The TransDock with IntelliTune costs $99.99 and lets you not only broadcast music from the iPod to your car's radio but also show video from the iPod on your in-car video system. A flexible gooseneck plugs into the accessory outlet and lets you position the iPod where it's conveniently to hand but out of harm's way.
- **TuneBase and TuneCast** The TuneBase and TuneCast series from Belkin (www.belkin.com) provide a variety of ways to play audio from an iPod or iPhone through a car stereo. For example, the TuneCast Auto with ClearScan for iPhone and iPod ($79.99) powers the iPod or iPhone from the accessory outlet and transmits audio wirelessly to the car stereo.
- **LiquidAUX Deluxe** The Kensington LiquidAUX Deluxe for iPhone and iPod ($99.95; http://store.apple.com) charges the iPod from the accessory outlet and transmits audio via an audio cable to the car stereo. There's even a wireless remote control for backseat drivers.

Bike Mounts

If you want to mount the iPod on your bike, your options are more limited. Here are a couple of examples:

- **iPod Mobility Pack** The iPod Mobility Pack ($19.95; http://store.apple.com) from Marware includes a bike holder, swivel clip, and car holder that work with Marware cases that use the Multidapt clip system. The Bike Holder Accessory lets you strap the iPod to your bike's handlebars so that you can manipulate the music when you have a hand free.
- **iBikeMount** The iBikeMount from CertifiableSolutions.com (www.ibikemount .com; $29.99) attaches an iPhone to your bike's handlebars or another tube (for example, a baby stroller). This product is still in development at this writing, but it looks promising.

If you want to mount a speaker on your bike, head to UrbanOutfitters.com (www.urbanoutfitters.com) and search for the Bicycle iPod Speaker. This $50 item is a water-resistant speaker that clamps onto your bike's frame. You control the music via a remote control mounted on the handlebars.

 Almost everyone who pronounces on the subject of road safety is adamant that you shouldn't listen to audio using earphones when riding a bike lest you fail to hear the vehicles thundering past with their own music shaking the scenery. But if you do listen to an iPod or iPhone, keep your eyes on the road rather than on the device's screen. An iPod shuffle is great for biking, because there's no screen to distract you, you can easily attach the player to your clothing rather than to your bike, and you can work the buttons by touch.

Power Adapters and Battery Packs

Each iPod or iPhone comes with a USB cable that allows you to recharge it from a computer. You may want to get a power adapter so that you can recharge the device from an electrical outlet, or you may need to prolong your AC-free playing time by using a backup battery pack.

Incase Power Slider Case for iPhone 3G

If you use your iPhone heavily enough to run out of battery power, have a look at the Incase Power Slider Case for iPhone 3G ($99.95; http://store.apple.com). This case includes a built-in rechargeable lithium-ion polymer battery that can give you twice the battery life.

TuneJuice 2

The TuneJuice 2 and TuneJuice for iPhone from Griffin Technology ($29.99; www.griffintechnology.com) are external backup batteries that run off four AAA batteries. TuneJuice for iPhone is a better bet, because it also works with any iPod that has the Dock Connector port, and it recharges the battery. TuneJuice 2 provides up to 14 hours of extra power to an iPod, but it doesn't recharge the iPod's battery.

MicroPack

The MicroPack Portable Multimedia Dock and Battery from XtremeMac ($99.95; www.xtrememac.com) is a dock with a built-in lithium-ion rechargeable battery.

JBox and JBoxMini

The JBox from Macally ($49.99; www.macally.com) is an external lithium-ion battery that connects to any iPod or iPhone via a Dock Connector or a USB socket. The JBox gives up to eight hours extra battery life.

Macally also makes the JBoxMini ($29.99), a smaller device along the same lines. The JBoxMini gives up to four hours extra battery life.

Basic AC Power Adapters

If you want to be able to recharge an iPod without connecting it to a USB port, you can buy an Apple USB Power Adapter ($29; http://store.apple.com). Alternatively, you can find a third-party USB power adapter for less.

Car Adapters

If you drive extensively (or live in a vehicle), you may need to bolster the iPod's or iPhone's battery life. To recharge the device in your car, you need either an iPod-integration unit or a power adapter that'll run from your car's 12-volt accessory outlet or cigarette-lighter socket. Technically, such an adapter is an *inverter*, a device that converts DC into AC, but we'll stick with the term *adapter* here.

You can choose between a generic car adapter and a custom car adapter for the iPod or iPhone. Another option is an all-in-one device that combines a power adapter with a radio transmitter and (in some cases) a means of mounting the device, as discussed in "All-in-One Adapters for the Car," earlier in this chapter.

Generic Car Adapter

The simplest and most versatile option is to get a generic car adapter that plugs into your car's 12-volt accessory outlet or cigarette-lighter socket. Models vary, but the most effective types give you one or more conventional AC sockets. You plug an iPod or iPhone power adapter into one of these AC sockets, just as you would any other AC socket, and then plug the USB cable into the power adapter.

The advantage to these adapters is that you can run any electrical equipment off them that doesn't draw too heavy a load—a laptop, your cell phone charger, a portable TV, or whatever. The disadvantage is that such adapters can be large and clumsy compared with custom adapters.

Cost usually depends on the wattage the adapter can handle; you can get 50-watt adapters from around $20 and 140-watt adapters for around $50, whereas 300-watt adapters cost more like $80. A 50-watt adapter will take care of an iPod or iPhone and portable computer easily enough.

iPod- and iPhone-Specific Adapters

If the only thing you want to power from your car is the iPod or iPhone, you can get a car adapter designed specially for the device. Many different models are available, including the following:

- The Belkin Auto Kit for iPod with Dock Connector ($39.99; www.belkin.com) is a charger for iPods with the Dock Connector port. This kit also includes an adjustable amplifier and a 3.5mm audio-out jack for playing music from the iPod through the car stereo.
- The Griffin PowerJolt for iPhone ($19.99; www.griffintechnology.com) is an adapter with a USB socket and a USB-to–Dock Connector cable. The PowerJolt for iPhone (see Figure 4-5) can power any iPod as well as the iPhone.
- The XtremeMac InCharge Auto ($19.95; www.xtrememac.com) is an adapter into which you can plug the iPhone or any iPod that has a Dock Connector port.

FIGURE 4-5   You can power the iPod or iPhone from a car's cigarette-lighter socket or 12-volt accessory outlet with an adapter such as the PowerJolt.

World Travel Adapters

If you travel abroad with an iPod or iPhone, the lightest and easiest way to recharge it is from your laptop—provided that you have your computer with you, and you have access to an electric socket so that you don't flatten your computer's battery by charging the iPod or iPhone.

If you need to recharge the iPod or iPhone directly from the electric socket, get an adapter that lets you plug the iPod's or iPhone's power adapter into electric sockets in different countries. The adapter can handle multiple voltages, so you can plug it safely in even in countries that think 240 volts is just a refreshing tingle.

For such adapters, you have the choice between a set of cheap and ugly adapters and a set of stylish and sophisticated adapters. You can get the cheap and ugly adapters from any competent electrical-supply shop; they consist of an assortment of prong-converter receptacles into which you plug the power adapter U.S. prongs. The resulting piggyback arrangement is clumsy, and sometimes you have to jiggle the adapters to get a good connection. But these adapters are inexpensive (usually from $5 to $10) and functional, and they work for any electrical gear that can handle the different voltages.

The stylish and sophisticated adapters are designed by Apple and are (collectively) called the World Travel Adapter Kit. The kit costs $39 from the Apple Store (http://store.apple.com) or an authorized reseller. You slide the U.S. prongs off the iPod or iPhone power adapter and replace them with a set of prongs suited to the country you're in. The kit includes six prongs that'll juice up any iPod (except the iPod shuffle) or the iPhone in continental Europe, the United Kingdom, Australia, Hong Kong, South Korea, China, and Japan, as well as in the United States. These adapters also work with Apple laptops, but they won't help you plug in any of your other electrical equipment.

 If you're going somewhere sunny that lacks electricity, or you live somewhere sunny that suffers frequent power outages, consider a solar charger such as the Solio Hybrid 1000 ($79.95; www.solio.com/v2).

Remote Controls

If you connect an iPod to your stereo (as discussed in "Connect an iPod or iPhone to a Stereo" in Chapter 5), you'd probably appreciate being able to control the iPod from across the room. You can do so by using a wireless remote control.

Apart from price and looks, consider the following points when evaluating a remote control:

- Does it use infrared (IR) or radio frequency (RF)? RF typically gives better range and works around corners. On the other hand, if you have a universal remote control, you may be able to teach it the commands from an IR iPod control so that you can control the iPod remotely using the universal remote.
- Do you simply want to play back music, or do you need to be able to control other features, such as displaying photos or running videos?

Here are a couple of remote controls to consider:

- **HomeDock Deluxe Music Remote**   The HomeDock Deluxe Music Remote from Digital Lifestyle Outfitters ($149.99; www.dlo.com) is a remote-control kit that works with all iPods that have a Dock Connector port (but not with the iPhone). You place the iPod in the HomeDock Deluxe, which you connect to your stereo, and then control the iPod using the Music Remote. The Music Remote includes a display that allows you to navigate the iPod's screens.
- **Aerolink**   The Aerolink family of remote controls from Engineered Audio, LLC ($45 each; www.engineeredaudio.com) includes radio-frequency (RF) remotes designed for the iPods that have Dock Connector ports. The transmitter is a five-button key fob that offers control buttons but no screen.

Microphones

If you have an iPod nano or iPod classic, you may want to add a microphone so that you can use the iPod to take audio notes.

Tip To record on the iPhone, all you need is a suitable application. You can find various applications in the App Store by searching for "record" or "recorder." To record on the second-generation iPod touch, you need a recording application and an input with a microphone—for example, a headset with a microphone built in, such as the Apple Earphones with Remote and Mic ($29; http://store.apple.com).

At this writing, your best bet is the TuneTalk Stereo from Belkin ($69.95; http://store.apple.com). The TuneTalk Stereo is a digital recorder that clips onto the iPod's base and enables you to record CD-quality audio (16-bit, 44.1 KHz).

The TuneTalk Stereo has a real-time gain control. You can also plug in an external microphone and record through that instead of through the TuneTalk Stereo's two built-in microphones.

Portable Speakers for the iPod and iPhone

You can use the iPod as the sound source for just about any stereo system, as you'll see in "Connect an iPod or iPhone to a Stereo" in the next chapter. But if you travel with an iPod, or simply prefer a compact lifestyle, you may want portable speakers that will treat the iPod as the center of their universe. You can find a variety of iPod-specific speakers to meet most constraints of budgets and portability.

Some of the speakers mentioned here work for the iPhone as well. However, the iPhone has the advantage of having its own built-in speakers for low-volume listening.

Tip To boost the iPhone's built-in speakers, you can use an acoustic horn such as the AirCurve or the Ampli-Phone, both discussed earlier in this chapter.

Choosing Portable Speakers for the iPod or iPhone

If you've decided that you need portable speakers specifically for an iPod or iPhone, you've already narrowed down your choices considerably. Bear the following in mind when choosing portable speakers:

- *How much sound do the speakers make?* The best design in the world is useless if the speakers deliver sound too puny for your listening needs.
- *Do the speakers recharge the device?* Some speakers recharge the iPod or iPhone as it plays. Others just wear down the battery.
- *Do the speakers work with all iPods and with the iPhone?* Some speakers are designed only to work with a particular model. Others can recharge various iPods (for example, all models with the Dock Connector port) and the iPhone but can accept input from other players via a line-in port.
- *How are the speakers powered?* Some speakers are powered by replaceable batteries; others by rechargeable batteries; and others by AC power. A pairing of rechargeable batteries and AC power gives you the most flexibility.
- *Do the speakers include a remote control?* If you're planning to use the speakers from across the room, look for speakers that include a remote control.

Examples of Speakers for the iPod and iPhone

As with many iPod and iPhone accessories, there are far more speakers than you could shake even a large and threatening stick at. But here are five speakers worth looking at—for assorted reasons:

- **Bowers & Wilkins Zeppelin**   The Zeppelin from Bowers & Wilkins ($599.95; http://store.apple.com) is a zeppelin-shaped speaker that hides two 25-watt midrange/tweeter speakers and a 50-watt bass unit. Long on style but even longer on sound, the Zeppelin is the speaker to get if you've yet to hear of the credit crunch.
- **Edifier Luna 5**   An all-in-one speaker, the Luna 5 looks like a heavy-metal football standing on end on a round base in which the iPod or iPhone docks. The Luna 5 (see Figure 4-6) costs $349 and is available from various retailers. See the Edifier International website (www.edifier-international.com/minisite/lifestyle .html) for information.
- **Bose SoundDock II**   The SoundDock II from Bose ($299.00; www.bose.com) is one of the larger and more powerful speaker systems designed for the iPod. The SoundDock II works with all iPods that have a Dock Connector port. The SoundDock II runs on AC power and recharges the iPod as it plays.

FIGURE 4-6   The Luna 5 is capable of producing high-quality, room-shaking sound from an iPod or iPhone.

- **JBL OnStage III**   The OnStage III from JBL ($169.95; http://store.apple.com) is a round speaker unit that runs off AC power and delivers up to 10W per channel. The OnStage III is designed for iPods with the Dock Connector port, but you can also use other sound sources through an auxiliary audio input cable. The OnStage III weighs only 1lb and is portable enough to take traveling.
- **Altec Lansing inMotion**   The inMotion series from Altec Lansing (various prices; http://store.apple.com) includes portable and ultraportable stereo systems designed for iPods with Dock Connector ports. The larger models are AC powered, while the smaller models can run from batteries.

Radio Transmitters

Portable speakers are a great way of getting a decent amount of audio out of an iPod or iPhone when you're at home or traveling with a moderate amount of kit. But where portable speakers aren't practical, or when you need to travel light, you can use a radio transmitter to play audio from an iPod or iPhone through a handy radio. This is useful in hotels, in cars, in friends' houses—and even in your own home.

Choosing a Radio Transmitter

Many models of radio transmitters are available. Apart from price and esthetics, consider the following when choosing between them:

- *Does the transmitter fit only one model, or will it work for any device?* You may find that the choice is between a transmitter designed to fit only your current model of iPod or iPhone or a less-stylish transmitter that will work with any model—or indeed any sound source.
- *Is the transmitter powered by the iPod (or iPhone), or does it have its own power source?* Drawing power from the player's battery is a neater arrangement, because you don't have to worry about keeping the battery in the transmitter charged (or putting in new batteries) or connecting an external power supply. But drawing power from the player tends to limit the transmitter to working with certain models only.
- *Is the transmitter powerful enough for your needs?* Even among low-power transmitters that are legal for unlicensed use, power and range vary widely.
- *How many frequencies can the transmitter use?* Some transmitters are set to broadcast on a single frequency, which means you're out of luck if a more powerful local station happens to be using that frequency. Many transmitters offer several preset frequencies among which you can switch. Some transmitters provide a wide range of frequencies. Some provide "auto-tune" features to help you find a frequency that's free amid the radio storm.
- *Does the transmitter have other tricks?* Some transmitters are designed for use in your car or another vehicle, whereas others are general purpose.

Low-power radio transmitters are legal in the United States and the United Kingdom, but some other countries don't permit them. If you don't know whether your country permits radio transmitters, check before buying one.

Examples of Radio Transmitters

Here are three examples of radio transmitters:

- **PodFreq** The PodFreq from Sonnet Technologies ($29.95 to $79.95; www.sonnettech.com) is a family of relatively powerful radio transmitters built around the shape of an iPod case. The iPod slips inside the PodFreq (see Figure 4-7), and the PodFreq's aerial extends past the top of the iPod. The PodFreq offers a full range of digital tuning from 88.3 to 107.7 MHz, enabling you to avoid other stations even if the airwaves are jammed.

FIGURE 4-7 The PodFreq is one of the larger radio transmitters built for the iPod—and one of the most powerful.

FIGURE 4-8   The iTrip family offers models for the regular iPod and the iPod nano.

- **iTrip**   The iTrip family from Griffin Technology ($49.99 each; www.griffintechnology.com) consists of compact radio transmitters designed to work with most iPods. The iTrip models connect to the Dock Connector port, adding an extra section to the bottom of the iPod, and draw power from the iPod's battery rather than using batteries of their own. The iTrip (see Figure 4-8) lets you set it to broadcast on any frequency between 87.7 and 107.9 FM, so you should be able to get the signal through even in a busy urban area.
- **iBreath**   If you suspect your iPod has had too much to drink—just a second, let me try that again. If you want to ask your iPod if you've had too much to drink, consider getting the iBreath Breathalyzer & FM Transmitter ($89.99; www.davidsteele.com/). If you're too lubricated to drive, you can simply listen to the FM transmitter instead.

5

Use an iPod or iPhone as Your Home Stereo or Car Stereo

HOW TO...

- Equip an iPod or iPhone with speakers
- Connect an iPod or iPhone to your stereo
- Play music throughout your house from an iPod or iPhone
- Play music through an AirPort Express network
- Control iTunes from an iPod touch or iPhone
- Connect an iPod or iPhone to your car stereo
- Use your computer to play songs directly from an iPod or iPhone

By the time you've loaded hundreds or thousands of songs onto your iPod or iPhone, you'll probably have decided that headphones only get you so far. To enjoy your music the rest of the time, chances are that you'll want to play it from the iPod or iPhone and through your home stereo or your car stereo. This chapter shows you the various ways of doing so, from using cables to using radio waves.

Equip an iPod or iPhone with Speakers

The simplest way to get a decent volume of sound from an iPod or iPhone is to connect it to a pair of powered speakers (speakers that include their own amplifier). You can buy speakers designed especially for the iPod or iPhone (see the section "Portable Speakers for the iPod and iPhone" in Chapter 4), but you can also use any iPod or iPhone with any powered speakers that accept input via a miniplug connector (the size of connector used for the iPod's or iPhone's headphones).

Speakers designed for the iPod or iPhone tend to be smaller and more stylish than general-purpose speakers, but also considerably more expensive.

To get the highest sound quality possible from an iPod or iPhone, use a dock rather than the headphone port. Various models are available, from the utilitarian to the decorative. Connect the dock's line-out port to the speakers or receiver, and you're in business any time you've docked the iPod or iPhone.

Connect an iPod or iPhone to a Stereo

If you already have a stereo that produces good-quality sound, you can play songs from an iPod or iPhone through the stereo. There are three main ways of doing this:

- Connect the iPod or iPhone directly to the stereo with a cable, either via the device's headphone port or (better) via a dock.
- Use a radio transmitter to send the music from the iPod or iPhone to your radio, which plays it.
- Use your computer to play the music from an iPod or iPhone through an AirPort Express wireless access point that's connected to your stereo.

Connect an iPod or iPhone to a Stereo with a Cable

The most direct way to connect an iPod or iPhone to a stereo system is with a cable. For a typical receiver, you'll need a cable that has a miniplug at one end and two RCA plugs at the other end. Figure 5-1 shows an example of an iPod connected to a stereo via the amplifier.

Some receivers and boom boxes use a single stereo miniplug input rather than two RCA ports. To connect an iPod or iPhone to such devices, you'll need a stereo miniplug-to-miniplug cable. Make sure the cable is stereo, because mono miniplug-to-miniplug cables are common. A stereo cable has two bands around the miniplug (as on most headphones), whereas a mono cable has only one band.

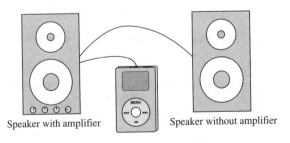

Speaker with amplifier   Speaker without amplifier

FIGURE 5-1 A miniplug-to-RCA-plugs cable is the most direct way of connecting an iPod or iPhone to your stereo system.

If you have a high-quality receiver and speakers, get a high-quality cable to connect the iPod or iPhone to them. After the amount you've presumably spent on the iPod or iPhone and stereo, it'd be a mistake to degrade the signal between them by sparing a few bucks on the cable.

 Tip   You can find various home-audio connection kits that contain a variety of cables likely to cover your needs. These kits are usually a safe buy, but unless your needs are peculiar, you'll end up with one or more cables you don't need. So if you do know which cables you need, make sure a kit offers a cost savings before buying it instead of the individual cables.

Connect the iPod or iPhone to your receiver as follows:

1. Connect the miniplug to the player's headphone port. If you have a dock, connect the miniplug to the dock's line-out port instead, because this gives better sound quality than the headphone port.
2. If you're using the headphone port, turn down the volume on the iPod or iPhone all the way.
3. Whichever port you're using, turn down the volume on the amplifier as well.
4. Connect the RCA plugs to the left and right ports of one of the inputs on your amplifier or boom box—for example, the AUX input or the Cassette input (if you're not using a cassette deck).

 Caution   Don't connect the iPod or iPhone to the Phono input on your amplifier. The Phono input is built with a higher sensitivity to make up for the weak output of a record player. Putting a full-strength signal into the Phono input will probably blow it.

5. Start the music playing. If you're using the headphone port, turn up the volume a little.
6. Turn up the volume on the receiver so that you can hear the music.
7. Increase the volume on the two controls in tandem until you reach a satisfactory sound level.

 Note   Too low a level of output from the player may produce noise as your amplifier boosts the signal. Too high a level of output from the player may cause distortion.

If you plug a player directly into your stereo, get a remote control for the player so that you don't need to march over to it each time you need to change the music. See "Remote Controls" in Chapter 4 for details of some of the remote controls available for the iPod and iPhone.

Use a Radio Transmitter Between an iPod or iPhone and a Stereo

If you don't want to connect the iPod or iPhone directly to your stereo system, you can use a radio transmitter to send the audio from the player to the radio on your stereo. See "Radio Transmitters" in Chapter 4 for examples of radio transmitters designed for the iPod and iPhone.

The sound you get from this arrangement typically will be lower in quality than the sound from a wired connection, but it should be at least as good as listening to a conventional radio station in stereo. If that's good enough for you, a radio transmitter can be a neat solution to playing music from the iPod or iPhone throughout your house.

 Using a radio transmitter has another advantage: You can play the music on several radios at the same time, giving yourself music throughout your dwelling without complex and expensive rewiring.

Use an AirPort Express, a Computer, and an iPod or iPhone

If you have an AirPort Express (a wireless access point that Apple makes), you can use it not only to network your home but also to play music from your computer, iPod, or iPhone through your stereo system.

To play music through an AirPort Express, follow these general steps:

1. Connect the AirPort Express to the receiver via a cable. The line-out port on the AirPort Express combines an analog port and an optical output, so you can connect the AirPort Express to the receiver in either of two ways:
   - Connect an optical cable to the AirPort Express's line-out socket and to an optical digital-audio input port on the receiver. If the receiver has an optical input, use this arrangement to get the best sound quality possible.
   - Connect an analog audio cable to the AirPort Express's line-out socket and to the RCA ports on your receiver.
2. If your network has a wired portion, connect the Ethernet port on the AirPort Express to the switch or hub using an Ethernet cable. If you have a DSL that you will share through the AirPort Express, connect the DSL via the Ethernet cable.
3. Plug the AirPort Express into an electric socket.
4. Install on your computer the software that accompanies the AirPort Express. Then use the AirPort Admin Utility for Windows or the AirPort Utility (on Mac OS X) to configure the network.
5. Connect the iPod or iPhone to your computer.
6. Launch iTunes if it isn't already running.
7. If the iPod or iPhone is set for automatic updating of songs and playlists, click its entry in the Source list to display the device's screens. On the Summary tab, select the Manually Manage Music and Videos option button, click the OK

button in the confirmation dialog box, and then click the Apply button to apply the changes.

8. Click the Choose which Speakers to use button (the large button at the bottom of the iTunes window) and choose the entry for the AirPort Express from the drop-down list. (This button appears only if iTunes has detected an AirPort Express within striking distance.)

9. Click the iPod's or iPhone's entry in the Source list to display its contents. You can then play the songs on the iPod back via your computer to the speakers connected to the AirPort Express.

10. To switch back to playing through the computer's speakers, Click the Choose which Speakers to use button at the bottom of the iTunes window again. This time, choose the Computer entry from the drop-down list.

 If you changed the iPod's or iPhone's updating preferences in Step 7, remember to change updating back to your preferred setting before you disconnect the device.

Figure 5-2 shows a typical setup for playing music from an iPod or iPhone through an AirPort Express.

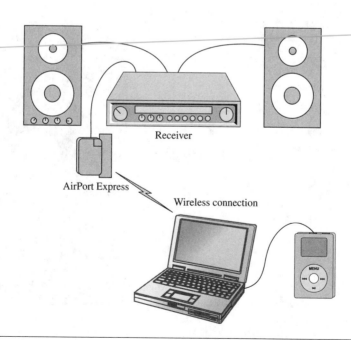

FIGURE 5-2   If you have an AirPort Express, you can play music on your computer or iPod or iPhone through your stereo system across the wireless network.

Control iTunes Remotely from an iPod touch or iPhone

If you have an iPod touch or iPhone, you can use it as a remote control to control iTunes on your PC or Mac across your wireless network. This is great when you want to be able to play music without getting up from your armchair—or from another room.

To use the iPod touch or iPhone as a remote control, follow these steps:

1. Download the free Remote application from the iTunes Store. You can download the application either directly onto the iPhone or iPod touch or onto your computer.
2. If you downloaded the Remote application onto your computer, synchronize the iPod touch or iPhone to install the application on it. (See Chapter 19 for instructions on installing applications.)
3. On the iPod touch or iPhone, go to the Home screen and touch the Remote icon to launch the Remote application. The application displays the Settings screen (shown on the left in Figure 5-3), without any libraries, because you haven't added any yet.

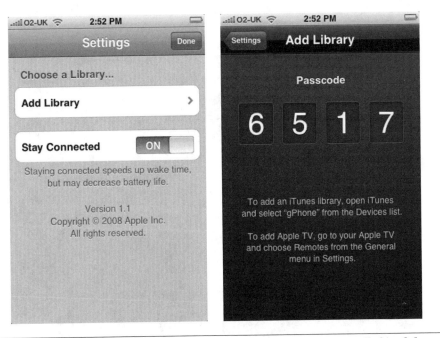

FIGURE 5-3 Touch the Add Library button on the Settings screen (left) of the Remote application to display the passcode for identifying the iPod touch or iPhone.

4. Touch the Add Library button to display the Add Library screen (shown on the right in Figure 5-3). This screen shows a one-time password that you use to identify the iPod touch or iPhone to iTunes.
5. On your computer, launch iTunes if it's not already running. When iTunes detects the Remote application running across the wireless network, it displays the iPhone or iPod touch in the Source list.

Note If iTunes on your computer doesn't show the iPod touch or iPhone in the Source list, you may need to reconfigure your wireless network. You don't need to connect the iPod touch or iPhone to your computer to give iTunes the passcode for the Remote application—in fact, you can't connect this way. You must make the connection across the wireless network, as you will when using Remote to control iTunes.

6. Click the iPod touch or iPhone in the Source list. iTunes prompts you for the passcode (see Figure 5-4).
7. After iTunes checks that the passcode is correct, it displays a screen telling you that the Remote can now control iTunes. Click the OK button to dismiss this screen.
8. On the iPod touch or iPhone, the library to which you've connected now appears on the Settings screen, as shown on the left in Figure 5-5. Touch the library to display its contents, as shown on the right in Figure 5-5.

FIGURE 5-4   Enter the passcode for the iPod touch or iPhone on this iTunes screen.

FIGURE 5-5 Once the library appears on the iPod touch or iPhone (left), touch its name to display its contents.

 If you want to keep the Remote application connected to the iTunes library, move the Stay Connected slider on the Settings screen to the On position. This setting eats up the iPod's or iPhone's battery life, so try using Remote without it and turn it on only if you need it.

From here, you can play songs and videos using much the same techniques as for songs and videos on the iPod touch or iPhone itself. For example, touch the Artists button at the bottom of the screen to display the list of artists.

Connect an iPod or iPhone to a Car Stereo

You can connect an iPod or iPhone to a car stereo in any of the following ways:

- Get a car with a built-in iPod or iPhone connection or add an after-market iPod- or iPhone-integration device.
- Use a cassette adapter to connect the iPod or iPhone to the car's cassette player.
- Use a radio-frequency device to play the device's output through the car's radio.
- Wire the device directly to the car stereo and use it as an auxiliary input device.

Each of these methods has its pros and cons. The following sections tell you what you need to know to choose the best option for your car stereo.

Use a Built-in iPod or iPhone Connection

At this writing, Apple claims that more than 90 percent of new cars sold in the United States have an option for connecting an iPod. (See the list at www.apple.com/ipod/carintegration.html.) So if you're in the market for a new car, add iPod connectivity to your list of criteria. Similarly, if you're buying a used car that's only a few years old, you may be able to get iPod connectivity built in.

If your car doesn't have its own means of integrating an iPod or iPhone, look for a third-party solution. Some adapters not only let you play back music from the device through the car's stereo and control it using the stereo system's controls, but also let you display the song information from the device on the stereo's display, making it easier to see what you're listening to.

Use a Cassette Adapter

If the car stereo has a cassette player, your easiest option is to use a cassette adapter to play audio from the iPod or iPhone through the cassette deck. You can buy such adapters for between $10 and $20 from most electronics stores or from an iPod specialist.

The adapter is shaped like a cassette and uses a playback head to input analog audio via the head that normally reads the tape as it passes. A wire runs from the adapter to the iPod or iPhone.

A cassette adapter can be an easy and inexpensive solution, but it's far from perfect. The main problem is that the audio quality tends to be poor, because the means of transferring the audio to the cassette player's mechanism is less than optimal. But if your car is noisy, you may find that road noise obscures most of the defects in audio quality.

If the cassette player's playback head is dirty from playing cassettes, audio quality will be that much worse. To keep the audio quality as high as possible, clean the cassette player regularly using a cleaning cassette.

 If you use a cassette adapter in an extreme climate, try to make sure you don't bake it or freeze it by leaving it in the car.

Use a Radio Transmitter

If the car stereo doesn't have a cassette deck, your easiest option for playing music from an iPod or iPhone may be to get a radio transmitter. This device plugs into the iPod or iPhone and broadcasts a signal on an FM frequency to which you then tune your radio to play the music. Better radio transmitters offer a choice of frequencies to allow you easy access to both the device and your favorite radio stations.

 See the section "Radio Transmitters" in Chapter 4 for a discussion of how to choose among the many radio transmitters offered and examples of transmitters designed for the iPod and iPhone.

Radio transmitters can deliver reasonable audio quality. If possible, try before you buy by asking for a demonstration in the store (take a portable radio with you, if necessary).

The main advantages of these devices are that they're relatively inexpensive (usually between $15 and $50) and they're easy to use. They also have the advantage that you can put the iPod or iPhone out of sight (for example, in the glove compartment—provided it's not too hot) without any telltale wires to help the light-fingered locate it.

On the downside, most of these devices need batteries (others can run off the 12-volt accessory outlet or cigarette-lighter socket), and less expensive units tend not to deliver the highest sound quality. The range of these devices is minimal, but at close quarters, other radios nearby may be able to pick up the signal—which could be embarrassing, entertaining, or irrelevant, depending on the circumstances. If you use the radio transmitter in an area where the airwaves are busy, you may need to keep switching the frequency to avoid having the transmitter swamped by the full-strength radio stations.

If you decide to get a radio transmitter, you'll need to choose between getting a model designed specifically for the iPod or iPhone and getting one that works with any audio source. Radio transmitters designed for the iPod or iPhone typically mount on the iPod or iPhone, making them a neater solution than general-purpose ones that dangle from the headphone socket. Radio transmitters designed for use with iPods or iPhones in cars often mount on the accessory outlet or dash and secure the device as well as transmitting its sound.

Tip A radio-frequency adapter works with radios other than car radios, so you can use one to play music through your stereo system (or someone else's). You may also want to connect a radio-frequency adapter to a PC or Mac and use it to broadcast audio to a portable radio. This is a great way of getting streaming radio from the Internet to play on a conventional radio.

Wire an iPod or iPhone Directly to a Car Stereo

If neither the cassette adapter nor the radio-frequency adapter provides a suitable solution, or if you simply want the best audio quality you can get, connect the iPod or iPhone directly to your car stereo. How easily you can do this depends on how the stereo is designed:

- If your car stereo is one of the few that has a miniplug input built in, get a miniplug-to-miniplug cable, and you'll be in business.
- If your stereo is built to take multiple inputs—for example, a CD player (or changer) and an auxiliary input—you may be able to simply run a wire from unused existing connectors. Plug the iPod or iPhone into the other end, press the correct buttons, and you'll be ready to rock-and-roll down the freeway.
- If no unused connectors are available, you or your local friendly electronics technician may need to get busy with a soldering iron.

If you're buying a new car stereo, look for iPod or iPhone integration or at least an auxiliary input that you can use with an iPod or iPhone.

PART II

Create and Manage Your Library

6

Create Audio Files, Edit Them, and Tag Them

HOW TO...

- Choose where to store your library
- Choose suitable audio-quality settings in iTunes
- Convert audio files from other audio formats to AAC or MP3
- Create AAC files or MP3 files from cassettes, vinyl, or other sources
- Remove scratches, hiss, and hum from audio files
- Trim or split song files
- Rename song files efficiently
- Save audio streams to disk

In Chapter 2, you learned how to start creating your library by copying music from your CDs and importing your existing music files. This is a great way to put songs on an iPod or iPhone quickly, but to get the most enjoyment out of your music, you'll probably want to customize iTunes' settings rather than use the defaults.

You may also want to do things with AAC files and MP3 files that iTunes doesn't support. For example, you may receive (or acquire) files in formats the iPod or iPhone can't handle, so you'll need to convert the files before you can use them on an iPod or iPhone. You may want to create song files from cassettes, LPs, or other media you own, and you may need to remove clicks, pops, and other extraneous noises from such recordings you make. You may want to trim intros or outros off audio files, split files into smaller files, or retag batches of files in ways iTunes can't handle. Last, you may want to record streaming audio to your hard disk.

Choose Where to Store Your Library

Because your library can contain dozens—or even hundreds—of gigabytes of files, you must store it in a suitable location if you choose to keep all your files in it.

By default, iTunes stores your library in a folder named iTunes Music. This folder, the library folder, contains not only songs (in subfolders named after the artist) but also other items. For example, iTunes stores your movies in the Movies folder within the library folder, your podcasts in the Podcasts folder, and your TV shows in the TV Shows folder.

 Instead of keeping all your song files in your library, you can store references to where the files are located in other folders. Doing so enables you to minimize the size of your library. But for maximum flexibility and to make sure you can access all the tracks in your library all the time, keeping all your song files in your library folder is best—if you can do so.

To change the location of your library from now on, follow these steps:

1. Display the iTunes dialog box or the Preferences dialog box:
   - In Windows, choose Edit | Preferences or press CTRL-COMMA or CTRL-Y to display the iTunes dialog box.
   - On the Mac, choose iTunes | Preferences or press ⌘-COMMA or ⌘-Y to display the Preferences dialog box.
2. Click the Advanced tab to display its contents. Figure 6-1 shows the Advanced tab of the iTunes dialog box in Windows.
3. Click the Change button to display the Browse For Folder dialog box (Windows) or Change Music Folder Location dialog box (Mac).
4. Navigate to the folder that will contain your library, select the folder, and then click the OK button (Windows Vista), Open button (Windows XP), or Choose button (Mac). iTunes returns you to the iTunes dialog box or Preferences dialog box.
5. Click the OK button to close the iTunes dialog box or the Preferences dialog box. iTunes displays a message box as it updates your iTunes library, as shown here.

6. If iTunes prompts you to decide whether to let iTunes move and rename the files in your new iTunes Music folder, as shown here, click the Yes button.

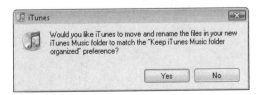

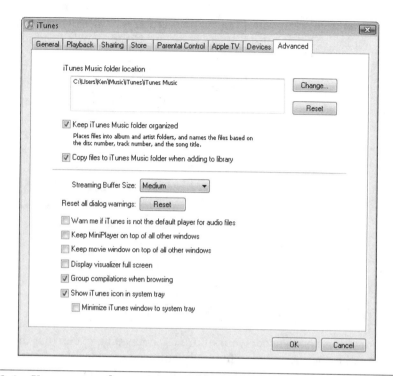

FIGURE 6-1   You may need to move your library folder from its default location to a folder that has more disk space available.

Note   To reset your library folder to its default location (the iTunes\iTunes Music folder in Windows or the iTunes/iTunes Music folder on the Mac), click the Reset button on the Advanced tab of the iTunes dialog box or the Preferences dialog box.

When you change the location of your library like this, iTunes doesn't actually move the files that are already in your library. To move the files, make sure the new folder contains enough space, and then follow these steps:

1. Display the iTunes dialog box or the Preferences dialog box again:
   - In Windows, choose Edit | Preferences or press CTRL-COMMA or CTRL-Y to display the iTunes dialog box.
   - On the Mac, choose iTunes | Preferences or press ⌘-COMMA or ⌘-Y to display the Preferences dialog box.
2. Click the Advanced tab to display its contents (see Figure 6-1).
3. Select the Keep iTunes Music Folder Organized check box.
4. Select the Copy Files To iTunes Music Folder When Adding To Library check box.
5. Click the OK button to close the iTunes dialog box or the Preferences dialog box.

6. Choose File | Library | Consolidate Library. iTunes displays a message box telling you that consolidating your library will copy all the songs to the iTunes Music folder, as shown here.

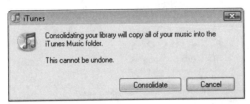

7. Click the Consolidate button. iTunes copies the files, showing you its progress (as shown here) until it has finished.

Configure iTunes for the Audio Quality You Want

Before you rip and encode your entire CD collection, check that the settings in iTunes are suitable for your needs. iTunes' default is to encode to AAC files at 128 Kbps in stereo: a fair choice for defaults, but you may well want to change them. Spend some time choosing the right settings for ripping and encoding so that you don't waste time ripping your CDs more than once.

First, decide which music format and audio quality you want. Then choose the appropriate settings in iTunes.

Choose the Best Audio Format for Your Needs

iTunes can encode audio in five formats: AAC, MP3, Apple Lossless Encoding, WAV, and AIFF. AAC, MP3, and Apple Lossless Encoding are compressed audio formats, whereas WAV and AIFF are not compressed.

AAC

AAC is the abbreviation for Advanced Audio Coding, a *codec* (*coder/decoder*) for compressing and playing back digital audio. AAC was put together by a group of heavy hitters in the audio and digital audio fields, including Fraunhofer IIS-A (the German company that developed MP3), Sony Corporation, Dolby Laboratories, AT&T, Nokia, and Lucent.

AAC is newer than MP3 (which is discussed in the next section), is generally agreed to deliver better sound than MP3, and is more tightly controlled than MP3. It is one of the key audio components of the MPEG-4 specification, which covers digital audio and video.

How to... Understand CD-Quality Audio and Lossy and Lossless Compression

CD-quality audio samples audio 44,100 times per second (a sampling rate of 44.1 KHz) to provide coverage across most of the human hearing range. Each sample contains 16 bits (2 bytes) of data, which is enough information to convey the full range of frequencies. There are two tracks (for stereo), doubling the amount of data. CD-quality audio consumes around 9MB (megabytes) of storage space per minute of audio, which means that around 74 minutes of music fits on a standard 650MB CD and 80 minutes on a 700MB CD. The data on audio CDs is stored in *pulse code modulation* (PCM), a standard format for uncompressed audio.

To make more music fit on your computer, iPod, or iPhone, you can compress it so that it takes up less space. AAC and MP3 use *lossy compression*, compression that discards the parts of the audio data that your ears won't be able to hear or that your brain won't be able to pick out even though your ears hear it. Lossy audio codecs use *psychoacoustics*, the science of how the human brain processes sound, to select which data to keep and which to discard. As a basic example, when one part of the sound is masked by another part of the sound, the encoder discards the masked part, because you wouldn't hear it even if it were there.

How much data the encoder keeps depends on a setting called the *bitrate*. Almost all encoders let you choose a wide range of bitrates. In addition, most MP3 encoders can encode either at a constant bitrate (CBR) or a variable bitrate (VBR). The pros and cons of CBR and VBR are discussed in the sidebar "Choose Between CBR and VBR, and a Suitable Stereo Setting, for MP3," later in this chapter.

The advantage of lossy compression is that a well-designed codec can produce good-sounding audio at a fraction of the file size of uncompressed audio. For example, AAC and MP3 sound good to most people at a bitrate of 128 Kbps, which produces files around a tenth of the size of the uncompressed audio. The disadvantage of lossy compression is that the audio can never sound perfect, because some data has been discarded.

Better than lossy compression is *lossless compression*, which reduces the file size without discarding any of the audio data. Apple Lossless Encoding is lossless compression and produces extremely high-quality results.

The advantage of lossless compression is that it produces audio that is as high in quality as the uncompressed audio. The disadvantage is that lossless compression reduces the file size by much less than lossy compression, because it doesn't discard audio data.

AAC files can be either protected with digital rights management (DRM) technology or unprotected.

The iTunes Store (discussed in Chapter 7) uses AAC for its songs, so if you buy songs from it, you won't have any choice about using AAC. You can convert unprotected AAC songs to other formats (for example, to MP3) but you lose audio quality in the conversion.

QuickTime includes an AAC codec. iTunes uses QuickTime's capabilities to encode audio and play back audio and video.

 AAC can work with up to 48 full-frequency audio channels. This gives it a huge advantage over MP3, which can work with only two channels (in stereo) or a single channel (in mono). If you're used to listening to music in stereo, 48 channels seems an absurd number. But typically, only a small subset of those channels would be used at the same time. For example, conventional surround-sound rigs use 5.1 or 7.1 setups, using six channels or eight channels, respectively. Other channels can be used for different languages, so that an AAC player can play a different vocal track for differently configured players. Other tracks yet can be used for synchronizing and controlling the audio.

Advantages of AAC   For music lovers, AAC offers higher music quality than MP3 at the same file sizes, or similar music quality at smaller file sizes. Apple claims that 128-Kbps AAC files sound as good as 160-Kbps MP3 files—so you can either save a fair amount of space and enjoy the same quality or enjoy even higher quality at the same bitrate. Around 24 Kbps, AAC streams provide quite listenable sound, whereas MP3 streams sound quite rough. (*Streaming* is the method of transmission used by Internet radio, in which you can listen to a file as your computer downloads it.)

Small file sizes are especially welcome for streaming audio over slow connections, such as modem connections. AAC streamed around 56 Kbps sounds pretty good (though not perfect), whereas MP3 sounds a bit flawed.

The main advantage of AAC for the music industry is that the format supports DRM. This means that AAC files can be created in a protected format with custom limitations built in. For example, most of the song files you can buy from the iTunes Store used to be protected by DRM so that, even if you distributed them to other people, those people couldn't play them. Happily, at this writing, Apple is phasing out the iTunes Store's use of DRM.

 To tell whether an AAC file is protected, click it in iTunes, choose File | Get Info, and then check the Kind readout on the Summary tab of the Item Information dialog box. If the file is protected, the Kind readout reads "Protected AAC Audio File." If not, Kind reads "AAC Audio File." Alternatively, check the file extension: The .m4p extension indicates a protected file, whereas the .m4a extension indicates an unprotected file.

Disadvantages of AAC   If you use iTunes and an iPod or iPhone, you'll probably find AAC's disadvantages easy enough to bear:

- AAC files are not widely available except by using iTunes and the iTunes Store. Even though Apple has made AAC the default format for iTunes and the iTunes Store, most other sources of digital audio files use other formats—typically either WMA or MP3.
- Encoding AAC files takes more processor cycles than encoding MP3 files. But any computer built in the last few years should be plenty fast enough.

- DRM can prevent you from playing AAC files on the computers or devices you want to. Even worse, whoever applied the DRM can change its conditions after you buy a song—for example, further restricting your rights.

MP3

Like AAC, MP3 is a file format for compressed audio. MP3 became popular in the late 1990s and largely sparked the digital music revolution by making it possible to carry a large amount of high-quality audio with you on a small device and enjoy it at the cost of nothing but the device, battery power, and time.

Among Mac users, MP3 has been overshadowed recently by AAC since Apple incorporated the AAC codec in iTunes, QuickTime, and the iPod (and later the iPhone). But MP3 remains the dominant format for compressed audio on computers running Windows (where its major competition comes from WMA, Microsoft's proprietary Windows Media Audio format) and computers running Linux.

MP3's name comes from the Moving Picture Experts Group (MPEG; www .chiariglione.org/mpeg/—not www.mpeg.org), which oversaw the development of the MP3 format. MP3 is both the extension used by the files and the name commonly used for them. (Technically, MP3 is the file format for MPEG-1 Layer 3.)

MP3 can deliver high-quality music in files that take up as little as a tenth as much space as uncompressed CD-quality files. For speech, which typically requires less fidelity than music, you can create even smaller files that still sound good, enabling you to pack that much more audio in the same amount of disk space.

Apple Lossless Encoding

Apple Lossless Encoding is an encoder that gives results that are mathematically lossless—there is no degradation of audio quality in the compressed files. The amount that Apple Lossless Encoding compresses audio depends on how complex the audio is. Some songs compress to around 40 percent of the uncompressed file size, whereas others compress to only 60–70 percent of the uncompressed file size.

Apple Lossless Encoding is a great way to keep full-quality audio on your computer—at least, if it has a large hard disk (or several large hard disks). Apple Lossless Encoding gives great audio quality on the iPod and iPhone as well, but it's not such a great solution for most people. This is for three reasons:

- The large amount of space that Apple Lossless Encoding files consume means that you can't fit nearly as many songs on an iPod or iPhone as you can using AAC or MP3.
- The Apple Lossless Encoding files are too large for the memory chip in the iPod classic to buffer effectively. As a result, the iPod has to read the hard drive more frequently, which reduces battery life. (This isn't a concern for the iPod nano, iPod touch, or iPhone, which use flash memory rather than a hard drive.)
- Most non-Apple hardware and software players can't play Apple Lossless Encoding files. If you want to be able to play your song files on various devices, either now or in the future, choose a format other than Apple Lossless Encoding.

The second-generation iPod shuffle doesn't play Apple Lossless Encoding files at all, even though it plays WAV files and AIFF files. But what you can do is select the Convert Higher Bit Rate Files To 128 Kbps AAC check box on the Settings tab for the iPod shuffle. You can then add Apple Lossless Encoding files to the iPod shuffle, with iTunes converting the files to AAC files on-the-fly. (iTunes converts other file formats that use a bitrate higher than 128 Kbps as well.)

WAV and AIFF

WAV files and AIFF files both contain uncompressed PCM audio, which is also referred to as "raw" audio. WAV files are PCM files with a WAV header, whereas AIFF files are PCM files with an AIFF header. The *header* is a section of identification information placed at the start of the file.

 AIFF tends to be more widely used on the Mac than in Windows, which favors WAV. However, iTunes can create and play both AIFF files and WAV files on both Windows and Mac OS X.

If you want the ultimate in audio quality, you can create AIFF files or WAV files from your CDs and use them on your computer and iPod or iPhone. However, there are three reasons why you probably won't want to do this:

- Each full-length CD will take up between 500MB and 800MB of disk space, compared to the 50MB to 80MB it would take up compressed at 128 Kbps. Apple Lossless Encoding gives a better balance of full audio quality with somewhat reduced file size.
- An iPod classic won't be able to buffer the audio effectively, will need to access the hard drive more frequently, and will deliver poor battery life. Other iPods and the iPhone don't have this limitation.
- Neither AIFF files nor WAV files have containers for storing tag information, such as the names of the artist, the CD, and the song. iTunes does its best to help by maintaining the tag information for AIFF files or WAV files in its database, but if you move the files (for example, if you copy them to a different computer), the tag information doesn't go with them. By contrast, Apple Lossless Encoding files have containers for their tag information.

That all sounds pretty negative—yet if you need the highest quality for music, WAV or AIFF is the way to go. Another advantage is that WAV files are widely playable—all versions of Windows, Mac OS X, and most other operating systems have WAV players. The AIFF format is not as widely used on Windows (although iTunes for Windows can play AIFF), as it is primarily a Mac format.

Choose the Best Format for iTunes, the iPod, and the iPhone

Choosing the best audio format for iTunes, the iPod, and the iPhone can be tough. You'll probably be torn between having the highest-quality audio possible when playing audio on your computer and packing the largest possible number of good-sounding songs on the player—and making sure it has enough battery life for you to listen to plenty of those songs each day.

For the highest possible audio quality on your computer, use Apple Lossless Encoding. (WAV and AIFF are also possible, but they use more space, have no tag containers, and offer no advantage over Apple Lossless Encoding.) For the largest possible number of songs on an iPod or iPhone, use AAC.

Unless your library has space for you to keep two copies of each song that you want to be able to play both on your computer and on the iPod or iPhone, you'll probably be best off going with AAC at a high enough bitrate that you don't notice the difference in quality between the AAC files and Apple Lossless Encoding files.

Did You Know?

Digital Audio Formats iTunes, the iPod, and the iPhone Can't Play

For most of the music you store on your computer and enjoy via iTunes or an iPod or iPhone, you'll want to use AAC, MP3, or whichever combination of the two you find most convenient. Both iTunes and the iPod and iPhone can also use WAV files and AIFF files.

For you as a digital audio enthusiast, other formats that may be of interest include the following:

- WMA is an audio format developed by Microsoft. It's the preferred format of Windows Media Player, the Microsoft audio and video player included with all desktop versions of Windows. WMA supports DRM, but its DRM is incompatible with iTunes and the iPod and iPhone.
- mp3PRO was designed to be a successor to MP3, delivering higher audio quality at the same bitrates, but it has now been discontinued.
- Ogg Vorbis is an open-source format that's patent free but not yet widely used. To play Ogg Vorbis files on an iPod or iPhone, you'll need to convert them to AAC or MP3. (You can also convert them to Apple Lossless Encoding, WAV, or AIFF, but doing so makes little sense, because Ogg Vorbis is a lossy format.) You can convert Ogg Vorbis files to WAV by using the freeware program Audacity (discussed later in this chapter) and then use iTunes to convert the WAV files to AAC or MP3, or convert them directly to AAC or MP3 by using Total Audio Converter (www.coolutils.com).
- FLAC, Free Lossless Audio Codec, is an open-source audio codec that creates lossless compressed files comparable in quality to Apple Lossless Encoding. To play FLAC files on an iPod or iPhone, you'll need to convert them to AAC or MP3. For Windows, the best tool is Total Audio Converter (www.coolutils.com). To add FLAC playback and conversion to iTunes on the Mac, try Fluke (http://cubicfruit.com/fluke).

AAC delivers high-quality audio, small file size, and enough flexibility for most purposes. But if you want to use the files you rip from a CD on a portable player that doesn't support AAC, or you need to play them using a software player that doesn't support AAC, choose MP3 instead. Similarly, if you want to share your music files with other people in any way other than sharing your library via iTunes, MP3 is the way to go—but remember that you need the copyright holder's explicit authorization to copy and distribute music.

Check or Change Your Importing Settings

To check or change the importing settings, follow these steps:

1. Display the iTunes dialog box or the Preferences dialog box:
   - In Windows, choose Edit | Preferences or press CTRL-COMMA or CTRL-Y to display the iTunes dialog box.
   - On the Mac, choose iTunes | Preferences or press ⌘-COMMA or ⌘-Y to display the Preferences dialog box.
2. Click the General tab if it's not already displayed.
3. In the When You Insert A CD drop-down list, choose what you want iTunes to do when you insert a CD: Show CD, Begin Playing, Ask To Import CD, Import CD, or Import CD And Eject.
   - Bear in mind that Show CD, Import CD, and Import CD And Eject all involve looking up the song names on the Internet (unless you've already played the CD and thus caused iTunes to look up the names before), so iTunes will need to use your Internet connection.
   - Avoid the Import CD And Eject setting unless your computer's optical drive can always open (or eject a CD) safely without hitting anything.
4. Click the Import Settings button to display the Import Settings dialog box. Figure 6-2 shows the Import Settings dialog box on iTunes for the Mac. The Import Settings dialog box on iTunes for Windows has the same controls.
5. In the Import Using drop-down list, choose the encoder for the file format you want:
   - The default setting is AAC Encoder, which creates compressed files in AAC format. AAC files combine high audio quality with compact size, making AAC a good format for both iTunes and the iPod or iPhone.
   - The other setting you're likely to want to try is MP3 Encoder, which creates compressed files in the MP3 format. MP3 files have marginally lower audio quality than AAC files for the same file size, but you can use MP3 files with a wider variety of software applications and hardware players.
   - Apple Lossless Encoding files have full audio quality but a relatively large file size. They're good for iTunes but typically too large for the iPod or iPhone.
   - AIFF files and WAV files are uncompressed audio files, so they have full audio quality (and are widely playable, as noted earlier) but take up a huge amount of space. You'll seldom need to use either of these formats.

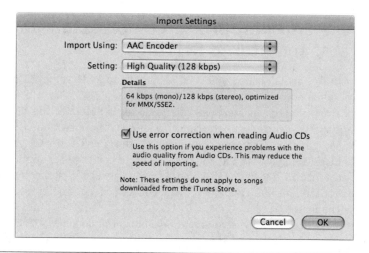

FIGURE 6-2 Configure your audio quality settings in the Import Settings dialog box.

6. In the Setting drop-down list, choose the setting you want to use:
   - For the AAC Encoder, the Setting drop-down list offers the settings High Quality (128 Kbps), iTunes Plus (which uses the 256 Kbps bitrate), Spoken Podcast, and Custom. When you select Custom, iTunes displays the AAC Encoder dialog box so you can specify custom settings. See the next section, "Choose Custom AAC Encoding Settings," for a discussion of these options.
   - For the MP3 Encoder, the Setting drop-down list offers the settings Good Quality (128 Kbps), High Quality (160 Kbps), Higher Quality (192 Kbps), and Custom. When you select Custom, iTunes displays the MP3 Encoder dialog box so you can specify custom settings. See "Choose Custom MP3 Encoding Settings," later in this chapter, for a discussion of these options.
   - The Apple Lossless Encoder has no configurable settings. (The Setting drop-down list offers only the Automatic setting.)
   - For the AIFF Encoder and the WAV Encoder, the Setting drop-down list offers the settings Automatic and Custom. When you select Custom, iTunes displays the AIFF Encoder dialog box or the WAV Encoder dialog box (as appropriate) so you can specify custom settings. See "Choose Custom AIFF and WAV Encoding Settings," later in this chapter, for a discussion of these options.
7. Select the Use Error Correction When Reading Audio CDs check box if you want to turn on the error-correction feature. Usually, you need error correction only if you get clicks or skips in your imported files without it.
8. Click the OK button to close the Import Settings dialog box.
9. Click the OK button to close the iTunes dialog box or Preferences dialog box.

How to... Choose an Appropriate Compression Rate, Bitrate, and Stereo Settings

To get suitable audio quality, you must use an appropriate compression rate for the audio files you encode with iTunes.

iTunes' default settings are to encode AAC files in stereo at the 128-Kbps bitrate using automatic sample-rate detection. iTunes calls those settings High Quality, and they deliver great results for most purposes. If they don't suit you, you can opt for the iTunes Plus setting, choose the Podcast setting to create files suitable for podcasting (in other words, with lower quality and a smaller file size), or specify custom AAC settings for the files you create. With AAC you can change the bitrate, the sample rate, and the channels.

iTunes' MP3 Encoder gives you more flexibility. The default settings for MP3 are to encode MP3 files in stereo at the 160-Kbps bitrate, using CBR and automatic sample-rate detection. iTunes calls those settings High Quality, and they deliver results almost as good as the High Quality settings with the AAC Encoder, although they produce significantly larger files because the bitrate is higher.

For encoding MP3 files, iTunes also offers preset settings for Good Quality (128 Kbps) and Higher Quality (192 Kbps). Beyond these choices, you can choose the Custom setting and specify exactly the settings you want: bitrates from 16 Kbps to 320 Kbps, CBR or VBR, sample rate, channels, the stereo mode, whether to use Smart Encoding Adjustments, and whether to filter frequencies lower than 10 Hz.

If possible, invest a few days in choosing a compression rate for your library. Choosing the wrong compression rate can cost you disk space (if you record at too high a bitrate), audio quality (too low a bitrate), and the time it takes to rip your entire collection again at the bitrate you prefer.

Choose a representative selection of the types of music you plan to listen to using your computer and iPod or iPhone. Encode several copies of each test track at different bitrates, and then listen to them over several days to see which provides the best balance of file size and audio quality. Make sure some of the songs test the different aspects of music that are important to you. For example, if your musical tastes lean to female vocalists, listen to plenty of those types of songs. If you prefer bass-heavy, bludgeoning rock, listen to that. If you go for classical music as well, add that to the mix. You may need to use different compression rates for different types of music to achieve satisfactory results and keep the file size down.

Choose Custom AAC Encoding Settings

To choose custom AAC encoding settings, follow these steps:

1. In the Import Settings dialog box, choose AAC Encoder in the Import Using drop-down list.

2. In the Setting drop-down list, choose the Custom item to display the AAC Encoder dialog box:

```
┌─────────────────────────────────────────────────────┐
│                      AAC Encoder                      │
│                                                       │
│     Stereo Bit Rate:  [ 128 kbps      ▲▼]             │
│                                                       │
│       Sample Rate:  [ Auto          ▲▼]               │
│                                                       │
│         Channels:  [ Auto          ▲▼]               │
│                                                       │
│                    ☐ Use Variable Bit Rate Encoding (VBR) │
│                    ☐ Optimize for voice               │
│                                                       │
│  ( Default Settings )          ( Cancel ) ( OK )      │
└─────────────────────────────────────────────────────┘
```

3. In the Stereo Bit Rate drop-down list, choose the bitrate. You can use from 16 Kbps to 320 Kbps. The default is 128 Kbps.
   - The 128 Kbps setting provides high-quality audio suitable for general music listening. You may want to experiment with higher bitrates to see if you can detect a difference. If not, stick with 128 Kbps so as to get the largest possible amount of quality music on the iPod or iPhone.
   - If you listen to spoken-word audio, experiment with the bitrates below 64 Kbps to see which bitrate delivers suitable quality for the material you listen to, and select the Optimize For Voice check box.
4. In the Sample Rate drop-down list, specify the sample rate by choosing Auto, 44.100 KHz, or 48.000 KHz. 44.100 KHz is the sample rate used by CD audio; unless you have a data source that uses a 48.000-KHz sampling rate, there's no point in choosing this option. For most purposes, you'll get best results by using the Auto setting (the default setting), which makes iTunes use a sampling rate that matches the input quality. For example, for CD-quality audio, iTunes uses the 44.100-KHz sampling rate.
5. In the Channels drop-down list, select Auto, Stereo, or Mono, as appropriate. In most cases, Auto (the default setting) is the best bet, because it makes iTunes choose stereo or mono as appropriate to the sound source. However, you may occasionally need to produce mono files from stereo sources.
6. If you want to use VBR encoding rather than CBR encoding, select the Use Variable Bit Rate Encoding (VBR) check box.
7. If you want to optimize the encoding for voice instead of music, select the Optimize For Voice check box. Normally, you'd do this only for podcasts and other spoken-word audio.
8. Click the OK button to close the AAC Encoder dialog box.

Choose Custom MP3 Encoding Settings

To choose custom MP3 encoding settings, follow these steps:

1. In the Import Settings dialog box, choose MP3 Encoder in the Import Using drop-down list.
2. In the Setting drop-down list, choose the Custom item to display the MP3 Encoder dialog box:

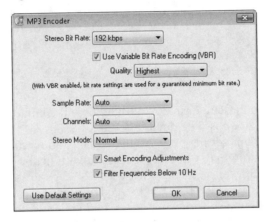

3. In the Stereo Bit Rate drop-down list, select the bitrate you want to use.
   - The choices range from 16 Kbps to 320 Kbps. 16 Kbps produces shoddy-sounding audio even for the spoken word, but it may be useful when you need to get long passages of low-quality audio into a small file. At the other extreme, 320 Kbps produces audio high enough in quality that most people can't distinguish it from CD-quality audio.
   - iTunes uses the bitrate you select as the exact bitrate for CBR encoding and as the minimum bitrate for VBR encoding.
   - See the section "Understand CD-Quality Audio and Lossy and Lossless Compression" earlier in this chapter for a discussion of CD-quality audio. "Choose an Appropriate Compression Rate, Bitrate, and Stereo Settings," also earlier in this chapter, offers advice on choosing a compression rate that matches your needs.
4. Select the Use Variable Bit Rate Encoding (VBR) check box if you want to create VBR-encoded files instead of CBR-encoded files.
   - See the sidebar "Choose Between CBR and VBR, and a Suitable Stereo Setting, for MP3" later in this chapter for a discussion of CBR and VBR.
   - If you select this check box, choose a suitable setting in the Quality drop-down list. The choices are Lowest, Low, Medium Low, Medium, Medium High, High, and Highest. iTunes uses the bitrates specified in the Stereo Bit Rate drop-down list as the guaranteed minimum bitrates. The Quality setting controls the amount of processing iTunes applies to making the file sound as close to the original as possible. More processing requires

more processor cycles, which will make your computer work harder. If your computer is already working at full throttle, encoding will take longer.

5. In the Sample Rate drop-down list, set a sample rate manually only if you're convinced you need to do so.
   - You may want to use a lower sample rate if you're encoding spoken-word audio rather than music and don't need such high fidelity.
   - Choices range from 8 KHz to 48 KHz (higher than CD-quality audio, which uses 44.1 KHz).
   - The default setting is Auto, which uses the same sample rate as does the music you're encoding. Using the same sample rate usually delivers optimal results.

6. In the Channels drop-down list, select Auto, Mono, or Stereo. The default setting is Auto, which uses mono for encoding mono sources and stereo for stereo sources.

7. In the Stereo Mode drop-down list, choose Normal Stereo or Joint Stereo. See the sidebar "Choose Between CBR and VBR, and a Suitable Stereo Setting, for MP3," later in this chapter, for a discussion of the difference between normal stereo and joint stereo. If you select Mono in the Channels drop-down list, the Stereo Mode drop-down list becomes unavailable because its options don't apply to mono.

8. Select or clear the Smart Encoding Adjustments check box and the Filter Frequencies Below 10 Hz check box, as appropriate. These check boxes are selected by default. In most cases, you'll do best to leave them selected.
   - Smart Encoding Adjustments allows iTunes to tweak your custom settings to improve them if you've chosen an inappropriate combination.
   - Frequencies below 10 Hz are infrasound and are of interest only to animals such as elephants, so filtering them out makes sense for humans.

 Note To restore iTunes to using its default settings for encoding MP3 files, click the Use Default Settings button in the MP3 Encoder dialog box.

9. Click the OK button to close the MP3 Encoder dialog box.

How to...

Choose Between CBR and VBR, and a Suitable Stereo Setting, for MP3

After choosing the bitrate at which to encode your MP3 files, you must choose between constant bitrate (CBR) and variable bitrate (VBR). You must also choose whether to use joint stereo or normal stereo.

CBR simply records each part of the file at the specified bitrate. CBR files can sound great, particularly at higher bitrates, but generally VBR delivers better quality than CBR. This is because VBR can allocate space more intelligently as the audio needs it. For example, a complex passage of a song will require more data to represent it accurately than will a simple passage, which in turn will require more data than the two seconds of silence before the massed guitars come crashing back in.

(continued)

The disadvantage to VBR, and the reason why most MP3 encoders are set to use CBR by default, is that many older decoders and hardware devices can't play it. If you're using iTunes and an iPod or iPhone, you don't need to worry about this. But if you're using an older decoder or hardware device, check that it can manage VBR.

So VBR is probably a better bet. A harder choice is between the two different types of stereo that iTunes offers: joint stereo and normal stereo. (iTunes also offers mono—a single channel that gives no separation among the sounds. The only reason to use mono is if your sound source is mono; for example, a live recording that used a single mono microphone.)

Stereo delivers two channels: a left channel and a right channel. These two channels provide positional audio, enabling recording and mixing engineers to separate the audio so that different sounds appear to be coming from different places. For example, the engineer can make one guitar sound as though it's positioned on the left and another guitar sound as though it's positioned on the right. Or the engineer might pan a sound from left to right so it seems to go across the listener.

Normal stereo (sometimes called *plain stereo*) uses two tracks: one for the left stereo channel and another for the right stereo channel. As its name suggests, normal stereo is the form of stereo that's usually used. For example, if you buy a CD that's recorded in stereo and play it back through your boom box, you're using normal stereo.

Joint stereo (sometimes called *mid/side stereo*) divides the channel data differently to make better use of a small amount of data storage. The encoder averages out the two original channels (assuming the sound source is normal stereo) to a mid channel. It then encodes this channel, devoting to it the bulk of the available space assigned by the bitrate. One channel contains the data that's the same on both channels. The second channel contains the data that's different on one of the channels. By reducing the channel data to the common data (which takes the bulk of the available space) and the data that's different on one of the channels (which takes much less space), joint stereo can deliver higher audio quality at the same bitrate as normal stereo.

Use joint stereo to produce better-sounding audio when encoding at lower bitrates, and use normal stereo for all your recordings at your preferred bitrate. Where the threshold for lower-bitrate recording falls depends on you. Many people recommend using normal stereo for encoding at bitrates of 160 Kbps and above, and using joint stereo for lower bitrates (128 Kbps and below). Others recommend not using normal stereo below 192 Kbps. Experiment to establish what works for you.

The results you get with joint stereo depend on the quality of the MP3 encoder you use. Some of the less-capable MP3 encoders produce joint-stereo tracks that sound more like mono tracks than like normal-stereo tracks. Better encoders produce joint-stereo tracks that sound very close to normal-stereo tracks. iTunes produces pretty good joint-stereo tracks.

Using the same MP3 encoder, normal stereo delivers better sound quality than joint stereo—at high bitrates. At lower bitrates, joint stereo delivers better sound quality than normal stereo, because joint stereo can retain more data about the basic sound (in the mid channel) than normal stereo can retain about the sound in its two separate channels. However, joint stereo provides less separation between the left and right channels than normal stereo provides. (The lack of separation is what produces the mono-like effect.)

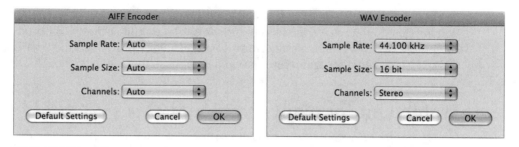

FIGURE 6-3   If you choose to encode to AIFF or WAV files, you can set encoding options in the AIFF Encoder dialog box (left) or the WAV Encoder dialog box (right).

Choose Custom AIFF and WAV Encoding Settings

The AIFF Encoder dialog box (shown on the left in Figure 6-3) and the WAV Encoder dialog box (shown on the right in Figure 6-3) offer similar settings. AIFFs and WAVs are essentially the same apart from the file header, which distinguishes the file formats from each other.

In either of these dialog boxes, you can choose the following settings:

- **Sample Rate**   Choose Auto (the default setting) to encode at the same sample rate as the original you're ripping. Otherwise, choose a value from the range available (8 KHz to 48 KHz).
- **Sample Size**   Select Auto to have iTunes automatically match the sample size to that of the source. Otherwise, select 8 Bit or 16 Bit, as appropriate. PCM audio uses 16 bits, so if you're encoding files from CDs, iTunes automatically uses a 16-bit sample size.
- **Channels**   Select Auto (the default setting) to encode mono files from mono sources and stereo files from stereo sources. Otherwise, select Mono or Stereo, as appropriate.

Deal with CDs That Your Computer Can't Rip

iTunes and your computer should be able to rip songs from any CD that uses the regular audio CD format. This standard is called Red Book, because it was published in a red binder. But you may run into audio discs that look like CDs but that use different formats and content-protection technologies to prevent you ripping them.

Until several years ago, it looked as though CD protection would become widespread, with record companies deploying content-protection technologies such as Macrovision's CDS-300 and SunnComm's MediaMax on ever more CDs. But then Sony BMG used a copy-protection system named Extended Copy Protection (XCP) on some audio discs in 2005 that installed what computer hackers call a rootkit on Windows computers that tried to play the discs. The rootkit severely compromised the computers' security, and caused a storm of protest. Sony BMG eventually withdrew the XCP-protected discs and offered to exchange those that had been bought.

Watch Out for Copy-Protected Discs

If you're unlucky, you may still run into copy-protected discs. These are bad news because they can

- Cause your computer to freeze, or make it unable to eject the disc.
- Install files on your PC (not on a Mac) without your permission.
- Restrict you to playing back low-quality audio.

Use these three indicators to spot copy-protected discs:

- **Look for the Compact Disc Digital Audio (CDDA) logo**   This isn't a reliable indicator, because some Red Book CDs don't have the logo, and some non–Red Book discs do. But if the disc doesn't have the logo, examine it carefully.
- **Look for a disclaimer, warning, or notice**   This will say something like "Will *not* play on PC or Mac," "This CD [*sic*] cannot be played on a PC/Mac," "Copy Control," or "Copy Protected."
- **Watch out for odd behavior**   If the disc attempts to install software that you must use to access the music on the disc, it's protected. Or if the disc won't play on your computer, or it will play but won't rip, it's most likely protected (it could also be scratched or damaged).

Deal with Copy-Protected Discs

Here are tricks you can try for dealing with copy-protected discs:

- **Turn off AutoPlay in Windows**   Most of the copy-protection technologies use Windows' AutoPlay feature to run and install software automatically. Turning AutoPlay off in Control Panel gives you some protection.
- **Use a different optical drive**   Some optical drives are more tolerant than others of the faults deliberately introduced on the CD by some copy-protection systems.
- **Use a heavy-duty ripper**   A heavy-duty ripper such as Exact Audio Copy (www.exactaudiocopy.de; free) can extract audio from CDs that are corrupted or scratched badly enough to defeat other rippers. Technically, using a program such as this to defeat copy-protection is illegal. However, using such a program on a scratched or damaged CD is fine.

How to... ## Eject Stuck Audio Discs from a Mac

If you get an audio disc stuck in your Mac, follow as many of these steps as necessary to eject it:

1. Restart your Mac. If it's too hung to restart by conventional means, press the Reset button (if it has one) or press ⌘-CTRL-POWER. At the system startup sound, hold down the mouse button until your Mac finishes booting. This action may eject the disc.
2. Restart your Mac again. As before, if the Mac is too hung to restart by conventional means, press the Reset button or press ⌘-CTRL-POWER. At the system startup sound, hold down ⌘-OPTION-O-F to boot to the Open Firmware mode.
3. Type **eject cd** and press RETURN. If all is well, the CD drive will open. If not, you may see the message "read of block0 failed. can't OPEN the EJECT device." Either way, type **mac-boot** and press RETURN to reboot your Mac.

If Open Firmware mode won't fix the problem, you'll need to take your Mac to a service shop.

Convert Other File Types to Formats an iPod or iPhone Can Play

Most iPods and the iPhone can play AAC files, MP3 files (including files in the Audible audiobook format), Apple Lossless Encoding files, AIFF files, and WAV files. The second-generation iPod shuffle can play all these file types except Apple Lossless Encoding. These common formats should take care of all your regular listening in iTunes and on the iPod or iPhone.

But if you receive files from other people, or download audio from the Internet (as described in Chapter 7), you'll encounter many other digital audio formats. This section describes a couple of utilities for converting files from other formats to ones the iPod or iPhone can use.

Convert a Song from AAC to MP3 (or Vice Versa)

Sometimes, you may need to convert a song from the format in which you imported it, or (more likely) in which you bought it, to a different format. For example, you may need to convert a song in AAC format to MP3 so that you can use it on an MP3 player that can't play AAC files.

What Happens When You Convert a File from One Compressed Format to Another

Don't convert a song from one compressed format to another compressed format unless you absolutely must, because such a conversion loses audio quality.

For example, say you have a WMA file. The audio is already compressed with lossy compression, so some parts of the audio have been lost. When you convert this file to an MP3 file, the conversion utility expands the compressed WMA audio to uncompressed audio, and then recompresses it to the MP3 format, again using lossy compression.

The uncompressed audio contains a faithful rendering of all the defects in the WMA file. So the MP3 file contains as faithful a rendering of this defective audio as the MP3 encoder can provide at that compression rate, plus any defects the MP3 encoding introduces. But you'll be able to play the file on the iPod or iPhone—which may be your main concern.

So if you still have the CD from which you imported the song, import the song again using the other compressed format rather than converting the song from one compressed format to another. Doing so will give you significantly higher quality. But if you don't have the CD—for example, because you bought the song in the compressed format—converting to the other format will produce usable results.

If the AAC file is a protected song you bought from the iTunes Store, you cannot convert it directly. Instead, you must burn it to a CD, and then rip that CD to the format you need.

To convert a song from one compressed format to another, follow these steps:

1. In iTunes, display the Advanced menu and see which format is listed in the Create Version command (for example, Create AAC Version or Create MP3 Version). If this is the format you want, you're all set, but you might want to double-check the settings used for the format.

You can also right-click a file (or CTRL-click on the Mac) and look at the Create Version item on the shortcut menu.

2. Display the iTunes dialog box or the Preferences dialog box:
   - In Windows, choose Edit | Preferences or press CTRL-COMMA or CTRL-Y to display the iTunes dialog box.
   - On the Mac, choose iTunes | Preferences or press ⌘-COMMA or ⌘-Y to display the Preferences dialog box.
3. Click the General tab to display its contents.

4. Click the Import Settings button to display the Import Settings dialog box.
5. In the Import Using drop-down list, select the encoder you want to use. For example, choose MP3 Encoder if you want to convert an existing file to an MP3 file; choose AAC Encoder if you want to create an AAC file; or choose Apple Lossless Encoder if you want to create an Apple Lossless Encoding file.

 Unless the song file is currently in WAV or AIFF format, it's usually not worth converting it to Apple Lossless Encoding, because the source file is not high enough quality to benefit from Apple Lossless Encoding's advantages over AAC or MP3.

6. If necessary, use the Setting drop-down list to specify the details of the format. (See "Check or Change Your Importing Settings" earlier in this chapter for details.)
7. Click the OK button to close the Import Settings dialog box.
8. Click the OK button to close the iTunes dialog box or the Preferences dialog box.
9. In your library, select the song or songs you want to convert.
10. Choose Advanced | Create *Format* Version. (The Create Version item on the Advanced menu changes to reflect the encoder you chose in Step 5.) iTunes converts the file or files, saves it or them in the folder that contains the original file or files, and adds it or them to your library.

 Because iTunes automatically applies tag information to converted files, you may find it hard to tell in iTunes which file is in AAC format and which is in MP3 format. The easiest way to find out is to issue a Get Info command for the song (for example, right-click or CTRL-click the song and choose Get Info from the shortcut menu) and check the Kind readout on the Summary tab of the Item Information dialog box.

After converting the song or songs to the other format, remember to restore your normal import setting in the Import Settings dialog box before you import any more songs from CD.

Convert WMA Files to MP3 or AAC

If you buy music from any of the online music stores that focus on Windows rather than on the Mac, chances are that the songs will be in WMA format. WMA is the stores' preferred format for selling online music because it offers DRM features for protecting the music against being stolen.

In iTunes for Windows, you can convert a WMA file to your current importing format (as set in the Import Settings dialog box) by dragging the file to your library or by using either the File | Add File To Library or the File | Add Folder To Library command. iTunes for the Mac doesn't have this capability—but if you have access to a PC running Windows, you can then copy or transfer the converted files to the Mac.

If you buy WMA files protected with DRM, you'll be limited in what you can do with them. In most cases, you'll be restricted to playing the songs with Windows Media Player (which is one of the underpinnings of the WMA DRM scheme), which won't let you convert the songs directly to another format. But most online music stores allow you to burn the songs you buy to CD. In this case, you can convert the WMA files to MP3 files or AAC files by burning them to CD and then use iTunes to rip and encode the CD as usual.

Create Audio Files from Cassettes or Vinyl Records

If you have audio on analog media such as cassette tapes, vinyl records, or other waning technologies, you may want to transfer that audio to your computer so you can listen to it using iTunes or an iPod or iPhone. Dust off your gramophone, cassette deck, or other audio source, and then work your way through the following sections.

 You may need permission to create audio files that contain copyrighted content. If you hold the copyright to the audio, you can copy it as much as you want. If not, you need specific permission to copy it, unless it falls under a specific copyright exemption. For example, the Audio Home Recording Act (AHRA) personal use provision lets you copy a copyrighted work (for example, an LP) onto a different medium so you can listen to it—but only provided that you use a "digital audio recording device," a term that doesn't cover computers.

Connect the Audio Source to Your Computer

Start by connecting the audio source to your computer with a cable that has the right kinds of connectors for the audio source and your sound card. For example, to connect a typical cassette player to a typical sound card, you'll need a cable with two RCA plugs at the cassette player's end (or at the receiver's end) and a male-end stereo miniplug at the other end to plug into your sound card. If the audio source has only a headphone socket or line-out socket for output, you'll need a miniplug at the source end too.

 Because record players produce a low volume of sound, you'll almost always need to put a record player's output through the Phono input of an amplifier before you can record it on your computer.

If your sound card has a line-in port and a mic port, use the line-in port. If your sound card has only a mic port, turn the source volume down to a minimum for the initial connection, because mic ports tend to be sensitive.

 If you have a Mac that doesn't have an audio input, consider an external audio interface such as the Griffin iMic (www.griffintechnology.com), which lets you record via USB.

Record on Windows

To record audio on Windows, you can use the minimalist sound-recording application, Sound Recorder, or add (and usually pay for) a more powerful application. This section discusses how to use Sound Recorder.

Sound Recorder doesn't automatically sync the recording with the playback, so unless you manage some cute cueing, you'll end up with empty audio at the beginning and end of the file. You can remove this empty audio later using iTunes; see the section "Trim Audio Files to Get Rid of Intros and Outros You Don't Like," later in this chapter, for details.

One of the best cross-platform solutions for recording, editing, and cleaning up audio files is Audacity (freeware; http://audacity.sourceforge.net). Audacity runs on Windows, Mac OS X, and Linux, using very nearly the same interface on each platform. The section "Record Audio with Audacity," later in this chapter, shows you how to use Audacity on the Mac (which doesn't come with an equivalent of Sound Recorder). However, the steps for using Audacity on Windows are almost identical. Audacity includes features for removing noise such as hiss and crackles from recordings.

The next two subsections show you how to specify the audio source on Windows Vista and then record using Sound Recorder. The two subsections after those show you how to specify the audio source and record using Sound Recorder on Windows XP.

Specify the Audio Source for Recording in Windows Vista

To set Windows Vista to accept input from the source so you can record from it, follow these steps:

1. Start your audio source playing so that you'll be able to check the volume level.
2. Right-click the Volume icon in the notification area, and then choose Recording Devices from the shortcut menu to display the Recording tab of the Sound dialog box (see Figure 6-4).
3. If the device you want to use is marked as Currently Unavailable (as in the figure), click the device, and then click the Set Default button. Windows makes the device available and moves the green circle with the white check mark from the other device to this device.
4. Verify that the signal level is suitable—for example, somewhere between the halfway point and the top of the scale for much of the input, as shown here.
5. To change the recording level for the device, click the device in the list box, and then click the Properties button. In the Properties dialog box for the device, click the Levels tab to display its contents (see Figure 6-5). You can then drag the input slider to the level needed. Click the OK button when you've finished.

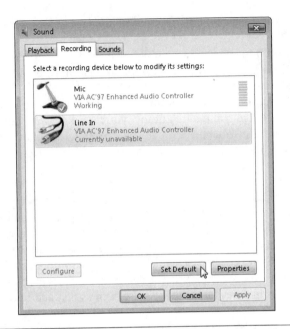

FIGURE 6-4 Before recording in Windows Vista, you may need to change the recording device on the Recording tab of the Sound dialog box.

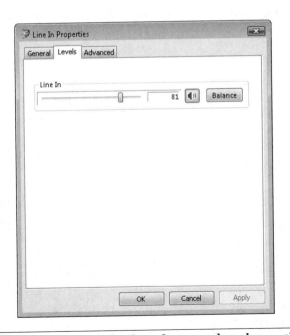

FIGURE 6-5 Use the Properties dialog box if you need to change the input level for a device.

You can also change the left–right balance by clicking the Balance button and then dragging the L and R sliders in the Balance dialog box.

Record with Sound Recorder in Windows Vista

To record with Sound Recorder in Windows Vista, follow these steps:

1. Choose Start | All Programs | Accessories | Sound Recorder to open Sound Recorder (shown here).

2. Get the audio source ready to play.
3. Click the Start Recording button when you're ready to start recording.
4. Click the Stop Recording button when you're ready to stop recording, and then stop the audio source. Sound Recorder automatically displays the Save As dialog box.
5. Type the filename, change the folder if necessary, and then click the Save button. Sound Recorder saves the file, closes it, and then automatically starts a new file in case you want to record something else.

Specify the Audio Source for Recording in Windows XP

To set Windows XP to accept input from the source so you can record from it, follow these steps:

1. If the notification area includes a Volume icon, double-click this icon to display the Volume Control window. Otherwise, choose Start | Control Panel to display the Control Panel, click the Switch To Classic View link if it appears in the upper-left corner, double-click the Sounds And Audio Devices icon, and then open the Volume Control window from there. For example, click the Advanced button in the Device Volume group box on the Volume tab of the Sounds And Audio Devices Properties dialog box.

 Depending on your audio hardware and its drivers, the Volume Control window may have a different name (for example, Play Control).

2. Choose Options | Properties to display the Properties dialog box. Then select the Recording option button to display the list of devices for recording (as opposed to the devices for playback). The left screen in Figure 6-6 shows this list.
3. Select the check box for the input device you want to use—for example, select the Line-In check box or the Microphone check box, depending on which you're using.
4. Click the OK button to close the Properties dialog box. Windows displays the Record Control window, an example of which is shown on the right in Figure 6-6. (Like the Volume Control window, this window may have a different name—for example, Recording Control.)
5. Select the Select check box for the source you want to use.
6. Leave the Record Control window open for the time being so you can adjust the input volume on the device if necessary.

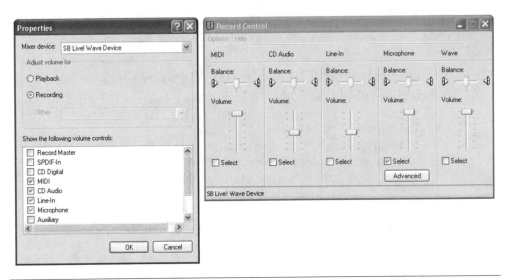

FIGURE 6-6 Click the Recording option button in the Properties dialog box (left) to display the Record Control window (right) instead of Volume Control.

Record with Sound Recorder in Windows XP

To open Sound Recorder, choose Start | All Programs | Accessories | Entertainment | Sound Recorder.

Sound Recorder works fine except that it can't record files longer than 60 seconds, which makes it next to useless for recording music. (This limitation doesn't apply to the version of Sound Recorder in Windows Vista.) But you can sidestep this limitation by creating a blank file longer than the longest item you want to record and then recording over this blank file. This takes a little effort but is worth the trouble.

There are two parts to making Sound Recorder record files longer than 60 seconds. The first part, which is compulsory, is to create a blank dummy file long enough to contain whatever you want to record. The second part, which is optional, is to make Sound Recorder open this file automatically when you start it so that you don't have to open it manually.

Create the Dummy File To create the blank dummy file, follow these steps:

1. Choose Start | All Programs | Accessories | Entertainment | Sound Recorder to launch Sound Recorder, shown here.
2. Mute your sound source.
3. Click the Record button (the button with the red dot) to start recording a blank file. Sound Recorder makes the file 60 seconds long, its default maximum.
4. Let the recording run until it stops automatically at 60 seconds.

5. Choose File | Save to display the Save As dialog box.
6. Save the file under a descriptive name such as Dummy.wav.
7. Choose Edit | Insert File to display the Insert File dialog box.
8. Select the file you saved and click the Open button to insert it in the open version of the file. This adds another 60 seconds to the file's length, doubling it.
9. Repeat the procedure of inserting the saved file in the open file until the open file reaches the length you need. It's best to have the dummy file substantially longer than the longest song you expect to record, so that you don't run out of recording time.

To increase the file's size more quickly, save the open file after inserting another one or two minutes in it. You can then insert the saved file, adding two or three minutes to the open file at a time.

10. When the file reaches the length you need, choose File | Save to save it.
11. Press ALT-F4 or choose File | Exit to close Sound Recorder.

Make Sound Recorder Open the Dummy File Automatically   To make Sound Recorder open the dummy file automatically, follow these steps:

1. Right-click the Sound Recorder entry on your Start menu and choose Properties from the shortcut menu to display its Properties dialog box (see Figure 6-7).

FIGURE 6-7   Use the Properties dialog box to configure Sound Recorder to open your dummy file automatically.

2. In the Target text box, enter the path and filename to the file you recorded, inside double quotation marks, after the path and filename of the executable, so that it looks something like this:

```
%SystemRoot%\System32\sndrec32.exe "C:\Documents and Settings\
Your Name\My Documents\Dummy.wav"
```

3. Click the OK button to close the Properties dialog box.

Now, when you start Sound Recorder, it automatically opens the dummy file. You can then record audio up to the length of the dummy file.

Record a Sound File   To record a file with Sound Recorder, follow these steps:

1. Choose Start | All Programs | Accessories | Entertainment | Sound Recorder to launch Sound Recorder and make it open the dummy file.

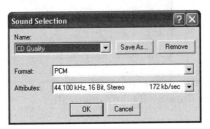

Note   If you didn't change the Sound Recorder shortcut, open your dummy file manually.

2. Get the audio source ready to play.
3. Click the Record button to start recording.
4. Start the audio playing.
5. To stop recording, click the Stop button.
6. Choose File | Save As to display the Save As dialog box, shown here.
7. Specify the location and name for the file. (Don't overwrite your dummy file.)
8. Make sure the Format field, at the bottom of the Save As dialog box, is displaying the format in which you want to save the file. This field gives brief details of the format—for example, "PCM 22 050 KHz, 8 Bit, Mono" or "Windows Media Audio V2, 160 Kbps, 48 KHz, Stereo." To set a different format, click the Change button and work in the Sound Selection dialog box:

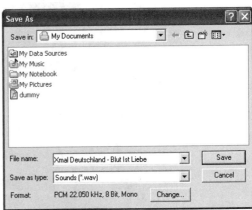

- To select a predefined set of attributes, select CD Quality, Radio Quality, or Telephone Quality in the Name drop-down list. If you're recording music you want to turn into an AAC file or MP3 file, choose the CD Quality item. You can define your own named formats by choosing appropriate settings in the Format drop-down list and Attributes drop-down list and then clicking the Save As button. You can then reuse these formats more quickly the next time you need the same settings.
- Otherwise, choose the format in the Format drop-down list and then select the appropriate attributes in the Attributes drop-down list. For example, you might choose PCM in the Format drop-down list and the 48 000 KHz, 16 Bit, Stereo setting in the Attributes drop-down list to record pulse code modulation audio at the highest quality that Sound Recorder supports.

9. Click the OK button to close the Sound Selection dialog box.
10. Click the Save button in the Save As dialog box to save the file.

The Format drop-down list in Sound Recorder includes an MPEG Layer-3 item, which creates MP3 files. Unfortunately, owing to a licensing issue, the encoder included with Windows XP can encode only up to 56 Kbps at 24 KHz, which makes it useless for high-quality audio. So you'll get much better results from creating WAV files with Sound Recorder and then using iTunes to encode them to MP3 files or AAC files.

Import the Sound File into iTunes and Convert It

After saving the sound file in an audio format that iTunes can handle (either the WMA format from Windows Vista or the WAV format from Windows XP), import the sound file into iTunes. If the file is WMA, iTunes automatically converts it to your current import format. If the file is WAV, you need to use the Advanced | Create Version command to convert the sound file to your preferred import format. Once you've done that, tag the compressed file with the appropriate information so that you can access it easily in iTunes and copy it to the iPod or iPhone.

Record Audio on the Mac

To record audio on the Mac, specify the audio source, and then download and install Audacity.

If you have iLife on your Mac, you can also use GarageBand to record audio.

Specify the Audio Source for Recording on the Mac

To specify the source on the Mac, follow these steps:

1. Choose Apple | System Preferences to display the System Preferences window.
2. Click the Sound item to display the Sound preferences.
3. Click the Input tab to display it (see Figure 6-8).

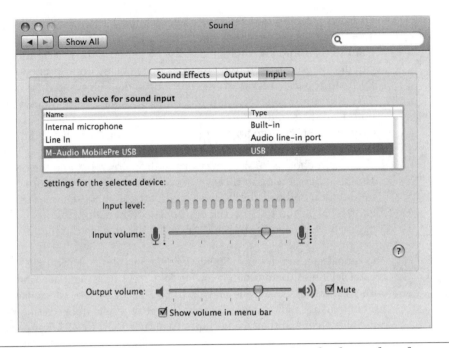

FIGURE 6-8 Configure your sound source on the Input tab of Sound preferences.

4. In the Choose A Device For Sound Input list box, select the device to use (for example, Line In).
5. Start some audio playing on the sound source. Make sure that it's representative of the loudest part of the audio you will record.
6. Watch the Input Level readout as you drag the Input Volume slider to a suitable level.

Install Audacity and Add an MP3 Encoder

Go to SourceForge (http://audacity.sourceforge.net) and download Audacity by following the link for the latest stable version and your operating system (for example, Mac OS X). At this writing, you download the file itself from one of various software-distribution sites.

Expand the downloaded file, and then drag the resulting Audacity folder to your Applications folder. Keep your browser open for the moment, and go back to the Audacity page. You'll need to download another file in a minute.

Set Up Audacity

The first time you run Audacity, choose the language you want to use—for example, English. You then see Audacity (see Figure 6-9).

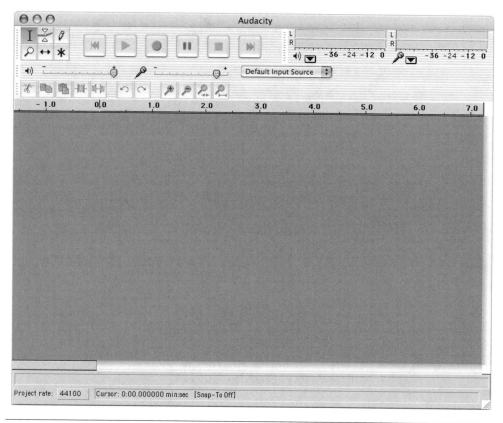

FIGURE 6-9   Audacity is a great freeware application for recording audio and fixing problems with it.

After you install Audacity, you'll need to add an MP3 encoder if you want to be able to create MP3 files with Audacity. (Instead of adding the MP3 encoder, you can create WAV files with Audacity and then use iTunes to create MP3 files or AAC files.)

Follow these steps to add an MP3 encoder to Audacity:

1. Download the latest stable version of the LAME encoder from the LAME Project home page (http://lame.sourceforge.net) or another site.
2. From the download package, extract the LameLib file and put it in a folder of your choosing, such as your ~/Library/Audio folder.
3. Display the Audacity Preferences dialog box by pressing ⌘-COMMA or choosing Audacity | Preferences.
4. Click the File Formats tab to display its contents (see Figure 6-10).
5. Check the MP3 Export Setup area. If the MP3 Library Version readout says "MP3 exporting plugin not found," you need to add an MP3 encoder.

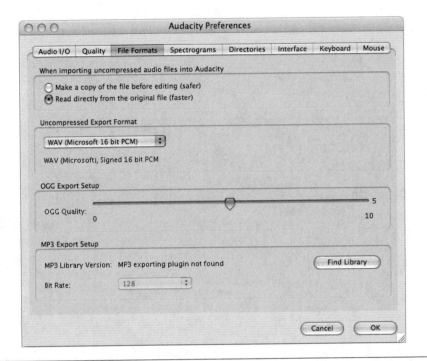

FIGURE 6-10   Use the File Formats tab of the Audacity Preferences dialog box to add an MP3 encoder to Audacity.

6. Click the Find Library button. Audacity displays the Export MP3 dialog box, which explains that you need to supply the LAME MP3 encoder and asks if you want to provide it.
7. Click the Yes button and use the resulting dialog box to find LameLib in the folder to which you extracted it in Step 2.
8. Click the Open button. Audacity adds the LAME version to the MP3 Library Version readout.
9. In the Bit Rate drop-down list, select the bitrate at which you want to export MP3 files. For example, choose 128 Kbps if you want acceptable-quality audio at small file sizes (so that you can cram more songs onto a low-capacity iPod or an iPhone) or choose 320 Kbps for maximum quality at the expense of file size.

Configure Input/Output and Quality Settings

With the Audacity Preferences dialog box still open, configure the audio input/output settings and the quality settings:

1. Click the Audio I/O tab to display its contents (see Figure 6-11).
2. Select your playback device, recording device, and the number of channels—for example, 2 (Stereo). You can also choose whether to play existing tracks while

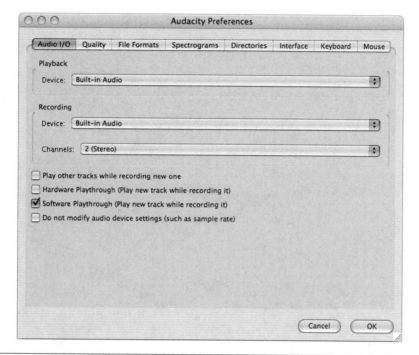

FIGURE 6-11   Choose your playback and recording devices, and the number of
channels, on the Audio I/O tab of the Audacity Preferences dialog box.

recording a new track (which you won't need to do if you're recording a single
audio track, such as a song) and whether to play the new track that's being
recorded (this can help you stop the recording at the appropriate point).

3. Click the Quality tab to display its contents (see Figure 6-12).
4. In the Default Sample Rate drop-down list, select the sample rate you want to
   use. If you don't know the rate you want, use 44100 Hz. Leave the other settings
   on the Quality tab at their defaults unless you know you need to change them.
5. Click the OK button to close the Audacity Preferences dialog box.

Record Audio with Audacity

To record audio with Audacity, follow these steps:

1. Start Audacity if it's not already running.
2. If necessary, choose a different sound source in the Default Input Source drop-
   down list on the right side of the window.
3. Cue your audio source.
4. Click the Record button (the button with the red circle) to start the recording
   (see Figure 6-13).

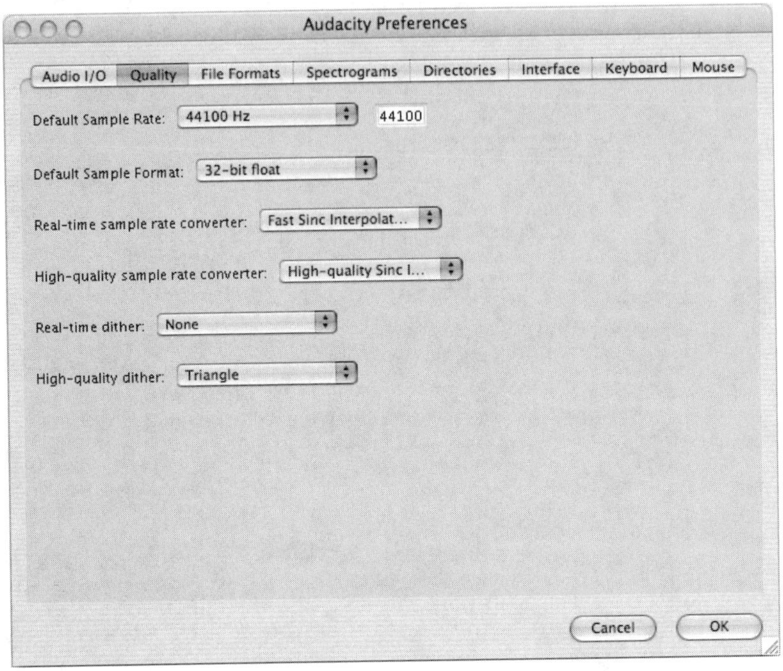

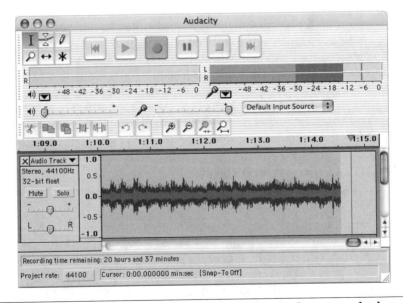

FIGURE 6-12   Choose the default sample rate on the Quality tab of the Audacity
Preferences dialog box.

FIGURE 6-13   Adjust the input volume if the signal is too low or too high.

If necessary, change the recording volume by dragging the Input Volume slider (the slider with the microphone at its left end). When you've got it right, stop the recording, create a new file, and then restart the recording.

5. Click the Record button again to stop recording.
6. Choose File | Save Project to open the Save Project As dialog box, specify a filename and folder, and then click the Save button.
7. When you are ready to export the audio file, choose File | Export As MP3 or File | Export As WAV.

How to... **Remove Scratches and Hiss from Audio Files**

If you record tracks from vinyl records, audio cassettes, or other analog sources, you may well get some clicks or pops, hiss, or background hum in the file. Scratches on a record can cause clicks and pops, audio cassettes tend to hiss (even with noise-reduction such as Dolby), and record players or other machinery can add hum.

All these noises—very much part of the analog audio experience, and actually appreciated as such by some enthusiasts—tend to annoy people accustomed to digital audio. The good news is that you can remove many such noises by using the right software.

Unless you already have an audio editor that has noise-removal features, your best choice is probably Audacity. This chapter has shown you how to install and use Audacity on the Mac, but the program also works on Windows.

To remove noise from a recording using Audacity, follow these steps:

1. In Audacity, open the project containing the song.
2. Select a part of the recording with just noise—for example, the opening few seconds of silence (except for the stylus clicking and popping along).
3. Choose Effect | Noise Removal to open the Noise Removal dialog box.
4. Click the Get Noise Profile button. The Noise Removal system analyzes your sample and applies the corresponding noise profile.
5. Select the part of the recording that you want to affect:
   - To affect the entire recording, choose Edit | Select | All. This is usually the easiest approach.
   - To affect only part of the recording, drag through it. For example, you might want to affect only the end of the recording if this is where all the scratches occur.

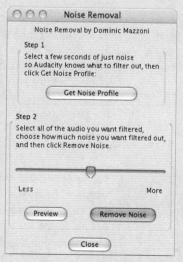

(continued)

6. Choose Effect | Noise Removal to open the Noise Removal dialog box again. This time, drag the slider in the Step 2 box along the Less–More axis to specify how much noise you want to remove. Click the Preview button to get a preview of the effect this will have, and adjust the slider as needed. When you're satisfied with the effect, click the Remove Noise button to remove the noise.

7. Choose File | Save to save your project.

Trim Audio Files to Get Rid of Intros and Outros You Don't Like

If you don't like the intro of a particular song, you can tell iTunes to suppress it by setting the Start Time option on the Options tab of the Item Information dialog box to the point where you want the song to start playing. Similarly, you can suppress an outro by using the Stop Time option, also on the Options tab.

You can also use these options to trim an audio file. Follow these steps:

1. In iTunes, right-click (or CTRL-click on the Mac) the song you want to shorten, and then choose Get Info from the shortcut menu to display the Item Information dialog box. (This dialog box's title bar shows the song name, not the words "Item Information.")

 If you've recorded songs that have empty audio at the beginning or end (or both), use this technique to remove the empty audio.

2. Click the Options tab to display its contents.
3. Set the Start Time, Stop Time, or both, as needed.
4. Click the OK button to close the Item Information dialog box.
5. Right-click (or CTRL-click on the Mac) the song, and then choose Create *Format* Version, where *Format* is the import format you've chosen in the Import Settings dialog box.
6. iTunes creates a shorter version of the song. It's a good idea to rename the song immediately to avoid confusing it with the source file. Alternatively, delete the source file if you no longer want to keep it.

 You can even use this trick to split a song file into two or more different files. For example, to create two files, work out where the division needs to fall. Create the first file by setting the Stop Time to this time and then performing the conversion. Return to the source file, set the Start Time to the dividing time, and then perform the conversion again.

Tag Your Compressed Files with the Correct Information for Sorting

The best thing about compressed audio formats such as AAC, MP3, and Apple Lossless Encoding—apart from their being compressed and still giving high-quality audio—is that each file format can store a full set of tag information about the song the file contains. The tag information lets you sort, organize, and search for songs on iTunes. The iPod and iPhone need correct artist, album, and track name information in tags to be able to organize your AAC files and MP3 files correctly. If a song lacks this minimum of information, iTunes doesn't transfer it to the device.

 You can force iTunes to load untagged songs on an iPod or iPhone by assigning them to a playlist and loading the playlist. But in most cases it's best to tag all the songs in your library—or at least tag as many as is practicable.

You can tag your song files using any tool you choose, but you'll probably want to use iTunes much of the time, because it provides solid if basic features for tagging one or more files at once manually. But if your library contains many untagged or mistagged files, you may need a heavier-duty application. This section shows you how to tag most effectively in iTunes and then presents two more-powerful applications—Tag&Rename for Windows, and MP3 Rage for the Mac.

Tag Songs Effectively with iTunes

The easiest way to add tag information to an AAC file or MP3 file is by downloading the information from CDDB (the CD Database) when you rip the CD. But sometimes you'll need to enter (or change) tag information manually to make iTunes sort the files correctly—for example, when the CDDB data is wrong or not available, or for existing song files created with software other than iTunes, such as song files you've created yourself.

 Often, MP3 files distributed illegally on the Internet lack tag information or include incorrect tags. That said, officially tagged files aren't always as accurate as they might be—so if you want your files to be as easy to find and manipulate as possible, it's worth spending some time checking the tags and improving them as necessary.

How to... **Tag Song Files After Encoding When Offline**

Even if you rip CDs when your computer has no Internet connection, you can usually apply the CD information to the song files once you've reestablished an Internet connection. To do so, select the album or the songs in your library and then choose Advanced | Get CD Track Names. If the CD's details are in CDDB, iTunes should then be able to download the information.

(continued)

If you imported the songs by using software other than iTunes, or if you imported the songs using iTunes on another computer and then copied them to this computer, iTunes objects with the "iTunes cannot get CD track names" dialog box shown here. In this case, you'll need to either reimport the songs on this computer or tag the songs manually.

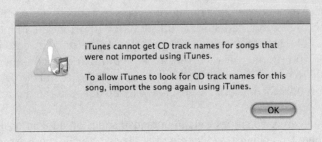

If you need to change the tag information for a whole CD's worth of songs, proceed as follows:

1. In iTunes, select all the song files you want to affect.
2. Right-click (or CTRL-click on the Mac) the selection and choose Get Info from the shortcut menu to display the Multiple Item Information dialog box. Alternatively, choose File | Get Info or press CTRL-I (Windows) or ⌘-I (Mac). Figure 6-14 shows the Windows version of the Multiple Item Information dialog box.

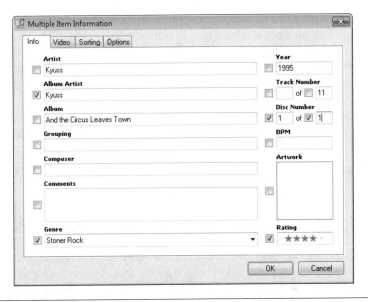

FIGURE 6-14 Use the Multiple Item Information dialog box to enter common tag information for all the songs on a CD or album at once.

Note By default, when you issue a Get Info command with multiple songs selected, iTunes displays a dialog box to check that you want to edit the information for multiple songs. Click the Yes button to proceed; click the Cancel button to cancel. If you frequently want to edit tag information for multiple songs, select the Do Not Ask Me Again check box in the confirmation dialog box to turn off confirmations in the future.

3. Enter as much common information as you can: the artist, year, album, total number of tracks, disc number, composer, comments, and so on. If you have the artwork for the CD available, drag it to the Artwork well on the Info tab.
4. Click the OK button to close the dialog box and apply the information to the songs.
5. Click the first song to clear the current selection. Right-click (or CTRL-click on the Mac) the song and choose Get Info from the shortcut menu to display the Item Information dialog box for the song. Click the Info tab to display it if iTunes doesn't display it automatically. Figure 6-15 shows the Windows version of the Item Information dialog box for the song "Catamaran." The song's title appears in the title bar of the dialog box.
6. Add any song-specific information here: the song name, the track number, and so on.

FIGURE 6-15   Use the Item Information dialog box (whose title bar shows the song's name) to add song-specific information.

7. If you need to change the song's relative volume, equalizer preset, rating, start time, or stop time, work on the Options tab.

8. If you want to add lyrics to the song (either by typing them in or by pasting them from a lyrics site), work on the Lyrics tab.

9. Click the Previous button or the Next button to display the information for the previous song or next song.

10. Click the OK button to close the Item Information dialog box when you've finished adding song information.

Change Tags with Tag&Rename on Windows

Tag&Rename, from Softpointer, Inc., is a powerful tag-editing application for various types of files, including AAC and MP3. You can download a free 30-day evaluation version from www.softpointer.com/tr.htm and from various other sites on the Internet.

How to... **Submit CD Information to CDDB Using iTunes**

If iTunes tells you a CD you want to rip doesn't have an entry in CDDB, you can submit an entry yourself. Users submitting entries like this have added many of the entries in CDDB for older or less widely known CDs. Mainstream entries are submitted by the record companies themselves when they release a new CD.

CDDB contains entries for an enormous number of CDs—so unless you have an unusual CD, chances are any CD you want to rip already has an entry in CDDB. You may find that your CD is listed under a slightly different title or artist name than you're expecting—for example, the artist might be listed as "Sixpack, Joe" rather than "Joe Sixpack." Check carefully for any close matches before submitting an entry so you don't waste your time. You may also find CDDB contains two or more entries for the same CD.

When submitting an entry to CDDB, type the CD title, artist name, and song titles carefully using standard capitalization, and double-check all the information before you submit it. Otherwise, if your entry is accepted and entered in CDDB, anyone who looks up that CD will get the misspellings or wrong information you entered.

Here's how to submit an entry to CDDB:

1. Enter the tag information for the CD.
2. Choose Advanced | Submit CD Track Names to display the CD Info dialog box, and then check the information in the Artist, Composer, Album, Disc Number, Genre, and Year fields. Select the Compilation CD check box if the CD is a compilation rather than a work by an individual artist.
3. Establish an Internet connection if you need to do so manually.
4. Click the OK button. iTunes connects to CDDB and submits the information.

Tag&Rename can derive tag information by breaking down a file's name into its constituents. For example, if you set Tag&Rename on the file Aimee Mann - Lost in Space - 06 - Pavlov's Bell.mp3, Tag&Rename can derive the artist name (Aimee Mann), the album name (Lost in Space), the track number (06), and the song name ("Pavlov's Bell") from the file and then apply that information to the tag fields.

Tag&Rename can also derive tag information from the folder structure that contains an MP3 file that needs tagging. For example, if you have the file 06 - Pavlov's Bell.mp3 stored in the folder Aimee Mann\Lost in Space, Tag&Rename will be able to tag the file with the artist name, album name, track name, and track number.

Change Tags with Media Rage on the Mac

Media Rage, from Chaotic Software (www.chaoticsoftware.com), is an impressive bundle of utilities for tagging, organizing, and improving your MP3 files. The tagging features in Media Rage include deriving tag information from filenames and folder paths and changing the tags on multiple files at once.

You can download a fully functional evaluation version of Media Rage from the Chaotic Software website.

Save Audio Streams to Disk So You Can Listen to Them Later

If you enjoy listening to Internet radio, you may want to record it so that you can play it back later. iTunes doesn't let you save streaming audio to disk because recording streaming audio without specific permission typically violates copyright. So you need to use either a hardware solution or a third-party application to record streams.

Save Audio Streams to Disk Using Hardware

To solve the problem via hardware, use a standard audio cable to pipe the output from your computer's sound card to its line-in socket. You can then record the audio stream as you would any other external input by using an audio-recording application such as those discussed earlier in this chapter—for example, Sound Recorder or Audacity.

The only problem with using a standard audio cable is that you won't be able to hear via external speakers the audio stream you're recording. To solve this problem, get a stereo Y-connector. Connect one of the outputs to your external speakers and the other to your line-in socket. Converting the audio from digital to analog and then back to digital like this degrades its quality, but unless you're listening to the highest-bitrate Internet radio stations around, you'll most likely find the quality you lose to be a fair trade-off for the convenience you gain.

Save Audio Streams to Disk Using Software

To solve the problem via software, get an application that can record the audio stream directly. Here are two applications for Windows:

- **Zinf (www.zinf.org)** Zinf is a freeware open-source music player that can record audio streams to files.
- **Total Recorder (www.highcriteria.com)** Total Recorder comes in three editions: Standard, Professional, and Developer. You can download an evaluation version to make sure that Total Recorder works with your PC and provides the features you need.

Here are two applications for the Mac:

- **RadioLover (www.bitcartel.com/radiolover)** RadioLover lets you record one or more radio streams at once.
- **Audio Hijack Pro (www.rogueamoeba.com/audiohijackpro)** Audio Hijack Pro lets you record the audio output from any application. You can set timers to record the items you want.
- **Radioshift (www.rogueamoeba.com/radioshift)** Radioshift lets you record Internet radio streams.

7

Buy and Download Songs, Videos, and More Online

HOW TO...

- Understand what the iTunes Store is
- Understand digital rights management (DRM)
- Set up an account with the iTunes Store
- Configure iTunes Store settings
- Access the iTunes Store
- Buy songs, videos, and movies from the iTunes Store
- Listen to songs and watch videos and movies you've purchased
- Authorize and deauthorize computers for the iTunes Store
- Buy and download music from other online music stores
- Download music from other online sources

Instead of creating song files by ripping your own CDs, tapes, and records, you can buy songs online. You can also buy videos, movies, audio books, and other content.

If iTunes has its way, your first stop for buying content will be the iTunes Store, Apple's online service for songs, videos, movies, and more. This chapter discusses what the iTunes Store is, how it works, and how to use it. Because the iTunes Store works in almost exactly the same way on Mac OS X and Windows, this chapter discusses both operating systems together and, for balance, shows some screens from each.

This chapter also discusses digital rights management (DRM), because you'll benefit from understanding the essentials of DRM before buying content online. The end of the chapter discusses other online sources of songs, from online music stores other than the iTunes Store to free sources.

Understand Digital Rights Management (DRM)

Currently, the movie and music industry bodies are engaged in a vigorous struggle with consumers over how music and video are sold (or stolen) and distributed:

- The record companies have applied copy-protection mechanisms to some audio discs to prevent their customers from making unauthorized pure-digital copies of music.
- Most video content is sold with copy-protection applied. For example, regular DVDs use the Content Scramble System (CSS) to protect their content. High-definition DVDs use the Advanced Access Content System (AACS) for protection.
- Some consumers are trying to protect their freedom to enjoy the music and video they buy in the variety of ways that law and case law have established to be either definitely legal or sort-of legal. For example, legal precedents that permit the use of VCRs, personal video recorders (PVRs), and home audio taping suggest that it's probably legal to create compressed audio files from a CD, record, or cassette, as long as they're for your personal use.
- Other people are deliberately infringing the media companies' copyrights by copying, distributing, and stealing music and video via peer-to-peer (P2P) networks, recordable CDs and DVDs, and other means.
- Also participating in this struggle is the movie industry, which suffers similar piracy problems. VCRs and personal video recorders (PVRs) provide plenty of precedent for making copies of copyrighted works for personal use and sharing them with other people (for example, on videotape or DVD), but widespread distribution of digital video files on P2P networks is another matter entirely.

Behind this struggle lies digital rights management (DRM), technologies for defining which actions a user may take with a particular work and restricting the user to those actions, preferably without preventing them from using or enjoying the work in the ways they expect to.

Understand That DRM Is Neither "Good" nor "Bad"

DRM is often portrayed by consumer activists as being the quintessence of the Recording Industry Association of America's and Motion Picture Association of America's dreams and of consumers' nightmares. The publisher of a work can use DRM to impose a wide variety of restrictions on the ways in which a consumer can use the work.

For example, some digital books are delivered in an encrypted format that requires a special certificate to decrypt, which means that the consumer can read them only on one authorized computer. DRM also prevents the consumer from printing any of the book or copying any of it directly from the reader application. As you'd imagine, these restrictions are unpopular with most consumers, and such books have largely failed in the marketplace: Consumers prefer traditional physical books that they can read wherever they want to, lend to a friend, photocopy, rip pages out of, drop in the bath, and so on.

But how good or bad DRM is in practice depends on the implementation. DRM can also be a compromise—for example, when Apple launched the iTunes Store, the only way it could persuade the record companies to make the songs available was by agreeing to apply DRM to the songs to limit what buyers could do with them.

The compromise worked adequately for both the record companies and the consumers. In May 2007, however, Apple convinced EMI to make songs available without DRM and at a higher quality. Following this move, other record companies have begun to make songs available without DRM. In January 2009, Apple announced that it would phase out DRM from the iTunes Store completely.

Music is almost ideal for digital distribution, and the record companies are sitting on colossal archives of songs that are out of print but still well within copyright. It's not economically viable for the record companies to sell pressed CDs of these songs, because demand for any given CD is likely to be relatively low. But demand is there, as has been demonstrated by the millions of illegal copies of such songs that have been downloaded from P2P services. If the record companies can make these songs available online with acceptable DRM (or without DRM), they'll almost certainly find buyers.

 Some enterprising smaller operators *have* managed to make an economic proposition out of selling pressed CDs or recorded CDs of out-of-print music to which they've acquired the rights. By cutting out middlemen and selling directly via websites and mail order, and in some cases by charging a premium price for a hard-to-get product, such operators have proved that making such music available isn't impossible. Many independent musicians are also selling directly to the public, either on CD or over the Internet, which gives them creative control over their music as well as direct feedback from their fans.

Historically, video has not been a good candidate for digital distribution, because the files have been too big to transfer easily across the Internet. But now that faster broadband connections are becoming increasingly widespread, and YouTube is used for everything from promoting music to promoting presidential candidates, distributing even full-quality video files is workable.

Know a Store's DRM Terms Before You Buy Any Protected Songs

Before you buy any song (or video, or movie) that is protected by DRM, make sure you understand what the DRM involves, what restrictions it places on you, and what changes the implementer of the DRM is allowed to make.

In most cases, when you "buy" a song that is protected by DRM, you buy not the song but a license to play the song in limited circumstances—for example, on a single computer or several computers, or for a limited length of time or a limited number of plays. You may or may not be permitted to burn the song to disc for storage or so that you can play it in conventional audio players (rather than on computers). In most cases, you are not permitted to give or sell the song to anyone else, nor can you return the song to the store for a refund or exchange. This may all seem too obvious to state— but it's completely different from most other things you buy, from a CD to a car.

The store that sells you the license to the song usually retains the right to change the limitations on how you can use the song. For example, the store can change the number of computers on which you can play the song, prevent you from burning it to disc, or even prevent you from playing it anymore. Any restrictions added may not take place immediately if your computer isn't connected to the Internet, but most online music stores require periodic authentication checks to make sure the music is still licensed for playing.

In general, "buying" DRM-protected songs online compares poorly to buying a physical CD, even though you have the option of buying individual songs rather than having to buy the entire contents of the CD. While you don't own the music on the CD, you own the CD itself, and can dispose of it as you want. For example, you can create digital copies of its contents (assuming that the CD is not copy-protected), lend the CD to a friend, or sell the CD to an individual or a store. However, you can't distribute the digital copies freely without specific permission.

Before buying from an online store such as the iTunes Store, check the terms and conditions to make sure you know what you're getting and what you're not. For example, most video and movie files you buy from the iTunes Store are encumbered with DRM. In most cases, if the same content is available on a conventional medium (such as a DVD or a video cassette), buying it on that medium gives you more flexibility than buying a digital file.

Buy Songs, Videos, and Movies from the iTunes Store

So far, the iTunes Store is one of the largest and most successful attempts to sell music online. (The latter part of this chapter discusses other online music services, including Amazon.com, Wal-Mart, the second-generation Napster, and eMusic.) The iTunes Store is far from perfect, and its selection is still very limited compared to what many users would like to be able to buy, but it's an extremely promising start. At this writing, the iTunes Store is available to iTunes users on Windows and the Mac.

Here's the deal with the iTunes Store:

- Until January 2009, most songs cost $0.99 each for a DRM-protected version and $1.29 for a DRM-free version (if there was one). But in January 2009, Apple announced it would start phasing out DRM completely—and pricing songs at different levels ($0.69, $0.99, and $1.29).

If you have songs bought from the iTunes Store that are protected by DRM, you can upgrade them for 30 cents per song, 30 percent of the cost of an album, or 60 cents for a music video.

- The cost of albums varies, but costs tend to be around what you'd pay for a discounted CD in many stores. Some CDs are available only as "partial CDs," which typically means that you can't buy the songs you're most likely to want. Extra-long songs (for example, those 13-minute jam sessions used to max out a CD) are sometimes available for purchase only with an entire CD.
- Most video items cost $1.99 or more, but you can also buy them in bulk and save. For example, you might buy a whole season of *Desperate Housewives*.
- You can listen to a 30-second preview of any song to make sure it's what you want. After you buy a song, you download it to your music library.
- You can burn songs to CD an unlimited number of times, although you can burn any given playlist only seven times without changing it or re-creating it under another name.
- The songs you buy are encoded in the AAC format (discussed in the section "AAC" in Chapter 6). The videos and movies you buy are in the MPEG-4 video format and are protected with DRM.
- You can play the songs you buy on any number of iPods or iPhones that you synchronize with your PC or Mac. You may also be able to play the songs on other music players that can use the AAC format (for example, some mobile phones can play AAC files).
- You can play the DRM-protected items you buy on up to five computers at once. These computers are said to be "authorized." You can change which computers are authorized for the items bought on a particular iTunes Store account.
- You can download each item you buy only once (assuming the download is successful). After that, the item is your responsibility. If you lose the item, you have to buy it again. This means that you must back up the items you buy or risk losing them.
- You can rent a movie and watch it on your computer, iPod, iPhone, or Apple TV. You can watch a rented movie on only one device at a time. So when you transfer a rented movie from your computer to one of the other devices mentioned above, it disappears from the iTunes library on your computer.

Know the Disadvantages of Buying from the iTunes Store

As of summer 2008, the iTunes Store offered more than eight million songs and had sold more than five billion songs altogether.

For customers, it's great to be able to find songs easily, buy them almost instantly for reasonable prices, and use them in enough of the ways they're used to (play the songs on their computer, play them on their iPod or iPhone, or burn them to disc).

For the record companies, the appeal is a still largely untapped market that can provide a revenue stream at minimal cost (no physical media are involved) and with an acceptably small potential for abuse. (For example, most people who buy songs from the iTunes Store won't share them with others.)

Before you buy from the iTunes Store, though, make sure you know the disadvantages:

- Even though the AAC format provides relatively high audio quality, the songs sold by the iTunes Store are significantly lower quality than CD-quality audio.
- When you buy a CD, you own it. You can't necessarily do what you want with the music—not legally, anyway. But you can play it as often as you want on whichever player, lend it to a friend, sell it to someone else, and so on. By contrast, when you buy a song from the iTunes Store, you're not allowed to lend it to other people, or to sell it.

As well as songs, the iTunes Store sells video files and movies. As with songs, the convenience of buying via download is wonderful, but there are still disadvantages:

- Even the high-definition format provides lower quality than a high-definition DVD.
- You buy not a tangible object but a license to use the file. You can't resell the file—in fact, you can't even give it to someone else.
- You need to back up your purchases to physical media to avoid loss.
- If the video or movie file is protected by DRM (as most are), Apple can change your rights to use it, or simply stop you from playing it.

Set Up an Account with the iTunes Store

To use the iTunes Store, you need a PC or a Mac running iTunes as well as a .Mac account, an Apple ID, or an AOL screen name. (An Apple ID is essentially an account with the iTunes Store and takes the form of an e-mail address. The .Mac service is Apple's online service. If you have a .Mac account, you have an Apple ID, but you don't have to get a .Mac account to get an Apple ID.)

To get started with the iTunes Store, click the iTunes Store item in the Source list in iTunes. (Alternatively, double-click the iTunes Store item to display a separate iTunes Store window.) iTunes accesses the iTunes Store and displays its home page, of which Figure 7-1 shows an example on the Mac.

To sign in or to create an account, click the Sign In button. iTunes displays the Sign In To Download Music From The iTunes Store dialog box (see Figure 7-2).

If you have a .Mac account or an Apple ID, type it in the Apple ID text box, type your password in the Password text box, and click the Sign In button. Likewise, if you have an AOL screen name, select the AOL option button, type your screen name and password, and click the Sign In button.

 Note Remember that your Apple ID is the full e-mail address, including the domain—not just the first part of the address. For example, if your Apple ID is a MobileMe address, enter **yourname@me.com** rather than just **yourname.**

FIGURE 7-1 The iTunes Store home page

The first time you sign in to the iTunes Store, iTunes displays a dialog box pointing out that your Apple ID or AOL screen name hasn't been used with the iTunes Store and suggesting that you review your account information:

Click the Review button to review your account information. (This is a compulsory step. Clicking the Cancel button doesn't skip the review process, as you might hope—instead, it cancels the creation of your account.)

FIGURE 7-2 From the Sign In dialog box, you can sign in to an existing account or create a new account.

To create a new account, click the Create New Account button and then click the Continue button on the Welcome To The iTunes Store page. The subsequent screens then walk you through the process of creating an account. You have to provide your credit card details and billing address. Beyond this, you get a little homily on what you may and may not legally do with the items you download, and you must agree to the terms of service of the iTunes Store.

Understand the Terms of Service

Almost no one ever reads the details of software licenses, which is why the software companies have been able to establish as normal the sales model in which you buy not software itself but a limited license to use it, and you have no recourse if it corrupts your data or reduces your computer to a puddle of silicon and steel. But you'd do well to read the terms and conditions of the iTunes Store before you buy music from it, because you should understand what you're getting into.

 The iTunes window doesn't give you the greatest view of the terms of service. To get a better view, click the Printable Version link at the very bottom of the scroll box or direct your browser to www.apple.com/legal/itunes/us/service.html.

The following are the key points of the terms of service:

- You can play DRM-protected items that you download on five Apple-authorized devices—computers, iPods, or iPhones—at any time. You can authorize and deauthorize computers, so you can (for example) transfer your DRM-protected items from your old computer to a new computer you buy.
- You can use, export, copy, and burn songs for "personal, noncommercial use." Burning and exporting are an "accommodation" to you and don't "constitute a

grant or waiver (or other limitation or implication) of any rights of the copyright owners." If you think that your being allowed to burn what would otherwise be illegal copies must limit the copyright owners' rights, I'd say you're right logically but wrong legally.

- You're not allowed to burn videos. Period.
- After you buy and download songs and videos, they're your responsibility. If you lose them or destroy them, Apple won't replace them. (You have to buy new copies of the songs and videos if you want to get them back.)
- You agree not to violate the Usage Rules imposed by the agreement.
- You agree that Apple may disclose your registration data and account information to "law enforcement authorities, government officials, and/or a third party, as Apple believes is reasonably necessary or appropriate to enforce and/or verify compliance with any part of this Agreement." The implication is that if a copyright holder claims that you're infringing their copyright, Apple may disclose your details without your knowledge, let alone your agreement. This seems to mean that, say, Sony Music or the RIAA can get the details of your e-mail address, physical address, credit card, and listening habits by claiming a suspicion of copyright violation.
- Apple and its licensors can remove or prevent you from accessing "products, content, or other materials."
- Apple reserves the right to modify the Agreement at any time. If you continue using the iTunes Store, you're deemed to have accepted whatever additional terms Apple imposes.
- Apple can terminate your account for your failing to "comply with any of the provisions" in the Agreement—or for your being suspected of such failure. Terminating your account prevents you from buying any more songs and videos immediately, but you might be able to set up another account. More seriously, termination may prevent you from playing songs and videos you've already bought—for example, if you need to authorize a computer to play them.

Configure iTunes Store Settings

By default, iTunes displays a Store category in the Source list with an iTunes Store item and (once you've bought a song or video from the iTunes Store) a Purchased item below it. iTunes also uses 1-Click buying and downloading. You may want to remove the iTunes Store category or use the shopping basket. To change your preferences, follow these steps:

1. Display the iTunes dialog box or the Preferences dialog box:
   - In Windows, choose Edit | Preferences or press CTRL-COMMA or CTRL-Y to display the iTunes dialog box.
   - On the Mac, choose iTunes | Preferences or press ⌘-COMMA or ⌘-Y to display the Preferences dialog box.
2. Click the Parental Control tab (Windows) or Parental button (Mac) to display the Parental Controls. Figure 7-3 shows the Parental Controls on the Mac.

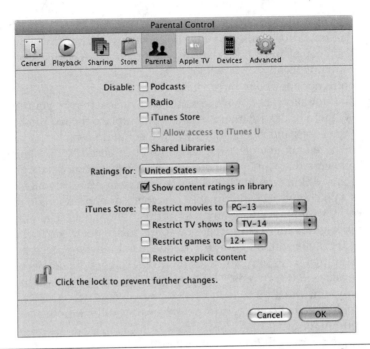

FIGURE 7-3 The Parental Control tab of the iTunes dialog box or Preferences dialog box lets you disable the iTunes Store or restrict the content it displays.

3. In the Disable area, select the iTunes Store check box if you want to remove the Store category from the Source list. Select the Allow Access To iTunes U check box if you want to leave iTunes U's educational content enabled. If you want to prevent anyone else from reenabling the iTunes Store, click the lock icon and then go through User Account Control for the iTunes Parental Controls Operation (on Windows Vista) or authenticate yourself (on the Mac).

4. If you didn't disable the iTunes Store, choose content ratings and restrictions:
   • Select your country in the Ratings For drop-down list.
   • Select the Show Content Ratings In Library check box if you want iTunes to display content ratings.

5. In the iTunes Store area, choose whether to restrict movies, TV shows, games, and explicit content. For example, to restrict movies to the PG rating, select the Restrict Movies To check box, and then choose PG in the drop-down list. Click the Store tab (Windows) or Store button (Mac) to display the Store tab. Figure 7-4 shows the Store tab on the Mac. The Store tab in Windows has the same controls.

6. Select the Buy And Download Using 1-Click option button or the Buy Using A Shopping Cart option button, as appropriate. 1-Click is great for impulse shopping and instant gratification, whereas the shopping cart enables you to round up a collection of songs, weigh their merits against each other, and decide which ones you feel you must have.

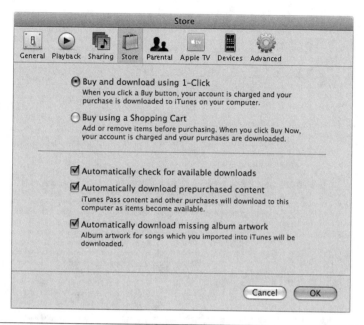

FIGURE 7-4   Configure the settings on the Store tab of the iTunes dialog box or the Preferences dialog box before you buy any songs unexpectedly.

 If you have a slow connection, use the Buy Using A Shopping Cart option to queue up a stack of tracks to download overnight when the download won't compete with your other online activities for your meager bandwidth.

7. Select the Automatically Check For Available Downloads check box if you want iTunes to look for new episodes of podcasts to which you've subscribed. Clear this check box if you prefer to check for new episodes manually.
8. Select the Automatically Download Prepurchased Content check box if you want iTunes to automatically download content you've bought using prepurchase features such as iTunes Pass (a kind of season ticket for items that come in episodes).
9. Select the Automatically Download Missing Album Artwork check box if you want iTunes to try to download the artwork for songs you import. This is usually helpful. You can add further artwork later as needed.
10. Click the OK button to apply your choices and close the dialog box.

Find the Songs, Videos, and Movies You Want

You can find songs and videos in the iTunes Store in several ways that will seem familiar if you've used other online stores:

- You can meander through the interface looking for songs and videos by clicking links from the home page.

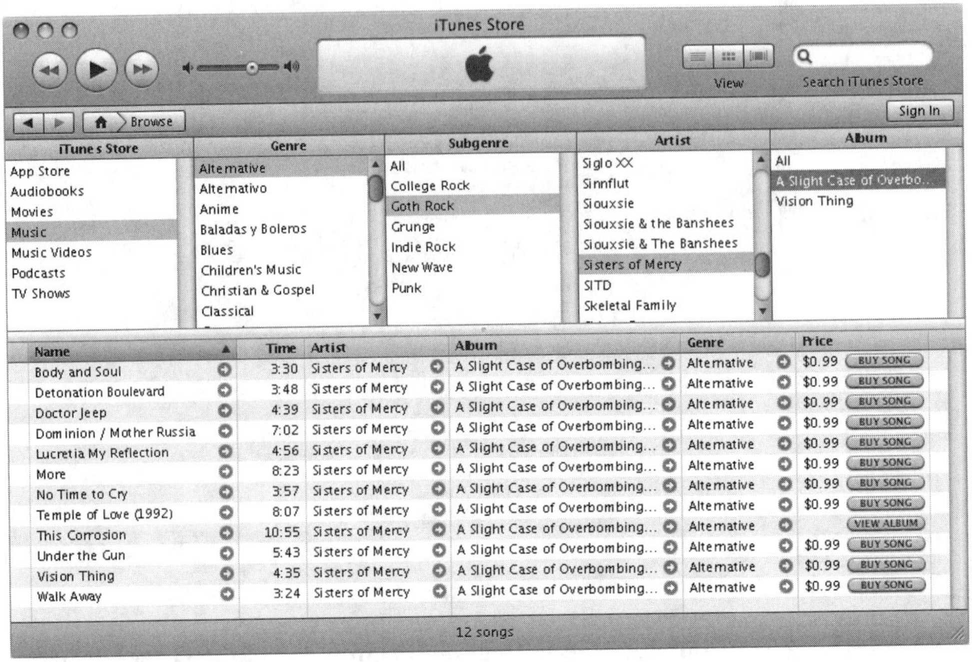

FIGURE 7-5   Use the Browse feature to browse through the iTunes Store's offerings.

- You can browse by genre, subgenre, artist, and album. Click the Browse button, click the Browse link in the Quick Links area on the home page, choose View | Show Browser, or press CTRL-B (Windows) or ⌘-B (Mac) to display the Browse interface (see Figure 7-5).
- You can search for specific music or videos either by using the Search iTunes Store box or by clicking the Power Search link (in the Quick Links box on the right of the home page) and using the Power Search page to specify multiple criteria. Figure 7-6 shows the Power Search page with some results found. You can sort the search results by a column heading by clicking it. Click the column heading again to reverse the sort order.

Preview Songs, Videos, and Movies

One of the most attractive features of the iTunes Store is that it lets you preview a song, video, or movie before you buy it. This feature helps you ensure both that you've found the right song, video, or movie and that you like it.

For some songs, the previews are of the first 30 seconds. For most songs, the previews feature one of the most distinctive parts of the song (for example, the chorus or a catchy line). For videos and movies, the previews are 20 seconds of the most identifiable highlights.

Double-click a song's or video's listing to start the preview playing. To view the trailer for a movie, click the View Trailer button.

FIGURE 7-6 Use the Power Search feature to search for songs by song title, artist, album, genre, and composer. The + sign indicates that a song is available in the unprotected iTunes Plus format.

Understand A******s, "Explicit," and "Clean"

The iTunes Store censors supposedly offensive words to help minimize offense:

- Songs or videos deemed to have potentially offensive lyrics are marked EXPLICIT in the Name column. Where a sanitized version is available, it's marked CLEAN in the Name column. Some of the supposedly explicit items contain words no more offensive than "love." Some supposedly explicit songs are instrumentals.
- Strangely, other songs and videos that contain words that are offensive to most people aren't flagged as being explicit. So if you worry about what you and yours hear, don't trust the iTunes Store ratings too far.
- Any word deemed offensive is censored with asterisks (**), at least in theory. (In practice, some words sneak through.) When searching, use the real word rather than censoring it yourself.

Request Songs or Other Items You Can't Find

Eight million songs sounds like an impressive number, but it's a mere jugful in the bucket of all the songs that have ever been recorded (and that music enthusiasts would like to buy). As a result, the iTunes Store's selection of music pleases some users more than others. Not surprisingly, Apple and the record companies seem to be concentrating first on the songs that are most likely to please (and to be bought by) the most people. If you want the biggest hits—either the latest ones or longtime favorites—chances are that the iTunes Store has you covered. But if your tastes run to the esoteric, you may not find the songs you're looking for in the iTunes Store.

If you can't find a song or other item you're looking for in the iTunes Store, you can submit a request for it. If a search produces no results, the iTunes Store offers you a Request link that you can click to display the iTunes Request form for requesting songs, videos, films, or other items.

Beyond the immediate thank-you-for-your-input screen that the iTunes Store displays, requesting items feels unrewarding at present. Apple doesn't respond directly to requests, so unless you keep checking for the items you've requested, you won't know that they've been posted. Nor will you learn if the items will ever be made available. Besides, given the complexities involved in licensing items, it seems highly unlikely that Apple will make special efforts to license any particular item unless a truly phenomenal number of people request it. Instead, Apple seems likely to continue doing what makes much more sense—licensing as many items as possible that are as certain as possible to appeal to plenty of people.

Navigate the iTunes Store

To navigate from page to page in the iTunes Store, click the buttons in the toolbar. Alternatively, use these keyboard shortcuts:

- In Windows, press CTRL-[to return to the previous page and CTRL-] to go to the next page.
- On the Mac, press ⌘-[to return to the previous page and ⌘-] to go to the next page.

Buy an Item from the iTunes Store

To buy an item from the iTunes Store, simply click the Buy button. For example, to buy a song, click the Buy Song button.

If you're not currently signed in, iTunes displays the Sign In To Download Music From The iTunes Store dialog box, as shown here.

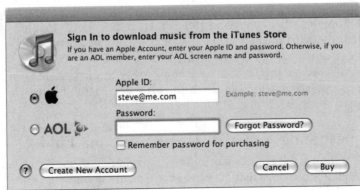

Type your ID and password. Select the Remember Password For Purchasing check box if you want iTunes to remember your password so that you don't need to enter it in the future. Then click the Buy button. iTunes then displays a confirmation message box like this:

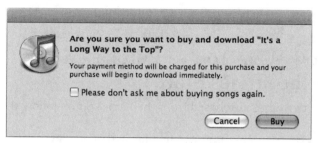

Click the Buy button to make the purchase. Select the Don't Warn Me About Buying Songs Again check box if you don't want to have to confirm your purchases in the future. Leave this check box cleared if you're feeling the credit crunch and want to rein in your impulse buying.

iTunes then downloads the song or video to your library and adds an entry for it to your Purchased playlist.

Listen to Songs or Watch Videos You've Purchased

When you download a song or video from the iTunes Store, iTunes adds it to the playlist named Purchased in the Source list. When you click the Purchased playlist, iTunes automatically displays a message box to explain what the playlist is. Select the Do Not Show This Message Again check box before dismissing this message box, because otherwise it will soon endanger your sanity.

The Purchased playlist is there to provide a quick-and-easy way to get to all the items you buy. Otherwise, if you purchase items on impulse without keeping a list, they might vanish into your huge media library.

To delete the entry for an item in the Purchased playlist, right-click it (or CTRL-click it on the Mac), choose Clear from the shortcut menu, and click the Yes button in the confirmation message box. However, unlike for regular files, iTunes doesn't offer you the opportunity to delete the file itself—the file remains in your library on the basis that, having paid for it, you don't actually want to delete it.

You can drag items that you haven't purchased to the Purchased playlist as well.

Restart a Failed Download

If a download fails, you may see an error message that invites you to try again later. If this happens, iTunes terminates the download but doesn't roll back the purchase.

To restart a failed download, choose Store | Check For Available Downloads. If you're not currently signed in, type your password in the Enter Account Name And Password dialog box, and then click the Check button. iTunes attempts to restart the failed download and also checks for any other items (such as new podcast episodes) that are lined up for downloading to your computer.

Review What You've Purchased from the iTunes Store

To see what you've purchased from the iTunes Store, follow these steps:

1. Click the Account button (the button that displays your account name), enter your password, and then click the View Account button to display the Apple Account Information window.
2. Click the Purchase History button to display details of the items you've purchased.
3. Click the arrow to the left of an order date to display details of the purchases on that date.
4. Click the Done button when you've finished examining your purchases. iTunes returns you to your Apple Account Information page.

Authorize and Deauthorize Computers for the iTunes Store

As mentioned earlier in this chapter, when you buy a DRM-protected item from the iTunes Store, you're allowed to play it on up to five different computers or devices at a time. iTunes implements this limitation through a form of license that Apple calls *authorization*. iTunes tracks which computers are authorized to play items you've purchased and stops you from playing the items when you're out of authorizations.

If you then want to play items you've purchased on another computer, you need to *deauthorize* one of the authorized computers so as to free up an authorization for use on the extra computer. You may also need to specifically deauthorize a computer to prevent it from playing the items you've bought. For example, if you sell or give away your Mac, you'd probably want to deauthorize it. You might also need to deauthorize a computer if you're planning to rebuild it.

 Your computer must be connected to the Internet to authorize and deauthorize computers.

Authorize a Computer to Use the iTunes Store

To authorize a computer, simply try to play a DRM-protected item purchased from the iTunes Store. For example, access a shared computer's Purchased playlist and double-click one of the items. iTunes displays the Authorize Computer dialog box:

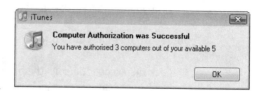

Enter your Apple ID and password and then click the Authorize button. iTunes accesses the iTunes Store and (all being well) authorizes the computer. iTunes starts playing the item and displays the Computer Authorization Was Successful dialog box, as shown here. Click the OK button.

Deauthorize a Computer from Using the iTunes Store

To deauthorize a computer so that it can no longer play the items you've purchased from the iTunes Store, follow these steps:

1. Choose Store | Deauthorize Computer to display the Deauthorize Computer dialog box, shown here.

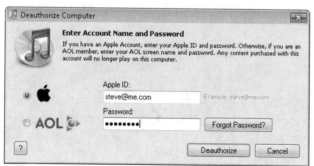

2. Type your Apple ID and password, and then click the Deauthorize button. iTunes deauthorizes the computer and displays a message box to tell you it has done so, as shown here.

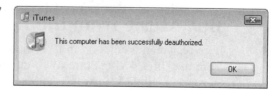

Deauthorize a Computer You Can't Currently Access

The procedure you've just seen for deauthorizing a computer is easy—but you must be able to access the computer. If you've already parted with the computer, or if the computer has stopped working, this gives you a problem.

The solution is to deauthorize *all* your computers at once, and then reauthorize those you want to be able to use. But there are a couple of restrictions you need to know about first:

- You're allowed to deauthorize all your computers only once per year.
- You can only deauthorize all your computers when you've used the full five authorizations. (But you can quickly use up those authorizations in a pinch.)

To deauthorize all your computers, follow these steps:

1. Click the Account button (the button that displays your account name) and then enter your password to display the Apple Account Information window.
2. Click the Deauthorize All button. iTunes displays a confirmation dialog box, as shown here.

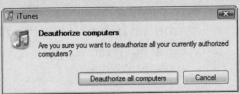

3. Click the Deauthorize All Computers button. iTunes deauthorizes all the computers, and then displays a message box to let you know it has done so.

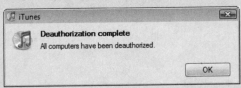

4. Click the OK button, and then click the Home button to return to the iTunes Store home screen.

Buy Music from the iTunes Wi-Fi Store

If you have an iPhone or an iPod touch, you can buy songs and albums over the air from the iTunes Wi-Fi Store. With either device, you can connect to the iTunes Wi-Fi Store via a wireless network—for example, your home wireless network or a wireless hotspot. With the iPhone, you can also connect via 3G or the Edge network, but downloads will be slower.

When you buy an item from the iTunes Wi-Fi Store, the iPhone or iPod touch downloads it, and you can play it immediately. The next time you synchronize the iPhone or iPod touch with your computer, iTunes copies the item, and you can then play it in iTunes as well.

To use the iTunes Wi-Fi Store, follow these steps:

1. Press the Home button to go to the Home screen unless you're already there.
2. Touch the iTunes button to display the iTunes Wi-Fi Store.
3. Touch the buttons onscreen to navigate to the song or item you want. For example:
   - Touch the Featured button to view the songs that the iTunes Wi-Fi Store is featuring.
   - Touch the Top Tens button to display a list of Top Tens in different categories—for example, Pop, Alternative, or Rock. Touch the Top Ten item you want to view.
   - To search, touch the Search button, touch the Search box to bring up the onscreen keyboard, and then type your search term. The iTunes Wi-Fi Store searches as you type, so you usually needn't touch the Search button to start the search. The left screen in Figure 7-7 shows the results of a successful search.
   - Touch one of the buttons at the top of the screen, such as New Releases, What's Hot, or Genres, to display a list of songs.

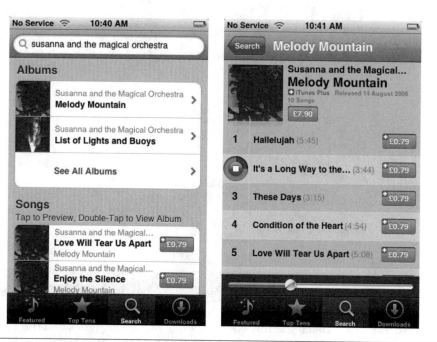

FIGURE 7-7   The results of a successful search on the iTunes Wi-Fi Store (left) and previewing a song (right)

4. When you've found a song or item you're interested in, touch a song to start playing its preview. If what starts playing is unbearable, touch the Stop button at the left of the item's listing (shown on the right in Figure 7-7) to end the torment.

5. To buy a song or other item, touch its price. The price changes to a Buy Now button, as shown on the left in Figure 7-8.

6. Touch the Buy Now button. The iTunes Wi-Fi Store adds the song to your Downloads list and prompts you for your password.

7. Type the password, and then touch the OK button. The iPhone or iPod touch starts downloading the song.

8. To see the progress of your downloads, touch the Downloads button and look at the Downloads screen (shown on the right in Figure 7-8).

9. Once the download is finished, you can touch the Purchased button on the Downloads screen to jump straight to the Purchased playlist and play the downloaded item.

To transfer your purchases from your iPhone or iPod touch to your iTunes library, connect the device to your PC, and then choose File | Transfer Purchases From *Device*, where *Device* is the name you've given the device.

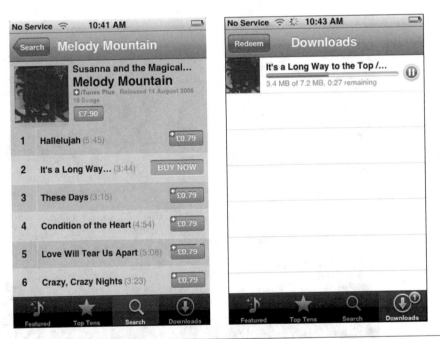

FIGURE 7-8   Touch the Buy Now button to buy a song (left), and use the Downloads screen to see how your downloads are coming along (right).

Create iPhone Ringtones from Songs You Buy from the iTunes Store

If you have an iPhone, you can create custom ringtones from songs you purchase from the iTunes Store that have the ringtone mark (a bell symbol) next to them. Each ringtone costs an additional $0.99.

To create a ringtone, follow these steps:

1. In iTunes, right-click the song, and then choose Create Ringtone from the context menu. iTunes displays the Ringtone controls (see Figure 7-9).

 At this writing, you can create ringtones only from songs you buy from the U.S. iTunes Store.

2. Drag the blue highlighted section to cover the part of the song that you want to turn into the ringtone.
3. Click the Preview button to hear what you've selected. The ringtone loops, so you can take your time. If necessary, reposition the blue highlighted section. Also if necessary, click the Stop button to stop the music.
4. You can lengthen or shorten the selection by positioning the mouse pointer over the starting or ending line so that it turns into a two-headed arrow, and then clicking and dragging.

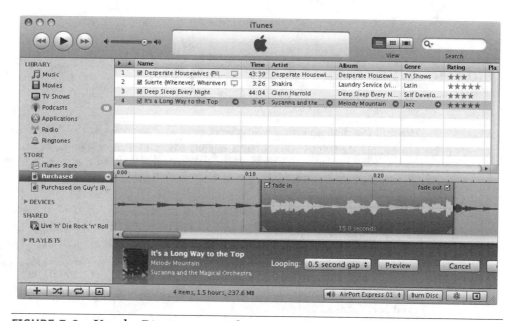

FIGURE 7-9   Use the Ringtone controls to create a custom ringtone from a song you've purchased from the iTunes Store.

5. If you want the ringtone to start with a bang rather than fading in, clear the Fade In check box at the beginning of the blue highlighted section. Similarly, if you don't want the ringtone to fade out, clear the Fade Out check box at the end of the blue highlighted section.

6. In the Looping drop-down list, choose the length of gap you want between each loop of the ringtone (assuming you don't answer the call). You can choose a gap of 0.5 second, 1 second, 2 seconds, 3 seconds, 4 seconds, or 5 seconds.

7. When you've arranged the ringtone to your liking, click the Buy button.

Buy Music from Other Online Music Stores

If you use an iPod or iPhone, the iTunes Store is the best of the large online music stores, because it sells songs in a format that the device can play, whereas most other online music stores use incompatible formats (such as WMA). But you may want to use other online music stores for a couple of reasons:

- Some sell songs that the iTunes Store doesn't have.
- Some offer subscription pricing that lets you download and listen to as much music as you want for a monthly fee.

This section discusses some of the main online music stores at this writing, starting with the one that is most likely to be of interest to iPod or iPhone owners—Amazon.com.

Did You Know?

Most Other Online Music Stores Work Only with Windows

Most of the online music services work only with Windows at the time of writing. To complicate things still more for anyone using an iPod or iPhone, most of the online music services use WMA files protected with DRM for their songs. Some services are also tied to specific hardware players, some to their own software players, and some to Windows Media Player.

To use protected WMA files with an iPod or iPhone, you must burn them to CD, and then rip and encode the CD to AAC files or MP3 files. You could also use Apple Lossless Encoding, but because the WMA files are lower quality than Apple Lossless Encoding, doing so makes little sense.

Most of the online music services permit you to burn songs to CD, but creating further copies of the songs could be interpreted to be against the terms and conditions of some services.

Amazon.com

Amazon.com (www.amazon.com) sells songs in the MP3 format, with most encoded at the 256-Kbps bitrate. Most songs cost $0.89 apiece, but there are special deals on many whole albums.

At this writing, you can download an individual song directly to your computer (and then add it to iTunes manually), but you need to use Amazon's custom download program to download a full album. This program automatically adds the songs you've bought to your iTunes library.

Walmart.com

Wal-Mart's website (www.walmart.com) includes an MP3 Music Downloads section that offers songs and albums. Songs from Walmart.com come as unprotected MP3 files, so you can use them freely.

You can download the songs one at a time using any web browser, but Wal-Mart also provides an MP3 Music Downloads Manager to streamline downloads of multiple songs on Windows Vista and Windows XP.

eMusic

eMusic (www.emusic.com) offers more than 3.5 million songs for download—and the songs are in the unprotected MP3 format, so you can use them freely in iTunes, on an iPod or iPhone, or on almost any other music player.

eMusic offers various pricing plans, including yearly subscriptions. Each plan has a free 14-day trial, but you must provide valid credit card details. You download the songs using eMusic's software.

Amie Street

Amie Street (http://amiestreet.com) is a website that offers DRM-free songs with two twists. First, members who are artists can sell their songs via Amie Street—no record deal needed. Second, a song's price varies depending on its popularity: It starts off being free, and the price increases (up to a maximum of $0.98) as it becomes more popular.

Napster 2.0

Napster 2.0 (www.napster.com) offers more than six million songs at this writing. Napster 2.0 has nothing to do with the pioneering file-sharing application Napster except the name and logo. Napster uses the WMA format protected with DRM and works only on the PC—there is no Mac client at this writing.

A standard Napster subscription allows you to download as much music as you want to your PC, where you can play it as often as you like using the Napster player. You can use up to three PCs for the same Napster account, but the terms and conditions specify that the account is for one person only, so you're not allowed to share it with your friends. If you discontinue your subscription, you lose access to all songs you've downloaded except for those you've bought.

If you want to burn a song to CD, you must pay; you must also pay if you want to transfer the song to a music player that supports WMA DRM.

Even if you pay, you can't transfer songs to an iPod or iPhone. You can put songs on the iPod or iPhone in only two ways:

- Buy the songs, burn them to CD, and then rip the CD to a format that the iPod or iPhone can play (for example, use iTunes to rip the CD to AAC files).
- Use an audio-grabbing utility (such as Total Recorder, discussed in Chapter 6) that captures the audio stream from the PC's sound card, or route the output from your sound card to an input that you can capture with a conventional audio application (such as Sound Recorder). These maneuvers are against the Napster terms and conditions and are illegal in most circumstances.

The Napster To Go service enables you to transfer as many songs as you want to a portable player that supports Windows Media Player 10 DRM. (The Napster website lists supported players.)

Napster's restrictions may appear to be onerous, but Napster can be a great way to listen to a wide variety of music for a fixed fee. Being able to "try before you buy" takes the gamble out of buying CDs (or individual songs) that you're not sure you'll like.

 Napster has been marketing its services aggressively to colleges and universities, which pay reduced fees for providing Napster access to all their students. Mac users are out of luck.

Real Rhapsody

Real Rhapsody (http://mp3.rhapsody.com) is a service that provides unlimited streaming access to several million songs. You can buy songs and put them on a variety of devices, but not on the iPod or iPhone. Like Napster, Rhapsody provides a good way to listen to a wide variety of music for a fixed fee.

Russian MP3 Download Sites

You can also find high-quality MP3 files—without DRM—for download on sites hosted in Russia and other former Eastern Bloc countries. These sites typically offer a wide selection of music at very low prices.

At this writing, the legal position of these sites is not clear. While these sites insist they are operating legally, most Western legal experts disagree. Music industry bodies, such as the RIAA, are actively trying to close these sites down.

Find Free Songs Online

Beyond the iTunes Store and the other online music stores discussed so far in this chapter, you'll find many sources of free music online. Some of this free music is legal, but much of it is illegal.

Find Free Songs on the Online Music Stores

Most of the major online music stores provide some free songs, usually to promote either up-and-coming artists or major releases from established artists. For example, the iTunes Store provides a single for free download each week. The stores typically make you create an account before you can download such free songs as they're offering.

Find Free Songs for Legal Download

Sadly, many of the sites that provided free songs in the early days of the Internet have closed down. However, the Internet still contains some sources of songs that are distributed for free by the artists who created them. Usually, the best way to discover these sites is to visit an artist's own website or an independent site such as GarageBand.com (www.garageband.com).

 If you're always looking for new music recommendations, try The Filter (www .thefilter.com). The website has a tool that lets you choose your three favorite artists and in response generates a playlist of music you might like. If you like the results, you can download a program that lets you create playlists on your computer and transfer them to an iPod or iPhone. Sites such as Pandora (www .pandora.com) and Musicovery (www.musicovery.com) also provide interesting recommendations.

Find Free Songs for Illegal Download

Beyond the legal offerings of the online music stores and the free (and legal) sites, you can find pretty much any song for illegal download on the Internet. Finding a song that you can't find anywhere else can be wonderful, and getting the song for free is even more so. But before you download music illegally, you should be aware of possible repercussions to your computer, your wallet, and even your future.

Threats to Your Computer

Downloading files illegally may pose several threats to your computer:

- Many companies that produce P2P software include other applications with their products. Some of these applications are shareware and can be tolerably useful; others are adware that are useless and an irritant; still others are spyware that report users' sharing and downloading habits.

To detect and remove spyware from your computer, use an application such as the free Ad-Aware from LavaSoft (www.lavasoft.com) or Spybot – Search & Destroy (www.safer-networking.org; make sure you use the hyphen in the name, as there is also a www.safernetworking.org site).

- Many of the files shared on P2P networks contain only the songs they claim to contain. Others are fake files provided by companies working for the RIAA and the record companies to "poison" the P2P networks and discourage people from downloading files by wasting their time.
- Other files *are* songs but also harbor a virus, worm, or Trojan horse. Even apparently harmless files can have a sting in the tail. For example, the tags in music files can contain URLs to which your player's browser component automatically connects. The site can then run a script on your computer, doing anything from opening some irritating advertisement windows, to harvesting any sensitive information it can locate, to deleting vital files or destroying the firmware on your computer.

Whether you're downloading songs illegally or not, use virus-checking software to scan all incoming files to your computer, no matter whom they come from—friends, family, coworkers, or the Internet.

Threats to Your Wallet, Your ID, and Your Future

Even if your computer remains in rude health, downloading files illegally poses several threats. Unless you use a service (such as Anonymizer, www.anonymizer.com) that masks your computer's IP address, any action that you take on the Internet can be tracked back to your computer.

Sharing digital files of other people's copyrighted content without permission is illegal. So is receiving such illegal files. The No Electronic Theft Act (NET Act) of 1997 and the Digital Millennium Copyright Act (DMCA) of 1998 provide savage penalties for people caught distributing copyrighted materials illegally. Under the DMCA, you can face fines of up to $500,000 and five years' imprisonment for a first offense, and double those for a second offense.

P2P networks also expose users to social-engineering attacks through the chat features that most P2P tools include. However friendly other users are, and however attractive the files they provide, it can be a severe mistake to divulge personal information. A favored gambit of malefactors is to provide a quantity of "good" (malware-free) files followed by one or more files that include a Trojan horse or keystroke logger to capture sensitive information from your computer.

Find P2P Software

At this writing, there are various P2P networks, some of which interoperate with each other. However, for legal reasons, P2P networks frequently change their nature or close.

To find up-to-date information on P2P software, consult a resource such as Wikipedia (http://en.wikipedia.org/wiki/Main_Page; see the "peer-to-peer file sharing" entry) or a search engine.

8

Create Video Files That Work with the iPod or iPhone

HOW TO...

- Create iPod or iPhone video files from your digital video camera
- Create iPod or iPhone video files from your existing video files
- Create video files from your DVDs

The iPods and iPhone are great for playing various kinds of video files—anything from music videos to TV shows or entire movies. You can play a movie either on the iPod's or iPhone's built-in screen or on a TV to which you connect the iPod or iPhone via a cable.

Apple's iTunes Store provides a fair selection of video content, including TV series and full-length movies, and you can buy or download video in iPod- or iPhone-compatible formats from various other sites online. But if you enjoy watching video on the iPod or iPhone, you'll almost certainly want to put your own video content on it. You may also want to rip files from your own DVDs so that you can watch them on the iPod or iPhone.

Create iPod or iPhone Video Files from Your Digital Video Camera

If you make your own movies with a digital video camera, you can easily put them on the iPod or iPhone. Use an application such as Windows Movie Maker (Windows) or iMovie (Mac) to capture the video from your digital video camera and turn it into a home movie.

What You Can and Can't Legally Do with Other People's Video Content

Before you start putting your videos and DVDs on the iPod or iPhone, it's a good idea to know the bare essentials about copyright and decryption:

- If you created the video (for example, it's a home video or DVD), you hold the copyright to it, and you can do what you want with it—put it on the iPod or iPhone, release it worldwide, or whatever. The only exceptions are if what you recorded is subject to someone else's copyright or if you're infringing on your subjects' rights (for example, to privacy).
- If someone has supplied you with a legally created video file that you can put on the iPod or iPhone, you're fine doing so. For example, if you download a video from the iTunes Store, you don't need to worry about legalities.
- If you own a copy of a commercial DVD, you need permission to rip (extract) it from the DVD and convert it to a format the iPod or iPhone can play. Even decrypting the DVD in an unauthorized way (such as creating a file rather than simply playing the DVD) is technically illegal.

Note Video formats are confusing at best—but the iPod, iPhone, and iTunes make the process of getting suitable video files as easy as possible. The iPod and the iPhone can play videos in the MP4 format up to 2.5 Mbps (megabits per second) or the H.264 format up to 1.5 Mbps. Programs designed to create video files suitable for the iPod and iPhone typically give you a choice between the MP4 format and the H.264 format. As a point of reference, VHS video quality is around 2 Mbps, while DVD is about 8 Mbps.

Create iPod or iPhone Video Files Using Windows Movie Maker

The versions of Windows Movie Maker included with Windows Vista and Windows XP can't export video files in an iPod-friendly format, so what you need to do is export the video file in a standard format (such as AVI) that you can then convert using another application.

Create an AVI File from Windows Movie Maker on Windows Vista

To save a movie as an AVI file from Windows Movie Maker on Windows Vista, follow these steps:

1. With your movie open in Windows Movie Maker, choose File | Publish Movie (or press CTRL-P) to launch the Publish Movie Wizard. The Wizard displays the Where Do You Want To Publish Your Movie? screen.

2. Select the This Computer item in the list box, and then click the Next button. The Wizard displays the Name The Movie You Are Publishing screen.
3. Type the name for the movie, choose the folder in which to store it, and then click the Next button. The Wizard displays the Choose The Settings For Your Movie screen (see Figure 8-1).
4. Select the More Settings option button, and then select the DV-AVI item in the drop-down list.

 The DV-AVI item appears as DV-AVI (NTSC) or DV-AVI (PAL), depending on whether you've chosen the NTSC option button or the PAL option button on the Advanced tab of the Options dialog box. NTSC is the video format used in most of North America; PAL's stronghold is Europe.

5. Click the Publish button to export the movie in this format. When Windows Movie Maker finishes exporting the file, it displays the Your Movie Has Been Published screen.

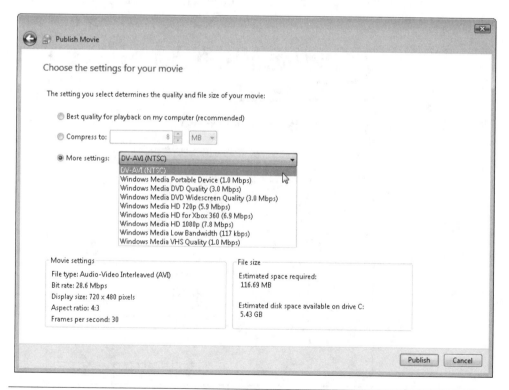

FIGURE 8-1 On the Choose The Settings For Your Movie screen, select the More Settings option button, and then pick the DV-AVI item in the drop-down list.

6. Clear the Play Movie When I Click Finish check box if you don't want to watch the movie immediately in Windows Media Player. Often, it's a good idea to check that the movie has come out okay.
7. Click the Finish button.

Now that you've created an AVI file, use one of the Videora Converter programs (discussed later in this chapter) to convert it to a format that works on the iPod or iPhone.

Create an AVI File from Windows Movie Maker on Windows XP

To save a movie as an AVI file from Windows Movie Maker on Windows XP, follow these steps:

1. Choose File | Save Movie File to launch the Save Movie Wizard. The Wizard displays its Movie Location screen.
2. Select the My Computer item, and then click the Next button. The Wizard displays the Saved Movie File screen.
3. Enter the name and choose the folder for the movie, and then click the Next button. The Wizard displays the Movie Setting screen (shown in Figure 8-2 with options selected).

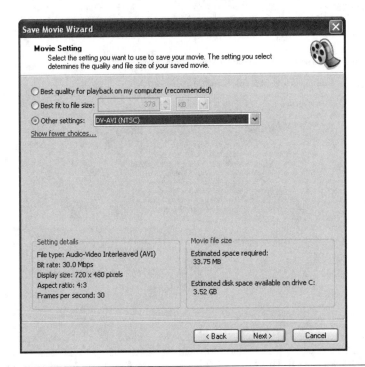

FIGURE 8-2   Click the Show More Choices link to make the Other Settings option button available, then select the Other Settings option button and pick the DV-AVI item from the drop-down list.

4. Click the Show More Choices link to display the Best Fit To File Size option button and the Other Settings option button.
5. Select the Other Settings option button, and then select the DV-AVI item in the drop-down list.

The DV-AVI item appears as DV-AVI (NTSC) or DV-AVI (PAL), depending on whether you've chosen the NTSC option button or the PAL option button on the Advanced tab of the Options dialog box.

6. Click the Next button to save the movie in this format. The Wizard displays the Completing The Save Movie Wizard screen.
7. Clear the Play Movie When I Click Finish check box if you don't want to test the movie immediately in Windows Media Player. Usually, it's a good idea to make sure the movie has come out right.
8. Click the Finish button.

Now that you've created an AVI file, use one of the Videora Converter programs (discussed later in this chapter) to convert it to a format that works on the iPod or iPhone.

Create iPod or iPhone Video Files Using iMovie

To use iMovie to create video files that will play on the iPod or iPhone, follow these steps:

1. With the movie open in iMovie, choose Share | iTunes to display the Publish Your Project To iTunes sheet (see Figure 8-3).
2. In the Sizes area, select the check box for each size you want to create. The dots show the devices for which that size is suitable. For example, if you want to play the video files on an iPhone or iPod touch, select the Mobile check box.

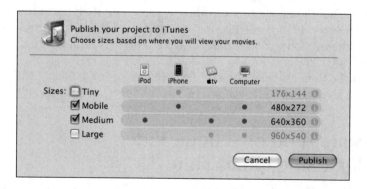

FIGURE 8-3   On the Publish Your Project To iTunes sheet in iMovie, choose which sizes of file you want to create—for example, Mobile for the iPhone and Medium for the iPod.

3. Click the Publish button, and then wait while iMovie creates the compressed file or files and adds it or them to iTunes. iMovie then automatically displays iTunes.

4. Click the Movies item in the Source list, and you'll see the movies you just created. Double-click a file to play it, or simply drag it to the iPod or iPhone to load it immediately.

Create iPod or iPhone Video Files from Your Existing Video Files

If you have existing video files (for example, files in the AVI format or QuickTime movies), you can convert them to iPod format in a couple of ways. The easiest way is by using the capabilities built into iTunes—but unfortunately, these work only for some video files. The harder way is by using QuickTime Pro, which can convert files from most known formats but which costs $30.

On Windows, you can also use the various Videora Converter programs, discussed later in this chapter.

Create iPod or iPhone Video Files Using iTunes

To create a video file for the iPod or iPhone using iTunes, follow these steps:

1. Add the video file to your iTunes library in either of these ways:
   - Open iTunes if it's not running. Open a Windows Explorer window (Windows) or a Finder window (Mac) to the folder that contains the video file. Arrange the windows so that you can see both the file and iTunes. Drag the file to the Library item in iTunes.
   - In iTunes, choose File | Add To Library, use the Add To Library dialog box to select the file, and then click the Open button (Windows) or the Choose button (Mac).
2. Select the movie in the iTunes window, and then choose Advanced | Convert Selection For iPod/iPhone. You can also right-click or CTRL-click (Mac) and choose Convert Selection For iPod/iPhone from the shortcut menu.

If the Convert Selection For iPod/iPhone command isn't available for the file, or if iTunes gives you an error message, you'll know that iTunes can't convert the file.

Create iPod or iPhone Video Files Using QuickTime

QuickTime, Apple's multimedia software for Mac OS X and Windows, comes in two versions: QuickTime Player (the free version) and QuickTime Pro, which costs $29.99.

On Mac OS X, QuickTime Player is included in a standard installation of the operating system; and if you've somehow managed to uninstall it, it'll automatically install itself again if you install iTunes. Likewise, on the PC, you install QuickTime Player when you install iTunes, because QuickTime provides much of the multimedia functionality for iTunes. The "Player" name isn't entirely accurate, because QuickTime provides encoding services as well as decoding services to iTunes—but QuickTime Player doesn't allow you to create most formats of video files until you buy QuickTime Pro.

QuickTime Player is a crippled version of QuickTime Pro, so when you buy QuickTime Pro from the Apple Store, all you get is a registration code to unlock the hidden functionality. To apply the registration code, choose Edit | Preferences | Register in Windows to display the Register tab of the QuickTime Settings dialog box. On the Mac, choose QuickTime Player | Registration to display the Register tab of the QuickTime dialog box.

 When you register QuickTime, you must enter your registration name in the Registered To text box in exactly the same format as Apple has decided to use it. For example, if you've used the name John P. Smith to register QuickTime, and Apple has decided to address the registration to *Mr. John P. Smith*, you must use **Mr. John P. Smith** as the registration name. If you try to use **John P. Smith**, registration fails, even if this is exactly the way you gave your name when registering.

To create an iPod- or iPhone-friendly video file from QuickTime, follow these steps:

1. Open the file in QuickTime, and then choose File | Export to display the Save Exported File As dialog box.
2. Specify the filename and folder as usual, and then choose Movie To iPod or Movie To iPhone in the Export drop-down list. Leave the Default Settings item selected in the Use drop-down list.
3. Click the Save button to start exporting the video file.

Create iPod or iPhone Video Files Using Videora Converters on Windows

If you have video files that you can't convert with iTunes on Windows, use a file conversion tool such as Videora iPod Converter or Videora iPhone 3G Converter (see Figure 8-4). You can download these tools for free from the Videora website (www.videora.com).

Videora makes a different tool available for each iPod and each iPhone, but any version of Videora Converter can create files for all iPods and iPhones: You just need to click the Settings button on the toolbar, open the Device drop-down list in the Video Conversion Defaults area of the Converter tab, and select your preferred device (for example, iPhone 3G).

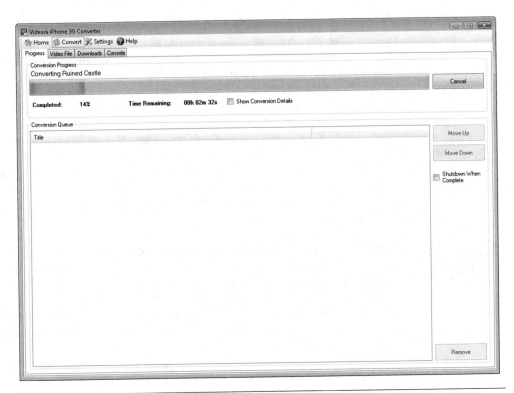

FIGURE 8-4 Videora iPhone 3G Converter lets you convert various types of videos to iPhone- and iPod-friendly formats.

Another way to convert video files from one format to another—on either Windows or the Mac—is to use an online file conversion tool such as Zamzar (www.zamzar.com). For low volumes of files, the conversion is free (though it may take a while), but you must provide a valid e-mail address. For higher volumes of files or higher priority, you can sign up for a paid account.

Create iPod or iPhone Video Files Using HandBrake on the Mac

If you have video files that you can't convert with iTunes on the Mac, try using the free conversion program HandBrake (http://handbrake.fr). Download HandBrake, install it to your Applications folder, run it from there, and then follow these steps:

1. Click the Source button on the toolbar to display an Open sheet.

HandBrake can also rip DVDs, provided you have a third-party decryption utility installed. See the end of the chapter for details.

2. Click the file you want, and then click the Open button. HandBrake shows the details of the file.

3. In the Title drop-down list, choose which title—which of the recorded items in the file—you want. Most files have only one title, so the choice is easy; DVDs have various titles.

4. If the file is broken up into chapters (sections), choose which ones you want. Pick the first in the Chapters drop-down list and the last in the Through drop-down list—for example, Chapters 1 through 4.

5. In the Destination area, change the name and path for the converted file if necessary.

6. If the Presets pane isn't displayed on the right side of the window, click the Toggle Presets button on the toolbar to display it. Figure 8-5 shows the HandBrake window with the Presets pane displayed.

7. In the Presets pane, choose the preset you want:
   - **iPhone/iPod Touch**   Use this setting for the iPhone or iPod touch.
   - **iPod High-Rez**   Use this setting to create files with a high enough resolution to play back on a TV connected to the iPod as well as on the iPod itself.
   - **iPod Low-Rez**   Use this setting to create files suitable for playing back on the iPod but not on a TV. (The advantage of this setting is that the files are far smaller than the High-Rez ones, so you can fit many more of them on the iPod.)

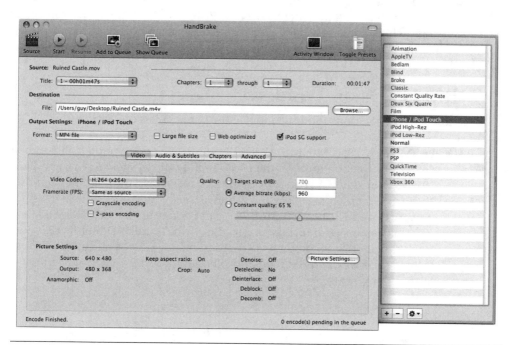

FIGURE 8-5   The Presets pane on the right side of the HandBrake window lets you instantly choose video settings for the iPhone, iPod touch, or iPod.

8. If necessary, change further settings. (Press ⌘-? to display the HandBrake User Guide for instructions.)

9. Click the Start button on the toolbar to start encoding the file.

Create Video Files from Your DVDs

If you have DVDs (and who doesn't?), you'll probably want to put them on the iPod or iPhone so that you can watch them without a DVD player. This section gives you an overview of how to create suitable files, first on Windows, and then on the Mac.

 Because ripping commercial DVDs without specific permission is a violation of copyright law, there are no DVD ripping programs from major companies. You can find commercial programs, shareware programs, and freeware programs on the Internet—but keep your wits firmly about you, as some programs are a threat to your computer through being poorly programmed, while others include unwanted components such as adware or spyware. Always read reviews of any DVD ripper you're considering before you download and install it—and certainly before you pay for it. As usual on the Internet, if something seems too good to be true, it most likely *is* too good to be true.

Before you start ripping, make sure that your discs don't contain computer-friendly versions of their contents. At this writing, some Blu-Ray discs include such versions, which are licensed for you to load on your computer and your lifestyle devices (such as the iPod and iPhone).

Rip DVDs on Windows

Here are two solutions for decrypting and ripping DVDs on Windows:

- **DVD43 and DVD Shrink** DVD43 is a free DVD-decryption utility that you can download from the links on the DVD43 – Download Sites page (www.dvd43.com). DVD43 opens the DVD up for ripping but doesn't rip the content from the DVD. To rip, use a program such as DVD Shrink (also free; www.official-dvdshrink.org).
- **AnyDVD and CloneDVD Mobile** AnyDVD from SlySoft ($49.99; www.slysoft .com) is a decryption utility that works with CloneDVD Mobile ($24.99; also from SlySoft). By using these two programs together, you can rip DVDs to formats that work on the iPod and iPhone. SlySoft offers 21-day trial versions of these programs.

How to... **Prevent DVD Player from Running Automatically When You Insert a DVD**

When you insert a movie DVD, Mac OS X automatically launches DVD Player, switches it to full screen, and starts the movie playing. This behavior is great for when you want to watch a movie, but not so great when you want to rip it.

To prevent DVD Player from running automatically when you insert a DVD, follow these steps:

1. Choose Apple | System Preferences to open System Preferences.
2. In the Hardware section, click the CDs & DVDs item.
3. In the When You Insert A Video DVD drop-down list, you can choose Ignore if you want to be able to choose freely which application to use each time. If you always want to use the same application, choose Open Other Application, use the resulting Open sheet to select the application, and then click the Choose button.
4. Choose System Preferences | Quit System Preferences or press ⌘-Q to close System Preferences.

Rip DVDs on the Mac

The best tool for ripping DVDs on the Mac is HandBrake, which you met earlier in this chapter. To rip DVDs with HandBrake, you must install VLC, a DVD- and video-playing application (free; www.videolan.org). This is because HandBrake uses VLC's DVD-decryption capabilities; without VLC, HandBrake cannot decrypt DVDs.

Once you've installed VLC, simply run HandBrake, click the Source button, click the DVD in the Source list, and then click the Open button. HandBrake scans the DVD. You can then choose which "title" (which of the recorded tracks on the DVD) to rip, and which chapters from it. The chapters are the bookmarks on the DVD—for example, if you press the Next button on your remote, your DVD player skips to the start of the next chapter.

9

Make Your Music Sound Great and Customize the iTunes Window

HOW TO...

- Play music with iTunes
- Make iTunes run automatically when you log on
- Improve the sound that iTunes produces
- Change the iTunes interface to meet your preferences
- Enjoy visualizations as you listen to music

In Chapter 2, you learned how to rip CDs and create playlists; in Chapter 7, you learned the ins and outs of creating high-quality audio files from both CDs and other sources, such as your records and tapes. This chapter shows you how to enjoy that music using iTunes and how to change the sound you get and the interface you see. But first, you may want to make iTunes run automatically when you log onto your PC or Mac.

Play Music with iTunes

By following the techniques described in Chapter 2 and Chapter 7, you've probably created a fair-sized library. Now it's time to enjoy your library, using as many of iTunes' features as you need.

Play Back Music with iTunes

To play back music with iTunes, follow these general steps:

1. Navigate to the album, playlist, or song you want to play, select it, and then click the Play button.
2. Drag the diamond on the progress bar in the display to scroll forward or backward through the current track.

201

How to... Run iTunes Frequently—or Always on Startup

Running iTunes from the iTunes icon on your desktop, from the Windows Start menu, or from the Dock works well enough for frequent use. But if you intend to run iTunes frequently, or always, you can do better.

In Windows, you can pin iTunes to the fixed part of the Start menu so that it always appears. To do so, navigate to the iTunes icon on the Start menu in Windows Vista or Windows XP, right-click it, and then choose Pin To Start Menu from the shortcut menu. If you keep the Quick Launch toolbar displayed, consider dragging an iTunes icon to the Quick Launch toolbar so that it's present there too.

To run iTunes even more quickly, configure a CTRL-ALT keyboard shortcut for it so that you can start iTunes by pressing the keyboard shortcut either from the Desktop or from within an application. Here's how to create the shortcut:

1. Right-click the iTunes icon on your Desktop or on your Start menu, and then choose Properties from the shortcut menu to display the iTunes Properties dialog box.
2. On the Shortcut tab, click in the Shortcut Key text box and then press the letter you want to use in the CTRL-ALT shortcut. For example, press I to create the shortcut CTRL-ALT-I.
3. Click the OK button to close the Properties dialog box.

But if you use iTunes whenever you're using your computer, the best solution is to make iTunes start automatically whenever you log on. To do so, follow these steps in Windows:

1. Right-click the iTunes icon on your Desktop or on your Start menu, and then choose Copy from the shortcut menu to copy the shortcut to the Clipboard.
2. On the Start menu's All Programs submenu, right-click the Startup folder and choose Open to open a Windows Explorer window showing the folder's contents.
3. Right-click in the Startup folder and choose Paste from the shortcut menu to paste a copy of the iTunes shortcut into the folder.
4. Click the Close button (the × button), press ALT-F4, or choose Organize | Close (on Windows Vista) or File | Close (on Windows XP) to close the Windows Explorer window.

To make iTunes start automatically on the Mac when you log in, simply right-click the iTunes icon on the Dock and select the Open At Login item from the shortcut menu.

3. Use the Shuffle button to shuffle the order of the tracks in the current album or playlist. Click once to shuffle the songs; click again to restore the songs to their previous order.

To reshuffle the current playlist on the Mac, OPTION-click the Shuffle button.

4. Click the Repeat button one or more times to repeat a playlist, album, or song:
   - **Repeat the current playlist or album** Click the Repeat button once, so that iTunes turns the arrows on the button to blue.
   - **Repeat the current song** Click the Repeat button again, so that iTunes adds to the blue arrows a blue circle bearing the number 1.
   - **Turn off repeat** Click the Repeat button a third time.

5. If you've scrolled the Song list so that the current song isn't visible, or switched to a different playlist or view, click the arrow button on the right side of the readout at the top of the iTunes window to go to the current song. Alternatively, press CTRL-L (Windows) or ⌘-L (Mac) to jump back to the current song. If you're still viewing the same playlist or category, you can also simply wait until the next song starts, at which point iTunes automatically scrolls back to it.

6. To open a Windows Explorer window (in Windows) or a Finder window (on the Mac) to the folder that contains the selected song file, press CTRL-R (Windows) or ⌘-R (Mac).

7. To toggle the display of the artwork viewer, click the Show Or Hide Song Artwork button. To display the Artwork column in List view, press CTRL-G (Windows) or ⌘-G (Mac).

8. On the Mac, you can also control iTunes by right-clicking or CTRL-clicking its Dock icon and making the appropriate choice from the shortcut menu, as shown here. In Windows, if you've chosen to display an iTunes icon in the notification area, you can control iTunes from the icon.

Tip You can change the information shown in the display window by clicking the items in it. Click the Play icon at the left of the display window to toggle between the track information and the equalization graph. Click the time readout to move between Remaining Time and Total Time.

How to... **Create a Gapless Album or Join Tracks Together Without Gaps**

iTunes' default settings are to create a separate file (AAC, MP3, Apple Lossless Encoding, AIFF, or WAV, depending on your preferences) from each song on CDs you rip.

For most CDs, this works well. But sometimes you'll want to rip a CD so that it plays back without any gaps between songs. For example, most live CDs have applause or banter rather than silence between songs, so having a break in the playback tends to be distracting.

To play back a CD without any gaps, you have two choices:

- **Create a gapless album** You can tell iTunes that an album shouldn't have a gap between songs. Creating a gapless album is a good idea when you will normally play the CD's songs in sequence rather than shuffle them.
- **Join two or more songs—or even the full CD—into a single file so that you can treat those songs (or CD) as a single unit** The advantage of this approach is that you can prevent Party Shuffle and other Smart Playlists from playing individual songs from the CD (or from your selection of songs) out of context. The disadvantage is that the joined-together songs tend to be long and hard to navigate through, especially on the iPod or iPhone.

You can create a gapless album either before or after you rip the CD:

- **Before you rip the CD** Right-click (or CTRL-click on the Mac) the CD's entry in the Source list and choose Get Info. In the CD Info dialog box, shown here, select the Gapless Album check box and then click the OK button.
- **After you rip the CD** Browse to the album, select it, and then choose File | Get Info. If iTunes asks whether you're sure you want to edit information for multiple tracks, click the Yes button. In the Multiple Item Information dialog box, choose Yes in the Gapless Album drop-down list, and then click the OK button. (Alternatively, right-click a song, choose Get Info, and then click the Options tab. Select the Part Of A Gapless Album check box, and then click the OK button.)

CD Info

Artist
Peter Hammill

Composer
Peter Hammill

Album | Disc Number
Chameleon in the Shadow of the Night | 1 | of | 1

Genre | Year
Progressive Rock | 1973

☐ Compilation CD   ☐ Gapless Album

(Cancel)   (OK)

To rip two or more tracks from a CD into a single file, select the tracks and then choose Advanced | Join CD Tracks. iTunes brackets the tracks, as shown here. These tracks then rip to a single file.

If you made a mistake with the tracks you joined, select one or more of the joined tracks and then choose Advanced | Unjoin CD Tracks to separate the tracks again.

Listen to Audiobooks on Your iPod or iPhone

Even if your iPod or iPhone is laden nearly to the gunwales with songs, you may be able to cram on a good amount of spoken-word audio, such as audiobooks and podcasts. This is because spoken-word audio can sound great at much lower bitrates than music requires.

The iTunes Store provides a wide variety of content, including audiobooks, magazines, plays, and poems. You can also get audiobooks from other sources, such as from the Audible.com website (www.audible.com), which offers subscription plans for audio downloads. (Audible.com provides many of the audiobooks on the iTunes Store.)

When playing many audiobooks, you can press CTRL-SHIFT–RIGHT ARROW (Windows) or ⌘-SHIFT–RIGHT ARROW (Mac) to go to the next chapter. Press CTRL-SHIFT–LEFT ARROW (Windows) or ⌘-SHIFT–LEFT ARROW (Mac) to go to the previous chapter.

Improve the Sound of Music

To make music sound as good as possible, you should apply suitable equalizations using iTunes' graphical equalizer. You can also crossfade one song into another, add automatic sound enhancement, and skip the beginning or end of a song.

Use the Graphical Equalizer to Make the Music Sound Great

iTunes includes a graphical equalizer that you can use to change the sound of the music (or other audio) you're playing. You can apply an equalization directly to the playlist you're currently playing, much as you would apply an equalization manually to a physical amplifier or receiver.

You can also apply a specific equalization to each song (or other item) in your iTunes library. Once you've done this, iTunes always uses that equalization when playing that song or item, no matter which equalization is currently applied to iTunes itself.

After playing an item that has an equalization specified, iTunes switches back to the equalization applied to iTunes itself for the next item that doesn't have an equalization specified.

Apply an Equalization to What's Currently Playing

To apply an equalization to what you're currently playing, follow these steps:

1. Display the Equalizer window (see Figure 9-1):
   - **Windows** Choose View | Show Equalizer.
   - **Mac** Choose Window | Equalizer or press ⌘-OPTION-2.
2. Select the equalization from the drop-down list. If you're playing an item, you'll hear the effect of the new equalization in a second or two.

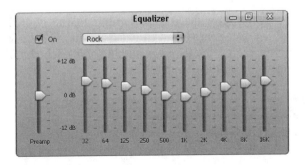

FIGURE 9-1 iTunes' Equalizer window offers preset equalizations, but you can also create custom equalizations.

Specify an Equalization for an Individual Item

To specify the equalization iTunes should use for a particular song or other item, follow these steps:

1. Select the item in your library or in a playlist.

It doesn't matter whether you apply the equalization to the item in the library or in a playlist, because applying the equalization even in a playlist affects the item in the library as a whole. So if you can access an item more easily through a playlist than through your library, start from the playlist.

2. Press CTRL-I (Windows) or ⌘-I (Mac), or choose Get Info from the File menu or the shortcut menu, to display the Item Information dialog box. This dialog box's title bar shows the item's name rather than the words "Item Information."
3. Click the Options tab to display its contents. Figure 9-2 shows the Options tab for iTunes for Windows. The Options tab for iTunes for the Mac has the same controls.
4. Select the equalization you want in the Equalizer Preset drop-down list.
5. Choose other options as necessary, and then click the OK button to close the Item Information dialog box. Alternatively, click the Previous button or the Next button to display the information for the previous item or next item in the Item Information dialog box so that you can continue applying equalizations.

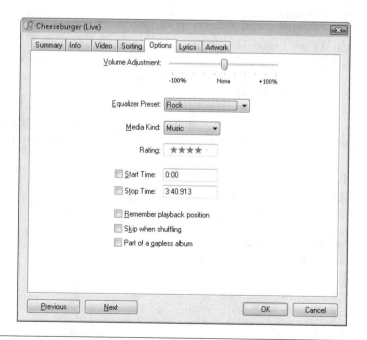

FIGURE 9-2   You can specify the equalization for a particular song or other item on the Options tab of the Item Information dialog box.

If the equalization you apply to an item is one of the equalizations built into the iPod or iPhone, the iPod or iPhone also automatically uses the equalization for playing back the item. But if the equalization is a custom one your iPod or iPhone doesn't have, the player can't use it. The iPod and iPhone don't pick up custom equalizations you create in iTunes. Equalizations don't apply to the iPod shuffle, because this player doesn't use equalizations.

Create a Custom Equalization That Sounds Good to You

The preset equalizations in iTunes span a wide range of musical types—but even if there's one named after the type of music you're currently listening to, you may not like the effects it produces. When this happens, try all the other equalizations, however unsuitable their names may make them seem, to see if any of them just happens to sound great with this type of music. (For example, some people swear the Classical equalization is perfect for many Grateful Dead tracks.) If none of them suits you, create a custom equalization that delivers the goods.

To create a new custom equalization, follow these steps:

1. Open the Equalizer window.
2. Drag the frequency sliders to the appropriate positions for the sound you want the equalization to deliver. When you change the first slider in the current preset, the drop-down list displays Manual.
3. If you need to change the overall volume of the song or item, drag the Preamp slider to a different level. For example, you might want to boost the preamp level on all the songs to which you apply a certain equalization.
4. Choose Make Preset from the drop-down list. iTunes displays the Make Preset dialog box.
5. Type the name for the equalization, and then click the OK button.

You can then apply your equalization from the drop-down list in the Item Information dialog box as you would any other preset equalization.

Delete and Rename Preset Equalizations

If you don't like a preset equalization, you can delete it. If you find an equalization's name unsuitable, you can rename it.

To delete or rename an equalization, start by following these steps:

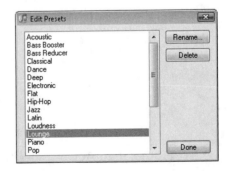

1. Select the Edit List item from the drop-down list in the Equalizer window. iTunes displays the Edit Presets dialog box.
2. Select the preset equalization you want to affect.

To rename the equalization, follow these steps:

1. Click the Rename button to display the Rename dialog box, shown here.

2. Type the new name in the New Preset Name text box.
3. Click the OK button. iTunes displays a dialog box like this, asking whether you want to change all songs currently set to use this equalization under its current name to use the equalization under the new name you've just specified.

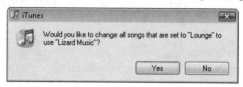

4. Click the Yes button or the No button as appropriate.
5. Click the Done button if you want to close the Edit Presets dialog box. If you want to work with other presets, leave it open.

To delete a preset equalization, follow these steps:

1. Click the Delete button.
2. iTunes displays a dialog box like the one shown here, asking you to confirm the deletion. Click the Delete button or the Cancel button, as appropriate.

3. To stop iTunes from confirming the deletion of preset equalizations, select the Do Not Warn Me Again check box before clicking the Delete button or the Cancel button. If you delete the preset, iTunes prompts you to choose whether to remove the equalization from all songs that are set to use it, as shown here. Click the Yes button or the No button as appropriate.

4. Click the Done button to close the Edit Presets dialog box.

Choose Crossfading, Sound Enhancer, and Sound Check Settings

The Playback tab of the iTunes dialog box (Windows) or the Preferences dialog box (Mac) offers options for crossfading playback, changing the Sound Enhancer, and controlling whether iTunes uses its Sound Check feature to normalize the volume of songs. Figure 9-3 shows the Playback tab of iTunes for the Mac. The Playback tab for iTunes for Windows has the same controls.

- **Crossfade Songs**   Makes iTunes fade in the start of the next song as the current song is about to end. This option lets you eliminate gaps between songs the way most DJs do. Drag the slider to increase or decrease the length of time that's crossfaded. This check box is selected by default. Turn off crossfading if you don't like it.

 Turning on crossfading prevents iTunes from using gapless playback for any song that does not have the gapless playback option explicitly turned on.

- **Sound Enhancer**   Applies iTunes' sound enhancement to the audio you're playing. The Sound Enhancer check box is selected by default, so you've probably been listening to it all along. Experiment with different settings on the Low–High scale by dragging the slider to see which setting sounds best to you—or turn off sound enhancement if you don't like it. Sound enhancement can make treble sounds appear brighter and can add to the effect of stereo separation, but the results don't suit everybody. You may prefer to adjust the sound manually by using the graphical equalizer.
- **Sound Check**   Controls whether iTunes uses its Sound Check feature to normalize the volume of different songs so that you don't experience widely varying audio levels in different songs. Many people find Sound Check useful. If you don't like Sound Check, or if you find that the extra processing power it requires makes your computer struggle to play music back satisfactorily, turn it off.

Skip the Boring Intro or Outro on a Song

If you disagree with the producer of a song about when the song should begin or end, use the Start Time and Stop Time controls on the Options tab of the Item Information dialog box (shown in Figure 9-2, earlier in this chapter) to specify how much of the track to lop off. This trimming works both in iTunes and on the iPod or iPhone.

To trim the intro, enter in the Start Time text box the point at which you want the song to start. For example, enter **1:15** to skip the first minute and a quarter of a song. When you start typing in the Start Time text box, iTunes selects the Start Time check box for you, so you don't need to select it manually.

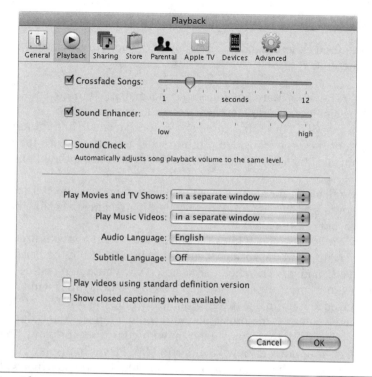

FIGURE 9-3   Choose crossfading, Sound Enhancer, and Sound Check options on the Playback tab of the iTunes dialog box or Preferences dialog box.

Similarly, you can change the value in the Stop Time text box to stop the song playing before its end. By default, the Stop Time text box contains a time showing when the song ends, down to thousandths of a second—for example, 4:56.769. When you reduce this time, iTunes selects the Stop Time check box automatically.

When skipping an intro or outro isn't enough, you can edit a song file down to only that part you want. See Chapter 6 for details.

Tweak the iTunes Interface

You can change the iTunes interface in several ways, which include resizing the window, turning off the display of the arrows linked to the iTunes Store, and changing the columns of data displayed.

This section also shows you how to control iTunes by using keyboard shortcuts, how to use iTunes' visualizations, and how to control iTunes with the iTunes widget on Mac OS X.

Resize the iTunes Window to the Size You Need

iTunes offers various window sizes to suit the amount of space you're prepared to dedicate to it:

- In Windows, iTunes has four sizes: normal, maximized, small, and minute. The small and minute sizes are considered mini mode.
- On the Mac, iTunes has three sizes: normal, small, and minute. The small and minute sizes are considered mini mode. You can also use the iTunes widget to control iTunes from the Dashboard instead of using the main iTunes window.

By default, iTunes opens in a normal window that you can resize by dragging any of its borders or corners (on Windows) or by dragging the sizing handle in the lower-right corner (on the Mac).

In Windows, you can click the Maximize button to maximize the window so that it occupies all the space on your screen (apart from the taskbar, if you have it displayed), and you can click the Restore Down button to restore the maximized window to its previous size. You can also toggle the iTunes window between its maximized and normal states by double-clicking the title bar.

Once you've set the music playing, you'll often want to reduce the iTunes window to its essentials so that you can get on with your work (or play). To do so, in Windows, press CTRL-M or choose View | Switch To Mini Player to display iTunes in mini mode.

On the Mac, there's no way of maximizing the iTunes window. You can click the Zoom button (the green button on the title bar) or press ⌘-CTRL-Z to toggle between

normal mode and mini mode (shown here). You can minimize the iTunes window by double-clicking the title bar, by clicking the Minimize button, or by pressing ⌘-M.

From here, you can drag the sizing handle in the lower-right corner to shrink iTunes down even further to its minute size. This can be handy when you're pushed for space, but it isn't very informative.

Here's how to restore iTunes to its normal size from mini mode:

- In Windows, press CTRL-M or click the Restore button.
- On the Mac, click the Zoom button, choose Window | Zoom, or press ⌘-CTRL-Z.

Change the Columns Displayed to Show the Information You Need

By default, iTunes displays the following columns: Name, Time, Artist, Album, Genre, My Rating, Play Count, and Last Played. You can change the columns displayed for the current item (for example, your music library or a playlist) by using either of two techniques.

How to...   Remove the iTunes Store Link Arrows on the Mac

Unless you're desperate to buy music or other items from the iTunes Store at a moment's notice, you'll probably find the arrows that iTunes displays in the Name, Artist, Album, and Composer columns an irritant rather than a boon. You can click an arrow to search the iTunes Store for related items.

iTunes used to display these arrows for all items that had related items available in the iTunes Store—and it used to let you turn the arrows off easily via a setting in the iTunes dialog box (Windows) or the Preferences dialog box (Mac). Now, iTunes displays the arrows only for the playing item and any other items you've selected, but it doesn't provide a setting for turning them off.

To remove the arrows on the Mac, follow these steps:

1. Click the Finder icon on the Dock, and then choose Go | Utilities to open the Utilities folder.
2. Double-click the Terminal icon to open a Terminal window.
3. Type the following command and press RETURN:

```
defaults write com.apple.iTunes show-store-arrow-links -bool FALSE
```

4. Choose Terminal | Quit Terminal to close the Terminal window.
5. Close iTunes, and then reopen it. Click a song, and the arrows won't appear.

If you want to restore the arrows, repeat the above steps, but change the FALSE value to TRUE.

To change the display of multiple columns in the same operation, press CTRL-J (Windows) or ⌘-J (Mac), or choose View | View Options, to display the View Options dialog box. Figure 9-4 shows the View Options dialog box for Windows; the View Options dialog box for the Mac has the same controls. The icon and label in the upper-left corner of the dialog box indicate which item's view you're customizing—for example, Music for your music library, or Party Shuffle for the Party Shuffle playlist. Select the check boxes for the columns you want to display, and then click the OK button to close the dialog box and apply your choices.

To change the display of a single column in the current item, right-click (or CTRL-click on the Mac) the heading of one of the columns currently displayed. iTunes displays a menu of the available columns, showing a check mark next to those currently displayed. Select an unchecked column to display it. Select a checked column to remove it from the display.

Note   The Play Count item stores the number of times you've played each item in iTunes. iTunes uses this information to determine your favorite items—for example, to decide which songs Smart Playlist should add to a playlist. You can also use this information yourself if you so choose. For example, you can create a Never Played playlist (with the criterion Play Count Is 0) to pick out all the items you've never played.

FIGURE 9-4 Use the View Options dialog box to specify which columns iTunes displays for the current item.

To change the order in which your selected columns appear, drag a column heading to the left or right. For example, if you want the Album column to appear before the Artist column, drag the Album column heading to the left until iTunes moves the column.

From the shortcut menu, you can also select the Auto Size Column command to automatically resize the column whose heading you clicked so that the column's width best fits its contents. Select the Auto Size All Columns command to automatically resize all columns like this.

 You can change the column width by dragging the bar at the right edge of a column heading to the left or right. Double-click this bar to set the column width to accommodate its widest entry.

Control iTunes via Keyboard Shortcuts

Controlling iTunes via the mouse is easy enough, but you can also control most of iTunes' features by using the keyboard. This can be useful both when your mouse is temporarily out of reach and when you've reduced the iTunes window to its small size or minute size, and thus hidden some of the controls.

Table 9-1 lists the keyboard shortcuts you can use to control iTunes. Most of these shortcuts work in any of iTunes' four display modes in Windows (normal, maximized, small, and mini) and iTunes' three display modes on the Mac (maximized, small, and mini), but the table notes the shortcuts that work only in some modes.

TABLE 9-1   Keyboard Shortcuts for iTunes

Action	Windows Keystroke	Mac Keystroke
Controlling Playback		
Play or pause the selected song.	SPACEBAR	SPACEBAR
Skip to the next song.	RIGHT ARROW CTRL–RIGHT ARROW	RIGHT ARROW ⌘–RIGHT ARROW
Skip to the previous song.	LEFT ARROW CTRL–LEFT ARROW	LEFT ARROW ⌘–LEFT ARROW
Rewind the song.	CTRL-ALT–LEFT ARROW	⌘-OPTION–LEFT ARROW
Fast-forward the song.	CTRL-ALT–RIGHT ARROW	⌘-OPTION–RIGHT ARROW
Skip to the next album in the list.	ALT–RIGHT ARROW	OPTION–RIGHT ARROW
Skip to the previous album in the list.	ALT–LEFT ARROW	OPTION–LEFT ARROW
Controlling the Volume		
Increase the volume.	CTRL–UP ARROW	⌘–UP ARROW
Decrease the volume.	CTRL–DOWN ARROW	⌘–DOWN ARROW
Toggle muting.	CTRL-ALT–UP ARROW CTRL-ALT–DOWN ARROW	⌘-OPTION–UP ARROW ⌘-OPTION–DOWN ARROW
Controlling the iTunes Windows		
Toggle the display of the iTunes main window.	n/a	⌘-OPTION-1
Toggle the display of the Equalizer window.	n/a	⌘-OPTION-2
Windows: Toggle between the mini player and full player. Mac: Minimize iTunes.	CTRL-M	⌘-M
Move the focus to the Find box.	CTRL-ALT-F	⌘-ALT-F
Display the Open Audio Stream dialog box.	CTRL-U	⌘-U
Controlling the Mini Player		
Increase the volume.	UP ARROW	UP ARROW
Decrease the volume.	DOWN ARROW	DOWN ARROW
Turn the iTunes volume to maximum.	SHIFT–UP ARROW	SHIFT–UP ARROW
Turn the iTunes volume to minimum.	SHIFT–DOWN ARROW	SHIFT–DOWN ARROW
Controlling the Visualizer		
Toggle the Visualizer on and off.	CTRL-T	⌘-T
Toggle full-screen mode on the Visualizer.	CTRL-F	⌘-F

Accompany Your Music with Visualizations

Like many music programs, iTunes can produce stunning visualizations to accompany your music. You can display visualizations at any of three sizes within the iTunes window (which can provide visual distraction while you work or play) or display them full screen to make your computer the life of the party.

Here's how to use visualizations:

- To start visualizations, press CTRL-T (Windows) or ⌘-T (Mac) or choose View | Show Visualizer.
- To stop visualizations, press CTRL-T (Windows) or ⌘-T (Mac) or choose View | Hide Visualizer.
- To change to another visualization mode on the Mac, choose View | Visualizer, and then choose Lathe, Jelly, or Stix from the submenu.
- To use the classic iTunes Visualizer, choose View | Visualizer | iTunes Classic Visualizer. (Choose View | Visualizer | iTunes Visualizer when you want to switch back.)
- To launch full-screen visualizations, press CTRL-F (Windows) or ⌘-F (Mac) or choose View | Full Screen.
- To stop full-screen visualizations, click your mouse button anywhere or press ESC or CTRL-T (Windows) or ⌘-T (Mac). Press CTRL-F (Windows) or ⌘-F (Mac) to switch back from full-screen visualizations to visualizations in a window.

Configure the iTunes Classic Visualizer to Get the Best Results

If you use the iTunes Classic Visualizer rather than the newer iTunes Visualizer, you can configure visualizations to make them look as good as possible on your computer. To configure visualizations, follow these steps:

1. If iTunes is displayed at its small or minute size, click the Restore button (Windows) or the green button on the window frame (Mac) to return iTunes to a normal window.
2. Start a song playing.
3. Start visualizations as described in the preceding section. For example, press CTRL-T (Windows) or ⌘-T (Mac).
4. Choose View | Visualizer | Options to display the Visualizer Options dialog box. Figure 9-5 shows the Visualizer Options dialog box for Windows on the left and the Visualizer Options dialog box for the Mac on the right.
5. Select and clear the check boxes to specify the options you want:
   - **Display Frame Rate** Controls whether iTunes displays the frame rate (the number of frames being generated each second) superimposed on the upper-left corner of the visualization. This check box is cleared by default. The frame rate is useless information that adds nothing to the visualization, but it can be useful as a point of reference. For example, you may want to compare the visualization frame rates generated by different computers, or you might

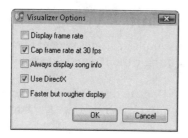 

FIGURE 9-5   Use the Visualizer dialog box to configure visualizations for Windows (on the left) and the Mac (on the right).

want to try the Faster But Rougher Display option (discussed in a moment) to see how much difference it produces. Bear in mind that the frame rate will vary depending on the size of the iTunes window, the complexity of the visualization, and what other tasks your computer is working on at the time.

- **Cap Frame Rate At 30 fps**   Controls whether iTunes stops the frame from exceeding 30 frames per second (fps). This check box is selected by default. iTunes is configured to cap the frame rate to reduce the demands on the visualization on your computer's graphics card and processor. The cap is at 30 fps because most people find that 30 fps provides smooth and wonderful visualizations—so there's no point in trying to crank out extra frames.
- **Always Display Song Info**   Controls whether iTunes displays the song information overlaid on the visualization all the time or just at the beginning of a song and when you change the Visualizer size while playing a song. This check box is cleared by default.
- **Use DirectX**   (Windows only.) Controls whether iTunes uses DirectX, a graphics-rendering system, to create the visualizations. This check box is selected by default if your computer supports DirectX (as most recent computers do). If this check box is selected, leave it selected for best results.
- **Use OpenGL**   (Mac only.) Controls whether iTunes uses OpenGL, a graphics-rendering system, to create the visualizations. This check box is selected by default. Leave it selected for best results.
- **Faster But Rougher Display**   Lets you tell iTunes to lower the quality of the visualizations to increase the frame rate. This check box is cleared by default. You may want to try selecting this check box on a less-powerful computer if you find the visualizations are too slow.

Tip   You can also trigger most of these options from the keyboard while a visualization is playing, without displaying the Visualizer Options dialog box. Press F to toggle the frame rate display, T to toggle frame rate capping, I to toggle the display of song information, and D to restore the default settings.

6. Click the OK button to close the Visualizer Options dialog box.

Control iTunes with the iTunes Widget on Mac OS X

If you're using Mac OS X, you can use the built-in iTunes widget to control iTunes from the Dashboard. To set the Dashboard to display the iTunes widget, follow these steps:

1. Click the Dashboard button on the Dock to display the Dashboard.
2. Click the + button superimposed on the left end of the Dock to display the bar showing the available widgets.
3. Click the iTunes widget, as shown here, to display it.

4. Click the × button superimposed on the left end of the Dock to close the widget bar.

You can then control iTunes by displaying the Dashboard and using the iTunes widget. Figure 9-6 shows the controls on the widget.

 Apart from clicking the Dashboard button on the Dock, you can display the Dashboard by pressing the hot key assigned to it on the Dashboard & Exposé tab of System Preferences (choose Apple | System Preferences and then click the Dashboard & Exposé icon). On this tab, you can also set an active screen corner for the Dashboard so that Mac OS X displays the Dashboard when you move the mouse pointer into that corner of the screen.

To open a playlist, click the Flip Widget button (the button showing the lowercase *i*). The iTunes widget rotates to show its other side. Select the playlist in the drop-down list and then click the Done button to flip the widget back to its regular position.

 If you use Yahoo! Widgets (free; http://widgets.yahoo.com), you can use similar widgets to run iTunes in both earlier versions of Mac OS X and Windows.

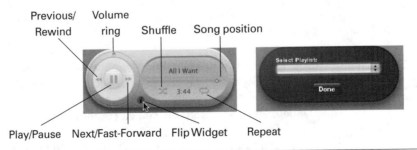

FIGURE 9-6 The iTunes widget lets you control your music from the Dashboard. Flip the widget (right) to select another playlist.

10

Manage Your Music and Video Library with iTunes

HOW TO...

- Browse quickly through your library
- Search for songs and other items
- Create regular playlists and Smart Playlists
- Create powerful playlists with iTunes' Genius
- Move your library from one folder to another
- Remove duplicate items from your library
- Use multiple libraries on the same computer
- Share your library with other iTunes users and access their shared library
- Build a media server for your household
- Enjoy podcasts

This chapter shows you how to use iTunes to manage your library of music and video files. You'll learn how to browse quickly by using the Browser panes, how to search for songs and videos, how to create playlists and Smart Playlists, and how to mix up your music with the iTunes DJ feature. After that, you'll meet iTunes' features for applying ratings and artwork to items, for consolidating your library so that it contains all your media files (or moving it to a different folder), and for removing any duplicate files that are wasting space.

Later in the chapter, you'll see how to export playlists so that you can share them with other people, import the playlists they share with you, and export your library to an XML file to store details of your playlists and ratings. You'll also learn how to build a media server for your household and how to enjoy podcasts.

Browse Quickly by Using the Browser Panes

iTunes provides the Browser panes (see Figure 10-1) to browse items quickly by artist, album, or genre. You can toggle the display of the Browser panes by choosing View | Show Browser or View | Hide Browser or by pressing CTRL-B (Windows) or ⌘-B (Mac).

 When you don't want to restrict the view by genre, select the All item at the top of the Genre pane so that you see all genres at once. Similarly, select the All item at the top of the Artist pane or the Album pane to see all the items in that pane.

Once the Browser panes are displayed, click an item in the Artist column to display the albums by that artist in the Album column. Then click an item in the Albums column to display that album in the lower pane.

 If you don't like having the Genre pane displayed on the Mac, open a Terminal window, type the command "defaults write com.apple.itunes show-genre-when-browsing -bool FALSE" (without the quotes), and then press RETURN. If you want to restore the Genre pane, issue the same command again, but use TRUE instead of FALSE.

The line of text at the bottom of the full iTunes window shows you how many songs or other items are in the current selection and how long they last. This readout has two formats for songs (5738 songs, 17.4 days, 22.98 GB, and 5738 songs, 17:10:06:58 total time, 22.98 GB) and three for items such as podcasts that contain episodes. To toggle between or cycle among the formats, click the item-and-time display.

FIGURE 10-1 iTunes' Browser panes let you browse by genre, artist, and album.

Use Views to Skim Through Your Library

Browsing can be an effective way of finding the songs or other items you want, but you may make better progress—or have more fun browsing—if you change the view iTunes is using.

iTunes provides three views: List view, Grid view, and Cover Flow view. You can switch among views by clicking the View buttons to the left of the Search box (as shown in the next illustration); by using the View | As List, View | As Grid, and View | As Cover Flow commands; or by pressing these keyboard shortcuts:

Windows	Mac	Switches to This View
CTRL-ALT-3	⌘-OPTION-3	List view
CTRL-ALT-4	⌘-OPTION-4	Grid view
CTRL-ALT-5	⌘-OPTION-5	Cover Flow view

Sort Your Songs in List View

List view is the view in which iTunes normally starts. List view shows a simple list of the songs in the selected item—for example, your library or a playlist. Figure 10-2 shows List view.

To move to the first item in the current sort column that matches a certain letter or sequence of letters, click in the list, and then type the letter or sequence. For example, with the list sorted by the Album column, you might type **Tang** to jump to the first item by Tangerine Dream.

To sort the songs in List view, click the heading of the column by which you want to sort. Click once for an ascending sort (alphabetical order and smaller numbers before larger numbers). Click again for a descending sort (reverse alphabetical order, larger numbers before smaller numbers). The column heading shows an upward-pointing arrow for an ascending sort and a downward-pointing arrow for a descending sort.

The exception is the Album column, which works a little differently:

- Click the column heading (but not the sort arrow) to cycle through the views: Album, Album By Artist, and Album By Year.
- Click the sort arrow to reverse the direction of the sort.

Disclosure triangle for Artwork column

FIGURE 10-2 In List view, you can sort the songs quickly by any column heading. Click the disclosure triangle if you want to display the Artwork column.

You can display a column of artwork at the left side of List view by clicking the disclosure triangle in the upper-left corner or by choosing View | Show Artwork Column.

See Your Songs as Pictures on a Grid

In Grid view, iTunes displays the items as a grid of cover pictures or frames. For example, for songs, you see a grid of album covers (see Figure 10-3), allowing you to browse through your albums quickly by the pictures. You can click the tabs at the top of Grid view to switch among albums, artists, genres, and composers for songs, or among other items for movies, TV shows, and podcasts.

To switch to Grid view, click the Grid View button to the left of the Search box. In Grid view, you can sort by clicking the column headings as described in the previous section.

FIGURE 10-3   Grid view lets you pick an album or other item quickly from its cover art.

Flick Through Your CDs in Cover Flow View

If you've ever had a record collection, you'll remember the joy of browsing through the records by cover, finding the record you wanted by color and picture. (If you haven't done this—finding a record by reading the tiny print on its spine was far less fun.)

Cover Flow view is the iTunes equivalent of that experience—and it's pretty good. In Cover Flow view (see Figure 10-4), iTunes displays a carousel of covers. You can click a cover to move to it or scroll the scroll bar to move in larger jumps.

Full Screen

FIGURE 10-4 In Cover Flow view, you can click the Full Screen button to view your album covers full screen.

Search for Particular Songs or Other Items

Sometimes you may need to search for particular songs. You can also turn up interesting collections of unrelated songs by searching on a word that appears somewhere in the artist name, song name, or album name.

To search all categories of information, type the search text in the Search box. iTunes searches automatically as you type. To constrain the search to artists, albums, composers, or songs, click the drop-down button and make the appropriate choice from the menu, as shown here.

To clear the Search box after searching, click the × button:

Use Playlists, Smart Playlists, and iTunes DJ

Typically, a CD presents its songs in the order the artist or the producer thought best, but often you'll want to rearrange the songs into a different order—or mix the songs from different CDs and files in a way that suits only you. To do so, you create playlists in iTunes, and iTunes automatically shares them with the iPod or iPhone so that you can use them there as well.

You'll probably want to start by creating playlists that contain songs. But playlists can also contain other items, such as TV shows, movies, or podcasts.

You can create playlists manually or use iTunes' Smart Playlist feature to create playlists automatically based on criteria you specify.

Create a Playlist Manually

To create a standard playlist, follow these steps:

1. Click the + button in the Source list, choose File | New Playlist, or press CTRL-N in Windows or ⌘-N on the Mac. iTunes adds a new playlist to the Source list, names it *untitled playlist* (or the next available name, such as *untitled playlist 2*), and displays an edit box around it.
2. Type the name for the playlist, and then press ENTER (Windows) or RETURN (Mac), or click elsewhere, to apply the name.
3. Click the Music item in the Source list to display your songs. If you want to work by artist and album, press CTRL-B (Windows) or ⌘-B (Mac), or choose View | Show Browser, to display the Browser panes.
4. Select the songs you want to add to the playlist and then drag them to the playlist's name. You can drag one song at a time, multiple songs, a whole artist, or a whole CD—whatever you find easiest. You can also drag an existing playlist to the new playlist.
5. Click the playlist's name in the Source list to display the playlist.
6. Drag the songs into the order in which you want them to play.

 For you to be able to drag the songs around in the playlist, the playlist must be sorted by the track-number column. If any other column heading is selected, you won't be able to rearrange the order of the songs in the playlist.

You can also create a playlist by selecting the songs or other items you want to include and then pressing ⌘-SHIFT-N (Mac) or choosing File | New Playlist From Selection. iTunes organizes the songs into a new playlist provisionally named *untitled playlist* and displays an edit box around the title so that you can change it immediately. Type the new name, and then press ENTER (Windows) or RETURN (Mac), or click elsewhere, to apply the name.

To delete a playlist, select it in the Source list and press DELETE (Windows) or BACKSPACE (Mac). Alternatively, right-click the playlist (or CTRL-click it on the Mac) and choose Delete from the shortcut menu. iTunes displays a confirmation dialog box:

Click the Delete button to delete the playlist. If you want to turn off the confirmation for playlists you delete from now on, select the Do Not Ask Me Again check box before clicking the Delete button.

iTunes also offers more complex ways of deleting playlists and their contents:

- If you choose not to turn off confirmation of deleting playlists, you can override confirmation by pressing CTRL-DELETE (Windows) or ⌘-DELETE (Mac) when deleting a playlist.
- On the Mac, to delete a playlist *and the songs it contains* from your library, select the playlist and press OPTION-DELETE. iTunes displays a confirmation dialog box for the deletion, as shown here. Click the Delete button. As before, you can select the Do Not Ask Me Again check box to suppress this confirmation dialog box in the future, but because you're removing song files from your library, it's best not to do so.

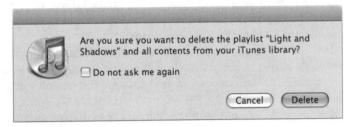

- On the Mac, to delete a playlist and the songs it contains from your library *and* to temporarily suppress the confirmation dialog box while doing so, select the playlist and press ⌘-OPTION-DELETE. iTunes prompts you to decide whether to move the selected songs to the Trash or keep them in the iTunes Music folder, as shown here. Click the Keep Files button or the Move To Trash button as appropriate. If you click the Move To Trash button, iTunes deletes only those songs that are in your iTunes Music folder, not those that are in other folders.

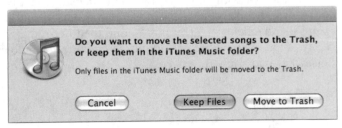

Automatically Create Smart Playlists Based on Your Ratings and Preferences

Smart Playlist is a great feature that lets you instruct iTunes how to build a list of songs automatically for you.

You can tell Smart Playlist to build playlists by artist, composer, or genre; to select up to a specific number of songs at random, by artist, by most played, by last played, or by song name; and to automatically update a playlist as you add tracks to or remove tracks from your library. For example, if you tell Smart Playlist to make you a playlist of songs by The Killers, Smart Playlist can update the list with new Killers tracks after you import them into your library or buy them from the iTunes Store.

By using Smart Playlist's advanced features, you can even specify multiple rules. For example, you might choose to include songs tagged with the genre Gothic Rock but exclude certain artists by name that you didn't want to hear.

 Smart Playlist maintains playlists such as the My Top Rated playlist, the Recently Played playlist, and the Top 25 Most Played playlist, which iTunes creates by default.

Here's how to create a Smart Playlist:

1. Press CTRL-ALT-N (Windows) or ⌘-OPTION-N (Mac), or choose File | New Smart Playlist, to display the Smart Playlist dialog box (see Figure 10-5). On the Mac, you can also OPTION-click the Add button.
2. Make sure the Match The Following Rules check box is selected so that you can specify criteria. (The other option is to create a random Smart Playlist, which can sometimes be entertaining.) If you create multiple rules, this check box offers the choices Match All Of The Following Rules and Match Any Of The Following Rules. Choose the appropriate one.

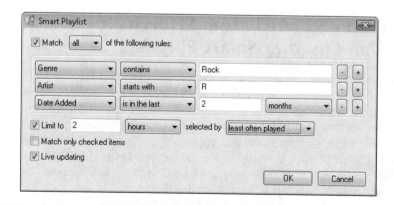

FIGURE 10-5   Smart Playlists are playlists that iTunes automatically populates with songs that match the criteria you specify.

3. Use the controls in the first line to specify the first rule:
   - The first drop-down list offers an extensive range of choices: Album, Album Artist, Album Rating, Artist, Bit Rate, BPM, Category, Comment, Compilation, Composer, Date Added, Date Modified, Description, Disc Number, Genre, Grouping, Kind, Last Played, Last Skipped, Name, Play Count, Playlist, Podcast, Rating, Sample Rate, Season, Show, Size, Skip Count, Sort Album, Sort Album Artist, Sort Artist, Sort Composer, Sort Name, Sort Show, Time, Track Number, Video Kind, and Year.
   - The second drop-down list offers options suitable to the item you chose in the first drop-down list—for example, Contains, Does Not Contain, Is, Is Not, Starts With, or Ends With for a text field, or Is, Is Not, Is Greater Than, Is Less Than, or Is In The Range for the bitrate.
4. To create multiple rules, click the + button at the end of the line. iTunes adds another line of rule controls, which you can then set as described in Step 3. To remove a rule, click the – button at the end of the line.
5. To limit the playlist to a maximum number of tracks, time, or disk space, select the Limit To check box and then specify the limit and how iTunes should select the songs. For example, you could specify Limit To 30 Songs Selected By Least Often Played or Limit To 8 Hours Selected By Random.
6. To make iTunes omit songs whose check boxes you've cleared, select the Match Only Checked Items check box.
7. Select the Live Updating check box if you want iTunes to update the playlist periodically according to your listening patterns. If you prefer not to update the playlist, clear this check box.
8. Click the OK button to close the Smart Playlist dialog box. iTunes creates the playlist, assigns a name to it (for example, *untitled playlist*), and displays an edit box around the name so you can change it.
9. Type the new name for the playlist and then press ENTER (Windows) or RETURN (Mac).

How to... **Use the Playlist Item Effectively When Creating Smart Playlists**

The Playlist item in the first drop-down list in the Smart Playlist dialog box lets you specify a relationship between the Smart Playlist you're creating and an existing playlist (either Smart or regular).

For example, you might specify in a Smart Playlist the criterion "Playlist Is Not Recently Played" to prevent any songs that appear in your Recently Played playlist from appearing in the Smart Playlist. Similarly, you could create a Smart Playlist called, say, "Rock Types" that uses several rules to define all the types of music you consider "rock": Genre Contains Rock, Genre Is Alternative, Genre Contains Gothic, and so on.

You could then use the criterion Playlist Is Rock Types in a Smart Playlist to create a subset of your rock music—for example, 90s rock or rock by artists not named Bryan or Brian.

A Smart Playlist limited by size can be a good way of selecting songs for an iPod or iPhone whose capacity is substantially less than the size of your library. For example, you might create a Smart Playlist with the parameter Limit To 950 MB for loading on an iPod shuffle or with the parameter Limit To 12 GB for an iPhone.

Mix Up Your Music with iTunes DJ

If you like having someone else choose music for you, you may well love iTunes' iTunes DJ feature. iTunes DJ (see Figure 10-6) automatically selects music for you based on four parameters that you specify.

To use iTunes DJ, follow these steps:

1. Click the iTunes DJ item in the Source list.

 If the Source list doesn't include iTunes DJ, press CTRL-COMMA (Windows) to display the iTunes dialog box or ⌘-COMMA (Mac) to display the Preferences dialog box. On the General tab, select the iTunes DJ check box in the Show area, and then click the OK button to close the dialog box.

2. At the bottom of the pane, select the source for iTunes DJ in the Source drop-down list.

FIGURE 10-6   iTunes DJ is like a giant Smart Playlist.

3. Click the Settings button to display the iTunes DJ Settings dialog box (see Figure 10-7).
4. In the Display area, choose how many recently played songs and how many upcoming songs to display. The display of recently played songs lets you see details of a song you didn't recognize—or start it playing again.
5. Select the Play Higher Rated Songs More Often check box if you want iTunes DJ to weight the selection toward songs you've given a higher rating.
6. If you want to let guests control your library from an iPod touch or iPhone:
   - Select the Allow Guests To Request Songs With Remote For iPhone Or iPod Touch check box.
   - Type a welcome message in the Welcome Message text box.
   - Select the Enable Voting check box if you want guests to wrangle over which song plays when.
   - If you want to keep uninvited guests out, select the Require Password check box and type a password in the text box.
7. Click the OK button to close the iTunes DJ Settings dialog box.
8. Click the Play button to start the songs playing.
9. If you don't like the selection, click the Refresh button to display a new selection of songs.

If you find that iTunes DJ dredges up many songs you don't like, you can use it as a means of finding songs for playlists. From the songs that iTunes DJ picks, select those you want to hear, and drag them to a playlist. Click the Refresh button to find more songs, add those you want to hear to the playlist, and repeat the process until you've got a long enough playlist. Then start that playlist playing.

Create Powerful Playlists with iTunes' Genius

iTunes' Genius is a feature with two facets:

- Genius can automatically create a Smart Playlist based on a single song you've chosen. Genius picks the songs from your iTunes library.
- Genius can automatically recommend songs from the iTunes Store that are related to the song you've chosen. The relationship varies from the obvious to the surprisingly tenuous.

Genius's ability to create Smart Playlists is great, and I'd be surprised if you aren't tempted to test it. The disadvantage is sharing the contents of your iTunes library with Apple. But because of the second part of Genius—the recommendations from the iTunes Store—there's no way to use one feature without using the other as well.

Turn On Genius

Before you can create playlists with Genius, you need to turn Genius on and allow it to analyze the songs in your iTunes library so that it knows the material it has to work with.

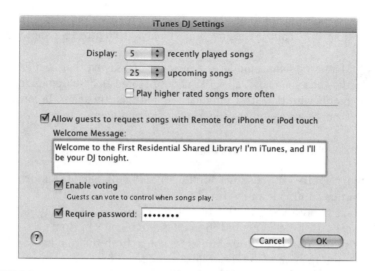

FIGURE 10-7   Use the iTunes DJ setting dialog box to tell iTunes which songs you want and who may control them.

Using Genius involves transmitting the details of the songs in your iTunes library to Apple; without this, the feature can't work as it's designed to work. Apple uses your iTunes Store account to store the data, so you must create an iTunes Store account if you don't already have one. See Chapter 7 for how to create an iTunes Store account.

When you first launch iTunes, it normally displays the Genius Sidebar on the right of the window. At any other time, you can choose Store | Turn On Genius to display the What Is Genius? screen, which includes the Turn On Genius button.

Click the Turn On Genius button, and—if you haven't already used the iTunes Store on this computer—either provide the details of your existing iTunes Store account or sign up for a new account. Genius then transmits the details of your songs to Apple. When it has finished, Genius creates a new playlist called Genius and displays an information screen telling you how to use Genius.

Create a Playlist with Genius

To create a playlist with Genius, simply click the song, and then click the Genius button in the lower-right corner of the iTunes window. You can also right-click the song (or CTRL-click on the Mac) and choose Start Genius from the context menu.

When you're playing a song, you can quickly create a Genius playlist from it. Simply click the Genius icon on the right side of the display panel.

From the songs in your library, Genius creates a playlist with the song you picked as the first song, calls it Genius, and displays it. Figure 10-8 shows an example.

If starting Genius produces a message box saying that "Genius is unavailable" for the song you chose, click OK, choose Store | Update Genius to update your Genius profile with the latest information, and then try again. If you strike out a second time, choose another song as your starting point.

From here, you can customize your Genius playlist as needed:

- **Start again** If the songs don't appeal to you, click the Refresh button to make Genius crank out a new list.
- **Start from a song in the playlist** To create a new playlist based on one of the songs, click the song, and then click the Genius button.
- **Edit the playlist** You can delete songs from the playlist, or drag them up and down it to change the order, just as you can for any other playlist.

FIGURE 10-8 Genius quickly creates a custom playlist for you.

- **Lengthen or shorten the playlist**   Choose a different number of songs from the Limit To drop-down list: 25 Songs, 50 Songs, 75 Songs, or 100 Songs. Genius uses 25 songs at first, but then uses whichever number you last used.
- **Save the playlist**   Click the Save Playlist button to save the playlist under the name of its first song. You can then change the name if you want.

Get Recommendations from Genius

As mentioned above, Genius also displays in its sidebar recommended songs from the iTunes Store based on what you're listening to. Click a Play button next to a song to play a snippet of it, or click the arrow button to display the song in the iTunes Store— or simply ignore the recommendations if you're not interested.

The Genius Sidebar (see Figure 10-9) can be useful for finding related songs or bands, but it can also feel like in-your-face marketing. You can hide the Genius

Show/Hide Genius
Sidebar button

FIGURE 10-9   The Genius Sidebar shows you songs related to the one you're listening to. You can easily turn it off if you don't like it.

Sidebar at any point by clicking the Show/Hide Genius Sidebar button in the lower-right corner of the iTunes window, by choosing View | Hide Genius Sidebar, or by pressing CTRL-SHIFT-G (Windows) or ⌘-SHIFT-G (Mac).

Turn Off Genius

If you tire of Genius, you can turn it off by choosing Store | Turn Off Genius and clicking the Turn Off Genius button in the Are You Sure You Want To Turn Off Genius? dialog box (shown here).

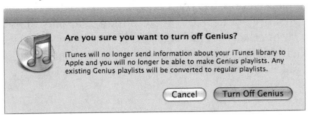

Genius copies your current Genius playlist to a regular playlist. You can then rename it if necessary.

If you need to turn on Genius again, choose Store | Turn On Genius.

Apply Ratings to Items

iTunes' Rating feature lets you assign a rating of no stars to five stars to each item in your library. You can then sort the songs by rating or tell Smart Playlist to add only songs of a certain ranking or better to a playlist. (See "Automatically Create Smart Playlists Based on Your Ratings and Preferences," earlier in this chapter, for a discussion of Smart Playlist.)

You can apply a rating in three ways:

- Select the song in iTunes, and then click in the Rating column to select the number of stars.
- Right-click a song or several selected songs (or CTRL-click on the Mac), choose Rating from the shortcut menu, and then select the appropriate number of stars from the submenu. This technique is useful when you've selected several songs and want to apply the same rating to them.
- Use the Rating box on the Options tab of the Item Information dialog box (press CTRL-I in Windows or ⌘-I on the Mac, or choose Get Info from the File menu or the shortcut menu) to specify the number of stars.

You can also rate a song on any iPod (apart from the iPod shuffle) or on an iPhone:

- **iPod classic or iPod nano** Press the Select button twice from the Now Playing screen while the song is playing, scroll left or right to select the appropriate number of stars, and then press the Select button again.

- **iPhone or iPod touch**   Touch the Information button to display the album information, then touch the star rating you want. Touch the album cover icon to return to the song.

iTunes picks up the rating the next time you synchronize the iPod or iPhone.

Add Artwork to Items

iTunes lets you add artwork to songs and other items, and then display the artwork while the item is playing or is selected.

Most songs or other items you buy from the iTunes Store include artwork—for example, the cover of the single, EP, album, or CD that includes the song, or the cover of a video. And once you've created an account with the iTunes Store, you can have iTunes automatically add art to songs in your library that do not already have art.

Better yet, when you add songs to your library, or when you convert songs in your library to another format, iTunes adds art to the songs from online sources wherever possible.

Set iTunes to Automatically Add Art from the iTunes Store to Songs

To set iTunes to download art from the iTunes Store for songs that do not have art, follow these steps:

1. Click the iTunes Store item in the Source list to access the iTunes Store.
2. If iTunes doesn't automatically sign you in, click the Sign In button, type your name and password in the Sign In dialog box, and then click the Sign In button.
3. Choose Advanced | Get Album Artwork. iTunes displays a confirmation dialog box, as shown here.

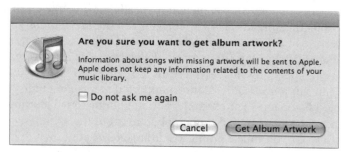

4. Select the Do Not Ask Me Again check box if you want to suppress this confirmation dialog box when you give the command in the future.
5. Click the Get Album Artwork button.

Set iTunes to Automatically Download Missing Album Artwork

To set iTunes to download missing album artwork automatically, follow these steps:

1. Create an account for the iTunes Store, and then sign in to it.
2. Display the iTunes dialog box or the Preferences dialog box:
   - In Windows, choose Edit | Preferences or press CTRL-COMMA or CTRL-Y to display the iTunes dialog box.
   - On the Mac, choose iTunes | Preferences or press ⌘-COMMA or ⌘-Y to display the Preferences dialog box.
3. Click the Store tab to display its contents.
4. Select the Automatically Download Missing Album Artwork check box. iTunes displays a confirmation message box, as shown here.

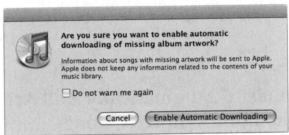

5. Select the Do Not Warn Me Again check box if you want to suppress this confirmation when you turn automatic downloading on in the future.
6. Click the Enable Automatic Downloading button to close the confirmation message box.
7. Click the OK button to close the iTunes dialog box or Preferences dialog box.

Add Artwork to Songs Manually

If iTunes can't find art for a song automatically, or if you want to add another piece of art to a song that already has art, you can add the art manually. You can use either the artwork pane in the iTunes window or the Artwork box in the Item Information dialog box or the Multiple Item Information dialog box. The artwork pane is usually easiest.

You can apply any image you want to a song, provided that it is in a format that QuickTime supports. (QuickTime's supported formats include JPG, GIF, TIFF, PNG, BMP, and PhotoShop.) For example, you might download album art or other pictures from an artist's website and then apply that art to the song files you ripped from the artist's CDs. Or you might prefer to add images of your own to favorite songs or to songs you've composed yourself.

 Amazon.com (www.amazon.com) has cover images for millions of CDs and records. For most music items, you can click the small picture on the item's main page to display a larger version of the image. Another source is Allmusic (www.allmusic .com), a service that requires registration.

Add Artwork to Songs by Using the Artwork Pane

To add an image by using the artwork pane, follow these steps:

1. Open iTunes, and then select the song or songs you want to affect.
2. If the artwork pane isn't displayed (below the Source list), display it by clicking the Show Or Hide Artwork button.
3. If the title bar of the artwork pane says Now Playing, click the title bar to change it to Selected Item.
4. Open a Windows Explorer window or a Finder window to the folder that contains the image you want to use for the artwork, or open a browser window to a URL that contains the image. For example, open an Internet Explorer window to Amazon.com, and then navigate to the image you want.
5. Arrange iTunes and the Windows Explorer window, Finder window, or browser window so that you can see them both.
6. Drag the image to the artwork pane and drop it there.
7. Add further images to the song or songs if you want while you have them selected.

 Most CD cover images are relatively small in dimensions and are compressed, so their file size is fairly small. Adding an image to a song increases its file size a little, but not by a large amount. If you add a large image to a song, iTunes uses a compressed version of the image rather than the full image.

Add Artwork to Songs by Using the Item Information Dialog Box or the Multiple Item Information Dialog Box

Follow these steps to add artwork by using the Item Information dialog box (for a single song) or the Multiple Item Information dialog box:

1. Select the songs, right-click (or CTRL-click on the Mac), and choose Get Info from the shortcut menu to display the dialog box. (You can also choose File | Get Info or press CTRL-I in Windows or ⌘-I on the Mac to display the dialog box.)
2. Display the tab you need:
   - **Item Information dialog box**   Click the Artwork tab.
   - **Multiple Item Information dialog box**   Click the Info tab.
3. Open a Windows Explorer window or a Finder window to the folder that contains the picture you want to use for the artwork, or open a browser window to a URL that contains the picture.
4. Drag the image to the Artwork box in the Multiple Item Information dialog box or the open area on the Artwork tab of the Item Information dialog box.
5. If you're using the Item Information dialog box, add further images as needed. To change the order of the images, drag them about in the open area (see Figure 10-10). You may need to reduce the zoom by dragging the slider to get the pictures small enough to rearrange.

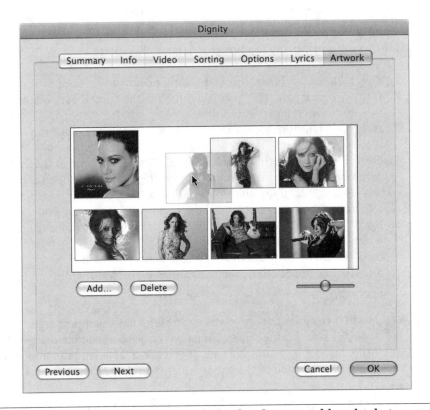

FIGURE 10-10 The Item Information dialog box lets you add multiple images to a song and rearrange them into the order you want.

When you've added two or more pictures to the same song, the artwork pane displays a Previous button and a Next button for browsing from picture to picture.

You can display the current picture at full size by clicking it in the artwork pane. Click the Close button (the × button) to close the artwork window.

 Adding artwork to your songs can be not only esthetic but also practical. For a way of selecting music by cover art that's even neater than iTunes' Cover Flow view, see "Improve the iTunes Interface with Clutter (Mac)" in Chapter 14.

To remove the artwork from a song, right-click (or CTRL-click on the Mac) the song and choose Get Info from the shortcut menu. Click the Artwork tab of the Item Information dialog box, click the picture, and then click the Delete button.

How to... **Copy a Picture from a Song to Other Songs**

You can also paste a picture into the Artwork box or the Artwork tab. For example, if your library already contains one song that has a picture you want to apply to other songs, you can copy the picture from that song, and then paste it into the other songs. Follow these steps:

1. Display the artwork pane if it isn't already displayed. If the artwork pane is showing Now Playing, click its title bar to make it show Selected Item.
2. Click the song that contains the picture you want to use.
3. Right-click (or CTRL-click on the Mac) the picture in the artwork pane, and then choose Copy from the shortcut menu.
4. Select the songs to which you want to apply the picture.
5. Right-click (or CTRL-click on the Mac) in the selection, and then choose Get Info from the shortcut menu to display the Multiple Item Information dialog box.
6. Right-click in the Artwork box, and then choose Paste from the shortcut menu.
7. Click the OK button to close the dialog box.

Consolidate Your Music Library So You Can Always Access All Its Songs

As you saw earlier in this book, you can set iTunes to copy to your iTunes Music folder the file for each song that you add to your library from another folder. Alternatively, you can have iTunes add a reference to the song in its original folder.

Whether iTunes copies the song or simply adds the reference is controlled by the Copy Files To iTunes Music Folder When Adding To Library check box. You'll find this on the Advanced tab in the iTunes dialog box (Windows) or the Preferences dialog box (Mac).

If you add references, when your external drives, network drives, or removable media aren't available, the songs stored on those drives or media won't be available. For example, when you grab your laptop and head over to a friend's house, you'll be able to play only the songs on the laptop's own drive.

 Use the Consolidate command when you want to move your library to another folder.

To make sure you can play the music you want wherever you want, you can *consolidate* your library, making iTunes copy all the files currently outside your library folder to the library folder.

Understand the implications before you consolidate your library:

- Consolidation can take a long time, depending on the number of files to be copied and the speed of the network connection you're using. Don't consolidate your library just as the airport shuttle is about to arrive.
- The drive that holds your library must have enough space free to hold all your files. If lack of space was the reason you didn't copy the files to your music library in the first place, you probably don't want to consolidate your library.
- Files on removable media such as CDs, DVDs, or USB sticks won't be copied unless the medium is in the drive at the time.

To consolidate your library, follow these steps:

1. Choose File | Library | Consolidate Library. iTunes displays the following dialog box:

2. Click the Consolidate button. iTunes displays the Copying Files dialog box as it copies the files to your library.

If consolidation goes wrong, see "Letting iTunes Copy All Song Files to Your Library Runs You Out of Hard-Disk Space" in Chapter 15 for help.

Remove Duplicate Items from Your Library

Even if your library isn't huge, it's easy to get duplicate songs or videos in it, especially if you add folders of existing files as well as rip and encode your CDs and other audio sources. Duplicates waste disk space, particularly on an iPod or iPhone, so iTunes offers a command to help you identify them so that you can remove them.

To remove duplicate items, follow these steps:

1. In the Source list, click the appropriate item in the Library category. For example, to look for duplicate songs, click the Music item. If you want to confine the duplicate-checking to a playlist, click that playlist in the Source list.
2. Choose File | Show Duplicates. iTunes displays a list of duplicate items. Figure 10-11 shows an example on Windows.

FIGURE 10-11 Use the File | Show Duplicates command to display a list of duplicate songs and videos in a playlist or in your library.

Caution iTunes identifies duplicates by artist and name, not by album, length, or other often-useful details. Before deleting any duplicates, check that they're actually duplicates, not just different versions or mixes of the same item.

3. Decide which copy of each item you want to keep. To find out where an item is stored, right-click it (or CTRL-click it on the Mac) and choose Show In Windows Explorer (Windows) or Show In Finder (Mac) from the shortcut menu. You'll see a Windows Explorer window or a Finder window that shows the contents of the folder that includes the file.

Tip If your library contains various file formats, you may find it helpful to display the file type in iTunes so that you can see which item is which format. For example, when you have duplicate song files, you might want to delete the MP3 files rather than the AAC files. Right-click (or CTRL-click on the Mac) the heading of the column after which you want the Kind column to appear, and then select the Kind item from the shortcut menu.

4. To delete an item, select it and press DELETE (Windows) or BACKSPACE (Mac). Click the Remove button in the confirmation dialog box; select the Do Not Ask Me Again check box first if you want to turn off the confirmation.

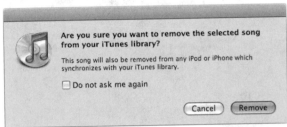

5. If the file is stored in your library folder, iTunes prompts you to move it to the Recycle Bin (Windows) or to the Trash (Mac). Click the Keep File button if you want to keep the file or the Move To Recycle Bin button or Move To Trash button if you want to get rid of it.

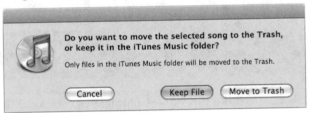

To display all items again, click the Show All button at the bottom of the iTunes window.

Export and Import Playlists

If you create a great playlist, chances are that you'll want to share it with others. You can do so by exporting the playlist so that someone else can import it—provided that they have the items in their library. Follow these steps:

1. Select the playlist in the Source list.
2. Choose File | Library | Export Playlist to display the Save As dialog box (Windows) or the Save dialog box (Mac).
3. Specify the filename for the list, and then choose the folder in which to store it.
4. Choose the format for the file. Windows lets you choose between Text Files and XML Files. Mac OS X lets you choose among Plain Text, Unicode Text, and XML. XML is the best choice for exporting a playlist to another copy of iTunes. When you're exporting a playlist for use with another program, use Text Files or Plain Text instead.
5. Click the Save button to save the playlist.

You can then share the playlist with someone else—for example, by sending it via e-mail.

When you receive a playlist, you can import it by choosing File | Library | Import Playlist, selecting the file in the Import dialog box (change the Files Of Type setting in Windows if necessary), and then clicking the Open button. iTunes checks the playlist against your library and creates a playlist that contains as many of the items as you have available. If one or more items are unavailable, iTunes warns you, as shown here.

Export Your Library

You can export the details of your entire library and all your playlists as a backup in case your computer suffers data loss or damage. To export the library, choose File | Library | Export Library, specify the name and folder in the Save As dialog box (Windows) or the Save dialog box (Mac), and then click the Save button.

As well as your playlists, your exported library contains details of your play count, ratings, equalizations, and other item-specific settings you've applied, such as start times and stop times.

Use Multiple Libraries on the Same Computer

Normally, you put all your songs, videos, and other items into a single iTunes library. This has several advantages, including simplicity and having all of your media items instantly accessible from iTunes.

However, in some cases you may want to create different libraries for different categories of items. For example, you can have a family library containing songs that are safe for the kids, and an adult library that contains explicit material. Or you can have a library that contains only the songs on your laptop, plus a library that contains all those songs and those that appear on your removable drives or network drives.

You already have the standard library that iTunes has created for you, so your first step is to create a new library.

Create a New Library

To create a new library, follow these steps:

1. If iTunes is running, close it. For example, press ALT-F4 (Windows) or ⌘-Q (Mac).
2. Start iTunes using the special command for changing libraries:
   - **Windows** Hold down SHIFT while you click the iTunes icon. For example, click the Start button, click All Programs, click the iTunes folder, and then SHIFT-click the iTunes icon. Keep holding down SHIFT until the Choose iTunes Library dialog box appears.

- **Mac** Hold down OPTION while you click the iTunes icon—for example, in the Dock. Keep holding down OPTION until the Choose iTunes Library dialog box appears.

3. iTunes displays the Choose iTunes Library dialog box. The next illustration shows the Windows version of this dialog box.

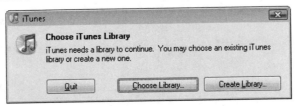

4. Click the Create Library button. iTunes displays the New iTunes Library dialog box. The next illustration shows the Windows version of this dialog box.

5. Type the name for the new library folder, choose the folder in which to store it, and then click the Save button. iTunes closes the New iTunes Library dialog box, creates the new library, and then opens itself, showing the contents of the new library.
6. Add songs and other items to the library using the techniques you learned in Chapter 9.

Switch to Another Library

When you start iTunes normally, the program loads the library you used last time. To switch from one library to another, follow these steps:

1. If iTunes is running, close it. For example, press ALT-F4 (Windows) or ⌘-Q (Mac).
2. Start iTunes using the special command for changing libraries:
   - **Windows** Hold down SHIFT while you click the iTunes icon. For example, click the Start button, click All Programs, click the iTunes folder, and then

SHIFT-click the iTunes icon. Again, keep holding down SHIFT until the Choose iTunes Library dialog box appears.

- **Mac** Hold down OPTION while you click the iTunes icon—for example, in the Dock. As before, keep holding down OPTION until the Choose iTunes Library dialog box appears.

3. iTunes displays the Choose iTunes Library dialog box.

4. Click the Choose Library button. iTunes displays the Open iTunes Library dialog box. The next illustration shows the Windows version of this dialog box.

5. Open the folder in which you stored the library, select the iTunes Library.itl file, and then click the Open button.

6. iTunes opens, showing the contents of the library you selected.

Share Items and Access Shared Items

Listening to your own music collection is great, but it's often even better to be able to share your music with your friends or family—and to enjoy as much of their music as you can stand. iTunes provides features for sharing your music with other iTunes users on your network and for playing the music they're sharing. You may also want to share music with other users of your computer—which, interestingly, requires a little more effort. Similarly, you may want to share other file types that iTunes supports.

Share Your Library with Other Local iTunes Users

You can share either your entire library or selected playlists with other users on your network. You can share most items, including MP3 files, AAC files, Apple Lossless Encoding files, AIFF files, WAV files, and links to radio stations. You can't share Audible files or QuickTime sound files.

Technically, iTunes' sharing is limited to computers on the same TCP/IP subnet as your computer is on. (A *subnet* is a logical division of a network.) If your computer connects to a medium-sized network, and you're unable to find a computer that you know is connected to the same network somewhere, it may be on a different subnet.

At this writing, you can share your library with up to five other computers per day, and your computer can be one of up to five computers accessing the shared library on another computer on any given day. (The sharing privileges used to be more generous: five concurrent computers at any time. See the sidebar "Apple May Change the Details of Library Sharing" for details.)

Did You Know?

Apple May Change the Details of Library Sharing

If you read through the license agreements for iTunes and the iTunes Store, you'll notice that Apple reserves the right to change the details of what you can and can't do with iTunes and the files you buy. This isn't unusual, but it's worth taking a moment to consider.

At this writing, Apple has made several changes. Some changes are no big deal. For example, Apple has reduced the number of times you can burn an individual playlist to CD from ten times to seven times. (You can create another playlist with the same songs and burn that seven times too, and then create another.)

More of a big deal are the changes Apple has made to sharing songs and other files on the network. When Apple first added sharing to iTunes, it could share songs not only on the computer's local network but also across the Internet. Apple quickly reduced this to the local network only, which seemed fair enough. iTunes could share music with five other computers at a time—enough to reach a good number of people, especially in a dorm situation with many people sharing music and listening to shared music.

Since then, Apple reduced the sharing from five computers at a time to five computers *per day* total. This still works fine for most homes, but on bigger networks, it's very restrictive. Once a computer has shared library items with its five computers for the day, you'll see one of the messages shown here if you try to connect.

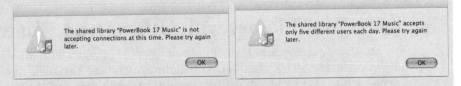

All the changes so far have been restrictive and have benefited the media providers (such as the record companies) rather than iTunes users. Further changes seem likely, so if iTunes doesn't behave as described here, check the latest license agreement on the Apple website.

The shared library remains on the computer that's sharing it, and when a participating computer goes to play a song or other item, that item is streamed across the network. This means that the item isn't copied from the computer that's sharing it to the computer that's playing it in a way that leaves a usable file on the playing computer.

When a computer goes offline or is shut down, library items it has been sharing stop being available to other users. Participating computers can play the shared items but can't do anything else with them; for example, they can't burn shared songs to CD or DVD, download them to an iPod or iPhone, or copy them to their own libraries.

To share some or all of your library, follow these steps:

1. Display the iTunes dialog box or the Preferences dialog box:
   - In Windows, choose Edit | Preferences or press CTRL-COMMA or CTRL-Y to display the iTunes dialog box.
   - On the Mac, choose iTunes | Preferences or press ⌘-COMMA or ⌘-Y to display the Preferences dialog box.
2. Click the Sharing tab to display it. Figure 10-12 shows the Sharing tab of the iTunes dialog box with settings chosen.
3. Select the Share My Library On My Local Network check box. (This check box is cleared by default.) By default, iTunes then selects the Share Entire Library option button. If you want to share only some playlists, select the Share Selected Playlists option button, and then select the check boxes in the list box for the playlists you want to share.

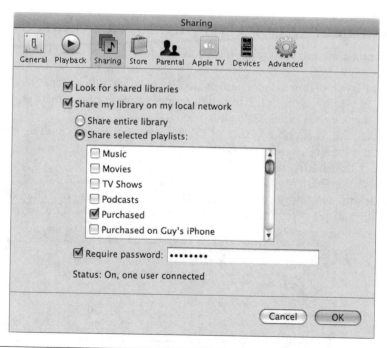

FIGURE 10-12   On the Sharing tab of the iTunes dialog box or the Preferences dialog box, choose whether to look for shared libraries and whether to share part or all of your library.

4. By default, your shared library items are available to any other user on the network. To restrict access to people with whom you share a password, select the Require Password check box, and then enter a strong (unguessable) password in the text box.

> If there are many computers on your network, use a password on your shared music to help avoid running up against the five-users-per-day limit. If your network has only a few computers, you may not need a password to avoid reaching this limit.

5. Click the General tab to display its contents. In the Shared Name text box near the bottom of the dialog box, set the name that other users trying to access your library will see. The default name is *username*'s Library, where *username* is your username—for example, Anna Connor's Library. You might choose to enter a more descriptive name, especially if your computer is part of a well-populated network (for example, in a dorm).
6. Click the OK button to apply your choices and close the dialog box.

> When you set iTunes to share your library, iTunes displays a message reminding you that "Sharing music is for personal use only"—in other words, remember not to violate copyright law. Select the Do Not Show This Message Again check box if you want to prevent this message from appearing again.

Disconnect Other Users from Your Shared Library

To disconnect other users from your shared library, follow these steps:

1. Display the iTunes dialog box or the Preferences dialog box:
   - In Windows, choose Edit | Preferences or press CTRL-COMMA or CTRL-Y to display the iTunes dialog box.
   - On the Mac, choose iTunes | Preferences or press ⌘-COMMA or ⌘-Y to display the Preferences dialog box.
2. Click the Sharing tab to display it.
3. Clear the Share My Library On My Local Network check box.
4. Click the OK button. If any other user is connected to your shared library, iTunes displays this message box to warn you:

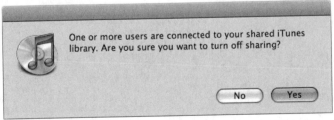

5. Click the Yes button or the No button, as appropriate. If you click the Yes button, anyone playing an item from the library will be cut off abruptly without notice.

Access and Play Another Local iTunes User's Shared Library

To access another person's shared library, you must first set your computer to look for shared libraries. You may already have done so when you turned on sharing on your own computer.

Set Your Computer to Look for Shared Libraries

First, set your computer to look for shared libraries. Follow these steps:

1. Display the iTunes dialog box or the Preferences dialog box:
   - In Windows, choose Edit | Preferences or press CTRL-COMMA or CTRL-Y to display the iTunes dialog box.
   - On the Mac, choose iTunes | Preferences or press ⌘-COMMA or ⌘-Y to display the Preferences dialog box.
2. Click the Sharing tab to display its contents.
3. Select the Look For Shared Libraries check box.
4. Click the OK button to close the dialog box.

Access Shared Libraries on Your Local Network

Once you've selected the Look For Shared Libraries check box on the Sharing tab of the iTunes dialog box or the Preferences dialog box, iTunes automatically detects shared libraries when you launch the program while your computer is connected to a network. If iTunes finds shared libraries or playlists, it displays them in the Source list. Click a shared library to display its contents. Figure 10-13 shows an example of browsing the music shared by another computer.

If a shared library has a password, iTunes displays the Shared Library Password dialog box.

Type the password, and then click the OK button to access the library. Select the Remember Password check box before clicking the OK button if you want iTunes to save the password to speed up future access to the library.

 Double-click the entry for a shared library in the Source list to open a separate window that shows its contents.

Disconnect a Shared Library

To disconnect a shared library you've connected to, take one of these actions:

- Click the Eject icon next to the library in the Source list.
- Click the library in the Source list, and then press CTRL-E (Windows) or ⌘-E (Mac).

FIGURE 10-13 Computers sharing libraries appear in the iTunes Source list, allowing you to quickly browse the songs and other items that are being shared.

- Click the library in the Source list, and then choose Controls | Disconnect *Library* from the shortcut menu (where *Library* is the name of the shared library).
- Right-click the library in the Source list (or CTRL-click on the Mac), and then choose Disconnect from the shortcut menu.

Share Your Music More Effectively with Other Local Users

As you saw in the previous section, iTunes makes it easy for you to share either your music library or specific playlists with other iTunes users on your local area network (LAN). You can share with up to five different computers per day, and of course your computer must be attached to the network and powered on for them to be able to access your music.

You may also want to share your music with other users of your computer. The security features built into Windows Vista, Windows XP, and Mac OS X mean that you have to do a little work to share it.

This section focuses on music files, but you can use the same approach for other media files—for example, video files.

Share Your Library with Other Users of Your PC

Windows automatically prevents other users from accessing your personal files, assigning each user a user account and keeping them out of other users' accounts. The result of this is that your iTunes library, which is stored by default in your Music\iTunes\iTunes Music folder on Windows Vista or the My Music\iTunes\iTunes Music folder on Windows XP, is securely protected from other users of your computer. That's great if you want to keep your music to yourself, but not so great if you want to share it with your friends, family, or coworkers.

 Windows Media Player, the audio and video player that Microsoft includes with Windows at this writing, gets around this restriction by making the music and video files that any user adds to their music library available to all users. This is great if you want to share all your files but less appealing if you want to keep some of them private.

The easiest way to give other users access to your library is to move it to the Public Music folder (on Windows Vista) or the Shared Music folder (on Windows XP). This is a folder created automatically when Windows is installed, and which Windows automatically shares with other users of your computer but not with other computers on the network.

Here's where to find this folder:

- **Windows Vista**   The Public Music folder is located in the Public folder.
- **Windows XP**   The Shared Music folder is located in the \Documents and Settings\All Users\Documents\My Music folder.

Alternatively, you can put the library in another shared folder. This example uses the Public Music folder on Windows Vista and the Shared Music folder in Windows XP. If you're using another folder, substitute it where appropriate.

Moving your library to the Public Music folder or the Shared Music folder involves two steps: moving the files, and then telling iTunes where you've moved them to.

To move your library files to the Public Music folder or the Shared Music folder, follow these steps:

1. Close iTunes if it's running. (For example, press ALT-F4 or choose File | Exit.)
2. Open your library folder:
   - **Windows Vista**   Choose Start | Music to open a Windows Explorer window showing your Music folder.
   - **Windows XP**   Choose Start | My Music to open a Windows Explorer window showing your My Music folder.
3. Double-click the iTunes folder to open it. You'll see an iTunes Music Library.xml file, an iTunes Music Library.itl file, and an iTunes Music folder. The first two files must stay in your library folder. If you remove them, iTunes won't be able to find your library, and it will create these files again from scratch.

4. Right-click the iTunes Music folder, and then choose Cut from the shortcut menu to cut it to the Clipboard.

5. Open the Public Music folder or the Shared Music folder:
   - **Windows Vista** In the Music folder, double-click the shortcut to the Sample Music folder. The Sample Music folder is in the Public Music folder. In the Address bar, click the Public Music item to display the folder's contents.
   - **Windows XP** In the Other Places task pane, click the Shared Music link to display the Shared Music folder. (If the Shared Music folder doesn't appear in the Other Places task pane, click the My Computer link, click the Shared Documents link, and then double-click the Shared Music folder.)

6. Right-click an open space in the Public Music folder or the Shared Music folder, and then choose Paste from the shortcut menu to paste the iTunes Music folder into the folder.

7. Close the Windows Explorer window. (For example, press ALT-F4 or choose File | Close.)

Next, you need to tell iTunes where the song files and other media files are. Follow these steps:

1. Start iTunes. (For example, double-click the iTunes icon on your desktop.)
2. Press CTRL-COMMA or choose Edit | Preferences to display the iTunes dialog box.
3. Click the Advanced tab to display its contents.
4. Click the Change button to display the Browse For Folder dialog box.
5. Navigate to the Public Music folder or the Shared Music folder, and then click the OK button to close the Browse For Folder dialog box.
6. Click the OK button to close the iTunes dialog box.

After you've done this, iTunes knows where the files are, and you can play them back as usual. When you rip further song files from CD or import files, iTunes stores them in the Public Music folder or Shared Music folder.

You're all set. The other users of your PC can do either of two things:

- Move their library to the Public Music folder or Shared Music folder, using the techniques described here, so that all files are stored centrally. Instead of moving the library folder itself, move the folders it contains. Users can then add songs they import to the shared library, and all users can access them.
- Keep their library separate, but add the contents of the shared library folder to it. Here's how:
  1. Choose File | Add Folder To Library to display the Browse For Folder dialog box.
  2. Navigate to the Public Music folder or Shared Music folder.
  3. Select the iTunes Music folder.
  4. Click the Open button. iTunes adds all the latest songs to your library.

Whichever approach the other users of your PC choose, the songs that they add to the shared library don't appear automatically in your library. To add all the latest tracks, use the Add Folder To Library command, as described in the previous list.

Share Your Library with Other Users of Your Mac

Mac OS X's security system prevents other users from accessing your Home folder or its contents—which by default includes your library. So if you want to share your library with other users of your Mac, you need to change permissions to allow others to access your Home folder (or parts of it) or move your library to a folder they can access.

The easiest way to give other users access to your songs and other items is to put your library in the Users/Shared folder and put an alias to it in its default location. To do so, follow these steps:

1. Use the Finder to move the iTunes Music folder from your ~/Music/iTunes folder to the /Users/Shared folder.
2. Press ⌘-COMMA (or ⌘-Y) or choose iTunes | Preferences to display the Preferences dialog box.
3. Click the Advanced button to display the Advanced tab.
4. Click the Change button, and then use the resulting Change Music Folder Location dialog box to navigate to and select the /Users/Shared/iTunes Music folder.
5. Click the Choose button to close the Change Music Folder Location dialog box and enter the new path in the iTunes Music Folder Location text box on the Advanced tab.
6. Make sure the Keep iTunes Music Folder Organized check box is selected.
7. Click the OK button to close the Preferences dialog box.

If you want other users to be able to put song files in the shared library (for example, if they import songs from CD), you need to give them Write permission for it. To do so, follow these steps:

1. Open a Finder window to the /Users/Shared folder.
2. CTRL-click or right-click the iTunes Music folder, and then choose Get Info from the shortcut menu to display the iTunes Music Info window, shown here.
3. In the Ownership & Permissions area, click the Details arrow to expand its display, if necessary.
4. In the Others drop-down list, select the Read & Write item instead of the Read Only item.

5. Click the Apply To Enclosed Items button. Mac OS X displays this dialog box:

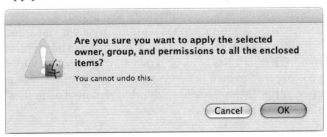

6. Click the OK button.
7. Click the Close button (the × button) to close the Info window for the library folder.

After you move your library to the /Users/Shared folder, the other users of your Mac can do one of two things:

- Move their library to the /Users/Shared folder, using the technique described here, so that all files are stored centrally. Users can then add songs they import to the shared library, and all users can access them.
- Keep their library separate, but add the contents of the shared library folder to it. Here's how:
  1. Press ⌘-O or choose File | Add To Library to display the Add To Library dialog box.
  2. Navigate to the /Users/Shared/iTunes Music folder.
  3. Click the Choose button. iTunes adds all the latest songs to the library.

Whichever approach the other users of your Mac choose, the songs that they add to the shared library don't appear automatically in your library. To add all the latest tracks, use the Add To Library dialog box, as described in the previous list.

Build a Media Server for Your Household

If you find that trying to play songs stored in libraries that keep disappearing off the network is too tedious, another option is to build a media server for your household. You can either build a server from scratch on a new computer or change the role of one of your existing computers—even a pensioned-off computer that's too old to run Mac OS X or Windows Vista or XP at a decent speed.

Whether you buy (or build) a new computer or repurpose an existing computer will color your choices for your server. Here are notes on the key components for the server:

- **Operating system**   The server can run Windows or Mac OS X if you have a copy that you can spare; if not, you might consider using a less expensive (or even free) operating system, such as one of the many distributions of Linux.
- **Processor**   The server can run on a modest processor—even an antiquated one by today's standards, such as a 500-MHz or faster processor for a Windows or Linux server or a slower G3 processor for a Mac server.

- **RAM**   The server needs only enough RAM to run the operating system unless you'll need to run applications on it. For example, 256MB of RAM is adequate for a server running Windows XP or an older version of Mac OS X. Windows Vista requires 512MB or (preferably) 1GB.
- **Disk space**   The server must have enough disk space to store all the songs and other files you want to have available. A desktop computer is likely to be a better bet than a notebook computer, because you can add internal drives to it. Alternatively, you might use one or more external USB or FireWire drives to provide plenty of space.
- **Network connection**   The server must be connected to your network, either via network cable or via wireless. A wireless connection is adequate for serving a few computers, but in most cases, a wired connection (Fast Ethernet or Gigabit Ethernet) is a much better choice.
- **Monitor**   If the server will simply be running somewhere convenient (rather than being used for other computing tasks, such as running applications), all you need is an old monitor capable of displaying the bootup and login screens for the operating system. After that, you can turn the monitor off until you need to restart or configure the server.
- **Keyboard and mouse**   Like the monitor, the keyboard and mouse can be basic devices, because you'll need to use them only for booting and configuring the server.
- **CD-ROM drive**   Your server needs a CD-ROM drive only if you'll use it for ripping. If you'll rip on the clients, the server can get by without one.
- **Sound card**   Your server needs a sound card only if you'll use it for playing music or other media files.
- **Reliability**   Modest your server may be, but it must be reliable—otherwise the music won't be available when you want to play it. Make sure also that the server has plenty of cooling, and configure its power settings so that it doesn't go to sleep.
- **Location**   If you choose to leave your server running all the time, locate it somewhere safe from being switched off accidentally. Because the running server will probably make some noise, you may be tempted to hide it away in a closet. If you do, make sure there's enough ventilation so that it doesn't overheat.

To set up the server, follow these general steps. The specifics will depend on which operating system you're using for the server.

1. Create a folder that will contain the songs.
2. Share that folder on the network so that all the users you want to be able to play music are allowed to access it.
3. On each of the client computers, move the library into the shared folder.

Enjoy Podcasts

A *podcast* is a downloadable show that you can play in iTunes or transfer to an iPod or iPhone. Some podcasts are downloadable versions of professional broadcast radio shows, while others are put together by enthusiasts.

Apple makes a wide selection of podcasts available through the iTunes Store, so getting started listening to podcasts or watching video podcasts is easy. You can also find many more podcasts on the Internet.

Configure Podcast Settings

Before you start working with podcasts, you should configure podcast preferences. These preferences cover how iTunes handles podcasts and which podcasts are synchronized with the iPod or iPhone. To control how iTunes handles podcasts, follow these steps:

1. Click the Podcasts item in the Source list to display the Podcasts screen (see Figure 10-14).
2. Click the Settings button to display the Podcast Settings dialog box (see Figure 10-15).

FIGURE 10-14 Click the Settings button on the Podcasts screen to choose your podcast settings.

FIGURE 10-15   Choose podcast settings in the Podcast Settings dialog box.

3. In the Check For New Episodes drop-down list, choose the appropriate frequency: Every Hour, Every Day, Every Week, or Manually. This setting applies to all the podcasts to which you subscribe.
4. In the Settings For drop-down list, pick the podcast for which you want to choose custom settings. (You can't do this until you've subscribed to a podcast, so you may want to come back to these settings later.)
5. If you want to use iTunes' default settings for the podcast, select the Use Default Settings check box. These settings are to download the most recent episode available and to keep all episodes of podcasts rather than jettisoning older ones that have passed their use-by dates.
6. In the When New Episodes Are Available drop-down list, choose what to do: Download All, Download The Most Recent One, or Do Nothing.
7. In the Keep drop-down list, choose which episodes of the podcasts to keep: All Episodes, All Unplayed Episodes, Most Recent Episodes, or the last 2, 3, 4, 5, or 10 episodes.
8. Click the OK button to close the dialog box.

Once you've set up iTunes to handle podcasts, tell the iPod or iPhone which podcasts you want to synchronize. Follow these steps:

1. Connect the iPod or iPhone to your computer if it's not already connected.
2. Click the iPod's or iPhone's entry in the Source list to display its contents.
3. Click the Podcasts tab to display that tab's contents (see Figure 10-16).
4. To synchronize podcasts automatically, select the Sync check box, and then choose which episodes in the drop-down list: All; 1, 3, 5, or 10 Most Recent; All Unplayed; 1, 3, 5, or 10 Most Recent Unplayed; All New; or 1, 3, 5, or 10 Most Recent New.

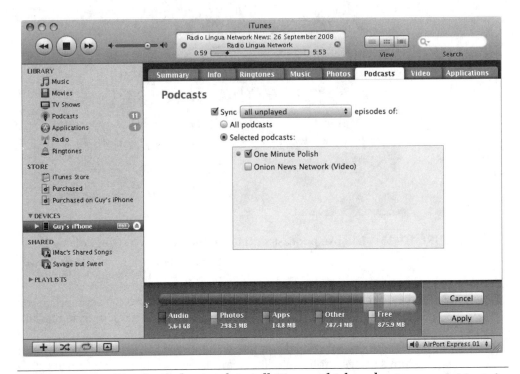

FIGURE 10-16   Use the Podcasts tab to tell iTunes which podcasts you want to put on the iPod or iPhone.

5. Choose which podcasts to synchronize by selecting either the All Podcasts option button or the Selected Podcasts option button (and then selecting the check box for each podcast that you want to have updated).
6. Click the Apply button to apply the changes. iTunes synchronizes the podcasts with the iPod or iPhone.

Explore Podcasts on the iTunes Store

To explore podcasts on the iTunes Store, click the iTunes Store item in the Source list, and then click the Podcasts link in the iTunes Store box on the home page. iTunes displays the Podcasts page (see Figure 10-17).

From here, you can follow the links to the various podcasts. When you find a podcast that interests you, you can either click the Get Episode button to download a particular episode or click the Subscribe button to subscribe to the podcast. When you click the Subscribe button, iTunes displays a confirmation dialog box, as shown

FIGURE 10-17   You can find a wide variety of podcasts on the Podcasts page of the iTunes Store.

here. Select the Do Not Ask About Subscribing Again check box if you want to suppress confirmation in the future, and then click the Subscribe button to proceed with the subscription.

Add Podcasts from the Internet

If the range of podcasts available on the iTunes Store doesn't sate your appetite, you can find many other podcasts on the Internet. To add a podcast whose URL you know, choose Advanced | Subscribe To Podcast to display the Subscribe To Podcast dialog box (shown here), type or paste the URL of the podcast, and then click the OK button.

Listen to Podcasts

To listen to the podcasts that you've subscribed to, click the Podcasts item in the Source list to display your podcasts. You can choose different views by clicking the Podcasts tab, Categories tab, or New tab at the top of the Podcasts screens.

To play the latest episode of a podcast, hover the mouse pointer over it for a moment, and then click the Play Selected button that appears.

To play a particular episode, double-click the podcast that you want to open, and then double-click the episode.

You can then control the podcast by using the iTunes play controls as usual. From here, you can unsubscribe from a podcast by selecting it and clicking the Unsubscribe button. When you do so, iTunes adds a Subscribe button to the podcast, so that you can easily subscribe to it again if you choose.

To play a podcast on the iPod, choose the Podcasts item on the Music menu; on the iPhone, go to the iPod, touch the More button, and then touch the Podcasts item. Select the podcast you want to play, and then use the device's play controls as usual.

If you want to create your own podcasts, you can find plenty of suitable software online—but you may already have all you need if you have a Mac. GarageBand, the music-composition tool that comes as part of the iLife suite, is quite capable of creating podcasts. Use the File | Export To iTunes command to export the resulting file to iTunes, select it in iTunes, and then use the Advanced | Convert Selection To command to convert it to the format in which you want to distribute it (for example, AAC using the Podcast quality).

PART III

Learn Advanced Techniques and Tricks

11

Use Multiple iPods or iPhones, Multiple Computers, or Both

HOW TO...

- Move an iPod classic or iPod nano from Windows to the Mac or from the Mac to Windows
- Move an iPhone or iPod touch from Windows to the Mac or from the Mac to Windows
- Change the computer to which an iPod or iPhone is linked
- Synchronize several iPods or iPhones with the same computer
- Load an iPod from two or more computers

This chapter starts by walking you through the processes of moving an iPod classic or iPod nano from a Mac to a PC, and vice versa. After that, it shows you how to do the same with an iPhone or an iPod touch, as these devices behave differently. Then it shows you how to change the computer to which an iPod or iPhone is linked—a useful skill when you upgrade your computer.

The chapter explains the nuances of synchronizing several iPods or iPhones with the same computer, and it walks you through loading an iPod from two or more computers at the same time. At this writing, you can synchronize the iPhone only with one computer at a time. However, you can load nonmedia items—such as contacts—on the iPhone from different computers if necessary.

Move an iPod from the Mac to Windows—and Back

Ideally, you'd be able to plug your iPod into any computer—PC or Mac—and simply load media files onto it or copy them from it. But there are three complications:

- Apple has designed the iPod to synchronize only with a single computer at a time. So when you connect the iPod to another computer, you need to decide whether to switch the iPod's synchronization to that computer.
- For copyright reasons, iTunes doesn't let you copy music and video files from the iPod to a computer. (Chapter 13 shows you ways to work around this limitation—for example, to recover your iTunes library after your computer crashes.)
- The iPod classic and iPod nano use a different file system when used with Macs than when used with Windows. (See the sidebar "Which File System Does Your iPod Use" for details.) As a result, you may have to "restore" the iPod's software when moving it between a PC and a Mac.

Did You Know?

Which File System Does Your iPod Use?

The iPod classic and the iPod nano ship with their disks or memory partitioned using the Mac OS Extended file system. When you connect a new iPod classic or iPod nano to a Windows PC, iTunes on the PC detects that the iPod needs to be reformatted, and it reformats the iPod using the FAT32 file system without notifying you. If the iPod contains files, iTunes warns you before reformatting the iPod. More on this topic later in this chapter.

The Mac OS Extended file system works better for the Mac than FAT32 does, but Windows can't read Mac OS Extended; so the iPod uses FAT32 for Windows instead. FAT32 works with Mac OS X as well as with Windows, so once you've formatted an iPod for Windows, you don't necessarily need to reformat it if you need to use it with a Mac again.

All three generations of the iPod shuffle use the FAT32 file system for both Windows and the Mac, so there's no need to convert an iPod shuffle from one format to another.

The iPhone performs some tricks to stop you from accessing its contents directly via a file-management program (such as Windows Explorer or the Finder) rather than through iTunes. To Windows, the iPhone's accessible storage uses the Design Rule for Camera File System (DCF). To Mac OS X, all the iPhone's storage appears to be inaccessible. You do not need to reformat an iPhone when moving it between Windows and the Mac or vice versa.

Like the iPhone, the iPod touch makes its storage inaccessible to programs other than iTunes. Unlike the iPhone, however, the iPod touch doesn't have a camera, so it doesn't need to make even part of its file system available to Windows Explorer.

If you reformat an iPod, you'll lose all its contents—every file you've stored on it. If the iPod contains valuable files, back them up to your PC or Mac before reformatting the iPod.

Move an iPod from the Mac to Windows

If you've used an iPod classic or iPod nano only with a Mac, and you move it to Windows, you must reformat the hard disk or flash memory. This permanently removes all the contents of the iPod. Follow the procedure described in the upcoming section "Move a Mac-Formatted iPod to Windows."

If you've used an iPod classic or iPod nano with Windows, and then moved it to the Mac without reformatting it, and you then move it back to Windows, you won't need to reformat the iPod. Follow the procedure described in "Move a FAT32-Formatted iPod from the Mac Back to Windows."

If you have an iPod shuffle or iPod touch, it is formatted with FAT32, so use the procedure described in "Move a FAT32-Formatted iPod from the Mac Back to Windows," even if you've been using the iPod only with a Mac.

Move a Mac-Formatted iPod to Windows

To move an iPod from the Mac to Windows, follow these steps:

1. Make sure the PC has iTunes installed—preferably the latest version:
   - If the PC doesn't have iTunes installed, download the latest version from www.apple.com/itunes/download/ and install it.
   - If the PC does have iTunes installed, choose Help | Check For Updates to see if a newer version of iTunes is available.
2. If nobody has used iTunes on that computer, run iTunes and complete the iTunes Setup Assistant. Close iTunes again.
3. Connect the iPod to the PC. If the iPod is formatted with the Mac OS Extended file system, the iPod Software tells you that it needs to be reformatted, as shown here. If so, follow Steps 4 and 5. Otherwise, go to Step 6.
4. Click the OK button to launch iTunes. iTunes tells you that the iPod is Mac-formatted, as shown here.

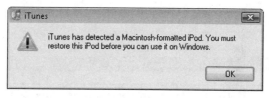

5. Click the OK button to close the message box.

6. Click the Restore button on the Summary tab of the iPod's control screen to format the iPod using the FAT32 file system and to reinstall the iPod firmware on it. iTunes displays a confirmation message box, as shown here, to make sure you know that all items and data will be erased.

7. Click the Restore button, and then allow the restore process to continue. iTunes downloads the latest version of the iPod Software if necessary, and then installs the software. During the process, iTunes displays for 10 seconds the informational message box shown here. Either click the OK button to dismiss the message box, or allow the countdown to complete, after which iTunes closes the message box automatically.

8. iTunes displays the Set Up Your iPod screen (see Figure 11-1). Type the name you want to give the iPod, decide whether to sync songs and photos with the iPod automatically (and if so, choose the source or folder for the photos), and then click the Done button. The first time you set up an iPod, you can also choose whether to register it.

FIGURE 11-1 In the Set Up Your iPod screen, specify the name for the iPod, and choose whether to sync songs, videos, and photos with it.

9. If you choose to sync songs and videos to the iPod automatically, and the iPod doesn't have enough space to contain them all, iTunes lets you know of the problem, as shown here. Click the Yes button if you want iTunes to create a playlist for the iPod. Click the No button if you want to choose songs for the iPod yourself.

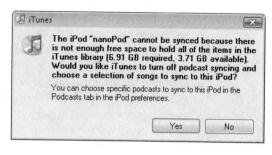

10. When the restore operation (and synchronization, if you chose that option) has completed, the iPod appears in the Devices list with the name you gave it and its full set of control screens. Figure 11-2 shows an example.

Move a FAT32-Formatted iPod from the Mac Back to Windows

If an iPod is formatted with FAT32, you can move it freely between Windows and the Mac. The iPod will be formatted with FAT32 if you have formatted it on Windows using the iPod Updater. If you've then moved the iPod back to the Mac without

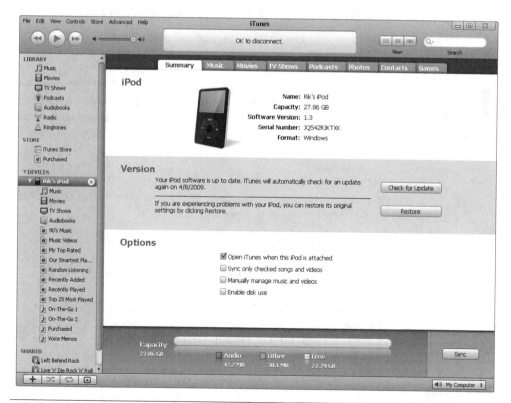

FIGURE 11-2 The iPod appears in the Devices list with its full set of control screens when the restore operation is complete.

reformatting it, the iPod will still be formatted with FAT32 rather than the Mac OS Extended file system. The same applies if the iPod is an iPod shuffle or an iPod touch, because these iPods use only the FAT32 file system.

To move a FAT32-formatted iPod from the Mac back to Windows:

1. Connect the iPod to the PC. iTunes detects the iPod and displays the dialog box shown here, warning you that the iPod is linked to another library and asking if you want to change the link and replace all its contents.

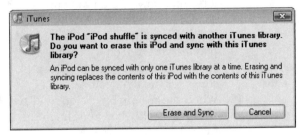

2. Click the Erase And Sync button to associate the iPod with the Windows library and overwrite the Mac library.

Wait while iTunes associates the iPod with the Windows library and then syncs the songs, videos, and other items with the iPod.

Move an iPod from Windows to the Mac

To move an iPod from Windows to the Mac, follow these steps:

1. For best results, update iTunes to the latest version available.

The easiest way to check that iTunes is up to date is to choose Apple | Software Update to check for updates. If Software Update identifies any iTunes updates, or other updates that your Mac requires, install them before moving the iPod to your Mac.

2. Connect the iPod to the Mac. When iTunes detects the iPod, it displays a dialog box such as that shown here, pointing out that the iPod is linked to a different library and asking if you want to replace that library.

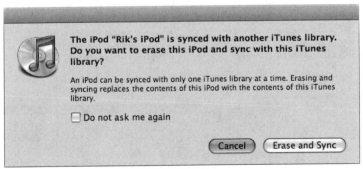

3. Click the Erase And Sync button. iTunes replaces the library on the iPod with the library on the Mac. This may take some time if the library is extensive.

 If the iPod is synced with another photo library, iTunes prompts you to decide whether to replace the photos on the iPod with those on your Mac. Click the Yes button or the No button as appropriate.

At this point, you've set up the iPod to work with your Mac, but you've left it using the FAT32 file system. FAT32 works fine with Mac OS X but is marginally less efficient than the Mac OS Extended file system, so you won't be able to fit quite as many files on the iPod with FAT32 as with Mac OS Extended.

If you intend to use the iPod with the Mac for the long term, and if the iPod doesn't contain any valuable files that you want to keep, you may choose to convert it to Mac OS X Extended to pack on as many items as possible. To do so, restore the iPod by following the process described in the section "Restore an iPod on Mac OS X" in Chapter 15.

 You must reformat the iPod with the Mac OS Extended file system if you want to update the iPod to the latest version of the iPod software using the Mac.

Move an iPhone or iPod touch Between Windows and the Mac

The iPhone and iPod touch use the same file system when connected to either a Windows computer or a Mac. This means that transferring an iPhone or iPod touch from Windows to the Mac, or from the Mac to Windows, is usually painless, because you do not need to restore the device and thus wipe out all its current contents.

However, when you connect the iPhone or iPod touch to another computer, you still need to decide whether to replace the device's songs, videos, information, and so on with the corresponding media file or information from the new computer, as described in the next section.

Change the Computer to Which an iPod or iPhone Is Linked

Apple has designed the iPod and iPhone so that they can synchronize with only one computer at a time. This computer is known as the *home* computer—home to the iPod or iPhone, not necessarily in your home. However, you can use two or more Macs, or two or more Windows PCs, to load files onto the same iPod. See the section "Load an iPod from Two or More Computers at Once," later in this chapter, for details. This doesn't work with the iPhone, which is limited to a single computer at a time for media files.

Linking an iPod or iPhone to another computer replaces all the songs, playlists, and other items on the device with those on the other computer. Be sure you want to change the link before you proceed. You can restore your previous library by linking again to the first computer, but, even with USB 2.0 file-transfer speeds, you'll waste a good deal of time if your library is large.

To change an iPod's or iPhone's home computer, follow these steps:

1. Make sure the other computer contains an up-to-date version of iTunes. If necessary, set up iTunes and install any relevant updates.

 If you're moving an iPod formatted with the Mac OS Extended file system to Windows, you'll need to restore it as described in "Move an iPod from the Mac to Windows," earlier in this chapter. This doesn't apply to the iPhone.

2. Connect the iPod or iPhone to the other PC or Mac.
3. For an iPod, iTunes displays the following dialog box warning you that the iPod is synced to another iTunes library and asking if you want to change the sync to the current computer's iTunes library.

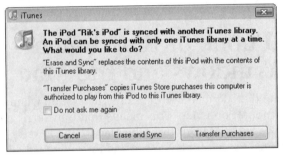

 When you connect an iPhone to a computer other than its home computer, iTunes doesn't ask if you want to change the synchronization for the iTunes library unless you select the Sync Music check box on the Music tab of the iPhone's control screens and then click the Sync button.

4. If you're sure you want to replace all the items on the device, click the Erase And Sync button. Click the Transfer Purchases button if you want to transfer items you've purchased from the iTunes Store from the iPod to your iTunes library.
5. If you don't transfer any purchased items, iTunes prompts you to copy them from your device to the iTunes library, as shown here. Click the Transfer button if you want to copy the items; if you don't, you'll lose them.

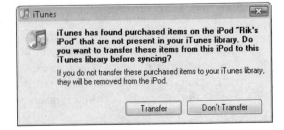

How to...   # Deal with Purchased Items Your Computer Isn't Authorized to Play

If you try to transfer purchased items but your computer isn't authorized to play them, iTunes displays a dialog box such as the one shown here.

Click the + button in the lower-left corner to see a list of the files, and then click the OK button (there's no alternative). iTunes then cancels the erase and sync operation and displays a dialog box telling you it has done so.

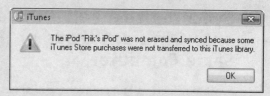

Click the OK button to close this dialog box, choose Store | Authorize Computer to open the Authorize Computer dialog box, type your password, and then click the Authorize Computer button.

Once you've authorized the computer, click the Sync button on the Summary tab of the device's control screens to start the erase and sync operation again. This time, you'll be able to transfer your purchases to the computer.

Because changing the iPod or iPhone to a different home computer replaces the entire iTunes library, the initial synchronization may take a long time, depending on how big the library is and whether it's stored on a local drive or a network drive.

Synchronize Several iPods or iPhones with the Same Computer

As you've seen earlier in this book, usually a computer and an iPod (or iPhone) have a mutually faithful relationship—but, as discussed in the previous section, the iPod or iPhone can decide to leave its home computer and set up home with another computer. It can even switch from Windows to the Mac or vice versa.

For most people, such fidelity (or serial fidelity) works fine. But if you have several iPods or iPhones and one computer, you can sync all the iPods and iPhones from that computer. Keep the following points in mind:

- Even if your computer has plenty of USB ports, it's best not to plug in more than one iPod or iPhone at once. That way, neither you nor iTunes becomes confused, and synchronization can take place at full speed.
- Each iPod and iPhone has a unique ID number that it communicates to your computer on connection, so your computer knows which device is connected to it. You can even give two or more devices the same name if doing so amuses you rather than confuses you.
- You can configure different updating for each iPod or iPhone by choosing options on the iPod screens or iPhone screens when the device is connected.

How to... ## Synchronize a Full—Different—Library onto Different iPods or iPhones from the Same Computer

Synchronizing two or more iPods or iPhones with the same computer works well enough provided that each user is happy using the same library or the same playlists (perhaps a different selection from the set of playlists). But if you want to synchronize the full library for each iPod or iPhone, yet have a different library on each, you need to take a different approach.

In most cases, the easiest solution is to have a separate user account for each separate user who uses an iPod or iPhone with the computer. Having separate user accounts is best in any case for keeping files and mail separate.

Place the music files that users will share in a folder that each user can access. In iTunes, make sure that the Copy Files To iTunes Music Folder When Adding To Library check box on the Advanced tab of the iTunes dialog box (in Windows) or the Preferences dialog box (on the Mac) is cleared so iTunes doesn't copy all the files into the music library.

If you have enough free space on your hard disk, you can set up your own libraries under your own user account and store all your music files in them. But unless your hard disk is truly gigantic, sharing most of the files from a central location is almost always preferable.

Another possibility is to start iTunes using a different library from within the same user account. To start iTunes using a different library:

- **Windows** Hold down SHIFT as you click the iTunes icon to start iTunes.
- **Mac** Hold down OPTION as you click the iTunes icon to start iTunes.

See the section "Use Multiple Libraries on the Same Computer" in Chapter 10 for more details on using multiple libraries.

When you use the same user account on Windows or the Mac to synchronize multiple iPods, Apple recommends that you use the same synchronization settings for each. However, this isn't an absolute requirement—which is just as well, because the iPods have such different capacities and capabilities. If you find yourself having problems synchronizing different iPods using different synchronization settings, consider creating a separate user account for synchronizing a particular iPod.

Load an iPod from Two or More Computers at Once

As you read earlier in this chapter, you can synchronize an iPod or iPhone with only one computer at a time—the device's home computer. You can change the home computer from one computer to another, and even from one platform (Mac or PC) to the other, but you can't actively synchronize the iPod or iPhone with more than one computer at once.

But you *can* load songs, videos, or other items onto the iPod from computers other than the home computer. If the iPod is formatted using the FAT32 file system, you can use a mixture of Macs and PCs to load files onto the iPod. If the iPod is formatted using the Mac OS Extended file system, you can use only Macs. You can't load songs onto the iPhone from computers other than the home computer at this writing, but you can load other items, such as photos or contacts. See the following section for details.

All the computers you use must have iTunes installed and configured, and you must configure the iPod for manual updating on each computer involved—on the home computer as well as on each other computer. Otherwise, synchronizing the iPod with the home computer after loading tracks from other computers will remove those tracks because they're not in the home computer's library.

Configure an iPod for Manual Updating

The first step in loading an iPod from two or more computers is to configure it for manual updating. You'll need to do this on the iPod's home computer first, and then on each of the other computers you plan to use.

To configure the iPod for manual updating, follow these steps:

1. Connect the iPod to your Mac or PC. Allow synchronization to take place. (If you need to override synchronization, see the sidebar "Temporarily Override Automatic Synchronization.")
2. Click the iPod's entry in the Source list to display the iPod screens.

3. Select the Manually Manage Music check box. iTunes displays a message box warning you that you'll need to eject the iPod manually before disconnecting it, as shown here.

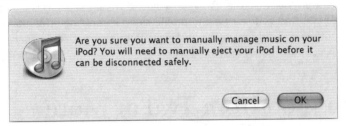

Are you sure you want to manually manage music on your iPod? You will need to manually eject your iPod before it can be disconnected safely.

Cancel   OK

4. Click the OK button to return to the iPod screens. iTunes selects the Enable Disk Use check box (if it wasn't already selected) and makes it unavailable so that you can't clear it manually.
5. Click the Apply button to apply the changes.

Load Files onto an iPod Manually

After you've configured an iPod for manual updating, you can load files onto it manually by following these general steps:

1. Connect the iPod to the computer that contains the files you want to load. The iPod appears in the Source list in iTunes.
2. Drag song files from your iTunes library, or from a Windows Explorer window or a Finder window, and then drop them on the iPod or on one of its playlists.
3. After loading all the songs you want from this computer, eject the iPod by clicking the Eject button next to its name in the Source list.

If you don't eject the iPod after configuring it for manual updating, you may lose data or corrupt the iPod's contents when you disconnect it.

You can then disconnect the iPod from this computer, move it to the next computer, and then add more song files by using the same technique.

How to... **Temporarily Override Automatic Synchronization**

If an iPod is configured for automatic synchronization, you can override this setting by holding down keys when you connect the iPod:

- Windows   Hold down CTRL-SHIFT.
- Mac   Hold down ⌘-OPTION.

Once the iPod appears in the Source list in iTunes, you can let go of the keys.

From this point on, to add further song files to the iPod from your home computer, you must add them manually. Don't synchronize the iPod with your home computer, because synchronization will delete from the iPod all the song files that do not appear in your library.

Load an iPhone from Two or More Different Computers at Once

At this writing, you can load songs and videos on an iPhone from only one computer at a time—but you can load other items, such as information (contacts, calendars, e-mail, and bookmarks) or photos, from a different computer.

In general, loading an iPhone this way is a recipe for confusion, but you may occasionally find it useful. In particular, you may want to merge information from two (or more) separate computers onto the iPhone so that you can carry it all with you.

To load an iPhone from two or more computers at once, follow these steps:

1. Connect the iPhone to the home computer—the computer that will supply the iPhone with songs and video files.
2. Sync the iPhone as described earlier in this book. If you want to load only some items from the home computer, select the Sync Only Checked Songs And Videos check box on the Summary tab of the iPhone's screens.
3. Disconnect the iPhone from the home computer, and then connect it to the computer that will provide the information or photos.
4. On the Summary tab of the iPhone's screens, select the Sync Only Checked Songs And Videos check box.
5. To sync information, follow these steps:
   - Click the Info tab to display its contents.
   - To sync contacts, select the Sync Contacts From check box (Windows) or the Sync Address Book Contacts check box. On Windows, choose the contacts source in the drop-down list. Choose whether to sync all contacts or just selected groups.
   - To sync calendars, select the Sync Calendars From check box (Windows) or the Sync iCal Calendars check box (Mac). On Windows, choose the Calendars source in the drop-down list. Choose whether to sync all calendars or just those you select.
   - To sync e-mail, select the Sync Selected Mail Accounts From check box (Windows) or Sync Selected Mail Accounts check box (Mac). On Windows, choose the program in the drop-down list—for example, Outlook. Select the check box for each e-mail account you want to sync (you might have only one available).
   - To sync bookmarks on Windows, select the Sync Bookmarks From check box, and then choose the browser in the drop-down list. On the Mac, select the Sync Safari Bookmarks check box.

- In the Advanced area (shown next), select the Contacts check box, the Calendars check box, the Mail Accounts check box, or the Bookmarks check box if you want to replace the existing information on the iPhone rather than add to it.

- Click the Apply button. The iPhone displays the following dialog box, telling you that the iPhone's information is synced with a different user account and asking whether you want to merge the information or replace it.

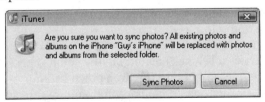

- Click the Merge Info button. iTunes merges the information.
6. To add photos from the new computer, follow these steps:
    - Click the Photos tab to display its contents.
    - Select the Sync Photos From check box, and then choose the source folder or program in the drop-down list.
    - Choose whether to sync all photos or just some of them.
    - Click the Apply button. iTunes displays the following dialog box, checking that you want to replace the existing photos on the iPhone with photos from the new computer.

- Click the Sync Photos button.
7. When you've finished, disconnect the iPod from the second computer.

12

Use an iPod as an External Drive or Backup Device

HOW TO...

- Decide whether or not to use an iPod as an external drive
- Enable disk mode on an iPod using Windows
- Enable disk mode on an iPod using a Mac
- Transfer files to and from an iPod
- Turn your iPhone into an external drive
- Back up an iPod so you don't lose your music or data

Apple sells the iPods primarily as portable media players—and they're the best ones around. But to a computer, the iPod is essentially an external USB drive with sophisticated audio and video features. This chapter shows you how to use an iPod as an external drive for backup and portable storage.

 One external-drive feature this chapter *doesn't* show you is how to transfer files from an iPod's library onto your computer. Chapter 13 covers this subject.

At this writing, Apple does not let you use an iPhone or iPod touch as a drive, so most of the coverage in this chapter does not apply to these devices. However, you can use a third-party program (such as DiskAid, Air Sharing, or PhoneView) to store data on an iPhone or iPod touch, as described later in the chapter.

Decide Whether to Use an iPod as an External Drive

If all you want from an iPod is huge amounts of music and video to go, you may never want to use an iPod as an external drive. Here's why you should think about it again:

- *An iPod provides a great combination of portability and high capacity.* You can get smaller portable-storage devices (for example, USB keys, CompactFlash drives, SmartMedia cards, and Memory Sticks), but they're an extra expense and an extra device to carry with you. An iPod classic lets you carry around serious amounts of data, but even an iPod nano has enough space to carry several gigabytes of your most important files along with your songs and videos. On an iPod shuffle, you'll feel the pinch a bit more—but you can still take your essential files with you.
- *You can take all your documents with you.* For example, you could take home that large PowerPoint presentation you need to get ready for tomorrow. You can even put several gigabytes of video files on an iPod if you need to take them with you (for example, to a studio for editing) or transfer them to another computer.
- *You can use an iPod for backup.* If you keep your vital documents down to a size you can easily fit on an iPod (and still have plenty of room left for songs, videos, and other files), you can quickly back up the documents and take the backup with you wherever you go.
- *You can use an iPod for security.* By keeping your documents on an iPod rather than on your computer, and by keeping the iPod with you, you can prevent other people from accessing your documents.

The disadvantages to using an iPod as an external drive are straightforward:

- Whatever space you use on the iPod for storing other files isn't available for music and video.
- If you lose or break the iPod, any files stored only on it will be gone forever.

Enable Disk Mode on the iPod

Before you can use an iPod as an external drive, you must enable disk mode. In disk mode, your computer uses an iPod as an external disk drive. You can copy to the iPod any files and folders that will fit on it.

 You can copy song files, video files, and playlists to an iPod in disk mode, but you won't be able to play them on the iPod. This is because when you copy the files, their information isn't added to the iPod's database the way it's added by iTunes and other applications designed to work with the iPod, such as Anapod Explorer or XPlay. So the iPod's interface doesn't know the files are there, and you can't play them.

From the computer's point of view, an external disk connected via USB works in largely the same way as any other disk. Here are the differences:

- The disk is external.
- The disk may draw power across the USB connection (as iPods do) rather than being powered itself (as high-capacity and high-performance external disks tend to be).
- If the iPod uses a USB connection, the USB controller and the USB cable or connection must supply enough power to feed the iPod. All USB connections supply power, but some don't supply enough for an iPod. (Other devices, such as USB keyboards and mice, require much less power than an iPod.) Apple refers to USB ports as "high-powered" (giving enough power for an iPod) and "low-powered" (not giving enough power).

 Using an iPod classic as an external disk with a connection that can't supply power may run down the battery quickly. Part of the problem is that the iPod can't use its caching capabilities when you use it as an external disk. (Caching works only for playlists and albums, when the iPod knows which files are needed next and thus can read them into the cache.) If the iPod isn't receiving power, check the battery status periodically to make sure the iPod doesn't suddenly run out of power.

Enable Disk Mode on an iPod Using Windows

To use an iPod as an external disk on a PC, enable disk mode. Follow these steps:

1. Connect the iPod to your PC as usual.
2. Launch iTunes if it doesn't launch automatically.
3. In the Source pane, click the iPod's icon to display the iPod screens.
4. For an iPod classic or an iPod nano, click the Summary tab if it isn't already displayed (see Figure 12-1). For an iPod shuffle, click the Settings tab if it isn't already displayed.
5. Select the Enable Disk Use check box. iTunes displays the following warning dialog box, telling you that using disk mode requires you to manually unmount the iPod before each disconnect, even when you're automatically updating music.

6. Select the Do Not Warn Me Again check box if you want to suppress this warning in the future, and then click the OK button. iTunes returns you to the Summary tab or Settings tab.

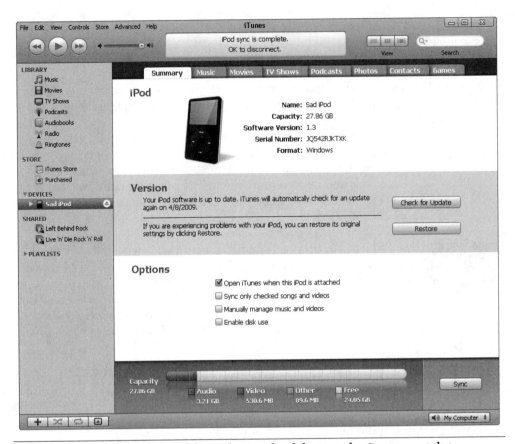

FIGURE 12-1 Select the Enable Disk Use check box on the Summary tab to enable disk mode on an iPod in Windows. For an iPod shuffle, this setting is on the Settings tab.

7. For second-generation iPod shuffle, drag the slider along the More Songs–More Data continuum to specify how much space you want to devote to data and how much to songs:

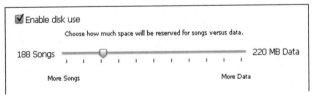

8. Click the Apply button to apply the changes.

Once you've enabled disk mode, the iPod appears to Windows Explorer as a removable drive. Windows Explorer automatically assigns a drive letter to the drive, so you can access it as you would any other drive connected to your computer.

To eject the iPod, take any of the following actions:

- In the Source pane in iTunes, click the Eject icon next to the iPod's name. (This is the easiest means of ejection.)
- In the Source pane in iTunes, right-click the icon for the iPod and then choose Eject.
- In Windows Vista, choose Start | Computer to open the Computer window. In Windows XP, choose Start | My Computer to open the My Computer window. Right-click the icon for the iPod and then choose Eject from the shortcut menu.

When the iPod displays the "OK to disconnect" message, you can safely disconnect it. On an iPod shuffle, make sure the iPod is showing a green light or a steady orange light rather than a flashing orange light before you disconnect it.

 Don't just disconnect the iPod without ejecting it. You might damage files or lose data.

Enable Disk Mode on an iPod Using a Mac

To use an iPod as an external disk on a Mac, enable disk mode. Follow these steps:

1. Connect the iPod to the Mac as usual.
2. Launch iTunes (for example, click the iTunes icon in the Dock) if iTunes doesn't launch automatically.
3. In the Source pane, click the iPod's entry to display the iPod's screens.
4. For an iPod classic or an iPod nano, click the Summary tab if it isn't already displayed (see Figure 12-2). For an iPod shuffle, click the Settings tab if it isn't already displayed.
5. Select the Enable Disk Use check box. iTunes displays the following warning dialog box, telling you that using disk mode requires you to unmount the iPod manually before each disconnect, even when synchronizing songs (instead of being able to have iTunes unmount the iPod automatically).

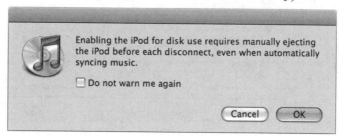

6. Select the Do Not Warn Me Again check box if you want to suppress this warning in the future, and then click the OK button. iTunes returns you to the Summary tab or Settings tab.

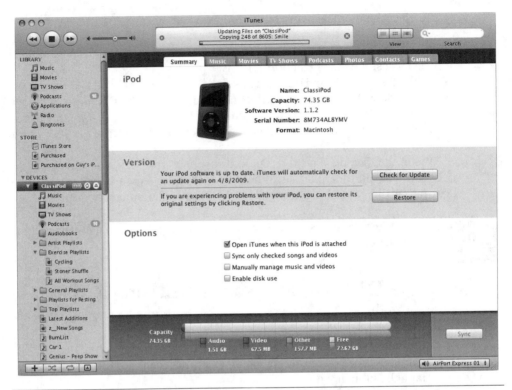

FIGURE 12-2 Select the Enable Disk Use check box on the Summary tab to enable disk mode on an iPod on the Mac. For an iPod shuffle, this setting is on the Settings tab.

7. For a second-generation iPod shuffle, drag the slider along the More Songs–More Data continuum to specify how much space you want to devote to data and how much to songs:

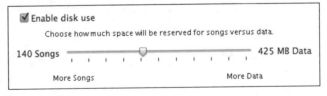

8. Click the Apply button to apply the changes.

How to... Force Disk Mode

If your USB port is underpowered, you may need to force an iPod to enter disk mode. To do so for an iPod classic or iPod nano, follow these steps:

1. Connect the iPod via USB as usual.
2. Toggle the Hold switch on and off, and then hold down the Select button and the Menu button for about five seconds to reboot the iPod.
3. When the iPod displays the Apple logo, hold down the Select button and Play button briefly. The iPod sends the computer an electronic prod that forces the computer to recognize it.

Once you've enabled disk mode, you'll need to eject the iPod manually after each connection. To eject the iPod, take any of the following actions:

- In the Source pane in iTunes, click the Eject icon next to the iPod's name. (This is the easiest means of ejection.)
- In the Source pane in iTunes, right-click the icon for the iPod and then choose Eject from the shortcut menu.
- Select the icon for the iPod on the desktop and then issue an Eject command from the File menu or the shortcut menu. (Alternatively, press ⌘-E.)
- Drag the desktop icon for the iPod to the Trash.

When an iPod displays the "OK to disconnect" message, you can safely disconnect it. On an iPod shuffle, make sure the iPod is showing a green light rather than an orange light before you disconnect it.

 Don't just disconnect the iPod without ejecting it. You might damage files or lose data.

Transfer Files to and from the iPod

When the iPod is in disk mode, you can transfer files to it by using the Finder (on the Mac), Windows Explorer (in Windows), or another file-management application of your choice. (You can transfer files by using the command prompt in Windows or the Terminal in Mac OS X, if you so choose.)

 If the iPod appears in the Computer window (on Windows Vista) or My Computer window (on Windows XP) as a drive named Removable Drive, and Windows Explorer claims the disk isn't formatted, chances are you've connected a Mac-formatted iPod to your PC. Windows Explorer can't read the HFS Plus disk format that Mac-formatted iPods use, so the iPod appears to be unformatted. (HFS Plus is one of the disk formats Mac OS X can use and is also called the Mac OS Extended format.)

You can create and delete folders on the iPod as you would any other drive. But be sure you don't mess with the iPod's system folders, such as the Calendars folder, the Contacts folder, the Notes folder, and the iPod_Control folder. The iPod_Control folder is a hidden folder, so it does not appear unless you have set Windows or Mac OS X to display hidden files.

 As mentioned earlier, don't transfer music or video files to an iPod by using file-management software if you want to be able to play the files on the iPod. Unless you transfer the files by using iTunes or another application designed to access the iPod's database, the details about the files won't be added to the iPod. You won't be able to play those files on the iPod because their data hasn't been added to its database of contents.

The exception to transferring files from an iPod is transferring files that you've put on the iPod by using iTunes or another application that can access the iPod's database. Chapter 13 shows you how to do this.

Put Files on an iPhone or iPod touch

At this writing, Apple doesn't provide a way to put an iPhone or iPod touch into disk mode so that you can transfer files to it. However, you can do so by using a third-party program that lets you use the iPhone or iPod touch as an external drive. This section shows you three such programs. You can find others on the Web or in the App Store (which you can access via iTunes on your computer or via the App Store application on the iPhone or iPod touch).

DiskAid (Windows and Mac OS X)

DiskAid from DigiDNA (www.digidna.net/diskaid) is a free utility that lets you mount your iPhone or iPod touch as an external disk. Figure 12-3 shows DiskAid at work on a Mac.

DiskAid's toolbar buttons let you easily create folders, copy items to and from the device, and delete items from the device. But you can also simply drag files and folders from a Windows Explorer window or a Finder window to the DiskAid window to add them to the device.

Air Sharing (Windows and Mac OS X)

Air Sharing from Avatron Software (www.avatron.com), which you can buy from the App Store, lets you access your iPhone or iPod touch across a wireless network connection rather than the USB connection that most other programs require. Not having to connect the device to your computer is an advantage, but you get slower file transfers, and the device doesn't get to recharge while you're using it.

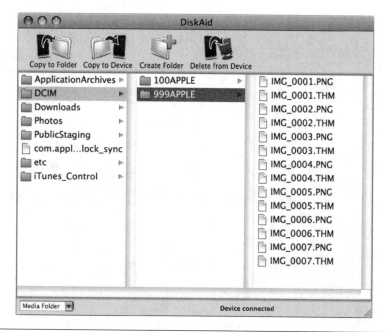

FIGURE 12-3   DiskAid gives you free access to your iPhone's or iPod touch's file system.

PhoneView (Mac OS X Only)

PhoneView (see Figure 12-4) from Ecamm Network (www.ecamm.com/mac/phoneview) lets you access your iPhone or iPod touch from your Mac. Ecamm provides a fully functional trial edition, which gives you seven days to find out how well PhoneView suits your needs.

Back Up an iPod So You Don't Lose Your Music or Data

If you synchronize your complete library with an iPod, and perhaps load your contacts, calendar information, and photos on the iPod as well, you shouldn't need to worry about backing up the iPod. That's because your computer contains all the data that's on the iPod. (Effectively, the iPod is a backup of part of your hard disk.) So if you lose the iPod, or it stops functioning, you won't lose any data you have on your computer.

If your computer's hard disk stops working, you may need to recover your library, contacts, calendar data, and photos from the iPod onto another computer or a new hard disk. You can transfer contacts, calendars, and full-resolution photos by enabling disk mode and using the Finder (Mac) or Windows Explorer (PC) to access the contents of

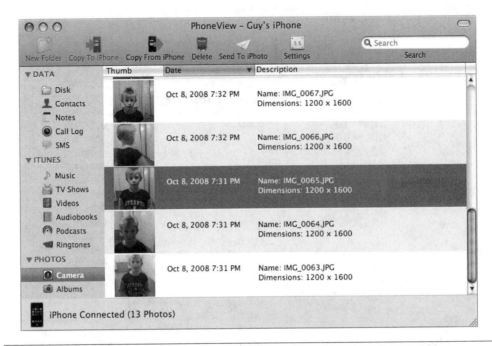

FIGURE 12-4 PhoneView lets you quickly access the contents of your iPhone or iPod to copy, add, or delete files.

the Contacts folder, the Calendars folder, and the Photos/Full Resolution folder. For instructions on recovering song and video files from an iPod, see Chapter 13.

So normally an iPod will be the vulnerable member of the tag team. But if you store files directly on an iPod, you should back them up to your computer to make sure you don't lose them if the iPod vanishes or its hard disk gives up the ghost.

To back up files, either use a file-management utility (for example, the Finder or Windows Explorer) to simply copy the files or folders to your computer, or use custom backup software to create a more formal backup. For example:

- **Windows Vista** Backup and Restore Center (Start | All Programs | Maintenance | Backup And Restore Center)
- **Windows XP** Backup Utility (Start | All Programs | Accessories | System Tools | Backup)

 If Backup Utility doesn't appear on the System Tools submenu in Windows XP, you may need to install it from your Windows XP CD or from the installation folder on your PC's hard disk. You'll find the files in the i386\MSFT\VALUEADD\ NTBACKUP folder.

- **Mac OS X** Backup application to .Mac iDisk (which you can access via any Internet connection)

13

Recover Your Songs and Videos from an iPod or iPhone

HOW TO...

- Know why the iPod and iPhone hide their song files and video files from you
- Understand how the iPod and iPhone store song files and video files
- Recover your songs and videos from an iPod or iPhone in Windows
- Recover your songs and videos from an iPod or iPhone on the Mac

As you saw in Chapter 2, you can copy all or part of your library onto an iPod or iPhone almost effortlessly by choosing suitable synchronization settings and then synchronizing the device. Normally, any songs and videos on the iPod or iPhone are also in your library, so you don't need to transfer the songs and videos from the player to your computer. But if you have a computer disaster, or if your computer is stolen, you may need to recover the songs and videos from the iPod or iPhone to your new or repaired computer.

This chapter shows you how to recover songs and videos from an iPod or iPhone on both Windows and the Mac. The chapter starts by explaining why the iPod and iPhone hide the song and video files. It then covers where the files are stored on the devices, how you can reveal them in Windows Explorer or the Finder, and why you need specialized tools to copy them from the devices. The chapter ends by showing you the best recovery utilities for Windows and the Mac.

Why the iPod and iPhone Hide Their Song and Video Files from You

For copyright reasons, the basic configuration of the iPod and iPhone prevents you from copying music and video files from the player's library to your computer. This restriction prevents you from loading files onto the player on one computer via iTunes and then downloading them onto another computer, which would most likely violate copyright by making unauthorized copies of other people's copyrighted material.

But if you turn on disk mode (as discussed in the previous chapter), you can use an iPod as a portable drive. (Apple doesn't offer disk mode on the iPhone or iPod touch, but you can use a third-party program to store files on these devices, as discussed in Chapter 12.) In disk mode, you can copy music and video files onto an iPod from one computer, connect the iPod to another computer, and copy or move the files from the iPod to that computer. The only limitation is that the files you copy this way aren't added to the iPod's music and video database, so you can't play them on the iPod.

Normally, you shouldn't need to copy songs and videos from an iPod or iPhone to your computer, because your computer will already contain all the songs and videos that the player contains. But there may come a time when you need to get the song files and video files out of the player's library for legitimate reasons. For example, if you drop your MacBook, or your PC's hard disk dies of natural causes, you may need to copy the music files and video files from the iPod or iPhone to a replacement computer or disk. Otherwise, you may risk losing your entire music and video collection.

To avoid losing data, you should back up all your valuable data, including any songs and videos that you can't easily recover by other means (such as ripping your CDs again), especially the songs and videos you've bought from the iTunes Store or other online stores. However, the amount of data—and, in particular, the size of many people's libraries—makes backup difficult, requiring either an external hard drive or multiple DVDs.

To help you avoid this dreadful possibility, iPod enthusiasts have developed some great utilities for transferring files from the player's hidden music and video storage to a computer.

Where—and How—the iPod and iPhone Store Song and Video Files

When you turn on disk mode, you can access the contents of the iPod's hard drive or flash memory by using Windows Explorer (in Windows) or the Finder (on the Mac). Until you create other folders there, though, you'll find only a few folders: Calendar, Contacts, Notes, and Photos (once you've synchronized photos). There's no trace of your song files and video files.

If you enable disk mode on an iPod shuffle, you'll find no folders at all, because the iPod shuffle can't hold contacts, calendars, or notes.

You can't see the song files and video files because the folders in which they are stored are formatted to be hidden in Windows and to be invisible on the Mac. Even if you make these folders visible, it doesn't help you much, because the iPod or iPhone

How to... **Make Visible the iPod's Hidden or Invisible Folders**

If you want to make visible the iPod's hidden or invisible folders, follow these instructions:

- **Windows Vista**   Choose Start | Computer, choose Organize | Folder And Search Options, and then click the View tab. Select the Show Hidden Files And Folders option button, and then click the OK button.
- **Windows XP**   Choose Start | My Computer, choose Tools | Folder Options, and then click the View tab. Select the Show Hidden Files And Folders option button, and then click the OK button.
- **Mac OS X**   Download and install TinkerTool from www.bresink.de/osx/TinkerTool.html. Run TinkerTool, select the Show Hidden And System Files check box on the Finder tab, and then click the Relaunch Finder button. Quit TinkerTool.

Once you've made the folders visible, open a Windows Explorer window or a Finder window, and double-click the iPod. Double-click the iPod_Control folder to see its contents.

automatically assigns each song or video a short and cryptic filename. You can copy these files back to your computer, but doing so would take a while, especially because the iPod or iPhone also stores the files in automatically named folders in apparently random order. The folders are named F00, F01, F02, and so on.

Windows Utilities for Transferring Song and Video Files from an iPod to Your PC

At this writing, there are several Windows utilities for transferring song and video files from an iPod to your PC. This section discusses two specialist utilities, iPod Access for Windows and iGadget.

The two heavy-duty iPod-management applications for Windows—Anapod Explorer and XPlay—also enable you to transfer media files to, and generally manage, an iPod, and are discussed in more detail in the next chapter.

iPod Access for Windows

iPod Access for Windows from Findley Designs (www.ipodaccess.com) lets you transfer files from an iPod to your PC. iPod Access for Windows (see Figure 13-1) costs $19.99, but you can download a limited evaluation version to see if the application works for you. You can also use iPod Access to play back songs directly from an iPod.

FIGURE 13-1 iPod Access for Windows can recover files from an iPod to a PC.

 Findley Designs also makes iPod Photo Access, a tool that lets you recover photos from an iPod or iPhone.

iGadget

iGadget from iPodSoft (www.ipodsoft.com) lets you transfer files from an iPod to a PC. iGadget (see Figure 13-2) costs $15 and also lets you transfer to an iPod weather forecasts, driving directions, gas prices, Outlook data, and other text.

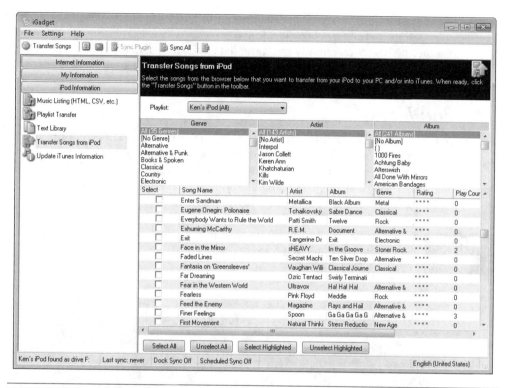

FIGURE 13-2   iGadget lets you recover songs and videos from an iPod to a PC.

Mac OS X Utilities for Transferring Song and Video Files from an iPod or iPhone to Your Mac

iPod enthusiasts have created an impressive array of utilities for transferring song and video files from an iPod to a Mac. This section discusses some of the leading utilities for doing so.

Note   If you don't like the look (or performance) of these utilities, search sites such as iLounge.com (www.ilounge.com), VersionTracker.com (www.versiontracker.com), MacUpdate (www.macupdate.com), and Apple's Mac OS X Downloads page (www.apple.com/downloads/macosx) for alternatives.

Different utilities work in different ways. The most basic utilities simply assemble a list of the filenames in the iPod's media folders, which leaves you with cryptic filenames. The best utilities read the database the iPod maintains of the files it holds, whereas other utilities plow painstakingly through each file on the iPod and extract information from its ID3 tags. Reading the iPod's database gives much faster results than assembling what's essentially the same database from scratch by scouring the tags. But if the database has become corrupted, reading the tags is a good recovery technique.

PodWorks

PodWorks from Sci-Fi Hi-Fi ($8; www.scifihifi.com/podworks) is a utility for transferring song and video files from an iPod or iPhone to your Mac. Figure 13-3 shows PodWorks in action with an iPhone. You can download an evaluation version that limits you to 30 days, copying 250 songs, and copying one song at a time—enough limitations to persuade you to buy the full version.

 Note   PodWorks has an extra trick: you can install PodWorks on your iPod so that you can use it on a computer you haven't used before.

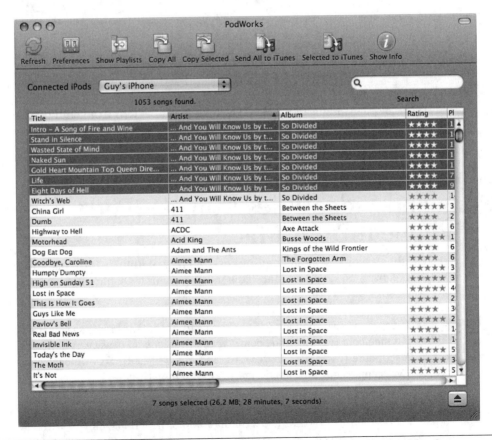

FIGURE 13-3   PodWorks can quickly recover songs and other media files from an iPod or iPhone.

iPod Access

iPod Access from Findley Designs (www.findleydesigns.com) also simplifies the process of transferring song and video files from an iPod to a Mac. iPod Access (see Figure 13-4) costs $19.99, but you can download a limited evaluation version to see if the application works for you. You can also use iPod Access to play back media files directly from the iPod.

iPodRip

iPodRip from The Little App Factory PTY Ltd. ($14.95; www.thelittleappfactory.com) integrates with iTunes and enables you to play back songs and other media files from either your library or an iPod or iPhone. iPodRip (see Figure 13-5; the application's title bar shows the device's name) comes in a trial version that you can use ten times before

FIGURE 13-4   iPod Access can recover songs and other media files from an iPod or simply play them back.

FIGURE 13-5 iPodRip is a utility that can recover files from an iPod or iPhone even if the device's database has been corrupted.

it cripples itself. iPodRip's SmartSync feature enables you to automatically copy to your library songs and videos that you've loaded onto an iPod using a different computer.

Apart from being able to recover media files using the data in the iPod's database, iPodRip can also perform a "hard recover" when the iPod's database is corrupted or missing. In a hard recover (see the illustration at right), iPodRip copies any songs found on the iPod to your desktop. When the database is corrupted or missing, iPodRip may not be able to find and recover all the files.

No songs found to display

Either your iPod is brand new and you will need to load songs on it or your database has become corrupt and can no longer be read.

If you would like iPodRip to recover any songs it finds on your iPod to your Desktop, please select 'Hard Recover'.

Hard Recover   Quit

Caution Before performing a "hard recover" with iPodRip, make sure you've updated the application to the latest available version, because the "No songs found to display" message can also mean that your iPod is using a new format that your version of iPodRip doesn't recognize; updating iPodRip may solve the problem.

14

Use the iPod or iPhone with Software Other Than iTunes

HOW TO...

- Understand why to use software other than iTunes to control the iPod or iPhone
- Manage the iPod or iPhone with Songbird on Windows or the Mac
- Manage the iPod with Anapod Explorer on Windows
- Manage the iPod or iPhone with XPlay on Windows
- Manage the iPod with Winamp on Windows
- Use Clutter to give iTunes a super-graphical interface on the Mac

Apple not only designed iTunes for the iPod and iPhone but also makes iTunes available for free to anyone who wants to download it—so you have a strong incentive to use iTunes to manage the iPod or iPhone. But if you choose not to use iTunes, there are some alternatives, particularly on Windows. This chapter introduces you to those alternatives, starting with the key question: Why use them at all?

Why Use Software Other Than iTunes to Control the iPod?

iTunes is one of the core applications that have made Mac OS X such a powerhouse for multimedia, and both iTunes and Mac OS X have been built to work with iPods and iPhones. As a result, iTunes is by far the best software for managing an iPod or iPhone on the Mac, unless you need features that iTunes cannot or will not provide, such as the ability to recover song and video files from the iPod or iPhone to the computer (see Chapter 13) or the ability to synchronize large amounts of your Entourage data with the iPod or iPhone.

iTunes for Windows, which was introduced several years after iTunes for Mac OS X, has caught up with the Mac version in functionality, even if it is still not as slickly integrated into the operating system (for the simple reason that Apple makes Mac OS X but not Windows). However, over the years of iTunes for Windows' development, third-party developers created other programs for managing iPods, both to allow you to avoid iTunes' teething troubles and to give you features that iTunes for Windows doesn't provide, such as Outlook integration or the ability to recover your iTunes library after your PC has disagreed violently with itself.

 Another reason to use other software is if iTunes doesn't run on your operating system. For example, iTunes for Windows requires Windows Vista or Windows XP. If you're brave enough to continue using an earlier version of Windows, such as Windows 2000, Windows 98, or Windows Me, you'll need to use other software.

Manage the iPod or iPhone with Songbird on Windows or the Mac

Songbird is an open-source software project that provides basic functionality for controlling an iPod or iPhone without using iTunes. Songbird makes it easy to import your iTunes library and to play back items from your library.

Songbird is available for Windows (it runs on Vista and XP), Mac OS X, and Linux. These are official builds with support; you can also find unsupported builds for other operating systems.

 At this writing, Songbird is at an early stage of development—but it *is* functional for essential tasks, and it is free.

Download and Install Songbird

To get Songbird, steer your web browser to the download page on the Songbird website (http://getsongbird.com/download). Click the download link for your operating system, and then launch the setup process when the download finishes.

Once you've downloaded and installed Songbird, the Songbird Setup assistant runs. Follow through the steps of the assistant to set Songbird up the way you prefer. The key decision comes on the Import Media page (shown on the left in Figure 14-1), where you can choose between scanning your computer for media files, importing the

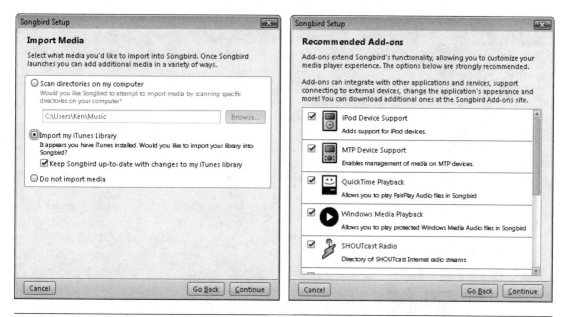

FIGURE 14-1   During Songbird setup, choose whether to import your iTunes library (left) and which add-ons to install (right).

contents of your iTunes library, and not importing media. If you have iTunes installed, as is normally the case, the best choice is to import your iTunes library and to select the Keep Songbird Up-to-Date With Changes To My iTunes Library check box.

On the Recommended Add-Ons page (shown on the right in Figure 14-1), decide which add-ons to include. You'll certainly want iPod Device Support if you plan to use an iPod or iPhone with Songbird. QuickTime Playback and Windows Media Playback support are also useful for most people.

Play Items and Manage the iPod or iPhone with Songbird

After setup completes, Songbird launches automatically and imports your iTunes library if you told it to. You can then play back items from your library via the easy-to-use interface shown in Figure 14-2.

FIGURE 14-2 Songbird's interface makes it easy to play back music and video. You can also listen to SHOUTcast radio stations.

To manage an iPod or iPhone, click its entry in the Source list on the left (see Figure 14-3). You can then use controls that will be familiar if you've worked with iTunes.

FIGURE 14-3   Songbird also lets you manage an iPod or iPhone.

Manage the iPod with Anapod Explorer on Windows

Anapod Explorer is a full-fledged utility for managing iPods on Windows. Anapod Explorer comes in a Trial Edition that's free but has limited features, and a Full Edition that costs between $20 and $30, depending on how many iPods you use and which model or models they are. For example, the iPod shuffle license for Anapod Explorer is less expensive than those for the iPod nano and the iPod classic. (If you're like most iPod users, further iPods probably lie in your future, so the Universal Edition is probably the best bet, though it's the most expensive.)

Anapod Explorer runs as a plug-in to Windows Explorer, so you work in a largely familiar interface, and you can use drag-and-drop to perform file transfers.

 Anapod Explorer works with Windows Vista, Windows XP, Windows 2000, Windows Me, and Windows 98 Second Edition. At this writing, Anapod Explorer does not yet work with the iPhone or iPod touch.

Get and Install Anapod Explorer

To get Anapod Explorer, go to the Red Chair Software, Inc. website (www .redchairsoftware.com) and either download the Trial Edition or buy one of the paid versions. Double-click the download file to open it.

 Windows Vista or Windows XP with Service Pack 2 may display an Open File— Security Warning dialog box warning you that the publisher of the Anapod Explorer distribution file cannot be verified. This is because the file is not signed with a digital signature. But if you've just downloaded the file from the Red Chair Software website, you can probably be confident that it contains only trustworthy code.

Anapod Explorer installs easily using a wizard. You can choose whether to create Desktop shortcuts and a group on the Start menu. Windows Vista or Windows XP with Service Pack 2 may display a Windows Security Alert dialog box at the end of the Anapod Explorer installation asking if you want Windows Firewall to keep blocking the Red Chair Manager from accepting connections from the Internet or a network (see Figure 14-4). You need to click the Unblock button to allow Red Chair Manager to accept connections before Anapod Explorer will work correctly.

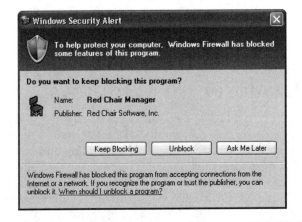

FIGURE 14-4 Windows XP with Service Pack 2 or later automatically blocks Red Chair Manager from accepting connections. You must unblock Red Chair Manager to get Anapod Explorer to work.

Red Chair Manager manifests itself as a controller named Anapod Manager, which is used to establish communication with and control the iPod. Anapod Manager runs by default when you launch Windows and displays an icon in the notification area. You can right-click this icon to launch Anapod Explorer or configure Anapod Manager.

Run Anapod Explorer

When the installation is complete, connect the iPod, and then open Anapod Explorer in one of the following ways:

- Right-click the Anapod Manager icon in the notification area, and then choose Open Anapod Explorer from the shortcut menu. This is usually the easiest way, and it gives you access to the Anapod Manager's other commands.
- Double-click the Anapod Explorer icon on your Desktop (if you chose to create one).
- Choose Start | All Programs | Red Chair Software | Anapod Explorer | Anapod Explorer.

 The first time you run Anapod Explorer, you must activate it for each iPod you will use with it.

You'll see a Windows Explorer window named Anapod Explorer. You can navigate around the Anapod Explorer window using standard Windows techniques.

 If the Open Anapod Explorer command on the Anapod Manager shortcut menu is grayed out, choose the Connect iPod item first to establish the connection with the iPod and then choose the Open Anapod Explorer item.

Transfer Items to and from the iPod with Anapod Explorer

To see the songs and other items on the iPod, click the Audio Tracks item under the Anapod Explorer heading (see Figure 14-5).

You can then add items to the iPod in any of these ways:

- Drag the files and drop them on the Audio Tracks item.
- Copy the files, right-click the Audio Tracks item, and then choose Paste.
- Select one or more files, right-click, click or highlight Send To on the shortcut menu, and then choose the iPod from the submenu.

You can also copy files from the iPod back to your PC by using either drag-and-drop or the Copy To Computer command on the shortcut menu.

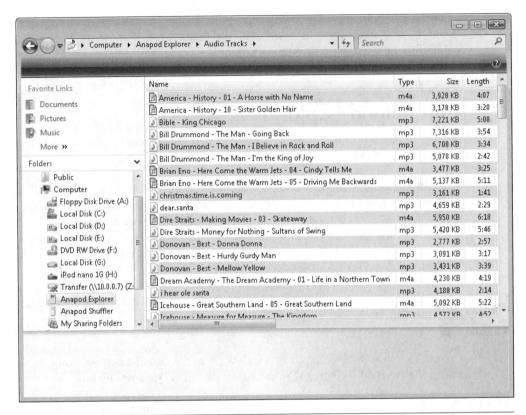

FIGURE 14-5 Anapod Explorer uses Windows Explorer as its interface.

Note Before disconnecting the iPod from your computer, right-click the Anapod Manager icon in the notification area and choose Disconnect iPod from the shortcut menu.

Manage the iPod or iPhone with XPlay on Windows

XPlay was originally developed to let Windows users synchronize Mac-formatted iPods with their PCs. XPlay now works with Windows-formatted iPods as well as Mac-formatted iPods, and also works with the iPhone. XPlay runs on Windows Vista and Windows XP.

XPlay lets you manage the songs and videos on the iPod or iPhone directly using Windows Explorer windows, but perhaps its strongest feature is that it lets you manage the iPod or iPhone from Windows Media Player. If you prefer Windows Media Player to iTunes, this is a compelling reason to choose XPlay.

Get and Install XPlay

To get XPlay, go to the Mediafour Corporation website (www.mediafour.com). The full version of XPlay costs $29.95, so before you pay, it's best to start by downloading the 15-day trial version of XPlay to make sure it works for you and that you like it.

The XPlay installation procedure is straightforward, but you may have to deal with Windows Security messages like the one shown here, and you will probably need to restart your PC to enable XPlay fully.

After the restart, XPlay may prompt you to stop synchronizing the iPod or iPhone with iTunes, as shown next. You'll probably want to click the Yes button to make sure you don't lose the changes you make in XPlay.

Explore the iPod or iPhone Using XPlay

Once you've installed XPlay, you can open XPlay and start exploring the iPod or iPhone in one of these ways:

- Double-click the iPod icon or iPhone icon in the notification area.
- Double-click the Explore My iPod With XPlay 3 icon on your Desktop.
- Choose Start | All Programs | XPlay 3 | Explore My iPod.

XPlay then opens a Windows Explorer window to the root of the drive that represents the iPod or iPhone. Double-click the Music & Videos item to view XPlay's representation of the device's music and video database (see Figure 14-6).

FIGURE 14-6 The XPlay Music & Videos item lets you access your media items in various ways. For example, you can access your music by playlists, albums, artists, genres, composers, or songs.

From here, you can drill down to view music, audiobooks, movies, music videos, playlists, podcasts, TV shows, and videos.

To copy files to the iPod or iPhone, drag-and-drop them on the device's icon.

Add Files to the iPod or iPhone Using Windows Media Player

With XPlay, you can also add files to the iPod or iPhone by opening Windows Media Player and clicking the Sync tab. The iPod or iPhone appears in the pane on the right (see Figure 14-7). Drag files to the Sync List pane, and then click the Start Sync button.

FIGURE 14-7   XPlay lets you add files to the iPod or iPhone directly from Windows Media Player.

Recover Media Files from the iPod or iPhone with XPlay

To copy song files from the iPod or iPhone to your PC using XPlay, drill down to the appropriate song or folder on the device. Then either drag the song or folder to a folder on your PC or right-click, choose Send To, and then select the destination folder. XPlay copies the file or files to a folder named after the iPod or iPhone within the folder you selected.

Prepare the iPod or iPhone for Disconnection

Before disconnecting the iPod or iPhone, eject the iPod or iPhone in one of these ways:

- **Notification area**   Right-click the iPod's or iPhone's icon, and then click Eject on the shortcut menu.
- **Windows Explorer window**   Click the iPod's or iPhone's button in the upper-right corner, and then click the Eject command.

Manage the iPod with Winamp on Windows

Winamp has been a favorite MP3 player for many music addicts since shortly after the MP3 revolution. Recent versions of Winamp can also communicate with the iPod classic, iPod nano, and iPod shuffle—which is great news if you're one of those addicts—but not with the iPod touch or iPhone.

Get and Install Winamp

To get started, download the latest version of Winamp from the Winamp website (www.winamp.com). Double-click the distribution file to run the installation, or simply accept Windows' offer to run the program.

 Winamp comes in a free version called Basic and a paid version called Pro. Start with the Basic version and see how you like it. You can upgrade easily to the Pro version if you like the application.

Installation is straightforward, but pay attention on the following screens:

- **Choose Start Options** Most people find the Start menu entry essential and the Quick Launch icon useful. The Desktop icon is much less useful unless you tend to leave swathes of desktop free of windows.
- **Get The Most Out Of Winamp** Decide whether to install the Winamp Remote feature (for playing your music remotely) and the Winamp Toolbar (which allows you to control Winamp from your web browser); whether to make Winamp Search your default search engine (which you probably don't want to do); and whether to sign up for 50 free MP3 downloads and one audiobook from eMusic (your call, but read the terms and conditions).

Winamp launches itself at the end of the installation and prompts you to choose a *skin* (a custom look). Winamp then asks you to add media files to its library so that it knows which songs you have. Figure 14-8 shows Winamp in a typical configuration, with the main window at the upper-left corner, the Playlist Editor window next to it, and the Media Library window below them both (with an iPod selected in it).

Choose How to Synchronize the iPod with Winamp

Next, connect the iPod to your computer, and tell Winamp how to synchronize it. Follow these steps:

1. In the Media Library window, expand the Portables category in the left pane, and then select the item for the iPod. You may need to collapse any expanded categories, or simply scroll down, to reach the Portables category.
2. Press CTRL-P or, on the main Winamp window, choose Options | Preferences to display the Winamp Preferences dialog box.

FIGURE 14-8   Winamp uses several windows, which you can position (or close) as you please.

3. Under the Media Library category, locate the Portables category, and then click the entry for the iPod (see Figure 14-9).
4. Choose synchronization settings:
   - **Sync tab**   Choose whether to update selected playlists or all playlists *except* those you select. Choose which podcasts you want to synchronize.
   - **AutoFill tab**   Choose whether to have Winamp automatically fill the iPod with songs, whether to prefer higher-rated songs over lower-rated songs, whether to include full albums only, and whether to automatically fill the iPod if you haven't done an AutoFill in the last however many hours (you choose the number).
   - **Transcoding tab**   Choose whether to transcode incompatible tracks—for example, to create MP3 files of tracks the iPod otherwise wouldn't be able to play. Click the Advanced Settings button if you want to force transcoding of high-bitrate-compatible tracks as well. This setting lets you put more music on the iPod, but the transcoding makes syncs take longer.
   - **View tab**   Choose how many filters to use, and choose which (for example, two filters: Artist and Album).
   - **Advanced tab**   Choose whether to use Gapless Playback (if the iPod supports it) and whether to add album art to songs as you transfer them to the iPod.
5. When you've finished choosing synchronization options, click the Close button to close the Winamp Preferences dialog box.

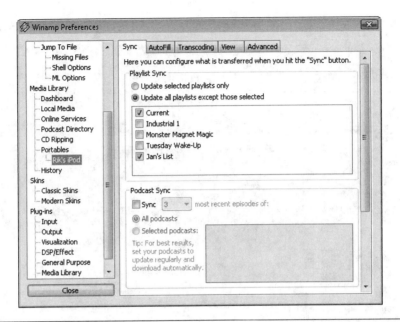

FIGURE 14-9 You'll find the iPod's settings in the Portables subcategory of the Media Library category.

Load the iPod from Winamp

Once you've chosen how to synchronize the iPod with Winamp, you can either sync it or AutoFill it.

Sync the iPod with Winamp

To sync the iPod with Winamp, follow these steps:

1. Select the iPod in the left pane in the Media Library window.
2. Click the Sync button at the bottom of the Media Library window. Winamp displays the Sync dialog box, as shown here.

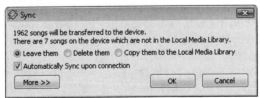

3. If there are songs on the iPod that are not in the media library, choose the appropriate option button: Leave Them, Delete Them, or Copy Them To The Local Media Library.

4. If you want to sync the iPod automatically when you connect it, select the Automatically Sync Upon Connection check box.

5. If you want to see the songs that Winamp will put on the iPod or remove from it, click the More button to expand the dialog box, as shown here. You can choose to remove songs from the selection.

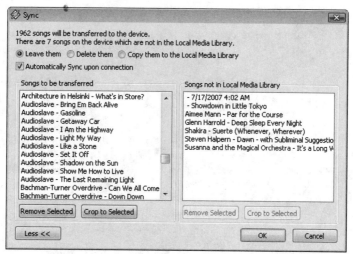

6. When you've finished choosing options, click the OK button. Winamp syncs the songs with the iPod.

Note   When you want to automatically fill the iPod from Winamp, click the AutoFill button at the bottom of the Media Library window, and then follow the prompts.

Eject the iPod

Before you disconnect the iPod, eject it. Select the iPod in the left pane of the Media Library window, and then click the Eject button in the lower-right corner of the Media Library window.

Improve the iTunes Interface with Clutter on the Mac

Sleek and effective as iTunes' interface is, it could be more visually compelling. If you'd like to be able to navigate your music collection by the covers of the CDs rather than by their names, download the freeware application Clutter (see Figure 14-10) from a site such as VersionTracker.com (www.versiontracker.com).

When you start playing a song in iTunes, Clutter tries to download the cover picture for the CD that contains the song. If Clutter can connect to the Internet and finds the picture at Amazon.com, it displays it in the Now Playing window. You can

FIGURE 14-10 Clutter is a free application that enables you to spread your music collection across your desktop and select music by its CD cover.

then drag the picture to your desktop and position it wherever you want it. Each CD cover is a separate window, so you can overlap the covers however you want.

If you start a song playing while your Mac isn't connected to the Internet, after connecting your Mac, you can force Clutter to search Amazon.com for the CD cover by pressing ⌘-F or choosing File | Find Cover On Amazon. If Amazon.com doesn't have the cover, you can search Google by pressing ⌘-G or choosing File | Search Google. Alternatively, you can drag a graphic to the Now Playing window from a browser window or a Finder window, so you can apply any graphic that you have or that you can find.

The main Clutter window shows the details of the song that's currently playing, and it provides a Play/Pause button, a Previous button, and a Next button. You can start the first available song on any CD playing by double-clicking that CD's cover on your desktop.

To get your desktop back again, quit Clutter (press ⌘-G). The next time you start Clutter, it places the CD covers across the desktop in the same arrangement as you left them.

15

Troubleshoot the iPod, iPhone, and iTunes

HOW TO...

- Understand what's in the iPod
- Understand what's in the iPhone
- Avoid things that may harm the iPod or iPhone
- Keep the iPod's or iPhone's operating system up to date
- Carry, clean, and look after the iPod or iPhone—and avoid voiding the warranty
- Troubleshoot the iPod classic, iPod nano, and iPod shuffle
- Troubleshoot the iPhone and iPod touch
- Troubleshoot iTunes problems on Windows
- Troubleshoot iTunes problems on the Mac
- Recover from iTunes running you out of disk space on Windows or the Mac

Apple designs and builds the iPods and iPhone to be as reliable as possible—after all, Apple would like to sell at least one iPod or iPhone to everyone in the world who has a computer, and they'd much prefer to be thwarted in this aim by economics or competition than by negative feedback. But even so, iPods and iPhones go wrong sometimes. Other times, iTunes has problems, either in communicating with the iPod or iPhone or in other ways.

This chapter shows you how to deal with problems with the iPod, the iPhone, and iTunes. The chapter focuses on the models that are current at this writing—the iPod classic, the fourth-generation iPod nano, the second-generation and third-generation iPod shuffle, the iPod touch, and the iPhone—but also provides general information about troubleshooting that will help you with older iPod models too.

Know What's in the iPod

The iPod classic is based around a hard drive that takes up the bulk of the space inside the case. The hard drive is similar to those used in the smaller portable PCs.

The iPod nano, iPod touch, and iPod shuffle use flash memory chips rather than a hard disk, which makes them more or less immune to shock.

Some of the remaining space is occupied by a rechargeable battery that provides between 8 and 20 hours of playback. The length of time the battery provides depends on the model of iPod and on how you use it. Like all rechargeable batteries, the iPod's battery gradually loses its capacity—but if your music collection grows, or if you find the iPod's nonmusic capabilities useful, you'll probably want to upgrade to a higher-capacity model in a couple of years anyway.

The iPod isn't user-upgradeable—in fact, it's designed to be opened only by trained technicians. If you're not such a technician, don't try to open the iPod if the iPod is still under warranty, because opening it voids the warranty. Open the iPod only if it's out of warranty and there's a problem you can fix, such as replacing the battery. See *iPod Repair QuickSteps*, also published by McGraw-Hill, for detailed instructions on replacing the battery and other components of iPods.

The iPod classic includes a 32MB memory chip that's used for running the iPod's operating system and for caching music from the hard drive. The cache reads up to 20 minutes of data ahead from the hard drive for two purposes:

- Once the cache has read the data, the iPod plays back the music from the cache rather than from the hard disk. This lets the hard disk *spin down* (stop running) until it's needed again. Because hard disks consume relatively large amounts of power, the caching spares the battery on the iPod and prolongs battery life.

After the hard disk has spun down, it takes a second or so to spin up again—so when you suddenly change the music during a playlist, there's a small delay while the iPod spins the disk up and then accesses the song you've demanded. If you listen closely (put the iPod to your ear), you can hear the disk spin up (there's a "whee" sound) and search (you'll hear the heads clicking).

- The hard disk can skip if you jiggle or shake the iPod hard enough. Modern hard drives can handle G loads that would finish off elite fighter pilots, so take this on trust rather than trying it out. If the iPod were playing back audio directly from the hard disk, such skipping would interrupt audio playback, much like bumping the needle on a turntable (or bumping a CD player, if you've tried that). But because the memory chip is solid state and has no moving parts, it's immune to skipping.

The length of time for which the caching provides audio depends on the compression ratio you're using and whether you're playing a playlist (or album) or individual songs. If you're playing a list of songs, the iPod can cache as many of the upcoming songs as it has available memory. But when you switch to another song beyond those cached, or to another playlist, the iPod has to start caching once again. This caching involves spinning the hard disk up again and reading from it, which consumes battery power.

 The iPod classic caches video as well, but because video files are much larger than audio files, playing them makes the hard disk work more than does playing songs.

Know What's in the iPhone and iPod touch

Much of the space behind the iPhone's touch screen is taken up by a large battery that can hold enough power for several days' standby, a day's worth of phone calls, or around 24 hours of audio playback. The iPod touch is slimmer and needs less power, because it doesn't need to keep tracking the telephone network, but it still needs a fair amount of energy to play back videos and music, connect to wireless networks, and run all the applications you pack onto it.

Then there's the storage (for example, 8GB, 16GB, or 32GB of flash memory); the processor, wireless chips, and assorted circuitry; an amplifier and speaker; and a microphone, camera lens, and sensor (in the iPhone only). Compared to the touch screen and the battery, these items are surprisingly small.

Apart from these items, the iPhone also contains the following:

- **Antenna**   The iPhone uses the antenna to connect to cell networks.
- **Ambient light sensor**   The iPhone automatically changes the brightness of the screen to make it visible in current light conditions. You can turn off the light sensor and adjust the brightness manually.
- **Accelerometer**   The accelerometer detects when you turn the iPhone and changes the display of supported programs to match the orientation. For example, when browsing in Safari, when you turn the iPhone to landscape orientation, Safari changes the display of the current webpage to landscape (which is normally better for browsing).
- **SIM card**   The SIM card lives in the slot at the top of the iPhone. You can take it out, but there's little reason to do so beyond curiosity unless you're planning to hack your iPhone with another SIM. (To open the SIM slot, push a blunt object such as the end of a straightened paperclip into the little hole.)

The iPod touch contains the accelerometer and ambient light sensor, but not the cell-phone antenna or SIM card. The iPod nano also has an accelerometer.

Avoid Things That May Harm the iPod or iPhone

This section discusses four items that are likely to make the iPod or iPhone unhappy: unexpected disconnections, fire and water (discussed together), and punishment. None of these should come as a surprise, and you should be able to avoid all of them most of the time.

Avoid Disconnecting the iPod or iPhone at the Wrong Time

When you synchronize the iPod or iPhone, always wait until synchronization is complete before disconnecting the player. The easiest way to be sure synchronization is complete is to watch the readout in iTunes. Alternatively:

- **iPod classic or iPod nano**   Make sure the iPod is showing the "OK to disconnect" message.
- **iPod shuffle**   Make sure the green light or amber light stays on steadily.
- **iPhone or iPod touch**   Make sure that the Sync screen is not showing. If the screen is blank, you're fine.

 Note If you have turned on disk mode for the iPod, you must eject the iPod manually after each sync.

Disconnecting at the wrong time may interrupt data transfer and corrupt files. In the worst case, you may need to restore the iPod or iPhone, losing any data on the player that wasn't already on your computer (for example, photos on an iPhone).

If you disconnect the iPod or iPhone from your Mac at the wrong time, your Mac displays the Device Removal dialog box, shown in Figure 15-1, telling you that you should have ejected it properly and that data may have been lost or damaged. If iTunes was transferring data to the iPod or iPhone when you disconnected it, you may also see another dialog box such as the one that appears at the bottom of Figure 15-1.

At this writing, iTunes for Windows tends not to notice if you disconnect an iPod or iPhone when it's telling you not to. If you find that the device's entry is showing up in the Source list in iTunes for Windows long after the iPod or iPhone has bolted, shut the stable door by clicking the Eject button to the right of the device's entry in the Source list.

After an unexpected disconnection, the iPod or iPhone simply figures out there's a problem and dusts itself down. The iPod classic or iPod nano then displays its main screen; the iPhone or iPod touch displays its Home screen.

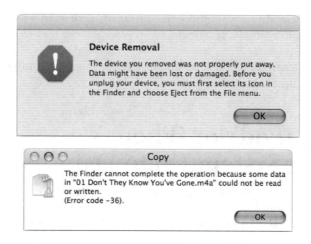

FIGURE 15-1   Mac OS X objects when you disconnect the iPod or iPhone at the wrong time.

Avoid Fire and Water

The iPods and iPhone have a wider range of operating temperatures than most humans, so if you keep the iPod or iPhone in your pocket, it will generally be at least as comfortable as you are.

Where an iPod or iPhone may run into trouble is if you leave it running in a confined space, such as the glove box of a car parked in the sun, that might reach searing temperatures. If you live somewhere sunny, take the iPod or iPhone with you when you get out of the car.

 If the iPod or iPhone gets much too hot or much too cold, don't use it. Give it time to return to a more normal temperature before trying to find out if it still works.

Further, the iPod and iPhone aren't waterproof, so don't expect to use them for swimming or in the bath unless you get a fully waterproof case (see Chapter 4).

Avoid Physically Abusing the iPod or iPhone

Apple has built the iPod and iPhone to be tough, so they will survive an impressive amount of rough handling. If you're interested in finding out how tough a particular model is without funding the experiment yourself, check out sites such as these:

- Ars Technica (http://arstechnica.com) performs real-world tests to destruction, such as dropping devices.

- Will It Blend (www.willitblend.com) tests devices in a blender, which is entertaining if less practical.

Use a case to protect the iPod or iPhone. Chapter 4 outlines some of the many options available.

Keep the iPod's or iPhone's Operating System Up to Date

To get the best performance from the iPod or iPhone, it's a good idea to keep its operating system (or *firmware*) up to date. To do so, follow the instructions in this section to update the iPod or iPhone on Windows or Mac OS X.

Update the iPod or iPhone on Windows

iTunes is set to check automatically for updates, and it displays a message box such as that shown here if it finds an update. Click the Download And Install button to download the update and install it immediately.

If you don't want iTunes to check for updates automatically, clear the Check For Updates Automatically check box on the General tab of the iTunes dialog box.

Alternatively, you can check for updates manually. Follow these steps:

1. Connect the iPod or iPhone to your computer. The computer starts iTunes (if it's not running) or activates it (if it is running).
2. In iTunes, click the iPod's or iPhone's entry in the Source list to display the iPod or iPhone screens.
3. Click the Summary tab if it's not automatically displayed. (For an iPod shuffle, click the Settings tab.)
4. Click the Check For Update button.

When the update is complete, the iPod or iPhone appears in the Source list in iTunes.

Update the iPod or iPhone on Mac OS X

You can get iPod or iPhone updates on Mac OS X in three ways:

- **iTunes**   iTunes checks periodically for updates. When it finds an update, iTunes displays a dialog box such as the one shown here. Click the Download And Install button to download the update and install it immediately.

If you don't want iTunes to check for updates automatically, clear the Check For Updates Automatically check box on the General tab of the Preferences dialog box for iTunes.

- **Software Update**   Choose Apple | Software Update to check for updates to Mac OS X and all Apple software. Mac OS X presents all updates to you in the Software Update dialog box. Click the Install button, and then enter your administrative password in the Authenticate dialog box. Mac OS X downloads the updates and installs them.

  Alternatively, you can check for updates manually. Follow these steps:

  1. Connect the iPod or iPhone to your computer. The computer starts iTunes (if it's not running) or activates it (if it is running).
  2. In iTunes, click the iPod's or iPhone's entry in the Source list to display the iPod or iPhone screens.
  3. Click the Summary tab if it's not automatically displayed. (For an iPod shuffle, click the Settings tab.)
  4. Click the Check For Update button.

  When the update is complete, the iPod or iPhone appears in the Source list in iTunes.

Carry and Store the iPod or iPhone Safely

Carrying and storing the iPod or iPhone safely is largely a matter of common sense:

- Use a case to protect the iPod or iPhone from scratches, dings, and falls. A wide variety of cases are available, from svelte-and-stretchy little numbers designed to hug your body during vigorous exercise, to armored cases apparently intended to survive *Die Hard* movies, to waterproof cases good enough to take sailing, swimming, or even diving. See Chapter 4 for details.

How to... **Clean the iPod or iPhone**

The iPhone and iPod touch come with a soft cloth for wiping smudges off the screen, which is made of scratch-resistant, optical-quality glass. Unless you do anything horrible to your iPhone or iPod touch, the cloth should be all you need.

To keep an iPod looking its best, you'll probably need to clean it from time to time. Before doing so, unplug it to reduce the chance of short disagreements with the basic principles of electricity. Treat the Dock Connector port and headphone port with due care; neither is waterproof.

Various people recommend different cleaning products for cleaning iPods. You'll find assorted recommendations on the Web—but unless you're sure the people know what they're talking about, proceed with great care. In particular, avoid any abrasive cleaner that may mar an iPod's acrylic faceplate or its polished back and sides.

Unless you've dipped the iPod in anything very unpleasant, you'll do best to start with Apple's recommendation: Simply dampen a soft, lint-free cloth (such as an eyeglass or camera-lens cloth) and wipe the iPod gently with it.

But if you've scratched the iPod, you may need to resort to heavier-duty cleaners. PodShop iDrops seems to have a good reputation; you can get it from Amazon.com and other online retailers, or directly from PodShop (http://podshop.com).

- If the iPod or iPhone spends time on your desk or another surface open to children, animals, or moving objects, use a dock or stand to keep it in place. A dock or stand should also make the iPod or iPhone easier to control with one hand. For example, if you patch the iPod or iPhone in to your stereo, use a dock or stand to keep it upright so you can push its buttons with one hand. See Chapter 4 for more information on docks and stands.

Understand Your Warranty and Know Which Actions Void It

Like most electronics goods, your iPod or iPhone almost certainly came with a warranty. Unlike with most other electronics goods, your chances of needing to use that warranty are relatively high. This is because you're likely to use the iPod or iPhone extensively and carry it with you. After all, that's what it's designed for.

Even if you don't sit on the iPod or iPhone, rain or other water doesn't creep into it, and gravity doesn't dash it sharply against something unforgiving (such as the sidewalk), the iPod or iPhone may suffer from other problems—anything from critters or debris jamming the Dock Connector port, to its flash memory becoming faulty or its hard drive getting corrupted, or its operating system getting scrambled. Perhaps most likely of all is that the battery will lose its potency, either gradually or dramatically. If any of these misfortunes befalls your iPod or iPhone, you'll probably want to get it repaired under warranty—provided you haven't voided the warranty by treating the iPod or iPhone in a way that breaches its terms.

All the iPods and the iPhone come with a one-year warranty. To find details of whether an iPod or iPhone is under warranty, enter your iPod's or iPhone's serial number and your country into Apple's Online Service Agent (https://selfsolve.apple.com).

Most of the warranty is pretty straightforward, but the following points are worth noting:

- You have to make your claim within the warranty period, so if the iPod or iPhone fails a day short of a year after you bought it, you'll need to make your claim instantly. Do you know where your receipt is?
- If the iPod or iPhone is currently under warranty, you can buy an AppleCare package for it to extend its warranty to two years. Most extended warranties on electrical products are a waste of money, because the extended warranties largely duplicate your existing rights as a consumer to be sold a product that's functional and of merchantable quality. But given the attrition rate among hard-used iPods and iPhones, AppleCare may be a good idea.
- Apple can choose whether to repair the iPod or iPhone using either new or refurbished parts, exchange it for another device that's at least functionally equivalent but may be either new or rebuilt (and may contain used parts), or refund you the purchase price. Unless you have valuable data on the iPod or iPhone, the refund is a great option, because you'll be able to get a new iPod or iPhone—perhaps even a higher-capacity one.
- Apple takes no responsibility for getting back any data on the iPod or iPhone. This isn't surprising because Apple may need to reformat the memory or hard drive or replace the player altogether. But this means that you must back up the iPod or iPhone if it contains data you value that you don't have copies of elsewhere.

You can void your warranty more or less effortlessly in any of the following easily avoidable ways:

- Damage the iPod or iPhone deliberately.
- Open the iPod or iPhone or have someone other than Apple open it for you. The iPod and iPhone are designed to be opened only by trained technicians. The only reason to open an iPod or iPhone is to replace its battery or replace a component—and you shouldn't do that yourself unless the iPod or iPhone is out of warranty (and out of AppleCare, if you bought AppleCare for it). If you're tempted to replace a battery, make sure you know what it involves: Replacing the battery in the iPhone and in some iPods requires a delicate touch with a soldering iron. See *iPod Repair QuickSteps* for the gory details.
- Modify the iPod or iPhone. Modifications such as installing a higher-capacity drive in an iPod classic would necessarily involve opening it anyway, but external modifications can void your warranty, too. For example, if you choose to trepan an iPhone so as to screw a holder directly onto it, you would void your warranty. (You'd also stand a great chance of drilling into something sensitive inside the case.)

Troubleshoot the iPod

When something goes wrong with the iPod, take three deep breaths before you do anything. Then take another three deep breaths if you need them. Then try to work out what's wrong.

Remember that a calm and rational approach will always get you further than blind panic. This is easy to say (and if you're reading this when the iPod is running smoothly, easy to nod your head at). But if you've just dropped the iPod onto a hard surface from a great enough height for gravity to give it some acceleration, left it on the roof of your car so it fell off and landed in the perfect position for you to reverse over it, or gotten caught in an unexpectedly heavy rainfall, you'll probably be desperate to find out if the iPod is alive or dead.

So take those three deep breaths. You may well *not* have ruined the iPod forever—but if you take some heavy-duty troubleshooting actions without making sure they're necessary, you might lose some data that wasn't already lost or do some damage you'll have trouble repairing.

Things can go wrong with any of the following:

- The iPod's hardware—anything from the Dock Connector port or headphone port to the battery, the hard disk, or the flash memory
- The iPod's software
- The cable you're using to connect the iPod to your computer
- Your computer's USB port or USB controller
- iTunes or the other software you're using to control the iPod

Given all these possibilities, be prepared to spend some time troubleshooting any problem.

Learn Troubleshooting Maneuvers for the iPod classic, iPod nano, and iPod shuffle

This section discusses several maneuvers you may need to use to troubleshoot the iPod: resetting the iPod, draining its battery, restoring its operating system on either Windows or Mac OS X, and running a disk scan.

Reset the iPod

If the iPod freezes so it doesn't respond to the controls, you can reset it:

1. Connect it to a power source—either a computer that's not sleeping or the iPod Power Adapter plugged into an electrical socket. (The iPod Power Adapter, or a generic equivalent, is a great weapon to have in your troubleshooting arsenal. You can buy it from the Apple Store.)

2. Reset the iPod: Move the Hold switch to the On position, and then move it back to the Off position. Hold down the Menu button and the Select button for about six seconds, until the iPod displays the Apple logo.
3. After you release the buttons, give the iPod a few seconds to finish booting.

If the iPod freezes when you don't have a power source available, try resetting it by using the preceding technique without the power source. Sometimes it works; other times it doesn't. But you've nothing to lose by trying.

 To reset a second-generation or third-generation iPod shuffle, move the switch to the Off position, and then move it back to the On position.

Drain the iPod's Battery

If you can't reset the iPod, its battery might have gotten into such a low state that it needs draining. This supposedly seldom happens—but the planets might have decided that you're due a bad day.

To drain the battery, disconnect the iPod from its power source and leave it for 24 hours. (Yes, I can imagine your pain.) Then try plugging the iPod into a power source. After the iPod has received power for a few seconds, reset the iPod: Move the Hold switch to the On position, and then move it back to the Off position. Hold down the Menu button and the Select button for about six seconds, until the iPod displays the Apple logo.

If draining the battery and recharging it revives the iPod, update the iPod's software with the latest version to try to prevent the problem from occurring again. See the section "Keep the iPod's or iPhone's Operating System Up to Date," earlier in this chapter, for details on how to update the operating system.

Restore the iPod

If the iPod is having severe difficulties, you may need to restore it. Restoring the iPod replaces its operating system with a new copy of the operating system that has Apple's factory settings.

 Restoring the iPod deletes all the data on the iPod's hard disk or flash memory— the operating system and all your songs, photos, videos, contacts, calendar information, and notes—and returns the iPod to its original factory settings. So restoring the iPod is usually a last resort when troubleshooting. Unless the iPod is so messed up that you cannot access its contents, back up all the data you care about that's stored on the iPod before restoring it.

Restore the iPod on Windows

To restore the iPod on Windows, follow these steps:

1. Connect the iPod to your PC via USB as usual. Allow iTunes to synchronize with the iPod if it's set to do so.

2. In iTunes, click the iPod's entry in the Source list to display the iPod screens.
3. Click the Summary tab if it's not already displayed. For an iPod shuffle, click the Settings tab.
4. Click the Restore button. iTunes warns you that you will lose all the songs and data currently stored on the iPod, as shown here.

5. Click the Restore button. iTunes formats the iPod's hard disk or flash storage, and then restores the iPod's operating system.
6. iTunes displays a message box on a 10-second countdown telling you (as shown here) that the iPod is restarting and that it will appear in the iTunes Source list after that. Either click the OK button to dismiss this message box, or wait for the timer to close it automatically.

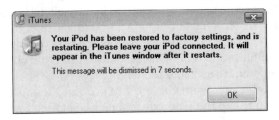

7. When iTunes notices the iPod after it restarts, iTunes displays the Set Up Your iPod screen. Type the name you want to give the iPod; choose whether to sync songs, videos, and photos with it; and then click the Done button.

After you disconnect the iPod, set the language it uses.

Restore the iPod on Mac OS X

To restore the iPod on Mac OS X, follow these steps:

1. Connect the iPod to your computer as usual. If the iPod is set to synchronize automatically with iTunes, allow it to do so.
2. In iTunes, click the iPod's entry in the Source list.
3. Click the Summary tab if it's not already displayed. For an iPod shuffle, click the Settings tab.
4. Click the Restore button to start the restore process. iTunes warns you that you will lose all the songs and data currently stored on the iPod, as shown next.

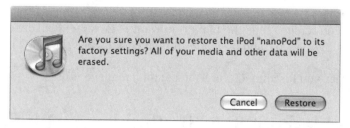

5. Click the Restore button if you want to proceed. Mac OS X displays the Authenticate dialog box to check that you have administrative rights.
6. Type your password in the Password text box, and then click the OK button. iTunes formats the iPod's hard disk or flash storage, and then restores the iPod's operating system.
7. iTunes displays a message box on a 10-second countdown telling you (as shown here) that the iPod is restarting and that it will appear in the iTunes Source list after that. Either click the OK button to dismiss this message box, or wait for the timer to close it automatically.

How to...   **Recover from a Disk Insertion Error on the Mac**

If something goes wrong while you're restoring the iPod, Mac OS X may display a Disk Insertion error message box such as the one shown here.

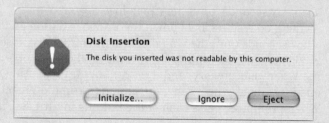

The large red exclamation icon makes the problem seem severe, but click the Ignore button rather than the Initialize button. (Clicking the Initialize button launches Disk Utility, the tool used for partitioning, repairing, and initializing regular hard disks, as opposed to the iPod.) Then try the Restore operation again. Usually, you'll be able to make it work after an attempt or two.

8. When iTunes notices the iPod after it restarts, iTunes displays the Set Up Your iPod screen. Type the name you want to give the iPod; choose whether to sync songs, videos, and photos with it; and then click the Done button.

After you disconnect the iPod, set the language it uses.

Troubleshoot Specific Problems with the iPod classic, iPod nano, and iPod shuffle

This section discusses how to troubleshoot specific problems with the iPod, starting with the more common problems and moving gradually toward the esoteric end of the spectrum.

The iPod Won't Respond to Keypresses

If the iPod won't respond to keypresses, follow as many of these steps, in order, as are necessary to revive it:

1. Check that the Hold switch on the iPod isn't on. If you're using a remote control that has a Hold switch, check that too.
2. Check that the battery is charged. When the battery is too low to run the iPod (for example, for playing back music), the iPod displays a low-battery symbol—a battery icon with an exclamation point—for a few seconds when you press a key. (You may miss this icon if you're using a remote or you're pressing the iPod's buttons without looking at the screen.) Connect the iPod to a power source (either a computer that's not asleep or the iPod Power Adapter, if you have one), give it a few minutes to recharge a little, disconnect it again, and then try turning it on.
3. Reset the iPod by holding down the Select button and the Menu button for about six seconds, until the Apple logo appears.
4. Enter diagnostic mode and run the KeyTest test or the WheelAndKey test like this:
   - Reset the iPod again. Hold down the Select button and the Menu button for about six seconds, until the Apple logo appears.
   - As the iPod restarts, hold down the Previous button and the Select button for a few seconds until the iPod displays the initial diagnostics screen.
   - Navigate to the test and run it. On the iPod classic, open the IO category, then the Wheel subcategory, and then run the KeyTest test. On the iPod nano, open the TouchWheel category, and then run the WheelAndKey test.
   - When prompted, press each of the buttons in turn. See if the iPod registers the presses.

Your Computer Doesn't React when You Plug In the iPod

If your computer (Mac or PC) doesn't react when you plug in the iPod, any of several things might have gone wrong. Try the actions described in the following subsections.

Unplug Any Other Devices in the USB Chain   If there's another device plugged into your computer's USB controller, try unplugging it. The problem may be that the controller can't supply power to another unpowered device as well as to the iPod.

 If the connection uses a hub, disconnect the hub and try a direct connection.

Check That the Cable Is Working   Make sure that the cable is firmly connected to the iPod (or its dock) and to the USB port on your computer. If you normally use a dock or connecting stand for the iPod, try the connection without it in case the dock or stand is causing the problem. (This doesn't apply to the second-generation iPod shuffle, which you cannot connect without its dock or a special cable.)

 If you're not sure the cable is working, and you have an iPod Power Adapter, you can run a partial check by plugging the cable into the iPod and the iPod Power Adapter, and then plugging the iPod Power Adapter into an electrical socket. If the iPod starts charging, you'll know that at least the power-carrying wires on the cable are working. It's likely that the data-carrying wires are working as well.

Check That the USB Port on the Computer Is Working   In most cases, the easiest way to check is by plugging in another device that you know is working. For example, you might plug in a USB scanner or external CD-ROM drive.

The iPod Says "Do Not Disconnect" for Ages when Connected to Your Computer

When you connect the iPod to your PC or Mac, the iPod displays the "Do not disconnect" message while it synchronizes with iTunes. When synchronization is complete, the iPod should display the charging indicator for as long as it's taking on power via the USB cable.

 But sometimes it doesn't. If the iPod displays the "Do not disconnect" message for long after synchronization should have finished, first try to remember if you've enabled disk mode on the iPod. If so, you always need to eject the iPod manually, so this message doesn't mean that there's a problem. You can eject the iPod in one of these ways:

- Click the Eject button next to the iPod's entry in the Source list in iTunes.
- Right-click the iPod in the Source list, and then choose Eject from the shortcut menu.
- Right-click the iPod's drive icon in a Computer window (Vista) or My Computer window (Windows XP), or CTRL-click the iPod's icon on your Mac desktop, and then choose Eject from the shortcut menu.
- On the Mac, from the Finder, drag the iPod to the Trash, or select it and press ⌘-E.

The iPod should then display the "OK to disconnect" message.

 If you haven't enabled disk mode on an iPod classic, the iPod's hard drive may have gotten stuck spinning. If you pick up the iPod to scrutinize it further, you'll notice it's much hotter than usual if the drive has been spinning for a while. Try unmounting it anyway using one of the methods described in the preceding list. The iPod should then display the "OK to disconnect" message, and you can disconnect it safely.

If that doesn't work, you may need to reset the iPod (see "Reset the iPod," earlier in this chapter). After the iPod reboots, you should be able to eject it by taking one of the actions listed previously.

Tip If you experience this problem frequently, try updating the iPod to the latest software version available. If there's no newer software version, or if an update doesn't help, use the AC adapter to recharge the iPod rather than recharging it from your computer.

The iPod Displays Only the Apple Logo When You Turn It On

If, when you turn on the iPod, it displays the Apple logo as usual but goes no further, there's most likely a problem with the iPod software. Try resetting the iPod first to see if that clears the problem. (See "Reset the iPod," earlier in this chapter.)

If resetting doesn't work, usually you'll need to restore the iPod as described in "Restore the iPod," earlier in this chapter. Restoring the iPod loses all data stored on it, so try several resets first.

Songs in Your Library Aren't Transferred to the iPod

If songs you've added to your library aren't transferred to the iPod even though you've synchronized successfully since adding the songs, there are two possibilities:

- First, check that you haven't configured the iPod for partial synchronization or manual synchronization. For example, if you've chosen to synchronize only selected playlists, the iPod won't synchronize new music files not included on those playlists.
- Second, check that the songs' tags include the artist's name and song name. Without these two items of information, iTunes won't transfer the songs to the iPod, because the iPod's interface won't be able to display the songs to you. You can force iTunes to transfer song files that lack artist and song name tags by adding the song files to a playlist, but in the long run, you'll benefit from tagging all your song files correctly.

Note For a second-generation iPod shuffle, there's another possibility: The songs may be in a format that the iPod shuffle cannot play without conversion. For example, the iPod shuffle cannot play songs in the Apple Lossless Encoding format. However, you can select the Convert Higher Bit Rate Songs To 128 Kbps AAC check box on the Settings tab for the iPod. iTunes then converts the Apple Lossless Encoding format or other unplayable files to AAC files. The only downside is that the conversion makes the process of loading the iPod shuffle much slower.

Troubleshoot the iPhone and the iPod touch

Unlike the iPods, which run their own operating systems, the iPhone and iPod touch actually run a version of Mac OS X. As a result, troubleshooting the iPhone and iPod touch sometimes is more like dealing with problems in Mac OS X than troubleshooting the other iPods.

Deal with Program Crashes

Normally, the programs in the iPhone and iPod touch just keep running: When you use the Home screen to switch to a different program, the program you were using before keeps running in the background, where you can't see it. When you go back to that program, you'll find it doing what it was doing before.

If a program stops responding, you can close it by "force-quitting" it—in other words, forcing it to quit. To force-quit a program, hold down the Home button for six seconds. Release the Home button when the iPhone or iPod touch displays the Home screen. In the background, the iPhone or iPod touch restarts the program, so if you touch its icon on the Home screen, you'll find it running again.

Restart, Reset, or Erase the iPhone or iPod touch

Usually, you'll keep the iPhone running all the time so that you can receive incoming calls even when you're not using any of its other functions. Similarly, you'll keep the iPod touch running so that you can play songs or videos, or access wireless networks. But if your iPhone or iPod touch gets seriously hung, so that it stops responding to the touch screen, you may need to restart it. If restarting doesn't work, you will need to reset it.

Restart the iPhone or iPod touch

To restart the iPhone or iPod touch, follow these steps:

1. Hold down the Sleep/Wake button until the screen shows the message "slide to power off."
2. Slide your finger across the screen. The iPhone or iPod touch shuts down.
3. Wait a few seconds, and then press the Sleep/Wake button again. The Apple logo appears, and the iPhone or iPod touch then starts.

Perform a Hardware Reset

If you're not able to restart the iPhone or iPod touch as described in the previous section, escalate the problem to the next level and perform a hardware reset. Hold down the Sleep/Wake button and the Home button together until the Apple logo appears on the screen.

Perform a Software Reset

If performing a hardware reset (as described previously) doesn't clear the problem, you may need to perform a software reset. This action resets the iPhone's or iPod touch's settings but doesn't erase your data from the device.

To perform a software reset, follow these steps:

1. Press the Home button to go to the Home screen unless you're already there.
2. Touch the Settings icon to reach the Settings screen.
3. Touch the General item to reach the General screen.
4. Scroll down to the bottom and touch the Reset item to reach the Reset screen.
5. Touch the Reset All Settings button, and then touch the Reset All Settings button on the confirmation screen.

Erase the Content and Settings on the iPhone or iPod touch

If even the software reset doesn't fix the problem, try erasing all content and settings. Before you do so, remove any content you have created on the iPhone or iPod touch— assuming the device is working well enough for you to do so. For example, send any notes that you have written on the iPhone or iPod touch to yourself via e-mail, or sync the iPhone to transfer any photos you have taken with its camera to your computer.

To erase the content and settings, follow these steps:

1. Press the Home button to go to the Home screen unless you're already there.
2. Touch the Settings icon to reach the Settings screen.
3. Touch the General item to reach the General screen.
4. Touch the Reset item to reach the Reset screen.
5. Touch the Erase All Content And Settings button, and then touch the Erase iPhone button or Erase iPod button on the confirmation screen.

After erasing all content and settings, sync the iPhone or iPod touch to load the content and settings back onto it.

Restore the iPhone or iPod touch

If you've tried all the other troubleshooting actions described earlier in this section, and your iPhone or iPod touch is still acting hinky, you need to restore it. The process is the same for Windows and the Mac; this section shows screens from Windows with an iPhone.

Restoring the iPhone or iPod touch wipes all the data off the device, resets the hardware, and reinstalls the software. Restoring an iPhone essentially returns the iPhone to the condition in which you bought it, except that the SIM remains activated. After restoring the iPhone, you sync it with iTunes again, and it picks up all the data from iTunes (and other programs, such as your address book) that it had before. Restoring an iPod touch is much the same except that it doesn't have a SIM.

Caution Before restoring the iPhone or iPod touch, remove any content that you've created on the device—for example, notes, photos (on the iPhone), or screen captures. Again, this assumes that the device is functioning well enough for you to remove the content.

To restore the iPhone or iPod touch, follow these steps:

1. Connect the iPhone or iPod touch to your computer, and wait for it to appear in the Source list in iTunes.
2. Click the iPhone's or iPod touch's entry in the Source list to display the iPhone screens or iPod screens.
3. Click the Summary tab if it's not already displayed.
4. Click the Restore button. If the device contains data that hasn't yet been backed up, iTunes prompts you to back it up, as shown here. Click the Back Up button or the Don't Back Up button, as appropriate.

5. Once any question of backup has been resolved, iTunes displays a confirmation message box, as shown here, to make sure you know that you're about to erase all the data from the device.

Note If a new version of the iPhone or iPod touch software is available, iTunes prompts you to restore and update the device instead of merely restoring it. Click the Restore And Update button if you want to proceed; otherwise, click the Cancel button.

6. Click the Restore button to close the message box. iTunes wipes the device's contents, and then restores the software, showing you its progress while it works.
7. At the end of the restore process, iTunes restarts the iPhone or iPod touch. iTunes displays an information message box, shown next, for 10 seconds while

it does so. Either click the OK button, or allow the countdown timer to close the message box automatically.

8. After the iPhone or iPod touch restarts, it appears in the Source list in iTunes. For an iPhone, instead of the iPhone's regular tabbed screens, the Set Up Your iPhone screen appears (see Figure 15-2).
9. To restore your data, make sure the Restore From The Backup Of option button is selected, and verify that the correct iPhone appears in the drop-down list.

How to... | ## Resolve the "SIM Card Is Not Installed" Error on an iPhone

If the iPhone shows you the message "The iPhone cannot be used with iTunes because the SIM card is not installed," as shown next, have a look at the SIM slot on top of the iPhone to make sure that it hasn't been popped out. Normally, opening the SIM slot requires human intervention, though not necessarily your own—for example, the iPhone seems to have an even greater attraction for children than for adults.

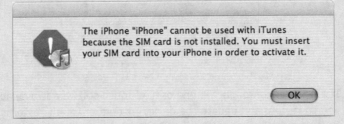

If the SIM slot is open, make sure the SIM is correctly aligned, and then push it back in. If the SIM slot seems fine, check the connection between the iPhone and the computer. This error can occur when the connection between the two is broken while iTunes is trying to access the iPhone—for example, if you bump the iPhone shortly after you put it in a dock.

FIGURE 15-2   After restoring the iPhone's system software, you will normally want
to restore your data from backup. The alternative is to set up the
iPhone as a new iPhone.

10. Click the Continue button. iTunes restores your data and then restarts the
iPhone, displaying another countdown message box while it does so, as shown
here. Either click the OK button, or allow the countdown timer to close the
message box automatically.

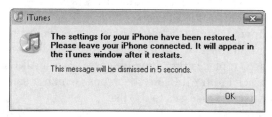

11. After the iPhone appears in the Source list in iTunes following the restart, you
can use it as normal.

Troubleshoot iTunes on Windows

This section shows you how to troubleshoot the problems you're most likely to
encounter when running iTunes on Windows.

iTunes Won't Start on Windows

If iTunes displays the Cannot Open iTunes dialog box saying that you can't open
iTunes because another user currently has it open, it means that Windows is using
Fast Switching and that someone else is logged on under another account and has

iTunes open. The following illustration shows the Cannot Open iTunes dialog box on Windows Vista, but this dialog box also appears on Windows XP.

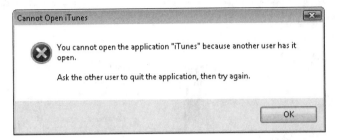

Click the OK button to dismiss the dialog box. If you know the other user's password, or if you know they have no password, switch to their account, close iTunes, and then switch back to your own account.

If you don't know the other user's password and you have a Standard user account (Windows Vista) or a Limited user account (Windows XP), you'll need to get them to log on and close iTunes for you.

If you have an Administrator account, you can use Task Manager to close iTunes. Follow these steps:

1. Right-click the taskbar, and then choose Task Manager from the shortcut menu to open Task Manager.
2. Click the Processes tab to display its contents. At first, as shown on the left in Figure 15-3, Task Manager shows only the processes running for your user session of Windows, not for other users' sessions.
3. Display processes for all users:
   - **Windows Vista** Click the Show Processes From All Users button, and then go through User Account Control for the Windows Task Manager feature. Task Manager replaces the Show Processes From All Users button with the Show Processes From All Users check box (which it selects), and then adds the other users' processes to the list.
   - **Windows XP** Select the Show Processes From All Users check box.
4. Select the iTunes.exe process in the Image Name column, as shown on the right in Figure 15-3. (If the list isn't sorted by the Image Name column, click the Image Name header to sort it that way.)
5. Click the End Process button. Task Manager displays the dialog box shown next, confirming that you want to end the process.

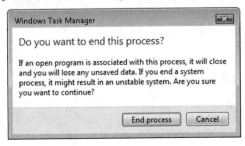

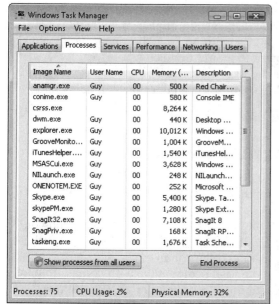
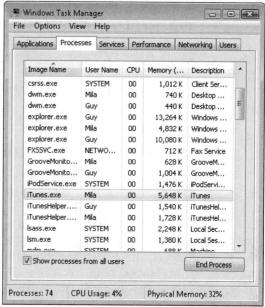

FIGURE 15-3   If someone else is running iTunes on a Windows Vista computer that uses Fast User Switching, you may need to use Task Manager to close iTunes before you can use it.

6. Click the End Process button. Task Manager closes the instance of iTunes in the other user's session.
7. Click the Close button (the × button) to close Task Manager.

You can now start iTunes as normal.

iTunes Doesn't Recognize the iPod

If the iPod doesn't appear in the Source list in iTunes, take as many of the following steps as necessary to make it appear there:

1. Check that the iPod is okay. If you find it's displaying an exclamation point or the Sad iPod symbol, you'll know iTunes isn't guilty this time.
2. Check that the iPod knows it's connected to your PC. The iPod should be displaying the Do Not Disconnect message. If it's not, fix the connection so that it does display this message.
3. Toggle the Hold switch on the iPod, and then restart the iPod by holding down the Play button and the Menu button together for several seconds. See if the iPod appears in the Source list in iTunes.

4. If restarting the iPod doesn't make it appear in iTunes, repeat the process for restarting it. This time, when the iPod displays the Apple symbol, hold down the Select button and the Play button for a moment to force disk mode. Forcing disk mode sends a request to the computer to mount the iPod as a drive.
5. Restart iTunes, and see if it notices the iPod this time.
6. If restarting iTunes doesn't make it recognize the iPod, restart Windows, and then restart iTunes.

iTunes Won't Play Some AAC Files

iTunes and AAC go together like bacon and eggs, but you may find that iTunes can't play some AAC files. This can happen for either of two reasons:

- You're trying to play a protected AAC file in a shared library or playlist, and your computer isn't authorized to play the file. In this case, iTunes skips the protected file.
- The AAC file was created by an application other than iTunes that uses a different AAC standard. The AAC file then isn't compatible with iTunes. To play the file, use the application that created the file, or another application that can play the file, to convert the file to another format that iTunes supports—for example, MP3 or WAV.

The iPod or iPhone "Is Linked to Another iTunes Library" Message

If, when you connect the iPod or iPhone to your computer, iTunes displays a message such as "The iPod 'iPod_name' is linked to another iTunes library," chances are that you've plugged the wrong iPod or iPhone into your computer. The message box also offers to change this device's allegiance from its current computer to this PC. Click the No button and check which iPod or iPhone this is before synchronizing it.

 For details about moving the iPod or iPhone from one computer to another, see "Change the Computer to Which an iPod or iPhone Is Linked," in Chapter 11.

iTunes Runs You Out of Hard-Disk Space on Windows

As you saw earlier in the book, iTunes lets you choose between copying to your library folder all the files you add to your library and leaving the files in other locations. Adding all the files to your library means you have all the files available in one place. This can be good, especially if your computer is a laptop and you want to be able to access your music and videos when it's not connected to your external drives or network drives. But if you have a large library, it may not all fit on your laptop's hard disk.

If your files are stored on your hard drive in folders other than your library folder, you have three choices:

- You can issue the File | Library | Consolidate Library command to make iTunes copy the files to your library folder, doubling the amount of space they take up. In almost all cases, this is the worst possible choice to make. (Rarely, you might want redundant copies of your files in your library so you can experiment with them.)
- You can have iTunes store references to the files rather than copies of them. If you also have files in your library folder, this is the easiest solution. To do this, clear the Copy Files To iTunes Music Folder When Adding To Library check box on the Advanced tab in the iTunes dialog box in Windows.
- You can move your library to the folder that contains your files. This is the easiest solution if your library is empty.

If you choose to consolidate your library, and there's not enough space on your hard disk, you'll see the following message box. "IBM_PRELOAD" is the name of the hard disk on the computer.

Clearly, this *isn't* okay, but iTunes doesn't let you cancel the operation. Don't let iTunes pack your hard disk as full of files as it can, because that may make Windows crash. Quit iTunes by pressing ALT-F4 or choosing File | Exit. If iTunes doesn't respond, right-click the taskbar and choose Task Manager to display Windows Task Manager. On the Applications tab, select the iTunes entry, and then click the End Task button. If Windows double-checks that you want to end the task, confirm the decision.

Once you've done this, you may need to remove the files you've just copied to your library from the folder. You can do this by using the Date Created information about the files and folders, because Windows treats the copy made by the consolidation as a new file.

To find the files and folders, search for them. The process differs on Windows Vista and Windows XP, so follow the instructions in the next sections for the OS you're using.

Search for the New Files and Folders on Windows Vista

To search for the new files and folders on Windows Vista, follow these steps:

1. Choose Start | Search to display a Search Results window.
2. Click the Advanced Search link at the right end of the toolbar to display the Advanced Search options.

3. In the Location drop-down list, click the Choose Search Location item to display the Choose Search Locations dialog box.

4. In the Change Selected Locations box, navigate to the folder that contains your iTunes Music folder. For example, if your iTunes Music folder is in its default location, follow these steps:
   - Click the triangle next to your username to expand its contents.

 If you're not sure where your iTunes Music folder is, switch to iTunes, press CTRL-COMMA, and look at the iTunes Music Folder Location box on the Advanced tab in the iTunes dialog box.

   - Click the triangle next to the Music folder to expand its contents.
   - Click the triangle next to the iTunes folder to expand its contents.
   - Click the iTunes Music folder to select its check box. Windows adds the folder to the Summary Of Selected Locations list box.

5. Click the OK button to close the Choose Search Locations dialog box and enter the folder you chose in the Location drop-down list in the Search Results window.

6. On the line below the Location drop-down list, set up the condition Date Created (in the first drop-down list), Is (in the second drop-down list), and today's date (in the third drop-down list).

7. Click the Search button. Windows searches and returns a list of the files and folders created.

8. If the Search Results window is using any view other than Details view, choose Views | Details to switch to Details view.

9. Display the Date Created column by taking the following steps:
   - Right-click an existing column heading, and then choose More from the shortcut menu to display the Choose Details dialog box.
   - Select the Date Created check box.
   - Click the OK button to close the Choose Details dialog box.

10. Click the Date Created column heading twice to make Windows Explorer sort the files by reverse date. This way, the files created most recently appear at the top of the list.

11. Check the Date Created column to identify the files created during the consolidation, and then delete them without putting them in the Recycle Bin. (For example, select the files and press SHIFT-DELETE.)

12. Click the Close button (the × button) to close the Search Results window.

After deleting the files (or as many of them as possible), you'll need to remove the references from iTunes and add them again from their preconsolidating location before iTunes can play them. When iTunes discovers that it can't find a file where it's supposed to be, it displays an exclamation point in the first column. Delete the entries with exclamation points and then add them to your library again.

Search for the New Files and Folders on Windows XP

To search for the new files and folders on Windows XP, follow these steps:

1. Choose Start | Search to display a Search Results window.
2. On the What Do You Want To Search For? screen, click the Pictures, Music, Or Video link. (If Search Companion displays the Search By Any Or All Of The Criteria Below screen instead of the What Do You Want To Search For? screen, click the Other Search Options link to display the What Do You Want To Search For? screen. Then click the Pictures, Music, or Video link.)
3. On the resulting screen, select the Music check box and the Video check box in the Search For All Files Of A Certain Type, Or Search By Type And Name area.
4. Click the Use Advanced Search Options link to display the remainder of the Search Companion pane.
5. Display the Look In drop-down list, select the Browse item to display the Browse For Folder dialog box, select your iTunes Music folder, and then click the OK button.

 If you're not sure where your iTunes Music folder is, switch to iTunes, press CTRL-COMMA, and look at the iTunes Music Folder Location box on the General subtab of the Advanced tab in the iTunes dialog box.

6. Click the When Was It Modified? heading to display its controls and then select the Specify Dates option button. Select the Created Date item in the drop-down list and then specify today's date in the From drop-down list and the To drop-down list. (The easiest way to specify the date is to open the From drop-down list and select the Today item. Windows XP then enters it in the To text box as well.)
7. Click the Search button to start the search for files created in the specified time frame.
8. If the Search Results window is using any view other than Details view, choose View | Details to switch to Details view.
9. Click the Date Created column heading twice to make Windows Explorer sort the files by reverse date. This way, the files created most recently appear at the top of the list.
10. Check the Date Created column to identify the files created during the consolidation and then delete them without putting them in the Recycle Bin. (For example, select the files and press SHIFT-DELETE.)

After deleting the files (or as many of them as possible), you'll need to remove the references from iTunes and add them again from their preconsolidating location before iTunes can play them. When iTunes discovers that it can't find a file where it's supposed to be, it displays an exclamation point in the first column. Delete the entries with exclamation points and then add them to your library again.

"iTunes Has Detected That It Is Not the Default Player" Message on Startup

When you start iTunes, you may see the message box shown next, telling you that "iTunes has detected that it is not the default player for audio files" and inviting you to go to the Default Programs control panel to fix the problem.

This message box doesn't indicate a problem as most people understand the word, but having it appear each time you start iTunes grows old fast, so you'll probably either want to suppress the message box or deal with the problem.

What's happened is that some other audio player has grabbed the associations for one or more of the audio file types that iTunes can play. For example, Windows Media Player may have taken the association for the MP3 file type. In this case, if you double-click an MP3 file in a Windows Explorer window, the file will play in Windows Media Player rather than in iTunes.

If you've set up your file associations deliberately to use different programs, simply select the Do Not Show This Message Again check box, and then click the No button. iTunes will drop the matter and not bug you again.

If you want to reassign the file associations to iTunes, click the Yes button. iTunes opens the Set Program Associations window (see Figure 15-4), which shows you the available associations and the programs to which they are assigned.

Select the check box for each file type you want to associate with iTunes, and then click the Save button.

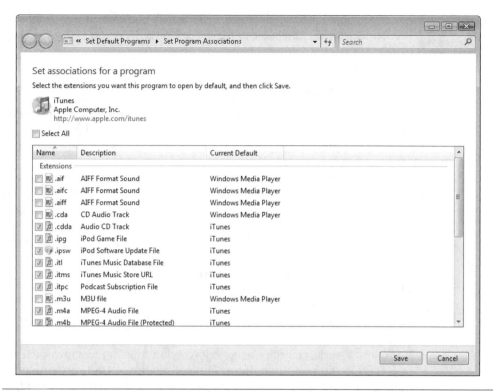

FIGURE 15-4   You can use the Set Program Associations window to reassign audio file associations to iTunes after other programs have grabbed them.

Troubleshoot iTunes on the Mac

This section shows you how to troubleshoot a handful of problems that you may run into when running iTunes on the Mac.

The iPod or iPhone "Is Linked to Another iTunes Library" Message

If, when you connect the iPod or iPhone to your computer, iTunes displays a message such as "The iPod 'iPod_name' is linked to another iTunes library," chances are that you've plugged the wrong iPod or iPhone into your computer. The message box also offers to change this device's allegiance from its current computer to this Mac. Click the No button and check which iPod or iPhone this is before synchronizing it.

For details about moving an iPod or iPhone from one computer to another, see the section "Change the Computer to Which the iPod or iPhone Is Linked" in Chapter 11.

Eject a "Lost" CD

Sometimes Mac OS X seems to lose track of a CD (or DVD) after attempting to eject it. It's as if the eject mechanism fails to get a grip on the CD and push it out, but the commands get executed anyway, so that Mac OS X believes it has ejected the CD even though the CD is still in the drive.

When this happens, you probably won't be able to eject the disc by issuing another Eject command from iTunes, but it's worth trying that first. If that doesn't work, use Disk Utility to eject the disc. Follow these steps:

1. Press ⌘-SHIFT-U or choose Go | Utilities from the Finder menu to display the Utilities folder.
2. Double-click the Disk Utility item to run it.
3. Select the icon for the CD drive or the CD itself in the list box.
4. Click the Eject button.
5. Press ⌘-Q or choose Disk Utility | Quit Disk Utility to quit Disk Utility.

If that doesn't work, you may need to force your Mac to recognize the drive. If it's a hot-pluggable external drive (for example, FireWire or USB), try unplugging the drive, waiting a minute, and then plugging it back in. If the drive is an internal drive, you may need to restart your Mac to force it to recognize the drive.

 See also the sidebar "Eject Stuck Audio Discs from a Mac" in Chapter 6 for instructions on ejecting an optical disc using the Mac's Open Firmware mode.

"You Do Not Have Enough Access Privileges" when Importing Songs

The following error occurs when you've moved the iTunes Music folder to a shared location and the user doesn't have Write permission to it.

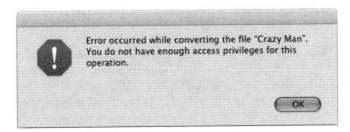

To fix this problem, an administrator needs to assign Write permission for the music folder to whoever received this error.

iTunes Runs You Out of Hard-Disk Space on the Mac

As you saw earlier in the book, iTunes can copy to your library folder all the files you add to your library. Adding all the files to your library means you have all the files available in one place. This can be good when (for example) you want your 'Book's hard disk to contain copies of all the song and video files stored on network drives so you can enjoy them when your computer isn't connected to the network. But it can take more disk space than you have.

If your files are stored on your hard drive in folders other than your library folder, you have three choices:

- You can use the Advanced | Consolidate Library command to cause iTunes to copy the files to your library. This doubles the amount of space the files take up and is usually the worst choice. (Rarely, you might want redundant copies of your files in your library so you can experiment with them.)
- You can have iTunes store references to the files rather than copies of them. If you also have files in your library folder, this is the easiest solution. To do this, clear the Copy Files To iTunes Music Folder When Adding To Library check box on the Advanced tab in the Preferences dialog box.
- You can move your library to the folder that contains your files. This is the easiest solution if your library is empty.

If you choose to consolidate your library, and your Mac doesn't have enough disk space, iTunes displays this message box to alert you to the problem.

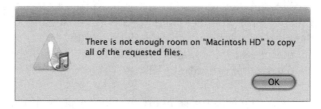

There is not enough room on "Macintosh HD" to copy all of the requested files.

Click the OK button to dismiss this message box—iTunes gives you no other choice. Worse, when you click the OK button, iTunes goes ahead and tries to copy all the files anyway.

This is a bad idea, so stop the copying process as soon as you can. To do so, quit iTunes by pressing ⌘-Q or choosing iTunes | Quit iTunes. If you can't quit iTunes gently, force quit it: OPTION-click the iTunes icon in the Dock, and then choose Force Quit from the shortcut menu. (Failing that, press ⌘-OPTION-ESC to display the Force Quit dialog box, select the entry for iTunes, and then click the Force Quit button.)

Once you've done this, remove the files you've just copied to your library from the folder. Unfortunately, Mac OS X maintains the Date Created information from the original files on the copies made by the consolidation, so you can't search for the files by date created on the Mac the way you can on Windows.

Your best bet is to search by date created to identify the folders that iTunes has just created in your library folder so that you can delete them and their contents. This approach will get all of the consolidated songs and videos that iTunes put into new folders, but it will miss any songs and videos that were consolidated into folders that already existed in your library.

For example, if the song file The Pretender.m4a is already stored in your library with correct tags, your library will contain a Foo Fighters/Echoes, Silence, Patience & Grace folder. If you then consolidate your library so that other songs from that album are copied, the files will go straight into the existing folder, and your search will miss it. The date-modified attribute of the Echoes, Silence, Patience & Grace folder will change to the date of the consolidation, but you'll need to drill down into each modified folder to find the song files that were added.

To search for the new folders, follow these steps:

1. Open a Finder window to the folder that contains your iTunes Music folder. For example, click the Finder icon on the Dock, click the Music item in the Sidebar, click the iTunes folder, and then click the iTunes Music folder.

 If you're not sure which folder the iTunes Music folder is in, look on the Advanced tab in iTunes' Preferences dialog box.

2. Press ⌘-F or choose File | Find to display the Search bar, and then click the iTunes Music button on it to tell Mac OS X to search in that folder.

3. In the top search line, set up this condition: Kind: Folders.

4. In the second search line, set up this condition: Created Date Is Today. Mac OS X searches for folders created today and displays a list of them.

5. Sort the folders by date created, identify those created during the consolidation by the time on the date, and then delete them.

6. Verify that the Trash contains no other files you care about, and then empty the Trash to get rid of the surplus files.

After deleting the files (or as many of them as possible), you'll need to remove the references from iTunes and add them again from their preconsolidating location before iTunes can play them. When iTunes discovers that it can't find a file where it's supposed to be, it displays an exclamation point in the first column. Delete the files with exclamation points and then add them to your library again.

PART IV

Make the Most of the iPod touch and iPhone

16

Make Phone Calls with the iPhone

HOW TO...

- Make phone calls with the iPhone
- Receive phone calls on the iPhone
- Make conference calls with the iPhone
- Get your messages with Visual Voicemail
- Choose phone settings for the iPhone
- Work with contacts on the iPhone and the iPod touch

Music, videos, photos, even file storage—so far in this book, you've learned how to get a wide variety of both entertainment and practical uses out of the iPhone. But what you haven't seen yet is how to make phone calls with it.

This chapter shows you how to make and receive phone calls on the iPhone—including conference calls, which on the iPhone are almost as easy as breaking an egg. You'll also learn how to set up Visual Voicemail and use it to retrieve your messages, how to choose settings for services such as call waiting, and how to add and edit contacts directly on the iPhone.

The information about contacts applies to the iPod touch as well. The rest of the chapter does not apply to the iPod touch.

Make and Receive Phone Calls

Making phone calls with the iPhone is about as easy as it possibly could be—provided that you have a signal. First, look at the signal-strength icon in the upper-left corner of the display. As long as there's at least one bar, you should be good to go.

Make a Phone Call

To make a phone call, follow these steps:

1. If you're planning to use the headphones and their microphone rather than the iPhone's built-in speaker and microphone, plug in the headphones and plant them in your ears. Or if you're using a Bluetooth headset, make sure it's connected and in place.
2. Press the Home button to go to the Home screen unless you're already there.
3. Touch the Phone button at the bottom of the screen to display whichever of the five Phone screens you were using last:
   - **Favorites** Displays a list of up to 20 favorite numbers you designate. This is handy for making quick calls to those numbers.
   - **Recents** Shows a list of calls you've made, received, and missed. The missed calls appear in red. Touch the Missed button at the top of the screen to see the list of missed calls so that you can easily return them. Touch the All button at the top of the screen to restore the full list. Touch the Clear button if you want to get rid of all the recents (for example, because you've dealt with all the missed calls).
   - **Contacts** Shows a list of your contacts, as on the left in Figure 16-1. You can display either all your contacts or just a group, such as your personal contacts. To choose a group, touch the Groups button at the upper-left corner of the Contacts screen, and then touch the group on the Groups screen.

 See the section "Work with Contacts on the iPhone or the iPod touch," later in this chapter, for a discussion of how to add contacts directly on the iPhone or iPod touch or edit existing contacts.

   - **Keypad** Displays a keypad so that you can dial a call, as shown on the right in Figure 16-1.
   - **Voicemail** Touch the message to which you want to reply, and then touch the Call Back button.
4. Choose the number you want to dial, either from the Phone screen you're on, or by touching the button for the Phone screen you want to access.

2. Touch the Add To Favorites button. If the contact has only a single phone number, the iPhone adds it. If the contact has two or more numbers, the iPhone displays the Add To Favorites screen, shown here, to let you choose which number to add to the Favorites.

3. Touch the number you want to add.
4. Touch the All Contacts button to return to the Contacts list.

To add a number to the Favorites list starting from the Favorites list itself, follow these steps:

1. Touch the + button in the upper-left corner to display the list of contacts.
2. Find the contact you want. If necessary, change the group of contacts displayed—for example, choose All Contacts if you want to pick from your full list of contacts.
3. Touch the contact's name to add them to your contacts. As before, if the contact has two or more numbers, the iPhone displays the Add To Favorites screen to let you choose which number to use.

To change the order of the Favorites list, follow these steps:

1. Touch the Favorites button to display the Favorites screen.
2. Touch the Edit button in the upper-left corner to switch the Favorites list into editing mode.
3. Touch the three bars at the right end of the contact you want to move, and then drag the contact up or down the screen.
4. When you've finished changing the order, touch the Done button.

To remove a favorite from the Favorites list, follow these steps:

1. Touch the Favorites button to display the Favorites screen.
2. Touch the Edit button in the upper-left corner to switch the Favorites list into editing mode.
3. Touch the red circle at the left of the favorite you want to remove. The iPhone adds a Remove button to it.
4. Touch the Remove button.
5. When you've finished removing favorites, touch the Done button.

FIGURE 16-1 The most convenient way to call a contact is by choosing their entry on the Contacts screen (left). You can also do things the hard way by using the keypad (right).

How to...

Control How the iPhone and iPod touch Sort Your Contacts List

The iPhone and iPod touch can sort your Contacts list into either "first, last" order (for example, "Jan Weiss") or "last, first" order (for example, "Weiss, Jan"). And the iPhone and iPod touch can also display the contacts in the same order as the sort order or in the other order.

To choose the sort order, follow these steps:

1. Press the Home button to go to the Home screen unless you're already there.
2. Touch the Settings icon to display the Settings screen.
3. Touch the Mail, Contacts, Calendars button to display the Mail, Contacts, Calendars screen.
4. Scroll down to the Contacts area and look at the Sort Order readout. It'll say either "Last, First" or "First, Last." To change the order, touch the Sort Order item, touch the other item on the Sort Order screen, and then touch the Phone button to return to the Phone screen.
5. Still in the Contacts area, look at the Display Order readout. This too will say either "Last, First" or "First, Last." To change the order, touch the Display Order item, touch the other item on the Display Order screen, and then touch the Settings button to return to the Settings screen.

Receive a Phone Call

Receiving a phone call is almost as easy as picking up the phone. Follow these steps:

1. When a call comes in, the iPhone rings—as you'd expect. The iPhone also switches to Phone mode and displays information on the call—the caller's name (if it's in your Contacts) or the phone number (if it's available). The left screen in Figure 16-2 shows an example. If you're listening to music, the iPhone fades the music, and then pauses it.

 If you've set the iPhone to vibrate, it vibrates as well. To turn vibration on or off, press the Home button, touch the Settings icon, and then touch the Sounds button. On the Sounds screen, touch the opposite setting on the Vibrate switch—for example, if it's set to On, touch the Off setting.

2. Touch the Answer button if you want to take the call. If you're using the iPhone's headset, click the button on the cord. The iPhone displays the control buttons shown in the right screen in Figure 16-2. If you want to send the call to voicemail, touch the Decline button, hold down the clicker on the headset cord, or simply don't answer for the set number of rings (the default is four rings).

 You can press either volume key or the Sleep/Wake button on the top of the iPhone to turn off the ringing before you answer the call—for example, because the phone ringing will disturb other people while you're trying to put your headset on. You can also turn the iPhone's ringer off completely by moving the Silencer switch on the left side of the iPhone toward the back, so that the orange dot appears.

FIGURE 16-2   You can accept or decline an incoming phone call (left) by using the touch screen or the headphone clicker button. When you're on a call, the iPhone displays the control buttons (right).

3. During the call, you can use the iPhone's other features freely, except for playing music or video. For example, if you need to take a note during the call, press the Home button, touch the Notes icon, and work on the Notes screen as usual.

4. To end the call, touch the End Call button. If you're using the iPhone's headset, click the button on the cord. If you were listening to music when the call came in, the iPhone restarts the music automatically for you.

Use the Onscreen Icons During Calls

When you make a call, the iPhone displays the icons shown on the right in Figure 16-2. Here's what you can do with them:

- **Mute** Touch this icon to mute the iPhone's microphone—for example, so that you can confer with someone near you without the person at the other end of the phone call being able to hear. Touch this icon again to remove the muting. You can still hear the person at the other end when your microphone is muted.
- **Hold** Touch this icon to put the whole call on hold. Hold is like muting on steroids: It interrupts the entire call, so neither end hears anything from the other. Touch the Hold icon again to remove the hold.
- **Keypad** Touch this icon to bring up the iPhone's keypad—for example, so that you can navigate your way through the voicemail hell that pretends to be customer service for all too many companies these days. Touch the Hide Keypad button when you've finished with the keypad. (Alternatively, touch the End Call button to end the call.)
- **Speaker** Touch this icon to switch from the earpiece to the speaker at the bottom of the iPhone. The speaker works only when you don't have the headset connected. Touch the Speaker icon again if you want to stop using the speaker.
- **Contacts** Touch this icon to display the Contacts list.
- **Add Call** Touch this icon to make a conference call or to make another call while putting the current call on hold. See the next two sections for details.

Put the Current Call on Hold and Make Another Call

If you make many calls, you probably use call waiting to let you interrupt an existing call to take an incoming call. If so, you'll love the iPhone's Add Call feature, as it not only lets you do this (see the next section) but also lets you make an outgoing call while putting the current call on hold.

To put the current call on hold and make another call, follow these steps:

1. In your current call, touch the Add Call button. The iPhone puts the current call on hold and displays whichever Phone screen you were using last—for example, Contacts.

2. Dial the second call as usual. For example, touch the Favorites icon, and then touch the favorite you want to call.

3. Make the call as usual. The only difference is that the name or number of the first call appears at the top of the screen, and two icons change, as shown here.

4. To switch to the caller who's on hold, touch the Swap button. You can also touch the caller's name or number at the top of the screen.
5. Touch the End Call button when you want to hang up the current call.

Receive an Incoming Call During an Existing Call

If you receive an incoming call during an existing call, you have three choices (see Figure 16-3):

- **Send the call to voicemail**   Touch the Ignore button.

FIGURE 16-3   You can put an existing call on hold to take an incoming call.

- **Put the current call on hold, and take the call**   Touch the Hold Call + Answer button.
- **End the current call, and take the call**   Touch the End Call + Answer button.

 If you've turned call waiting off, any call made to your phone while you're already on a call goes directly to voicemail.

Make Conference Calls

One of the iPhone's great features is that it enables you to make conference calls easily. Here's all you need to do to establish a conference call to two people:

1. Call the first person.
2. Put the first person on hold.
3. Call the second person, as described in the section "Put the Current Call on Hold and Make Another Call," earlier in this chapter.
4. Touch the Merge Calls button. You're then speaking to both the other people.
5. To add another person to the conference call, you can dial another number, and then touch the Merge Calls button to add that person to the conference call.
6. To hang up one of the participants, touch the blue button with the white arrow to display the Conference screen, and then touch the red button next to the participant's name.
7. To speak privately to one of the participants, touch the blue button with the white arrow to display the Conference screen, and then touch the Private button to the right of the participant's name.

Use Visual Voicemail

When someone leaves a message on your voicemail, you can access it easily through the iPhone's Visual Voicemail system.

First, though, you must set up your outgoing message. Follow these steps:

1. Press the Home button to go to the Home screen unless you're already there.
2. Touch the Phone button to display whichever Phone screen you were using last.
3. Touch the Voicemail button. The iPhone displays the Set Your Outgoing Message screen, shown on the left in Figure 16-4.
4. If you want to use the iPhone's automatic message (which gives your number in a female voice), touch the Default button. Otherwise, touch the Custom button, touch the Record button, and then record the outgoing message you want.
5. Touch the Play button to play the message, and verify that it's what you want. Then click the Save button.

FIGURE 16-4   After you set your outgoing message, you can access your voicemail messages in an easy-to-browse list.

To listen to your messages, follow these steps:

1. Press the Home button to go to the Home screen unless you're already there.
2. Touch the Phone button to display whichever Phone screen you were using last.
3. Touch the Voicemail button. The iPhone displays the Voicemail screen, shown on the right in Figure 16-4. The blue dots show the messages you haven't listened to yet.
4. Connect the headset or touch the Speaker button to switch the speaker on.
5. To listen to a message, touch it twice in quick succession.
6. To delete the current message, touch the Delete button. The iPhone doesn't ask you to confirm the deletion.
7. To call the person who left a message, touch the message, and then touch the Call Back button.

Choose Phone Settings for Your iPhone

The iPhone comes set for use as a phone, but you'll probably want to choose custom settings to make it behave the way you prefer. To do so, open the Phone settings screen like this:

1. Press the Home button to reach the Home screen unless you're already there.
2. Touch the Settings button to display the Settings screen.
3. Touch the Phone button to display the Phone settings screen (see Figure 16-5).

FIGURE 16-5 The Phone settings screen lets you turn on and off call forwarding, call waiting, and the display of your caller ID.

These are the settings you're most likely to want to change:

- **Call Forwarding** To forward calls your iPhone receives to another phone number, touch Call Forwarding, and then choose the details on the Call Forwarding screen. Move the Call Forwarding switch on this screen to the On position when you want to start forwarding.
- **Call Waiting** To choose whether your iPhone uses call waiting or leaves you undisturbed during calls, touch Call Waiting, and then move the Call Waiting switch to the On position or the Off position.
- **Show My Caller ID** To control whether your iPhone lets callers see your caller ID, touch Show My Caller ID, and then move the Show My Caller ID switch to the On position or the Off position, as appropriate.
- **Change Voicemail Password** When you want to change your voicemail password for security, touch this button, and then enter the new password on the Password screen.

When you've finished choosing settings, touch the Settings button to return to the Settings screen.

Work with Contacts on the iPhone or iPod touch

Normally, you'll add your contacts to the iPhone or iPod touch by synchronizing them from your address book, as described in Chapter 2. But sometimes you may want to create a contact directly on the iPhone or iPod touch—or perhaps edit a contact record when you learn a juicy new detail about the contact. You can do so easily enough, but the process of entering full contact details on the onscreen keyboard tends to be daunting.

You may also want to add information to an existing contact—or add a photo.

Create a New Contact on the iPhone or iPod touch

To add a contact, follow these steps:

1. From the Home screen, touch the Contacts icon to display the Contacts screen. If you're using the iPhone in Phone mode, touch the Contacts button to display the Contacts screen.
2. On the iPhone, in Phone mode, touch the Contacts button to display the Contacts screen. On the iPod touch, press the Home button, and then touch the Contacts icon on the Home screen to display the Contacts screen.
3. Touch the + button in the upper-right corner of the Contacts screen to display the New Contact screen, shown on the left in Figure 16-6.

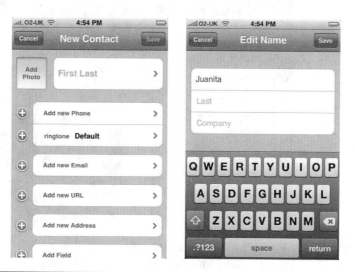

FIGURE 16-6 Creating a new contact on the iPhone or iPod touch is easy enough, but it can mean a whole bunch of one-fingered typing.

4. To enter the contact's name, touch the First Last button. The iPhone or iPod touch displays the Edit Name screen, shown on the right in Figure 16-6.

5. Type the contact's first name, last name, and company (if appropriate), and then click the Save button. The iPhone or iPod touch displays the New Contact screen, now with the name in place, as shown on the left in Figure 16-7.

6. Touch the next item of information you want to add. For example, touch the Add New Phone button to display the Edit Phone screen, shown on the right in Figure 16-7, on which you can enter the phone number and choose the phone type (mobile, home, work, and so on).

7. When you've finished adding the contact's details, touch the Save button. The iPhone or iPod touch displays the Info screen for the contact.

8. Touch the All Contacts button to return to the All Contacts screen. If you started adding the contact from within a group, touch the button to return to that group instead.

Add Data to an Existing Contact

Rather than add a whole new contact on the iPhone or iPod touch, you may want to add data to an existing contact. To do so, touch the contact's name on the All Contacts screen or the screen for a group, and then touch the Edit button on the Info screen for the contact.

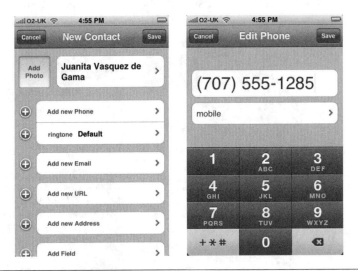

FIGURE 16-7 From the New Contact screen, touch the item of information you want to add, and then use the resulting screen to fill in the details.

If you meet with a contact in person and have your iPhone handy, you have a great opportunity to add a new photo for the contact if the contact record doesn't have one yet. Touch the contact's name to display the Info screen, touch the Edit button, and then touch the Add Photo button. On the panel that pops up, touch the Take Photo button, line the contact up against some attractive scenery, and then press the shutter button. On the Move And Scale screen, move or scale the photo as needed, and then touch the Set Photo button to apply it to the contact.

Delete a Contact

In business as in love, not all relationships work out—and you may sometimes need to delete a contact from the iPhone or iPod touch. To do so, follow these steps:

1. On the Contacts screen or a group screen, touch the contact's name to display the Info screen.
2. Touch the Edit button to start editing the record.
3. Scroll down to the bottom of the screen, touch the Delete Contact button, and then touch the Delete Contact button on the confirmation screen that appears.

17

Connect the iPhone or iPod touch to Wireless Networks and VPNs

HOW TO...

- Connect the iPhone or iPod touch to a wireless network
- Connect the iPhone or iPod touch to a virtual private network

To get the most out of your iPod touch or iPhone, you'll almost certainly want to connect it to a wireless network. For an iPod touch, this is the only way to access your e-mail, the Web, and all the charms and terrors of the Internet; for the iPhone, despite its third-generation wireless network connectivity, it's by far the fastest way to get these essential online features.

By connecting to your own wireless network at home, you can turn the iPod touch or iPhone into the ultimate Internet tablet—an always-at-hand tool for checking your mail, surfing the Web, or grabbing the latest information online. By connecting to a public wireless network, you can stay in high-speed touch when you're out on the town, in the train, or even on a plane.

If you use the iPhone or iPod touch for work as well as play, you may also need to connect it to your company's network via a virtual private network—a "secure tunnel" through the Internet that lets you access the company's network safely from wherever you happen to be.

Set Up a Wireless Network Connection

To connect to a wireless network, you need to know its name, which is called a *service set identifier*, or SSID. This is the name the wireless access point (or other device creating the network) has been set to call the network. If the wireless network has a password, as most do, you need to know that as well. You may also need to know the security type used for the network, which will be one of these three types:

- **WEP**   Wired Equivalent Privacy is the weakest form of protection used on wireless networks. WEP contains systemic errors that make cracking it easy for malefactors. Avoid using WEP if you have the choice. However, because many Wi-Fi hotspots still use WEP, you may find yourself forced to use it.
- **WPA**   WPA is the first level of Wi-Fi Protected Access (the second is WPA2, discussed next). WPA is far more secure than WEP—some experts compare WPA to a decent safe and WEP to a brown envelope—and is a good choice for home use.

 Both WPA and WPA2 also have an "Enterprise" version: WPA Enterprise and WPA2 Enterprise. These versions use a server to verify the identity of network users, whereas the regular or "Personal" versions of WPA and WPA2 use a password or passphrase. You'll find the Enterprise versions used widely in corporate networks.

- **WPA2**   WPA2 is the strongest level of wireless security in widespread use. Some wireless access points do not support WPA2, but if yours does, you might as well use WPA2, because the iPhone and iPod touch support it as well. There *is* such a thing as too much wireless network security, but this isn't it.

Armed with this information, you're ready to set up your wireless network connection. Follow these steps:

1. Press the Home button to reach the Home screen (unless you're already there).
2. Touch the Settings icon to display the Settings screen.
3. Touch the Wi-Fi icon to display the Wi-Fi Networks screen (shown on the left in Figure 17-1). This screen shows the open wireless networks that the iPhone or iPod touch can detect. *Open* means that a wireless network is broadcasting its network name.
4. Touch the button for the network you want to join. The iPhone or iPod touch displays the Enter Password screen for the network, as shown on the right in Figure 17-1.

 If the network you want to join doesn't appear in the list on the Wi-Fi Networks screen, it's probably *closed* (not broadcasting its SSID) rather than open. See the next section for instructions. If the network *is* open, most likely it's out of range of the iPhone or iPod touch.

5. Type the password. Passwords are usually case sensitive, so make sure you get it right. For security, the iPhone or iPod touch displays the character you just typed for a few seconds, then changes it to a security-conscious dot in case someone's peeking over your shoulder.
6. Touch the Join button. The iPhone or iPod touch joins the network.

FIGURE 17-1   Use the Wi-Fi Networks screen (left) to choose a network. The check mark shows the current connection (if there is one). Type the network password on the Enter Password screen.

 Wi-Fi network connections make the iPhone or iPod touch far more useful—but they use a lot of battery power. If you don't use Wi-Fi network connections, or use them only occasionally, turn Wi-Fi off to save battery life. On the Wi-Fi Networks screen, touch the right half of the Wi-Fi switch to turn Wi-Fi off. When you need to join a Wi-Fi network, revisit this screen, and touch the left half of the Wi-Fi switch.

Add a Wireless Network That's Not Listed

Closed wireless networks—ones configured not to broadcast their SSIDs, usually to deter casual attempts to connect—do not appear in the Choose A Network list on the Wi-Fi Networks screen. To join a closed wireless network, follow these steps from the Wi-Fi Networks screen:

1. Touch the Other button to display the Other Network screen (shown on the left in Figure 17-2).
2. In the Name box, type the name of the wireless network.
3. If the wireless network uses security (as most do), touch the Security button to display the Security screen (shown on the right in Figure 17-2).
4. Touch the appropriate button: WEP, WPA, WPA2, WPA Enterprise, or WPA2 Enterprise. (If you don't know which type of security the network uses, consult the network administrator.) The iPhone or iPod touch puts a check mark next to your choice.

FIGURE 17-2 Use the Other Network screen (left) to join a closed wireless network. Choose the security type on the Security screen.

5. Touch the Other Network button in the upper-left corner to go back to the Other Network screen again. This screen now shows the security type you chose on the Security line and displays a Password box under it.
6. Type the password, and then touch the Join button. The iPhone or iPod touch joins the network.

How to... **Turn Off the "Ask to Join Networks" Feature When in Busy Areas**

The Join Networks feature is useful when you want the iPhone or iPod touch to alert you to a wireless network you might need to join, but it can be a menace when you're somewhere in which there are many wireless networks. For example, if you wander down a business street or even a residential street, the iPhone or iPod touch may find dozens of wireless networks. Even at home, your neighbors may have you caged in a Wi-Fi prison.

In this case, the device is just wasting its battery power keeping track of the networks around. To stop it from doing so, go to the Wi-Fi Networks screen, and then touch the right half of the Ask To Join Networks switch.

Make the iPhone or iPod touch Forget a Wireless Network

When you no longer want to use a particular wireless network, tell the iPhone or iPod touch to forget it. To do so, open the wireless network's configuration screen, and then touch the Forget This Network button at the top. Touch the Forget Network button on the confirmation screen that the device displays.

If you find you need to join the wireless network again, join it as described earlier in this chapter. You will need to type the password for the network again.

Did You Know?

Why You Should Never Use a Wireless Access Point's Default Name

Normally, when you buy a wireless access point, it comes with a default network name, administrator name, and password that the manufacturer has programmed into it. The idea is that you can get your wireless network up and running in short order, and then change the network name and password (and perhaps the administrator name) for security.

Most people don't change the network name. Or the password.

As you can imagine, this is grim for security, because any attacker who knows the password for one of the default network names (which are widely published on the Web) can access the network. But it's doubly bad for the iPhone and iPod touch, because Apple set the devices up in a user-friendly but insecure way. Once you've connected to a wireless network successfully, the iPhone or iPod touch remembers the network and automatically connects to it again when it's within range—but without making sure that the network is the same network. So a malefactor can create a wireless network that has the same name (SSID) and password as a network you've used before, and the iPhone or iPod touch will happily connect to the malefactor's network. The malefactor can then attempt to grab your data off the device.

For this reason, it's a good idea not to use the manufacturer's default name (SSID) for any wireless network you set up. Using a unique network name will make it harder for a casual attacker to target your iPhone or iPod touch. However, a determined attacker who wants to target you specifically can use a "packet sniffer" program to eavesdrop on the network traffic and detect the wireless network settings you're using, after which they can implement this attack.

If you connect to a wireless network at a hotspot, you won't have the chance to change its network name or password—so be on your guard for anything unusual when connected. For example, if the iPhone or iPod touch can establish the connection to the wireless network, but you cannot access your e-mail as usual, you may have connected to the wrong network.

Apple may change the iPhone's and iPod touch's firmware or software to get around this problem. But even if it does, you're better off creating a unique name for your wireless network.

Solve Connection Problems on Any Wireless Network

In the early days, wireless networks were highly iffy—*if* you were lucky, you could connect to one; and *if* you were even luckier, the connection wouldn't drop at a critical moment.

These days, wireless networks are mostly pretty reliable. But you may still run into problems connecting to them. This section shows you how to deal with a couple of problems you may experience with any wireless network, be it private or public. The next section sorts out a connection problem with public wireless networks.

The iPhone Starts Using the Cellular Network Instead

When your iPhone is within range of a wireless network, you'll want to use the wireless network rather than the cellular network so that you can get the fastest possible connection and not eat up your calling plan. But you may find sometimes that, even when a wireless network icon appears on the screen, and the iPhone seems to have connected to the network, the iPhone is actually using the cellular network instead.

 You may run into this problem with the iPod touch as well. Because the iPod touch has no cellular connectivity, the symptoms will be different: It will simply be unable to establish an Internet connection.

This usually happens when your iPhone doesn't have permission to connect to the wireless network because the wireless router is set to accept connections only from certain network cards. The router's owner sets the restrictions by using the Media Access Control identification number for the hardware.

The Media Access Control number is usually referred to as the MAC number (spelled in capitals to distinguish it from Apple computers), and it's an ugly string in hexadecimal (the numbers 0–9, representing themselves, and the letters A–F, representing 10 through 15).

If you find this is happening, you need to add your iPhone's MAC address to the wireless router's approved list. How you do this depends on the router, but here's how to find the MAC address:

1. Touch the Home button to reach the Home screen.
2. Touch Settings to display the Settings screen.
3. Touch General to display the General screen.
4. Touch About to display the About screen.
5. Look at the Wi-Fi Address readout. You'll see a hexadecimal number such as 00:23:6D:CD:7D:75. This is what you need to add to the wireless router's list.

Solve the "Could Not Connect to Server" Error

If the iPhone or iPod touch gives you the error "could not connect to server" when you're trying to use something on the Internet, chances are that you're right at the limit of your wireless connection, and it has become intermittent.

If you have an iPod touch, you've only one choice: move closer to the wireless access point so that you can get a better signal. If you have an iPhone, you have two choices: move closer and use the wireless network (usually the better choice), or turn Wi-Fi off on the iPhone and use the cellular network instead. (You could also march briskly into the middle distance to get out of wireless range, but turning off Wi-Fi is usually smarter and easier.)

 If you know you're well within range of your wireless router, the problem may lie with the router itself. See if other computers are able to access the Internet through the router. If not, you may need to reset it.

Here's how to turn Wi-Fi off on the iPhone:

1. Press the Home button to reach the Home screen.
2. Touch Settings to display the Settings screen.
3. Touch the Wi-Fi button to display the Wireless Networks screen.
4. Touch the right half of the Wi-Fi switch to move it to the Off position.

Solve Connection Problems on Public Networks

If you're having problems connecting to the Internet through a Wi-Fi connection at a wireless hotspot, here's an easy solution: renew your DHCP lease to create a new connection to the hotspot. Dynamic Host Configuration Protocol (DHCP) is the technology used for allocating IP addresses efficiently to computers on a network.

To renew the DHCP lease, follow these steps:

1. Touch the Home button to reach the Home screen.
2. Touch Settings to display the Settings screen.
3. Touch Wi-Fi Networks to display the Wi-Fi Networks screen.
4. Touch the More Info button (the blue button with the arrow pointing to the right) next to the network's name to display the network information screen. This screen bears the network's name.
5. Make sure the DHCP button on the left is selected (if not, touch it).
6. Touch the Renew Lease button. The iPhone or iPod touch releases its connection with the wireless network and applies for a new connection. This gives the iPhone or iPod touch a different IP address (almost always; it's possible to get the same address again) and often resolves connection problems.

 You can renew the DHCP lease for any network, but if you've configured your home network so that the iPhone or iPod touch normally works with it, you won't normally need to renew the lease.

Connect to a Virtual Private Network

If you use an iPhone for company business, you may need to connect the iPhone to your company's network so that you can grab your e-mail or exchange data. When you're in the office, you'll probably connect via a wireless network, but when you're out of the office, you can connect across the Internet using a virtual private network, or VPN.

A *virtual private network* uses an insecure public network (such as the Internet) to connect securely to a secure private network (such as your company's network). A VPN acts as a secure "pipe" through the insecure Internet, providing a secure connection between your computer (or iPhone or iPod touch) and the company's VPN server.

Get the Information Needed to Connect to the VPN

To connect to a VPN, you need to know various pieces of configuration information, such as your username, the server's Internet address, and your password or other means of authentication. You also need to know which type of security to use: Layer 2 Tunneling Protocol (L2TP), Point-to-Point Tunneling Protocol (PPTP), or IP Security (IPSec).

Your company's network administrator will provide this information. They may provide it as a written list, which you enter manually in your iPhone, as described a little later in this chapter. But it's easy to get one or more items wrong, so usually an administrator will use the iPhone Configuration Utility (see Figure 17-3) to create a configuration file that you then install on your iPhone and that does the work for you. We'll start with this easier approach.

If you're the administrator, you'll find the iPhone Configuration Utility here: www .apple.com/support/iphone/enterprise. There are versions for both Windows and Mac OS X.

Set Up a VPN by Using a Configuration File

To set up a VPN on your iPhone by using a configuration file, all you need to do is get the configuration file onto your iPhone. Normally, the administrator will distribute the configuration file in one of these ways:

- **Via e-mail** This is an easy way of distributing configuration files as long as the administrator knows your e-mail account. If the configuration file is for a corporate e-mail account as well as for the VPN, however, you'll need to use another e-mail account (because the iPhone won't yet be able to access your corporate account). Open the e-mail message, touch the button for the attachment, and you'll see the Install Profile screen (shown on the left in Figure 17-4).

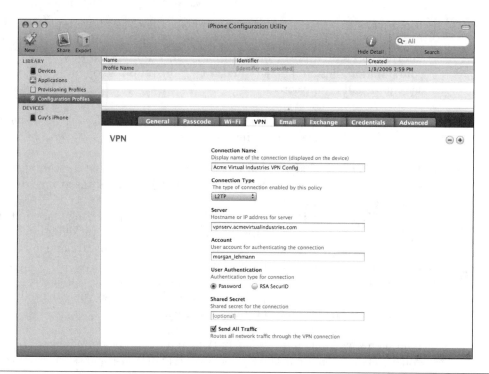

FIGURE 17-3   The iPhone Configuration Utility lets an administrator create configuration files for automatically connecting your iPhone to your company's network.

FIGURE 17-4   On the Install Profile screen (left), check the status of the profile (ideally, you'll see Trusted rather than Not Verified), and then touch the Install button to install it. Provide any required security information (right).

- **Via a website** The administrator can place the configuration file on a website from which you can download it using the iPhone. Typically this will be an internal corporate website or at least a password-protected website, because the configuration files aren't encrypted. Touch the button to open the file, and you'll see the Install Profile screen.

From the Install Profile screen, check the readout to the left of the Install button. You'll see one of these status descriptions:

- **Trusted** This is what you want to see. Trusted means that the configuration file has been signed by the company with a digital signature, so you can be sure you've got the right information.
- **Not Verified** This is not so good, but may be okay providing that you trust the person who sent it to you or the website from which you picked it up. Not Verified means that the configuration file does have a digital signature applied to it, but the identity of the certificate's holder hasn't been verified.
- **Unsigned** This should be a warning sign. Unsigned means that the configuration file has no digital signature applied to it, so you can't tell where it comes from: There's no audit trail on the file.

If all seems well, touch the Install button, and then provide the security information for which you are prompted. The right screen in Figure 17-4 shows an example of a password prompt.

Set Up a VPN Manually

If your administrator has supplied you with a list of configuration details for the VPN rather than with a configuration file, you'll need to set it up the hard way. Because you'll have to use the iPhone or iPod touch's onscreen keyboard, this is somewhat laborious, but you need to do it only once for any connection. Follow these steps:

1. Touch the Home button to reach the Home screen.
2. Touch Settings to display the Settings screen.
3. Touch General to display the General screen.
4. Touch Network to display the Network screen. The left screen in Figure 17-5 shows the Network screen for an iPhone 3G. The Network screen for an iPod touch has only the VPN and Wi-Fi items.
5. Touch VPN to display the VPN screen (shown on the right in Figure 17-5).
6. Touch the Add VPN Configuration button to display the Add Configuration screen, shown on the left in Figure 17-6.
7. Near the top of the screen, click the button for the security type the VPN uses: L2TP, PPTP, or IPSec. The iPhone or iPod touch displays a list of the information required for the connection.

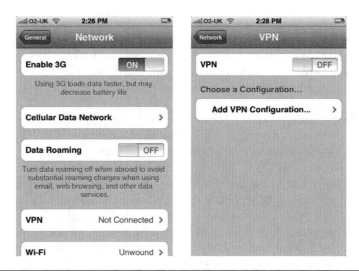

FIGURE 17-5   Touch the VPN button on the Network screen (left) to reach the VPN screen (right).

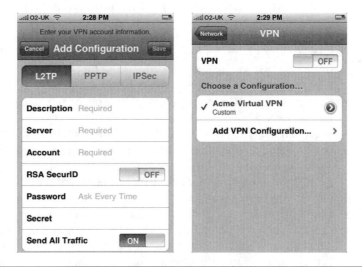

FIGURE 17-6   On the Add Configuration screen (left), enter the information for the connection. When you've saved the connection, move the slider on the VPN screen (right) to On to start the connection.

8. Type in the details for the VPN configuration on the screen:
   - **Description** This is the name under which the VPN appears in the list of VPNs. Choose a descriptive name that suits you.
   - **Server** Type the computer name (for example, vpnserv. acmevirtualindustries.com) or IP address (for example, 216.248.2.88) of the VPN server.
   - **Account** Type your login name for the VPN connection. Depending on your company's network, this may be the same as your regular login name, but in most cases it's different for security reasons.
   - **Password** If the administrator has given you a password rather that a certificate (discussed next), you can enter it here and have the iPhone provide it for you each time you connect. For greater security, you can leave the password area blank and enter the password manually each time you connect. This prevents anyone else from connecting using your iPhone, but it's laborious, especially if your password uses letters, numbers, and symbols (as a strong password should).
   - **RSA SecurID** (PPTP and L2TP only) If the administrator provided you with an RSA SecurID token, move this switch to On to use it. The iPhone or iPod touch then hides the Password field, because you don't need to use a password when you use the token.
   - **Use Certificate** (IPSec only) If the administrator provided you with a configuration file that installed a certificate for authenticating you on the connection, move this switch to On. To save you from temptation, the switch is available only when a certificate is installed.
   - **Secret** (L2TP only) Type the preshared key, also called the *shared secret*, for the VPN. This preshared key is the same for all users of the VPN (unlike your account name and password, which are unique to you).
   - **Group Name** (IPSec only) Type the name of the group to which you belong for the VPN.
   - **Send All Traffic** (L2TP only) Leave this switch set to On (the default position) unless the administrator has told you to turn it off. When Send All Traffic is on, all your Internet connections go to the VPN server; when it is off, Internet connections to parts of the Internet other than the VPN go directly to those destinations.
   - **Encryption Level** (PPTP only) Leave this set to Auto to have the iPhone or iPod touch try 128-bit encryption (the strongest) first, then weaker 40-bit encryption, and then None. Choose Maximum if you know you must use 128-bit encryption only. Choose None only in desperate circumstances—no sane administrator will recommend it.

9. When you've finished entering the information, touch the Save button to save the connection. The VPN connection then appears on the VPN screen (as shown on the right in Figure 17-6).

You're now ready to connect to the VPN, as described in the next section.

Connect to a VPN

After you've installed or created your VPN connection, you can connect to it quickly and easily. Follow these steps:

1. Touch the Home button to reach the Home screen.
2. Touch Settings to display the Settings screen.
3. Start the VPN connection in one of these ways:
   - **If you have only one VPN connection**   Move the On/Off switch on the VPN line (shown on the left in Figure 17-7) to the On position.
   - **If you have two or more VPN connections**   Touch the VPN button to display the VPN screen. In the Choose A Configuration list (shown on the right in Figure 17-7), make sure the correct VPN is selected; if not, touch the one you want. Then move the On/Off switch on the VPN line to the On position.

If the administrator set you up to authenticate yourself with a password, and you chose not to store the password in the VPN connection, you'll be prompted for your password. Enter it, and the iPhone or iPod touch establishes the connection.

Once you've established the connection, you'll be able to work on the VPN. What exactly you'll be able to do depends on the permissions the administrator has granted you, but you'll typically be able to access your e-mail and shared information resources.

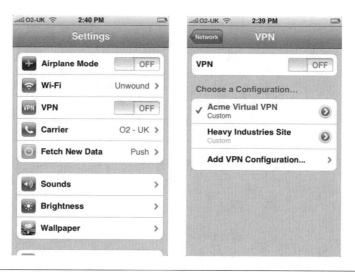

FIGURE 17-7   If you have a single VPN connection, you can turn it on from the Settings screen (left). If you have two or more connections, choose the connection on the VPN screen, and then turn it on.

Disconnect from a VPN

When you've finished using the VPN, close any files that you have been using, and then disconnect like this:

1. Touch the Home button to reach the Home screen.
2. Touch Settings to display the Settings screen.
3. Move the On/Off switch on the VPN line to the Off position.

18

Send E-mail and Surf the Web

HOW TO...

- Set up an e-mail account
- Send and receive e-mail and attachments
- Connect to Exchange Server
- Surf the Web with Safari

This chapter shows you how to set up your e-mail accounts on the iPhone or iPod touch and send and receive e-mail and attachments. The iPhone and iPod touch make it easy to set up personal accounts; but if you use the iPhone or iPod touch at work, you may also need to connect to Exchange Server for e-mail. To set up an Exchange account, you typically use a different technique.

Whether you use the iPhone or iPod touch for work or not, you'll almost certainly want to surf the Web with Safari.

Send and Receive E-mail

The iPhone and iPod touch can send and receive not only e-mail but also attachments, so you can receive files while out and about with your iPhone or iPod touch, and view them immediately.

The iPhone and iPod touch support various widely used file formats for attachments, including:

- **Word documents** Word 2007 format (DOCX) or Word 97–2003 format (DOC).
- **Excel workbooks** Excel 2007 format (XLSX) or Excel 97–2003 format (XLS).
- **Portable Document Format** PDF files, such as those produced by Adobe Acrobat or any program running on Mac OS X.
- **Text files** Plain text files, in the TXT format. The iPhone or iPod touch can't display Rich Text Files (RTF format).

First, you need to set up the iPhone or iPod touch to use your e-mail account. Then you can start sending and receiving.

Set Up an E-mail Account

As you'll know if you've set up an e-mail account manually on a computer (for example, in Windows Mail or Mac Mail), you need to know a handful of details and enter them accurately and in the right places. The process is tedious and can be frustrating.

Apple has largely bypassed this problem by teaching iTunes to grab the settings for your existing e-mail account and load them on the iPhone or iPod touch for you. So if you use one of the mail programs that iTunes supports, you won't actually need to type your username, password, mail servers, and so forth on the iPhone or iPod touch.

These are the Windows mail programs that iTunes supports at this writing:

- **Outlook** Either Outlook 2007 or Outlook 2003.
- **Outlook Express** The free e-mail program included with Windows XP and other versions of Windows before Windows Vista.
- **Windows Mail** The free e-mail program included with Windows Vista. (Windows Mail is an updated and renamed version of Outlook Express.)

These are the Mac mail programs that iTunes supports at this writing:

- **Mail** The mail program included with Mac OS X.
- **Entourage** The e-mail (and much more) program included in Office for the Mac—the Mac version of Outlook, if you will.

If you have another type of e-mail account, you can set it up manually on the iPhone or iPod touch. The iPhone or iPod touch provides help for setting up widely used web-mail accounts, such as Gmail, AOL, Yahoo! Mail, and Apple's own MobileMe service. Even if you have a different type of account, the device usually makes it pretty easy to set up.

Set Up an E-mail Account from Your Computer

To set up an e-mail account from your computer, follow these steps:

1. Connect the iPhone or iPod touch to your computer, and allow synchronization to take place.
2. In iTunes, click the iPhone's or iPod touch's entry in the Source pane to display the control screens for the device.
3. Click the Info tab, and then scroll down to the Mail Accounts area.
4. Select the Sync Selected Mail Accounts check box, and then choose the program in the drop-down list. If the program doesn't appear there, chances are that iTunes doesn't support it.
5. Click the Apply button. iTunes passes the details of the account to the iPhone or iPod touch.

How to... ## Connect the iPhone or iPod touch to Exchange Server

If you use your iPhone or iPod touch at a workplace that has a Microsoft Windows network, you may well need to connect it to Exchange Server, the Microsoft messaging server software.

Normally, you connect to Exchange Server by using a configuration file supplied by a network administrator at your workplace. See the section "Set Up a VPN by Using a Configuration File" in Chapter 17 for information on installing an Exchange account this way.

You can also set up an Exchange account manually from the Mail, Contacts, Calendars screen by using the technique described in "Set Up an E-mail Account Manually on the iPhone or iPod touch." Ask the administrator for the following information:

- Your e-mail address
- The domain name (this is usually necessary)
- Your username for the connection
- Your password for the connection
- The address of the mail server (you may not need this, but it's helpful to have just in case you do)

Set Up an E-mail Account Manually on the iPhone or iPod touch

If iTunes can't grab the details of the e-mail account you want to use with the iPhone or iPod touch, you'll need to set it up manually on the device. Follow these steps:

1. Press the Home button to go to the Home screen unless you're already there.
2. Touch the Settings button to display the Settings screen.
3. Scroll down, and then touch the Mail, Contacts, Calendars button to display the Mail, Contacts, Calendars screen, shown on the left in Figure 18-1.
4. Touch the Add Account button to display the Add Mail screen, shown on the right in Figure 18-1.
5. If the Add Mail screen shows your e-mail provider, touch its button. Otherwise, touch the Other button.
6. On the resulting screen, enter the details for the connection. Most of the mail screens look like the MobileMe screen shown here, and you enter the following information:
   - **Name** This is the name that your e-mail messages will be sent from—for example, your real name, or a variation of it.
   - **Address** This is the e-mail address for the account.

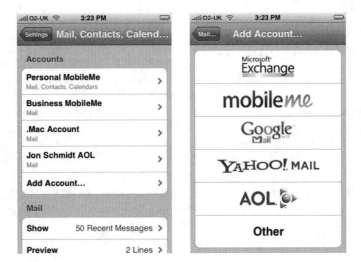

FIGURE 18-1   From the Mail, Contacts, Calendars screen, touch the Add Account button to reach the Add Mail screen. If your e-mail provider is listed here, touch it; if not, touch the Other button.

- **Password**   This is the password for the e-mail account.
- **Description**   This is the name under which the account appears on the iPhone or iPod touch. As soon as you enter the e-mail address for the account, the mail screen automatically copies the e-mail address to this field, but you'll often want to change it to a descriptive name.

7. Touch the Save button. The iPhone or iPod touch verifies the account information, and then adds the account to the Mail screen.

 When you set up an account using the Other screen, the iPhone or iPod touch tries to automatically detect the names of the mail servers and the settings required to access them. If the iPhone or iPod touch prompts you for additional information to set up the account, provide it.

You're now ready to send and receive e-mail using this e-mail account. But while you're at the Mail, Contacts, Calendars screen, let's look quickly at some of the configuration options you may want to set.

Configure Mail Settings

When you set up an e-mail account, the iPhone or iPod touch automatically applies standard settings to it. These settings work fine for many people, but you may want to change some of them. These settings apply to all the e-mail accounts you've set up on the iPhone or iPod touch: You can't apply them to one account but not to another.

How to...

Read Your Hotmail or Windows Live Mail from the iPhone or iPod touch

If you have a Hotmail account or Windows Live Mail, you may be able to access it by using the iPhone or iPod touch.

Microsoft and Apple claim that you must have a Windows Live Mail Plus account, which is the paid version of Windows Live Mail, to be able to use the iPhone or iPod touch. (See http://get.live.com/mailplus/features for the details and costs.) But if you search the Web, you'll find that many people report being able to use their Hotmail accounts from the iPhone or iPod touch without paying.

Whether *you* can do this may depend on when you set the account up and exactly which permissions it has accumulated over its lifetime. For example, in the olden days shortly after the turn of the millennium, you used to be able to manage free Hotmail accounts using Outlook Express. Microsoft put a stop to this long ago—but some people are still doing just that.

So if you have just a regular Hotmail account, it's worth trying to set it up from the Other screen. If it works, great; and if the iPhone or iPod touch gives you the message that you need Windows Live Mail Plus, at least you'll have tried—and you'll know you need either to pay for the upgrade or use third-party software.

These settings appear on the Mail, Contacts, Calendars screen below the list of your e-mail accounts. The left half of Figure 18-2 shows the mail settings.

FIGURE 18-2   It's worth spending a few minutes examining the mail settings on the Mail, Contacts, Calendars screen (left) in case the defaults cause you grief. You'll almost certainly want to customize your e-mail signature (right).

Here's what you need to know about the settings:

- **Show**   Controls how many recent messages Mail shows. Your choices are 25, 50, 75, 100, or 200 recent messages.
- **Preview**   Controls how many lines of the message Mail shows as a preview. Your choices are None, 1 Line, 2 Lines, 3 Lines, 4 Lines, or 5 Lines.
- **Minimum Font Size**   Controls the smallest font size used. Your choices are Small, Medium (the default), Large, Extra Large, or Giant.
- **Show To/Cc Label**   Controls whether Mail automatically shows the To label for a message (and the Cc label, if there is one) when you open the message. Move the switch to the On position or the Off position, as appropriate. You can display these labels manually by touching the Details button. Hiding the labels lets you see more of the message onscreen at once.
- **Ask Before Deleting**   Controls whether Mail prompts you to confirm each deletion of an e-mail message. Some people find the confirmation handy, while others find it irritating. Again, move the switch to the On position or the Off position, as appropriate.

 If you delete a message and then wish you hadn't, you can usually retrieve it from the Trash and move it back to your Inbox or another folder.

- **Always Bcc Myself**   Controls whether Mail automatically sends a blind carbon copy (one that the other recipients of the message can't see) to your e-mail address. On some e-mail systems, this is a convenient way of keeping copies of messages you send. Other e-mail systems provide a more sensible way of keeping copies, such as a Sent Items folder.
- **Signature**   Lets you set up text that Mail adds automatically to each new message you create. The iPhone's default signature is "Sent from my iPhone" and the iPod touch's is "Sent from my iPod touch," which is cute for the first couple of messages but not great for long-term use. (For example, you may not want your colleagues to know that you're actually working from the beach today.) To change the signature, touch the Signature bar, and then use the Signature screen (shown on the right in Figure 18-2) to compose a signature; alternatively, simply touch the Clear button to clear the current signature so that you can type whatever sign-off you want to use. Touch the Mail button when you've finished.

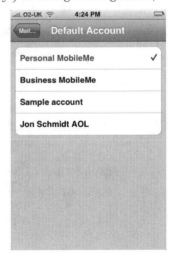

- **Default Account**   Controls which e-mail account Mail uses when you send a photo or a note (both discussed later in this chapter). If you've set up only one account, that will be the default account. If you've set up two or more, check the readout. If it shows the wrong account, touch the Default Account bar to display the Default Account screen (shown here), touch the account you want to use as the default, and then touch the Mail button.

How to...

Stop the iPhone or iPod touch from Checking a Particular E-mail Account

Sometimes you may need to prevent the iPhone or iPod touch from checking a particular e-mail account—for example, when you go on vacation and can leave your business e-mail to pile up for a few days. To do so, follow these steps:

1. Press the Home button to go to the Home screen unless you're already there.
2. Touch the Settings button to display the Settings screen.
3. Scroll down, and then touch the Mail, Contacts, Calendars button to display the Mail, Contacts, Calendars screen.
4. Touch the name of the e-mail account you want to switch off. The contents of the screen that appears depend on the type of account, but the next illustration shows a couple of examples.

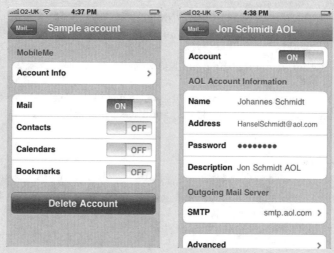

5. Move the Mail switch or the Account switch to the Off position.
6. Touch the Mail button in the upper-left corner to go back to the Mail, Contacts, Calendars screen.

When you want to start checking your e-mail again, repeat these steps, but move the switch to the On position.

When you've finished choosing mail settings, touch the Settings button to return to the Settings screen.

Send E-mail

To send e-mail, follow these steps:

1. Press the Home button to go to the Home screen unless you're already there.
2. Touch the Mail button to go to Mail.
3. If Mail displays the Accounts screen, touch the account you want to use.
4. Touch the Write Message button in the lower-right corner of the window (see Figure 18-3). The iPhone or iPod touch starts a new message from this account. If you chose in the settings to use a signature, the iPhone or iPod touch adds it to the end of the message for you.
5. Address the message:
   - If the recipient is in your Contacts list, touch the + button at the right end of the To line to display the Contacts screen. Touch the contact to add them to the To line.
   - Otherwise, type the e-mail address.

 To remove one of the recipients you've added, backspace over the name. The first backspace selects the address, and the second deletes it.

Write Message button

FIGURE 18-3 Touch the Write Message button (left) to start a new message (right) from the e-mail account you've selected.

6. If you need to add Cc recipients, touch the Cc field, and then add the address or addresses using the same techniques as in the previous step.
7. Add the subject line. Touch the Subject field, and then type the text.
8. Add the message content. Touch in the text area, and then type the text.

If you realize that you've started the e-mail message from the wrong e-mail account, don't worry—all is not yet lost. Touch the From field to display a spin wheel of your e-mail addresses, touch the address you want to use, and then touch elsewhere in the message to apply the change.

9. Touch the Send button.

Send Photographs via E-mail

You can send a photo that you've either taken on the iPhone or loaded onto the iPhone or iPod touch. Follow these steps:

1. Press the Home button to go to the Home screen unless you're already there.
2. Touch the Photos icon to display the Photo Albums screen.

If you're taking photos with the camera, you can start directly from there. Open the Camera Roll album, and then open the photo.

3. Touch the album that contains the photo, and then touch the photo to open it.
4. Touch the Picture Actions button in the lower-left corner of the screen, and then touch the Email Photo button on the pop-up screen (shown here). Mail starts a new message including the photo.

5. Address the message, type the subject line, type any text that's needed, and then touch the Send button.

You can also send a note created in the Notes application via e-mail by using a similar technique.

Receive E-mails and Attachments

Sending e-mail is only half the fun. You'll almost certainly receive it as well. To check, review, and deal with e-mail, follow these steps:

1. Press the Home button to go to the Home screen unless you're already there.
2. Touch the Mail button to go to Mail.
3. If Mail displays the Accounts screen, touch the account you want to view. You can see at a glance how many new messages are in each Inbox, as shown on the left in Figure 18-4.
4. On the screen for the account (see the example on the right in Figure 18-4), touch the Inbox to display its contents. The left screen in Figure 18-5 shows an example of an Inbox.
5. Touch the message you want to view. The iPhone or iPod touch displays its contents. The right screen in Figure 18-5 shows an example of a message with attachments.

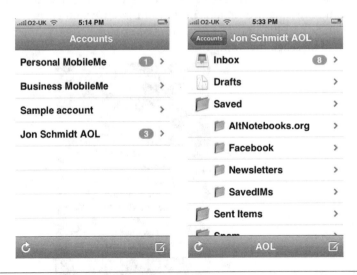

FIGURE 18-4 Mail lets you see at a glance how many messages are in each account. Touch the button in the lower-left corner to check for new messages.

FIGURE 18-5   Touch the Inbox (left) to display its contents, and then touch the message you want to open to display it.

 If an attachment appears as a button, you can touch the button to view the attachment. At this writing, the iPhone or iPod touch can display only some attachments, such as PDF files or graphics files. Touch the Message button in the upper-left corner of the screen to return from the attachment to the message.

6. To reply to the message or forward it, touch the button with the left-pointing arrow at the bottom of the screen, and then touch the Reply button or the Forward button on the panel that appears. Write the required text, address the message if you're forwarding it, and then touch the Send button.
7. To delete the message, touch the Delete button in the middle of the row at the bottom of the screen.
8. To file the message, touch the Move button, the button with the folder on it. Mail displays the list of folders for the mail account, as shown in Figure 18-6. Touch the destination folder. Mail moves the message there, and then displays the next message in the Inbox (if there is one).
9. To move through the messages, touch the Up button or the Down button in the upper-right corner of the screen.
10. To return to your Inbox, touch the Inbox button in the upper-left corner of the screen.

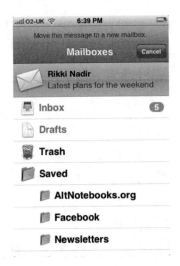

FIGURE 18-6   To remove a message from your inbox without deleting it, file it in one of the folders for the mail account.

Browse the Web with Safari

If you're used to browsing the Web on a big screen, you'll know how vital it is to have plenty of space so that you can see what's on each page. That may make you think that browsing the Web on the iPhone or iPod touch must be a nonstarter.

All credit to Apple, Safari on these devices is a marvel of miniaturization and makes browsing quite viable—even though you'll have to do plenty of zooming and scrolling to navigate most web pages:

- **Zoom**   Either pinch out with your fingers (or a finger and thumb) on the area you want to zoom in on, or double-touch a point to zoom in quickly on it. Pinch back in or double-touch again to zoom back out.
- **Scroll**   Flick your finger in the direction in which you want to move the page—up, down, left, right, or diagonally.

For best results, you'll usually want to turn the iPhone or iPod touch to landscape orientation almost immediately after switching to Safari.

Switch to Safari

First, switch to Safari. Follow these steps:

1. Press the Home button to go to the Home screen unless you're already there.
2. Touch the Safari icon at the bottom of the screen.

Get Your Bookmarks into Safari

Typing URLs into a web browser is a chore even on a full-sized keyboard. Typing URLs on the onscreen keyboard is pretty tedious, even though the software does its best to help by putting essential keys such as /, ., and .COM on the keyboard in Safari, as shown here.

If you browse extensively, you'll need to type some URLs on the onscreen keyboard sooner or later. But what you should do instead is create a bookmark in your web browser for each website you'll want to access frequently using your iPhone or iPod touch, and then synchronize those bookmarks with the device.

To synchronize your bookmarks with the iPhone or iPod touch, follow these steps:

1. Connect the iPhone or iPod touch to your computer, and allow synchronization to take place.
2. Click the device's entry in the Source pane to display its control screens.
3. Click the Info tab, and then scroll down to the Web Browser area.
4. Select the check box for synchronizing the bookmarks:
   - **Windows**   Select the Sync Bookmarks From check box, and then choose the browser in the drop-down list. If the browser doesn't appear there, chances are that iTunes doesn't support it.
   - **Mac**   Select the Sync Safari Bookmarks check box.

If iTunes can't import the bookmarks from your favorite browser, there is a workaround—even if it's an ugly one. Export the bookmarks from the browser, import them into Internet Explorer or Safari, and then synchronize the iPhone or iPod touch with Internet Explorer or Safari. You will not be able to keep your bookmarks synchronized with your preferred browser, but at least this gives you a way of getting your bookmarks from that browser onto the iPhone or iPod touch.

5. Click the Apply button. iTunes copies the bookmarks to the device.

FIGURE 18-7 The easiest way of getting to a website on the iPhone or iPod touch is to use a bookmark.

Go to a Bookmark

To go to a bookmark on the iPhone or iPod touch, follow these steps:

1. Touch the Bookmarks button at the bottom of the screen, as shown on the left in Figure 18-7 above.
2. The iPhone or iPod touch displays the Bookmarks screen you were using last. The first time, you will usually see the main Bookmarks screen, as shown on the right in Figure 18-8.
3. Touch the category of bookmarks you want to view. For example, touch the Bookmarks Menu button to display the Bookmarks Menu screen, as shown on the left in Figure 18-8.
4. Touch the bookmark for the webpage you want to display, as shown on the right in Figure 18-8. Safari opens the webpage.

Add a Bookmark on the iPhone or iPod touch

If you browse on the iPhone or iPod touch, you'll probably run into webpages that you want to bookmark for later reference. Not only can you do this, but iTunes syncs your bookmarks back to your browser, so you can use the bookmark on your computer as well.

To add a bookmark, follow these steps:

1. On the iPhone or iPod touch, browse to a webpage that deserves a bookmark.
2. Touch the + button at the bottom of the screen, and then touch Add Bookmark on the screen that appears (shown here).

FIGURE 18-8 Touch the bookmark category you want (left), and then touch the bookmark to display the page it marks (right).

3. The iPhone or iPod touch displays the Add Bookmark screen, shown on the left in Figure 18-9.
4. The device displays the page's title in the top text box. You can either accept this as the name for the bookmark, edit it by using the keyboard, or clear the name (touch the × button) and then type a new name.

Did You Know?

Why the iPhone and iPod touch Can't Show Flash Websites

If you've spent any time browsing the Web, you're probably familiar with Adobe Flash, a technology for adding multimedia, animations, and animated graphics to websites. Nearly as many people consider Flash a bane (because it creates large and unwieldy sites) as consider it a boon—but love it or hate it, Flash is very widely used.

Unfortunately for you and me, the iPhone and iPod touch don't support Flash, so if you browse to a website that uses Flash, Safari won't be able to display it properly.

Adobe is apparently working on a version of Flash for the iPhone (and iPod touch), but the main problem is that Flash appears to contravene Apple's guidelines for applications that run on the iPhone. This is because developers would be able to create applications in Flash and install them on the iPhone from webpages rather than having to get the applications approved by Apple and then sell or distribute them via the App Store.

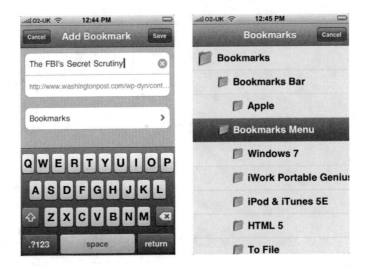

FIGURE 18-9 You can add a bookmark on the iPhone or iPod touch and have it be synchronized back to your computer.

5. To change the location in which the iPhone or iPod touch stores the bookmark, touch the bar indicating the current location (in the example, this is Bookmarks). On the resulting screen, shown on the right in Figure 18-9, touch the location you want. The device displays the Add Bookmark screen again, with the bar now showing the location you chose.
6. Touch the Save button to save the bookmark. The iPhone or iPod touch then returns you to the webpage from which you started the bookmarking process.

Go to Webpages You've Visited Before

To navigate among the webpages you've visited before in this session, touch the Back button or the Forward button at the lower-left corner of the screen.

The Back button is available as soon as you've navigated from one webpage to another. The Forward button becomes available when you use the Back button to go back to a webpage you've visited earlier.

Open Multiple Pages at the Same Time

Safari lets you open multiple pages at the same time, and then switch among them. This is handy when you want to view another webpage without closing the webpage you're currently viewing.

To open a new page in Safari, follow these steps:

1. Touch the button in the lower-right corner of the screen. Safari shrinks the current page and displays a New Page button and a Done button, as shown here.

2. Touch the New Page button. Safari displays a blank new page, as shown next. The button in the lower-right corner of the screen shows the number of pages you have open.

3. Go to a URL in one of the usual ways:
   - Touch the Address box to display the keyboard, type the URL, and then touch the Go button, as shown here.

- Touch the Bookmarks button to display your list of bookmarks, and then choose the bookmark you want.

To navigate from one open page to another, touch the button in the lower-right corner of the screen to shrink the current page and display the control buttons, as shown here. The dots below the page show you how many pages you have open, with the white dot showing which of the pages you're looking at.

Scroll left or right to reach the page you want to view, and then touch it to display it. To close a page, touch the × button that appears in its upper-left corner.

19

Install Applications and Play Games

HOW TO...

- Find, download, and install applications for the iPhone and iPod touch
- Synchronize your applications with iTunes
- Configure an application
- Update an application on the iPhone or iPod touch
- Navigate, rearrange, and delete applications
- Play games on the iPhone or iPod touch
- Jailbreak the iPhone or iPod touch and install non-approved applications

Perhaps the greatest thing about the iPhone and the iPod touch is the fact that they can run third-party software as well as the software Apple provides. Apple provides a wide selection of third-party software in its App Store, which is a division of the iTunes Store.

At this writing, Apple is driving to turn the iPhone and iPod touch into a platform for applications (including games) that will kill off competing handheld devices—Windows Mobile smartphones and devices, other smartphones such as the Palm Pre and Nokia's confusing offerings, the last few PDAs that haven't gone down in flames, and even game-focused devices such as the Nintendo DS and Sony PlayStation Portable. As a result, if you're looking for an application that fulfills a particular need, or for an entertaining game application, you'll be spoilt for choice.

And if the App Store can't provide what you're looking for, you can "jailbreak" your iPhone's or iPod touch's bonds so that you can install unapproved software. You'll learn about this drastic step toward the end of this chapter.

Find, Download, and Install Applications for the iPhone and iPod touch

For the iPhone or iPod touch, Apple provides a single source of software, the App Store. The App Store provides only applications that Apple has checked and approved for quality, content, and suitability, so that you can be sure not only that they'll run properly on the iPhone or iPod touch but also that you can download, install, and update them easily—and that they don't contain any unpleasant surprises (such as viruses or hidden adult content).

You can access the App Store either through iTunes or directly from the iPhone or iPod touch. If you have the choice, iTunes is easier, because you have more space for browsing and reading reviews. But browsing the App Store on the iPhone or iPod touch works fine too.

 Many developers provide free but limited versions of their applications in the hope of selling more copies of the paid and more powerful versions. If you're thinking of buying a paid application, always look to see if there's a free version that you can try first.

Browse the App Store Using iTunes

To browse the App Store using iTunes, follow these steps:

1. Click the iTunes Store item in the Source list to display the App Store in the main iTunes window. Double-click the iTunes Store item if you want to open a separate window (useful if you want to be able to keep playing music or videos in the main window).

 Here's another way to jump to the App Store: If the Applications item appears in the Source list, click it, and then click Get More Applications.

2. In the iTunes Store panel on the left of the main screen, click App Store to display the contents of the App Store. Figure 19-1 shows an example.
3. Follow links, categories, or recommendations to find an application that interests you. Click the application's icon to display full information about it. Figure 19-2 shows an example of such information.
4. If you decide to get an application, click the Get App button (for a free application) or the price button (for a paid application).
5. Follow through the process of signing in to the App Store (if you're not already signed in) and confirming the purchase (even if the application is free). iTunes then starts downloading the application. You can see the progress of the download by clicking the Downloads item in the Store category of the Source list.

After the download finishes, connect the iPhone or iPod touch to your computer, and then synchronize the applications to install the new applications on the device.

How to...

Find Useful Productivity Applications

Developers are adding hundreds of applications per month to the App Store, so it's almost impossible to provide solid recommendations. But here are ten productivity applications— all available from the App Store—that you may benefit from knowing about:

- **Todo**   Todo is a task-management tool that follows productivity guru David Allen's widely acclaimed Getting Things Done principles. Todo can synchronize with various online task-management services and with Microsoft Outlook (if you add the third-party ToodledoSync Application).
- **OmniFocus**   OmniFocus is a task-management tool that follows Getting Things Done principles. OmniFocus on the iPhone or iPod touch synchronizes with OmniFocus on the Mac (www.omnigroup.com/applications/omnifocus).
- **Things**   Things is a simple but powerful task-management tool that synchronizes with Things on the Mac (www.culturedcode.com/things/iphone).
- **WriteRoom**   WriteRoom provides a "clean-room" screen for writing without distractions. You can use the keyboard in landscape orientation, which gives you more room and makes typing faster. Better still, you can turn on document sharing, connect to your iPhone or iPod touch via a web browser, and type documents directly from a computer.
- **EasyWriter Pro**   EasyWriter Pro is an e-mail writing application that lets you work on a keyboard in landscape orientation for faster typing. You can check your spelling and insert boilerplate text clippings called snippets. Once you've written the message, you can transfer it to Mail to send it.
- **Jaadu VNC**   Jaadu VNC lets you take control of your Windows PC or Mac remotely from your iPhone or iPod touch. This application is relatively expensive, and you need to configure your PC or Mac for remote sharing before it will work.
- **Mocha VNC**   Mocha VNC lets you take control of your Windows PC or Mac remotely from your iPhone or iPod touch. As with Jaadu VNC, you will need to configure your PC or Mac for remote sharing. Start with Mocha VNC Lite, which has fewer features but is free.
- **Pennies**   Pennies is an expense-tracking application that will help you whip your budget under control.
- **Air Sharing**   Air Sharing lets you mount the iPhone or iPod touch as a wireless drive on a Windows PC or Mac so that you can transfer files to and from it or view documents stored on it.
- **SnapTell**   SnapTell is a shopping application that lets you quickly research products with the iPhone. You simply take a picture of the cover of a book, CD, DVD, or videogame, and SnapTell gives you links to online reviews and shopping sites.

Finally, here's an application that can save you money on applications:

- **AppSniper**   AppSniper is a tool for tracking applications that the App Store is offering at reduced prices. Many developers cut prices for a while to boost demand, and this is a handy tool for keeping tabs on applications you'd like to buy but aren't prepared to pay the full price for.

FIGURE 19-1 The App Store includes various categories and lists of applications that you can browse using the same techniques as you use for the other items in the iTunes Store.

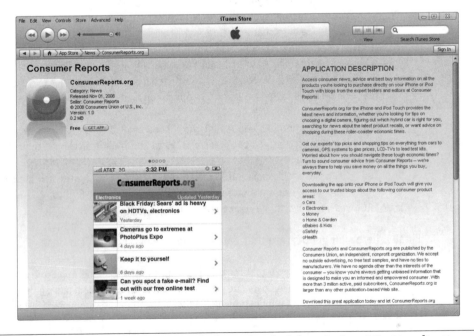

FIGURE 19-2 Each application includes a detailed description. Most applications worth using include customer ratings and comments.

Browse the App Store Using the iPhone or iPod touch

When you're using the iPhone or iPod touch, you can browse the App Store like this:

1. Press the Home button to go to the Home screen unless you're already there.
2. Touch the App Store icon to display the App Store screen.
3. Touch one of the buttons at the bottom of the screen to see the screen of applications you want to view:

   - **Featured**   This screen contains a New list (of the latest applications) and a What's Hot list (showing the applications that are currently most popular). The left screen in Figure 19-3 shows an example of the Featured screen.
   - **Categories**   This screen lets you browse the applications by different categories: Games, Entertainment, Utilities, Social Networking, Music, Productivity, and so on. The right screen in Figure 19-4 shows an example of the Categories screen.
   - **Top 25**   This screen contains lists of the top 25 paid applications and the top 25 free applications. The masses aren't always right, but they'll often point you to the most useful or most amusing applications.
   - **Search**   This screen lets you search by using keywords.
   - **Updates**   This screen lets you quickly find updates for applications that are already installed on the iPhone or iPod touch.

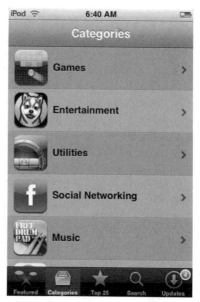

FIGURE 19-3   On the iPhone or iPod touch, you can browse the App Store using the Featured list (left) or the Categories list (right). You can also visit the Top 25 screen, search for applications, or update your existing applications.

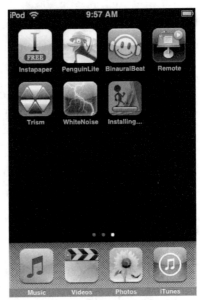

FIGURE 19-4 Check the Info screen (left) for details and reviews before buying or downloading an application. As the application installs and downloads, the Home screen shows you what's happening (right).

4. When you've found an application that looks promising, touch its icon to display the Info screen. The left screen in Figure 19-4 shows an example of the Info screen for a free application.
5. To get the application, touch the price button (for a pay application) or the Free button (for a free application), and then touch the Install button that replaces this button.
6. Enter your password when the iPhone or iPod touch prompts you for it. The iPhone or iPod touch then displays the Home screen, which shows you a progress readout as the application loads and installs (see the last icon in the right screen in Figure 19-4).

Once the application has finished installing, touch the icon to launch it.

The next time you connect the iPhone or iPod touch to your computer and synchronize, iTunes copies the application from the iPhone or iPod touch to the computer.

 Most applications are licensed per computer rather than per device. So if you buy an application for your iPhone and synchronize it back to iTunes, you can load the application on your iPod touch at its next synchronization.

Synchronize Your Applications with iTunes

To start with, you'll probably want to synchronize with iTunes all the applications you buy or get for free. This will give you the chance to see how well they work on the iPhone or iPod touch and decide whether you want to keep them.

Once you've done that, you may then want to prevent iTunes from loading an application onto a particular device. For example, if you synchronize both an iPhone and an iPod touch with the same computer, you may want to load some productivity applications on the iPhone and some games on the iPod touch, but not everything on both. Or you may want to load only some applications on the iPhone or iPod touch at a time, either to save space or to prevent the Home screen from becoming too cluttered and unwieldy.

To control how iTunes handles synchronization, follow these steps:

1. Connect the iPhone or iPod touch to your computer as usual.
2. Click the iPhone's or iPod touch's entry in the Source list to display its control screens.
3. Click the Applications tab to display the settings for synchronizing applications (see Figure 19-5).

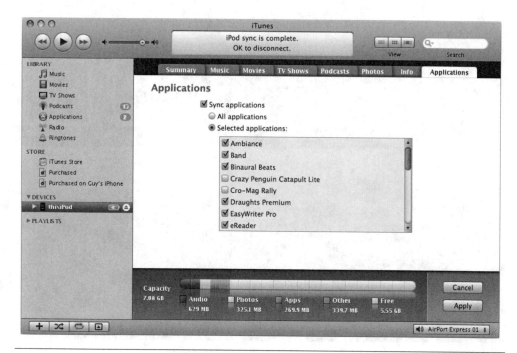

FIGURE 19-5   On the Applications tab of the iPhone's or iPod touch's control screens, choose whether to synchronize all applications or just some of them.

4. Select the Sync Applications check box if you want to synchronize applications, as usually you will.
5. Select the All Applications option button if you want to synchronize every application. Otherwise, click the Selected Applications option button, and then select the check box for each application you want to synchronize.
6. Click the Apply button to run the synchronization.

Configure an Application

Many applications for the iPhone or iPod touch come set up to run straight out of the virtual box, but most have settings that you can configure to make the applications run the way you want them to and give you the best results.

Many applications have Setup screens that are built directly into the application and intended for you to run through when starting to use the application. For example, Figure 19-6 shows the Setup arrangements for the Band application, which

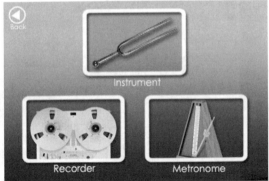
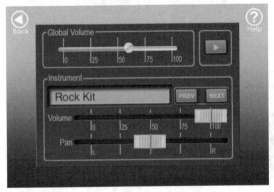
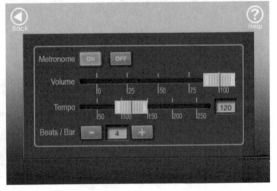

FIGURE 19-6 Many applications have their own setup screens that you access directly from the application.

lets you play and record music directly on the iPhone. From the main screen (shown at the top left), touch Setup to reach the Setup screen (top right). You can then touch Instrument, Recorder, or Metronome to display the configuration screen for that item (see the bottom two screens).

Some applications also add one or more screens of settings to the iPhone's or iPod touch's settings area. You can reach these settings from the iPhone's or iPod touch's Settings screen:

1. Press the Home button to reach the Home screen (unless you're already there).
2. Touch the Settings icon to display the Settings screen.
3. Scroll down to find the third-party applications (shown on the left in Figure 19-7), and then touch the application you want.
4. Choose settings on the resulting screen (the right screen in Figure 19-7 shows an example).
5. Touch Settings in the upper-left corner of the screen when you're ready to return to the Settings screen.

FIGURE 19-7 You can also find settings for some third-party applications on the iPhone's or iPod touch's main Settings screen (left). Touch the application's name to display its settings (right).

Update the Applications on the iPhone or iPod touch

You can update the applications on the iPhone or iPod touch either by using the device or by using iTunes. In most cases, using iTunes is faster and easier, so let's look at that first.

 Many updates to applications are free—especially updates that fix bugs with the application—but major updates and new versions tend to require payment. Check whether you'll need to pay for an upgrade before you install it.

Update an Application Using iTunes

Unless you're in a tearing hurry and you're not at your computer, the best way to update an application is by using iTunes. As before, this is because you can more easily see what you're doing, and you can access the Internet at the full speed of your Internet connection. Follow these steps:

1. In the Source list, click the Applications item in the Library category. iTunes displays a screen showing all the applications on the iPhone or iPod touch. Figure 19-8 shows an example.

FIGURE 19-8 The Applications screen lists the number of available updates that iTunes knows about. If none is available, click the Check For Updates button.

The number in the gray oval to the right of the Applications item in the Source list shows how many updates are available for your applications.

2. Click the Updates Available button to display the My App Updates screen (see Figure 19-9). If this button doesn't appear, click the Check For Updates button, which appears in its place. You'll either see details of the available updates or a message saying that no updates are available at the moment.
3. If all the updates are free, simply click the Download All Free Updates button to download them all. If not, you can pick and choose by using the Get Update buttons that appear on each update.
4. When you've finished applying updates, click the Done button.
5. Connect the iPhone or iPod touch and synchronize it as usual to update the applications.

 After you update an application from the App Store, you'll find an .ipa (iPhone application) file in the Recycle Bin on a Windows PC or in the Trash on the Mac. For example, if you update the Stanza e-book application, you'll find a file with a name such as Stanza 1.4.ipa in the Trash afterward. This file is the old version of the application, and you can safely get rid of it.

Update an Application Directly on the iPhone or iPod touch

When you're not at your computer and you need to get the latest update, you can update an application directly on the iPhone or iPod touch as well. You then

FIGURE 19-9 From the My App Updates screen, you can either update all your applications in one fell swoop or get updates for individual applications.

FIGURE 19-10   The number in the red circle on the App Store icon shows how many application updates are available. Touch the App Store icon and then touch the Updates icon to see which applications the updates are for.

synchronize the changes back to iTunes, making it ready to apply the updates to another iPhone or iPod touch you synchronize with the same computer.

To update the applications on the iPhone or iPod touch, follow these steps:

1. Press the Home button to reach the Home screen (unless you're there already). If updates are available, a red circle appears on the App Store icon, as shown on the left in Figure 19-10.
2. Touch the App Store icon to display the App Store screen.
3. Touch the Updates icon at the bottom of the screen to display the Updates screen. This screen (shown on the right in Figure 19-10) lists the applications for which updates are available.
4. Touch the Update All button if you want to update all the applications at once. Otherwise, touch an application to display the details of the update, and then touch the button to update it.

Navigate, Rearrange, and Delete Applications

When you add an application to the iPhone or iPod touch, the application appears at the end of the last screen of applications. As soon as you fill up one of the existing screens, the device provides a new screen—a second, a third, a fourth, and so on.

The iPhone or iPod touch displays a line of dots at the bottom of the Home screen to show how many screens of applications you have. The white dot represents the screen you're currently viewing. For example, the iPhone shown on the left in Figure 19-11 has three screens of applications, and the second is currently displayed.

To display the next screen of applications, drag your finger to the left horizontally across the screen, as shown on the right in Figure 19-11. Drag to the right to display the previous screen of applications. You can also touch a dot to the right of the current dot to display the next screen or a dot to the left of the current dot to display the previous screen.

Rearrange the Applications on the Screens

What you'll probably want to do is move the applications you use most to the first screen so that you can access them easily. Or you may want to sort your applications into different categories, such as work-related applications, games, and others.

To rearrange the applications, touch an application's icon and hold it down until the icons start jiggling about and a circle with an × appears at the upper-left corner of each application you've installed. The left screen in Figure 19-12 shows an example. Now drag the icon to where you want to place it. The iPhone or iPod touch moves the other icons out of the way.

FIGURE 19-11   The dots below the screen show how many screens of applications you have and which screen is displayed. Drag to the left (as shown on the right) or to the right to change the screen of applications.

FIGURE 19-12 Once the application icons start to jiggle (left), you can drag them to where you want them. To delete an application, touch a cross button, and then confirm the deletion (right).

To move an icon to another screen of applications, drag the icon off the side of the screen, wait until the iPhone or iPod touch displays the next screen, and then drag it to where you want.

 The screens don't have to be full of applications. You can create a new screen by dragging an application to it.

When you've finished rearranging the applications, press the Home button to stop the jiggling.

Delete an Application

As soon as you've synchronized an application after installing it, the application is installed both on the iPhone or iPod touch and on your computer. If you don't want to keep the application on the iPhone or iPod touch, you can delete it from there without affecting the copy in iTunes. And if you really don't want to keep the application at all, you can delete it from iTunes and remove it from the iPhone or iPod touch as well.

Delete an Application from the iPhone or iPod touch

You can delete an application from the iPhone or iPod touch in moments:

1. Touch the application's icon and hold it down until the icons start jiggling about.
2. Touch the circle with the × at the upper-left corner. The device displays a confirmation screen, as shown on the right in Figure 19-12.
3. Touch Delete. The iPhone or iPod touch deletes the application.

Delete an Application from iTunes and from the iPhone or iPod touch

When you want to get rid of an application completely, delete it from iTunes as follows. iTunes then removes it from the iPhone or iPod touch at the next synchronization.

1. Click the Applications item in the Source list to display the iPhone And iPod touch Apps screen.
2. Right-click (or CTRL-click on the Mac) the application and choose Delete from the shortcut menu. iTunes displays a confirmation dialog box, as shown here.

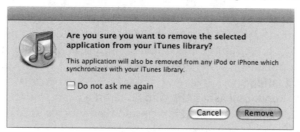

Are you sure you want to remove the selected application from your iTunes library?

This application will also be removed from any iPod or iPhone which synchronizes with your iTunes library.

☐ Do not ask me again

Cancel   Remove

3. Click the Remove button. iTunes removes the application.

Play Games on the iPhone or iPod touch

Always in your pocket or strapped to your body, the iPhone or iPod touch platform is poised to be the ultimate handheld gaming platform—unless Sony, Nintendo, or one of the many other players in this space mounts a credible challenge to Apple.

There's little to say about playing games on the iPhone or iPod touch beyond that the App Store has a wide selection of games, many of which take advantage of the device's accelerometer to determine tilt and movement as well as the touchscreen and audio features. Many of these—for example, the racing game Cro-Mag Rally and the last-tank-standing shooter iShoot—are well produced and fun to play, but not the kind of game that you'll find yourself playing over and over again.

With that rather boring criterion firmly in mind, here are five games that look like good bets for the long run:

- **Chess**   Chess lite is a great place to start, as it's free.
- **Checkers**   There are many free Checkers games, but most of them are hobbled by advertisements or poor programming (or both). If you're looking for an enjoyable game that works smoothly for either one or two players, look at Checkers Premium and its competitors.
- **Scrabble**   Scrabble is a colorful implementation of the classic game.
- **Trism**   Trism is a challenging game in which you rearrange colored triangular prisms on a grid.
- **Tetris**   There are various implementations of this classic computer game, but the one named TETRIS (in those shouting capitals) sets the benchmark at this writing.

Jailbreak the iPhone or iPod touch and Install Non-Approved Applications

As mentioned earlier in this chapter, the iPhone and iPod touch are a "locked" platform for applications. Any developer who wants to provide an application for the iPhone or iPod touch must submit it to Apple for approval. If Apple approves the application, up it goes on the App Store, and anyone who has an iPhone or iPod touch can buy it, download it, and use it.

Before Apple unleashed the App Store on a deeply suspecting world, enterprising hackers had "jailbroken" the iPhone's and iPod touch's virtual shackles so that they could install non-approved software on the devices. Even with the App Store up and active, some developers prefer not to go through the approval process, some on general principles and others secure in the knowledge that their applications offend enough of Apple's guidelines that approval isn't even a pipe dream.

If you want to install non-approved applications on the iPhone or iPod touch, you'll find plenty of tools and instructions online for jailbreaking the devices. As usual with the Internet, these tools and instructions are only a quick search away.

Before you take this step, however, make sure you understand the potential downside. Apple doesn't support jailbroken iPhones and iPod touches, and in fact plays Whack-a-Mole with the jailbreaking teams: Each update Apple releases to the iPhone and iPod touch software stands a good chance of putting a jailbroken device back in jail. If the update doesn't do that, it may even "brick" the device—knocking its functionality on the head, so that the device is useful only as a brick. The jailbreaking process itself isn't always successful, and it too can stop an iPhone or iPod touch from working.

Tip   "Bricking" is an evocative term, but neither an iPhone nor an iPod touch is actually any use as a brick. Either works well as a desk paperweight, though—if you still allow paper on your desk.

Index